Language Planning and Policy in Asia, Volume 1

PEFC™
PEFC/16-33-111
CATG-PEFC-052
www.pefc.org

LANGUAGE PLANNING AND POLICY
Series Editors: Professor Richard B. Baldauf Jr., *University of Queensland, Brisbane, Australia* and Professor Robert B. Kaplan, *University of Southern California, USA*

Other Books in the Series
Language Planning and Policy in Africa, Vol.1: Botswana, Malawi, Mozambique and South Africa
Richard B. Baldauf Jr. and Robert B. Kaplan (eds)
Language Planning and Policy in Africa, Vol. 2: Algeria, Côte d'Ivoire, Nigeria and Tunisia
Robert B. Kaplan and Richard B. Baldauf Jr. (eds)
Language Planning and Policy in Europe, Vol. 1: Hungary, Finland and Sweden
Robert B. Kaplan and Richard B. Baldauf Jr. (eds)
Language Planning and Policy in Europe, Vol. 2: The Czech Republic, The European Union and Northern Ireland
Richard B. Baldauf Jr. and Robert B. Kaplan (eds)
Language Planning and Policy in Europe, Vol. 3: The Baltic States, Ireland and Italy
Robert B. Kaplan and Richard B. Baldauf Jr. (eds)
Language Planning and Policy in Latin America, Vol. 1: Ecuador, Mexico and Paraguay
Richard B. Baldauf Jr. and Robert B. Kaplan (eds)
Language Planning and Policy in Pacific, Vol. 1: Fiji, The Philippines and Vanuatu
Richard B. Baldauf Jr. and Robert B. Kaplan (eds)
Language Planning and Policy: Issues in Language Planning and Literacy
Anthony J. Liddicoat (ed.)
Language Planning and Policy: Language Planning in Local Contexts
Anthony J. Liddicoat and Richard B. Baldauf Jr. (eds)

Other Books of Interest
Directions in Applied Linguistics
Paul Bruthiaux, Dwight Atkinson, William G. Eggington, William Grabe and Vaidehi Ramanathan (eds)
Language Decline and Death in Africa: Causes, Consequences and Challenges
Herman M. Batibo
Language Diversity in the Pacific: Endangerment and Survival
Denis Cunningham, D.E. Ingram and Kenneth Sumbuk (eds)
Language in Jewish Society: Towards a New Understanding
John Myhill
Linguistic Landscapes: A Comparative Study of Urban Multilingualism in Tokyo
Peter Backhaus
Multilingualism in European Bilingual Contexts: Language Use and Attitudes
David Lasagabaster and Ángel Huguet (eds)
Politeness in Europe
Leo Hickey and Miranda Stewart (eds)
The Defence of French: A Language in Crisis?
Robin Adamson

For more details of these or any other of our publications, please contact:
Multilingual Matters, St Nicholas House, 31-34 High Street, Bristol BS1 2AW
http://www.multilingual-matters.com

Language Planning and Policy in Asia, Vol. 1

Japan, Nepal, Taiwan and Chinese Characters

Edited by

Robert B. Kaplan and Richard B. Baldauf Jr.

MULTILINGUAL MATTERS
Bristol • Buffalo • Toronto

Library of Congress Cataloging in Publication Data
Language Planning and Policy in Asia/Edited by Robert B. Kaplan and Richard B. Baldauf Jr.
Language Planning and Policy
Includes bibliographical references.
1. Language planning–Asia. 2. Language policy–Asia. I. Kaplan, Robert B. II. Baldauf, Richard B. III. Series.
P40.5.L352A785 2008
306.44'95–dc22   2008012759

British Library Cataloguing in Publication Data
A catalogue entry for this book is available from the British Library.

ISBN-13: 978-1-84769-095-1 (hbk)

Multilingual Matters
UK: St Nicholas House, 31-34 High Street, Bristol BS1 2AW, UK.
USA: UTP, 2250 Military Road, Tonawanda, NY 14150, USA.
Canada: UTP, 5201 Dufferin Street, North York, Ontario M3H 5T8, Canada.

The articles in this book also appeared in the journal of *Current Issues in Language Planning* Vol. 6: 3 (2005); Vol. 9: 1 (2008) and *Journal of Multilingual and Multicultural Development* Vol. 20: 4&5 (1999).

The policy of Multilingual Matters/Channel View Publications is to use papers that are natural, renewable and recyclable products, made from wood grown in sustainable forests. In the manufacturing process of our books, and to further support our policy, preference is given to printers that have FSC and PEFC Chain of Custody certification. The FSC and/or PEFC logos will appear on those books where full certification has been granted to the printer concerned.

Printed and bound in Great Britain by MPG Books Ltd.

Contents

Series Overview

Since 1998, when the first polity studies on language policy and planning – addressing the language situation in a particular polity – were published in the *Journal of Multilingual and Multicultural Development*, 31[1] polity studies (and one issue on Chinese character modernization) have been published in that journal and (between 2000 and 2008) in *Current Issues in Language Planning*. These studies have all addressed, to a greater or lesser extent, 22 common questions or issues (Appendix A), thus giving them some degree of consistency. However, we are keenly aware that these studies have been published in the order in which they were completed. While such an arrangement is reasonable for journal publication, the result does not serve the needs of area specialists nor are the various monographs easily accessible to the wider public. As the number of available polity studies has grown, we have planned (where necessary) to update and republish these studies in coherent areal volumes.

The first such volume was concerned with Africa, both because a significant number of studies has become available and because Africa constitutes an area that is significantly under-represented in the language planning literature. Yet it is marked by extremely interesting language policy and planning issues, therefore in the first areal volume, we reprinted four polity studies – Botswana, Malawi, Mozambique and South Africa – as:

- *Language Planning and Policy in Africa, Vol. 1: Botswana, Malawi, Mozambique and South Africa* (2004) Richard B. Baldauf Jr. and Robert B. Kaplan (eds).

We hope that the first areal volume has served the needs of specialists more effectively. It is our intent to continue to publish other areal volumes as sufficient studies are completed. We will continue to do so in the hope that such volumes will be of interest to areal scholars and others involved in some way in language policies and language planning in geographically coherent regions. We have already been able to produce six areal volumes in addition to Africa Vol. 1 and the seven areal volumes presently in print cover 23 polities:

- *Language Planning and Policy in Africa, Vol. 2: Algeria, Côte d'Ivoire, Nigeria and Tunisia* (2007) Robert B. Kaplan and Richard B. Baldauf Jr. (eds)
- *Language Planning and Policy in Europe, Vol. 1: Hungary, Finland and Sweden* (2005) Robert B. Kaplan and Richard B. Baldauf Jr. (eds)
- *Language Planning and Policy in Europe, Vol. 2: The Czech Republic, The European Union and Northern Ireland* (2006) Richard B. Baldauf Jr. and Robert B. Kaplan (eds)
- *Language Planning and Policy in Europe, Vol. 3: The Baltics, Ireland and Italy* (2007) Robert B. Kaplan and Richard B. Baldauf Jr. (eds)
- *Language Planning and Policy in Latin America, Vol. 1: Ecuador, Mexico and Paraguay* (2007) Richard B. Baldauf Jr. and Robert B. Kaplan (eds)
- *Language Planning and Policy in the Pacific, Vol. 1: Fiji, the Philippines and Vanuatu* (2006) Richard B. Baldauf Jr. and Robert B. Kaplan (eds)

This volume – Asia, Vol. 1 – is another such volume:

- *Language Planning and Policy in Asia, Vol. 1: Japan, Nepal, Taiwan and Chinese Characters* (2008) Robert B. Kaplan and Richard B. Baldauf Jr. (eds)

The areas in which we are planning to produce additional volumes, and some of the polities that may be included are:

- **Europe**, including Cyprus and Luxembourg.
- **Asia**, including Bangladesh, Hong Kong, Malaysia, Singapore and Sri Lanka.
- **Africa**, including Cameroon, Niger, Senegal and Zimbabwe.

In the meantime, we will continue to bring out *Current Issues in Language Planning*, and add to the list of polities available for inclusion in areal volumes. At this point, we cannot predict the intervals over which such volumes will appear, since they will be defined by the ability of contributors to complete work on already contracted polity studies.

Assumptions Relating to Polity Studies

We have made a number of assumptions about the nature of language policy and planning that have influenced the nature of the studies presented. First, we do not believe that there is, yet, a broader and more coherent paradigm to address the complex questions of language policy/planning development. On the other hand, we do believe that the collection of a large body of more or less comparable data and the careful analysis of that data will give rise to a more coherent paradigm. Therefore, in soliciting the polity studies, we have asked each of the contributors to address some two-dozen questions (to the extent that such questions were pertinent to each particular polity); the questions were offered as suggestions of topics that might be covered (see Appendix A). Some contributors have followed the questions rather closely, others have been more independent in approaching the task. It should be obvious that, in framing those questions, we were moving from a perhaps inchoate notion of an underlying theory. The reality that our notion was inchoate becomes clear in each of the polity studies.

Second, we have sought to find authors who had an intimate involvement with the language planning and policy decisions made in the polity they were writing about, i.e. we were looking for insider knowledge and perspectives about the polities. However, as insiders are part of the process, they may find it difficult to take the part of the 'other' – to be critical of that process. But it is not necessary or even appropriate that they should be – this can be left to others. As Pennycook (1998: 126) argues:

> One of the lessons we need to draw from this account of colonial language policy [i.e. Hong Kong] is that, in order to make sense of language policies we need to understand both their location historically and their location contextually. What I mean by this is that we can not assume that the promotion of local languages instead of a dominant language, or the promotion of a dominant language at the expense of a local language, are

in themselves good or bad. Too often we view these things through the lenses of liberalism, pluralism or anti-imperialism, without understanding the actual location of such policies.

While some authors do take a critical stance, or one based on a theoretical approach to the data, many of the studies are primarily descriptive, bringing together and revealing, we hope, the nature of the language development experience in the particular polity. We believe this is a valuable contribution to the theoretical/paradigmatic development of the field. As interesting and challenging as it may be to provide a priori descriptions of the nature of the field based on specific paradigms (e.g. language management, language rights, linguistic imperialism) or to provide more general frameworks (e.g. Hornberger, 2006; Spolsky, 2004) – nor have we been completely immune from the latter ourselves (e.g. Kaplan & Baldauf, 2003: Chapter 12) – we believe that our current state of knowledge about language planning and policy is still partial and that the development of a sufficient database is an important prerequisite for adequate paradigm development.

Furthermore, we recognize that the paradigm on the basis of which language policy and planning is conventionally undertaken may be inadequate to the task. Much more is involved in developing successful language policy than is commonly recognized or acknowledged. There are several facets to this complexity of which we will mention but two. First, polity studies like those in this series might suggest that language planning is primarily a macro sociolinguistic activity. However, based on recent work on the micro or the local in language policy and planning (e.g. Canagarajah, 2005; Liddicoat & Baldauf, 2008b), it is becoming clear that the field is far more multidimensional than the previous literature has tended to suggest. The local is not only critical in carrying out top-down macro policy, but in some cases – often for political reasons – it is the only way that local language planning issues – for example, minority language development or work with oppressed languages or varieties – can be addressed. In addition, the availability of language and information through technology has democraticised language use and has lead to greater bottom-up pressures for language policy change.

This leads us to a second major facet – i.e. language policy development is a highly political activity with a variety of actors (Baldauf & Kaplan, 2003) or agents (Liddicoat & Baldauf, 2008a) working at different levels. Given its political nature, traditional linguistic research is necessary, but not in itself sufficient, and the publication of scholarly studies in academic journals is really only the first step in the complex process. Indeed, scholarly research itself may need to be expanded, to consider not only the language at issue but also the social landscape in which that language exists – the ecology of language and its social system. A critical step in policy development involves making research evidence understandable to the lay public; research scholars are not generally the ideal messengers in this context (Kaplan & Baldauf, 2007). We hope this series also may contribute to that end.

An Invitation to Contribute

We welcome additional polity contributions. Our views on a number of the issues can be found in Kaplan and Baldauf (1997); sample polity monographs have appeared in the extant issues of _Current Issues in Language Planning_ and in the volumes in this series. Interested authors should contact the editors, present a proposal for a monograph, and provide a sample list of references. It is also useful to provide a brief biographical note, indicating the extent of any personal involvement in language planning activities in the polity proposed for study as well as any relevant research/publication in LPP. All contributions should, of course, be original, unpublished works. We expect to work closely with contributors during the preparation of monographs. All monographs will, of course, be reviewed for quality, completeness, accuracy and style. Experience suggests that co-authored contributions may be very successful, but we want to stress that we are seeking a unified monograph on the polity, not an edited compilation of various authors' efforts. Questions may be addressed to either of us.

Richard B. Baldauf, Jr. (rbaldauf4@bigpond.com)
Robert B. Kaplan (rkaplan@olypen.com)

Note

1. Polities in print include: 1. Algeria; 2. The Baltics; 3. Botswana; 4. Cameroon; 5. Côte d'Ivoire; 6. Czech Republic; 7. Ecuador; 8. European Union; 9. Fiji; 10. Finland; 11. Hungary; 12. Ireland; 13. Italy; 14. Japan; 15. Luxembourg; 16. Malawi; 17. Mexico; 18. Mozambique; 19. Nepal; 20. Nigeria; 21. North Ireland; 22. Paraguay; 23. The Philippines; 24. South Africa; 25. Sri Lanka; 26. Sweden; 27. Taiwan; 28. Timor Leste; 29. Tunisia; 30. Vanuatu; and 31. Zimbabwe. A 32nd monograph on Chinese Character Modernization is also available.

References

Baldauf, R.B., Jr. and Kaplan, R.B. (2003) Language policy decisions and power: Who are the actors? In P.M. Ryan and R. Terborg (eds) _Language: Issues of Inequality_ (pp. 19–40). Mexico City: Universidad Nacional Autonoma de México.

Canagarajah, A.S. (ed.) (2005) _Reclaiming the Local in Language Policy and Practice_. Mahwah, NJ: Lawrence Erlbaum.

Hornberger, N.H. (2006) Frameworks and models in language policy and planning. In T. Ricento (ed.) _An Introduction to Language Policy: Theory and Method_ (pp. 24–41). Oxford: Blackwell.

Kaplan, R.B. and Baldauf, R.B., Jr. (2007) Language policy spread: Learning from health and social policy models. _Language Problems & Language Planning_ 31 (2), 107–129.

Kaplan, R.B. and Baldauf, R.B., Jr. (2003) _Language and Language-in-Education Planning in the Pacific Basin_. Dordrecht: Kluwer.

Kaplan, R.B. and Baldauf, R.B., Jr. (1997) _Language Planning From Practice to Theory_. Clevedon: Multilingual Matters.

Liddicoat, A.J. and Baldauf, R.B., Jr. (2008a) Language planning in local contexts: Agents, contexts and interactions. In _Language Policy and Planning: Language Planning in Local Contexts_ (pp. 1–14). Clevedon: Multilingual Matters.

Liddicoat, A.J. and Baldauf, R.B., Jr. (eds) (2008b) _Language Policy and Planning: Language Planning in Local Contexts_. Clevedon: Multilingual Matters.

Pennycook, A. (1998) _English and the Discourses of Colonialism_. London and New York: Routledge.

Spolsky, B. (2004) _Language Policy_. Cambridge: Cambridge University Press.

Appendix A

Part I: The Language Profile of ...

(1) Name and briefly describe the national/official language(s) (*de jure* or *de facto*).

(2) Name and describe the major minority language(s).

(3) *Name and describe the lesser minority language(s) (include 'dialects', pidgins, creoles and other important aspects of language variation).* The definition of minority language/dialect/pidgin will need to be discussed in terms of the sociolinguistic context.

(4) *Name and describe the major religious language(s).* In some polities religious languages and/or missionary policies have had a major impact on the language situation and provide *de facto* language planning. In some contexts religion has been a vehicle for introducing exogenous languages while in other cases it has served to promote indigenous languages.

(5) Name and describe the major language(s) of literacy, assuming that it is/they are not one of those described above.

(6) Provide a table indicating the number of speakers of each of the above languages, what percentage of the population they constitute and whether those speakers are largely urban or rural.

(7) Where appropriate, provide a map(s) showing the distribution of speakers, key cities and other features referenced in the text.

Part II: Language Spread

(8) Specify which languages are taught through the educational system, to whom they are taught, when they are taught and for how long they are taught.

(9) Discuss the objectives of language education and the methods of assessment to determine whether the objectives are met.

(10) To the extent possible, trace the historical development of the policies/practices identified in items 8 and 9 (may be integrated with 8/9).

(11) Name and discuss the major media language(s) and the distribution of media by socio-economic class, ethnic group, urban/rural distinction (including the historical context where possible). For minority language, note the extent that any literature is (has been) available in the language.

(12) How has immigration affected language distribution and what measures are in place to cater for learning the national language(s) and/or to support the use of immigrant languages.

Part III: Language Policy and Planning

(13) Describe any language planning legislation, policy or implementation that is currently in place.

(14) Describe any literacy planning legislation, policy or implementation that is currently in place.

(15) To the extent possible, trace the historical development of the policies/

practices identified in items 13 and 14 (may be integrated with these items).

(16) Describe and discuss any language planning agencies/organisations operating in the polity (both formal and informal).

(17) Describe and discuss any regional/international influences affecting language planning and policy in the polity (include any external language promotion efforts).

(18) To the extent possible, trace the historical development of the policies/ practices identified in items 16 and 17 (may be integrated with these items).

Part IV: Language Maintenance and Prospects

(19) Describe and discuss intergenerational transmission of the major language(s), and whether this is changing over time;

(20) Describe and discuss the probabilities of language death among any of the languages/language varieties in the polity, any language revival efforts as well as any emerging pidgins or creoles.

(21) Add anything you wish to clarify about the language situation and its probable direction of change over the next generation or two.

(22) Add pertinent references/bibliography and any necessary appendices (e.g. a general plan of the educational system to clarify the answers to questions 8, 9 and 14).

In addition, to the extent that it is either possible or relevant, authors should indicate who the 'actors' or 'agents' are in certain aspects of language policy and planning. Are there particular individuals/bodies/organisations that have played a major role in language planning activities and what has been their role?

Finally, while polity studies by definition are 'macro' descriptions of the sociolinguistic situation, there may be interesting 'micro' or 'local' language policy and planning occurring that would provide some extra depth and detail to the study.

Language Policy and Planning in Japan, Nepal and Taiwan + Chinese Characters: Some Common Issues

Robert B. Kaplan
Professor Emeritus, Applied Linguistics, University of Southern California Mailing Address: PO Box 577, Port Angeles, WA 98362 USA <rkaplan@ olypen.com>

Richard B. Baldauf Jr.
Professor, TESOL, School of Education, University of Queensland, QLD 4072 Australia <rbaldauf4@bigpond.com>

Introduction

This volume brings together three language policy and planning polity studies related to three countries in Asia as well as a study of Chinese characters[1], the dominant script form in the region. (See the 'Series Overview' for a more general discussion of the nature of the series, Appendix A for the 22 questions each study set out to address, and Kaplan *et al.* (2000) for a discussion of the underlying concepts for the studies themselves.) In this paper, in addition to providing an introductory summary of the material covered in these studies, we want to draw out and discuss some of the more general issues that these four studies have raised.

The polities covered do not in any useful sense constitute a geographic cluster, though as we note they do share some common elements in addition to the fact that all of them are in Asia. While both the Nepal and Taiwan study were initially completed about a decade ago – and have now been updated as unquestionably matters in those polities have changed over time – there are still some commonalities.

One of the important general issues raised by these studies has to do with literacy. Both China and Japan, at the end of the 19th century and the beginning of the 20th, recognized and began to try to solve the complex problem of trying to overcome widespread illiteracy in an environment of extremely complex writing systems. Character standardisation and simplification in China in the decades after the middle of the 20th century was driven by the need for mass literacy to push social reform. Literacy is still a pressing issue in Nepal, with women and minorities having very low literacy rates.

A second issue which has arisen out of the initial literacy concern is related to the use of script-based writing (except in Nepal) in the modern technological era and the ensuing problems of selecting, standardising and modernising character-based systems. A common standard based on Unicode for the overlapping character systems used in Japan, Taiwan and the People's Republic of China would increase the ease of intra- and inter-lingual written communication, making technological communication on the internet and on mobile devices like phones more reliable, and therefore making possible more widespread characters use. However, the mystique of the traditional forms, and their cultural associations, as well as different political agendas, have made agreement on standard forms of characters nearly impossible to achieve (see Zhao & Baldauf, 2008). One of the interesting things about these standards for characters is that they apply to government use and more generally to printed work. Although a guide for handwriting has fairly recently been published in Taiwan, handwritten texts in Japan and P.R. China are unregulated.

A third common issue is the increasing use of, demand for, and teaching of English as a first foreign language. It has even been suggested in Japan and Taiwan that English should be a second *de facto* national language (Kaplan & Baldauf, 2007). In all of the polities, there has been a move to begin the study of English earlier in order to gain communicative advantages that many people believe this will bring, and this demand has meant that English has begun to spread to primary schools, despite a lack of resources, especially of trained teachers (see, e.g., Butler, 2007 for Japan; Li, 2007 for P.R. China). In the character-using polities this spread also has implications for literacy in the national languages, as students are required to learn a new script form before mastering their own writing system. Furthermore, the growth of English as a world language has increasingly marginalized the study of other foreign languages in all these polities (see Baldauf *et al.*, 2007) as the demands for English take increasing quantities of language-related space in the curriculum.

A final common issue relates to the status of minority languages in each of these polities. In recent years, we have seen greater support for indigenous minority languages, especially in Taiwan where their study and greater public acceptance has become a mark of an alternate Taiwanese identity. Nevertheless, minority languages still remained squeezed by the need for the national language to be taught on the one hand and by the demand to learn English, the world language, on the other. In Japan, exogenous minority languages like Spanish, Portuguese or Korean, spoken by guest workers or returning ethnic nationals, are generally ignored by the government and the educational system, and students with these backgrounds are faced by submersion language-in-education policies. In Nepal until recently, there has been an almost total disregard of minority languages and their teaching, although some signs of bilingual programs are emerging.

Nepal

In the intervening decade since the initial study was first written, Nepal has been marked by continuous instability – protests, riots, civil war, bombings, strikes, school closures, and general unrest. The elected government and the parliament have been quite unstable; Parliament was frequently dissolved, and several political parties and their respective policies have been overturned. The Maoist 'people's war' commenced, and the build-up of the People's Liberation Army (PLA), as well as a larger people's militia, continued to undermine the elected government. At one point, the Maoists claimed to control two-thirds of the nation. Over 13,000 deaths can be attributed to both sides of the insurgency; schools were taxed or closed, often converted to training grounds and barracks. Originating in west Nepal, the unrest and civil war soon spread throughout the country.

On June 1, 2001, a massacre took place in the palace, murdering the reigning royal family and everyone in the immediate line of succession to the throne, an action regarded as devastating in a Hindu country where the king and his family were considered to be of divine descent. The official investigating commission blamed crown prince Dependra (who also died) for the massacre, but conspiracy theories were plentiful (see, e.g., Gregson, 2002; Raj, 2001; Willessee & Whittaker, 2004). Gyanendra – the younger brother of the murdered king, Birenda – and the new crown prince – Gyanendra's son Paras – were very unpopular and in some conspiracy theories were even suspected of having played a role in the massacre. Since the Maoist insurgency continued and the elected government was not able to control the uprising, in February 2005 King Gyanendra dissolved parliament and took complete control of the government. Civil and political rights were suppressed, large numbers of people, including politicians and journalists, were arrested and imprisoned, and the media were brought under the direct control of the King. Conflict between Maoist troops and the national army and police increased; indeed, many people who were not Maoist sympathizers opposed the actions of King Gyanendra and joined the insurgency. In April 2006 hundreds of thousands of people demonstrated against King Gyanendra in cities and villages throughout Nepal – a demonstration that became a spontaneous 19-day-long people's movement. On April 23, 2006, the leaders of the seven-party alliance[2] re-instated the parliament. On May 18, 2006, the House of Representatives stripped the King of his powers, declared Nepal to be a secular state, and removed the King as commander of the army. The House of Representatives removed the word *Royal* from the name of the Nepal Army, and designated the Prime Minister head of the Nepal Army. A hastily written interim constitution deprived Gyandendra of any administrative rights and removed from him all royal possessions of the massacred family members. Nepal, as a secular state, has pledged to secularize all Hindu symbols associated with the royal family, including the national anthem, and the national bird and flower, and to replace the image of the King on Nepalese currency with the image of Sagarmatha (Mount Everest). In November 2006, the seven-party alliance and the Maoist party signed a comprehensive peace agreement. An interim parliament was empanelled, and an interim constitution was framed, allowing the appointment of Maoist party members to ministerial positions in the interim government. Elections were scheduled to empanel a government body to write a new constitution. In the interim, under the supervision of United Nations peacekeepers, 31,000 Maoist soldiers, deprived of their weapons, have been placed in seven large camps and several smaller camps throughout Nepal. The Maoists have been granted amnesty and promised that consideration will be given to allowing some of them to be integrated into the Nepalese Army. Finally, in June 2007, the government agreed to give a monthly stipend of 3,000 rupees (US$46.00) to those confined in the camps.

Given these vast changes in the social and political environment, much that was reported a decade ago is no longer of any significance. The innumerable meetings that have occurred over the intervening decade have not specifically taken up the question of language in the polity. Unfortunately, the people's war and the unrest throughout Nepal have drastically limited or stopped the educational plans (i.e. expansion of education and introduction of second language education to first grade) reported in the initial (now decade) old study. For example, first language education was initiated for some Indo-European languages in the Terai and for Newari in the Kathmandu Valley. However, the lack of textbooks and of trained teachers, and the presence of ineffective management have seriously hindered the establishment of both first language education and first grade primary English education. In September 2007, the Ministry of Education and Sports issued a planning draft (for discussion) entitled 'School Sector Reform, Core Document: Policies and Strategies' (Ministry of Education and Sports, 2007). The report:

- emphasizes the need for a holistic and integrated approach to education, from grade one to grade twelve;
- notes the cultural and linguistic diversity of Nepal;
- states that a child's mother (first) language will be used as the medium of instruction up to the third grade;
- states that existing Sanskrit schools and other traditional schools may continue to operate if they follow the National Curriculum Framework (NCF);
- states that a regulatory framework will define 'the governance, management, quality, and finance functions' of English medium schools which will also follow the National Curriculum Framework;
- asserts that textbooks will be selected based on NCF guidelines;
- states that, in high school, the medium of instruction may be either Nepali or English as determined by the School Management Committee and the local government;
- states that priority will be given to recruiting and training for the teacher corps females, dalits, and other disadvantaged groups.
- avows that scholarships and training programs will be set up to improve the skills of disadvantaged teachers, especially for those who teach first language classes, and
- states that a minimum of 20 per cent of the national budget will be reserved for education.

These are important expectations; unfortunately, given the chaotic situation, they remain expectations.

Japan

Japan has long considered itself to be a mono-ethnic and therefore monolingual society, despite the existence of substantial old-comer ethnic minorities, and this – with the instrumental exception of English – has been reflected in its language planning and policy until quite recently. Increasing immigration (and hence emergent new-comer multilingualism), technological advances affecting the way people write and a perceived need to improve the teaching of English, however, mean that policies have begun to undergo rethinking. The study of Japan is divided into three main sections: the first discusses in detail the national language and minority languages; the next discusses language spread and maintenance through the education system and by other means; the last concludes with some thoughts on how language planning and policy might develop in the future, in order to give the reader a sense of how major language issues in Japan are evolving in such a manner that many of the policies developed during the 20th century may no longer be totally relevant.

Throughout its modern period (i.e. from the beginning of the Meiji period [1868] to the present), Japan has consistently represented itself in both internal and external discourse as a monolingual nation; for example, Internal Affairs and Communications Minister Aso Taro referred to Japan in a speech at the opening of the Kyushu National Museum in October 2005 as the only nation in the world having ' . . . one civilization, one language, one culture and one race' (*The Japan Times,* 18 October 2005). Official policies and a highly influential essentialist literary genre called *Nihonjinron* (theories of what it means to be Japanese) have both reflected and supported this view.

Historically, *Nihonjinron* theories have constituted a key influence on much of the government, academic and cultural discourse on Japanese society, including ideas about language. A large body of academic research has directly challenged those notions over the last two decades; however, they remain influential in some circles. In this discourse, the Japanese language is portrayed as somehow uniquely different from all other languages; at the same time, Japan is resolutely viewed as linguistically homogeneous despite all evidence to the contrary. The Japanese language is seen as too difficult for any but Japanese themselves to master by virtue of its orthography and its much-touted preference for ambiguity over directness. Race, language and culture are inextricably tied together, so that issues surrounding language carry a heavy burden of sensitive historical, political and cultural significance (Schneer, 2007). This has informed language policy to date, explaining in part the snail's pace at which planning and policy at the national level have responded to demographic change. The national language has been used as a key part of Japanese nation- and empire-building, and diversity has not been encouraged; indeed, in the early modern period the use of minority languages on both the northern and the southern borders was suppressed under a policy of assimilation designed to foster and reinforce the ideology of one whole and unified nation. In the colonies of Taiwan (1895 to 1945) and Korea (1905 to 1945), and later in the occupied territories during World War Two, inculcating use of the Japanese language became a key element in the formation of good subjects of the emperor. During this time, efforts were made to transform the language in both spoken and written form into something that could function as a modern standard – i.e., an effective instrument in the service of national unity. By the 1920s, several major steps in this process had been achieved: a standard language had been designated and was being disseminated through the education system and the national broadcaster (Japan Broadcasting Corporation, widely known as NHK). The classical-oriented written styles that had previously been the language of public life were well on their way to being replaced by a modern written Japanese based on contemporary speech rather than on centuries-old literary conventions.

Monolingualism is certainly a myth, built upon an equally shaky foundation of mono-ethnicity, but it has been an enduring and strongly entrenched pillar of what might be called the foundation myth of modern Japan. It is certainly true that nearly everybody in Japan does speak Japanese, that the language used for official purposes is Japanese and that the bulk of the population is Japanese. However, to insist that Japan is consequently monolingual disregards the existence of large ethnic communities[3] from Korea, China, Brazil and other parts of the world, of the languages of the indigenous Ainu people[4] and of the fact that Japanese students must study English for at least six years.

Language planning may be defined as consciously engineered change in the way language is used; i.e. not natural evolution but human intervention working to achieve specific desired purposes. Language planning of this sort, aimed at achieving particular linguistic and social outcomes in Japan, has covered many areas, among them standardization, script reform, language spread through the teaching of Japanese both as the national language and as a foreign language, the revival of the Ainu language and the teaching of English and other foreign languages. It is only relatively recently, except in the case of English, that language policy has included recognition of a language other than Japanese. At present, one of the most pressing issues for language planning and policy-making in Japan is the growing awareness of emergent multilingualism arising from increasing immigration over the last twenty years. The fact that this is occurring within the lingering framework of the monolingual myth accounts for the slow pace at which the national government has responded to these developments, as opposed to the greater responsiveness of local governments. Language policy change at the national level involves many years of discussion and consultation on issues that affect the nation as a whole. Local governments, however, enjoy greater freedom to respond as area-specific challenges arise, and what seems to be happening in Japan today is a more proactive stance in bottom-up rather than in top-down language planning initiatives. Local governments and NGOs are working to assist the increasing numbers of immigrants living in their areas, moving towards a greater recognition of the actual ecology of language in Japan.[5]

Japan's constitution makes no mention of any official language; it is simply taken for granted that the dominant (indeed only) historical contender is the national language. Native speakers refer to the language in two ways: when used by native speakers, it is called *kokugo* (i.e. the language of our country), but when it is taught to foreigners, it is called *nihongo* (i.e. the language of Japan). The distinction reflects an enduring belief that the Japanese language is a cultural property specific to, and a crucial part of, being Japanese. Nearly all of Japan's 128 million people speak and write Japanese, most as *kokugo*, some as *nihongo*. Standard Japanese, based on the speech of the Yamanote area of Tokyo, is spoken and understood throughout the country. The standard form was designated as such in 1916. The lexicon consists of approximately two-thirds loanwords and one-third words of Japanese origin (*wago*). Of the loanwords, the majority consists of words of Chinese origin (*kango*), borrowed over centuries of linguistic and cultural contact and absorbed into the lexicon to such a degree that most Japanese do not think of them as loanwords. *Kango* are perceived as being more formal in tone than words of Japanese origin, reflecting the centuries during which Sino-Japanese, a literary style heavily influenced by Chinese, was the major formal written variant used by the upper classes. The remainder of the lexicon consists of *gairaigo*, loanwords from languages other than Chinese (predominantly English), reflecting the historical specificities of Japan's contact with speakers of European languages. Estimates of the exact percentage of *gairaigo* differ: Backhouse (1993: 74, 76) suggests around six per cent, whereas Honna (1995: 45) puts it higher, at around ten per cent of the contents of a standard dictionary. English loanwords make up 60 to 70 per cent of the new words added to Japanese dictionaries each year (Hogan, 2003: 43).

In the absence of a native writing system, ideographic characters (*kanji*) were adopted from China (via Korea) around the 6th century CE. The characters had developed to fit the requirements of the Chinese language rather than those of the very different Japanese language; initially, they were used to write Chinese as a foreign language. Over time, however, characters were adapted to form two phonetic scripts (*hiragana* and *katakana*) in order to represent on paper the sounds and grammatical features of Japanese. These phonetic scripts developed in different parts of Japan for different purposes. *Hiragana* – a flowing and rounded script used in everyday letters and poems and in the literature written by the noblewomen of the Heian Period (794–1192 CE) – abbreviated the whole of a Chinese character until it was intelligible only to Japanese; *katakana* – more angular and used in Buddhist scriptures – extracted only one part of the relevant character. Originally there were several hundred symbols in each; however, they have been standardized at present to only 46 basic symbols, each representing the same syllables.

The prestige of Chinese characters as a mark of erudition was such that they did not fall out of use once the phonetic scripts were available, with the result that at present Japanese is written with a combination of several scripts:

- characters for nouns and the stems of inflected words;
- *hiragana* to show Japanese pronunciation where required and for the copula, pronouns and grammatical features such as inflections and postpositions;
- *katakana* for non-Japanese loanwords and for emphasis;
- Arabic numerals in phone numbers and other situations, and
- the Roman alphabet, though not an official script, nevertheless is prominent as a design feature in advertising and commerce.

Of the many thousands of characters available, current script policy recommends 1,945 of the most commonly occurring for general use, and these are taught in schools during the nine years of compulsory education. In practice, however, as many as 3,000–3,500 characters are needed in order to read the multiplicity of texts found in newspapers and advertisements (Seeley, 1991: 2). Combining the three scripts poses no particular problem once the basic principles are understood. The two phonetic syllabaries are easy to learn. Characters require more time, not only because they are much more numerous and complex in form but also because the pronunciation of each character may vary depending on the context in which it occurs; i.e. most will have at least one each of what are known as *kun* and *on* readings. The *kun* reading is the word's pronunciation in Japanese, the *on* reading represents an earlier Japanese attempt to approximate the pronunciation of the character in Chinese. *On* readings will usually be found in character compounds. Character shapes from the current list in general use range from the very simple to the quite complex; it is also often necessary to differentiate between which of several similar characters is used for a particular word. Emoticons (*kaomoji*) are also used in both handwriting and in online communication, whether by computer or mobile phone, to convey attitudinal information without words: (^-^), for instance, is one variation of a smiling face. A study by Katsuno and Yano (2002: 211) found that at least 20 dictionaries (hard copy and online) of *kaomoji* have been published since 1993. Mobile phones come with them already built in. A second area of text manipulation is the innovative and well documented *gyaru moji* (girl talk), in which users – usually young women, hence the name – manipulate text messages in a series of maneuvers, e.g. arranging the disarticulated component sections of characters in a vertical line. They may also include Roman letters, typographic or mathematical symbols, Greek letters, etc. in their messages. This orthographic play functions both for privacy (to protect the content of text messages from being understood by fellow passengers on crowded public transport) and as a kind of sub-cultural identity marker for this particular group of young women. Similar 'in-group' language play has been documented in postings to Channel 2, a well known unmoderated website (see Nishimura, 2004).

Talk of online language practices leads to the broader issue of what languages are used on the Internet in Japan. The Japanese language has established a strong online presence: the top six, in descending order, are English (31.3%), Chinese (15.0%), Spanish (8.7%), Japanese (7.4%), French (5.7%) and German (5.0%) (Internet World Statistics, 2007). Chinese and Japanese have risen to their high positions despite early views that their character-based orthographies were not suited for electronic use. An enabling factor in Japan's web presence is the capacity to access large amounts of information in the national language, an aspect usually linked with economic power. Japan is an economically advanced nation with a standard national written language that, in the 1980s, developed the technological capacity to reproduce that written language electronically. Japan:

- has a high literacy rate;
- does not recognize community languages in its language policies;
- exhibits no perceived pressing need to teach and use foreign languages – other than English – for international communication; and
- is an island country secure in its borders.

Its minority groups have, over time, been forcibly assimilated to speak Japanese. Japan has one of the world's largest domestic publishing industries, and a thriving translation industry means that most information is readily available in Japanese not long after it has appeared in other languages. In short, Japan is self-sufficient in developing a web presence and does not need to rely on another language to access information; consequently, the Internet, and particularly the web, in Japan is likely to remain largely monolingual. Within Japan, other languages are used on the Internet in personal emails and messaging, web-based language teaching sites, and major business and cultural websites.

Apart from these, the most proactive official use of other languages occurs at local government level, where foreign-language web pages offer instrumental benefits in facilitating the integration of non-Japanese residents into the community.

Publishing and printing are major industries in Japan. In 2004 there were 4,431 publishing companies, 7,778 bookstores and 2,759 libraries. Despite the stature of the publishing industry in comparative international terms, the industry recently suffered a seven-year slump in sales from which it began to emerge in 2004 thanks to the publication in that year of several very widely-selling books, first among them the translation of *Harry Potter and the Order of the Phoenix*. One area continuing to show lively sales activity is that of books relating to the Japanese language itself, in particular guides to correct usage. The translation industry in Japan plays a major part in the book trade, with many Japanese-language versions of foreign books available in any bookstore. About 5,000 translated works, most from English, are published in Japan annually (Aspect, 2006). Translation has always been important in Japan, from the early translations of the Chinese classics to the modern period's influx of translations of western books. It has provided one of Japan's major sources of information from other parts of the world. Around ten per cent of the books published each year are translations, mostly from English (Kondo & Wakabayashi, 1998: 492). What emerges is a picture of a highly literate population reading widely both domestic and translated books. The intricate writing system, although it may pose problems for children with learning difficulties or for recent migrants, is no barrier to the reading habits of the general public. Those habits are undergoing some change, in part owing to changes in the nature of publishing outlets, in part owing to the influence of electronic media and in part simply owing to the pressures of everyday life. Nevertheless, publishing and reading remain strong elements in Japan's language profile.

Japan has a range of language policies in place at national level, administered by a diverse collection of ministries and other government organizations. Policies relating to the national language and to the teaching of English in schools are administered by the Ministry of Education, Culture, Sports, Science and Technology (MEXT), before 2001 known as the Ministry of Education (MOE). Policies relating to other languages and to the teaching of Japanese overseas are implemented by the following bodies:

- Ainu maintenance (The Foundation for Research and Promotion of Ainu Culture, set up by the Hokkaido Development Agency and the Ministry of Education in September 1997);
- teaching of Japanese as a foreign language overseas (The Japan Foundation, within the Ministry of Foreign Affairs);
- foreign language teaching in schools, while under the control of MEXT in terms of curriculum, is supported by the Japan Exchange and Teaching (JET) program for foreign language teaching (under the Council of Local Authorities for International Relations [CLAIR], administered by three ministries, set up in 1987).

In addition to the official policies, informal language policies are administered by the print and visual media, which have strict regulations concerning the kinds of language that cannot be used in print or on screen because it is likely to offend readers/viewers. Other informal language promotion agencies concerned with other languages – i.e. Chinese, English, French, German, Spanish – are active in Japan (see List of Language Regulators http://en.wikipedia. org/wiki/List_of_language_regulators).

Of the current cluster of policies relating to the Japanese language itself, all deal with the written language, specifically with the orthography. In the case of Japanese, although the writing system had already existed for well over 1,000 years, there was much to be done in the 20th century in order to shape the written language to modern needs. Contemporary policies are the result of almost a century of deliberation on how best to rationalize what was formerly a much more unwieldy system of writing. The major policies in force today are:

- List of Characters for General Use, 1981;
- Modern Kana Usage, 1946, revised in 1986;
- Guide to the Use of Okurigana, 1959, revised in 1973;
- Notation of Foreign Loanwords, 1991.

The current List of Characters for General Use is the outcome of a revision of the earlier List of Characters for Interim Use, 1946, and also incorporates two earlier policies, one on the *on* and *kun* readings for characters (1948) and another on character shapes (1949). These policies were adopted by Cabinet on the basis of reports from the National Language Council, the body – located within the then Ministry of Education – responsible from 1934 to 2001 for investigating language matters and formulating recommendations for policy. In 2001 the Council was reorganized into the National Language Subdivision – the body in charge of language policy relating to *kokugo* – within the Committee for Cultural Affairs in the Agency for Cultural Affairs within the new MEXT super-ministry.

The irony of these policies setting out guidelines for orthography is that they are binding on government (including the education system and all government publications) but not on anyone else. The press largely adopted them voluntarily from the beginning and was indeed instrumental in pushing for them, since rationalization of the orthography was in the media's interest both in terms of printing technology and of boosting circulation figures. Private usage, however, is entirely up to the individual, although most people, having been socialized into writing in accordance with the policies through their years in the education system, write accordingly.

As previously noted, the contemporary List of Characters for General Use recommends a total of 1,945 characters necessary for general everyday writing, but recognizes that writing in specialist fields may require many more. The earlier List of Characters for Interim Use (1946) was slightly trimmer at 1,850 characters, but was more prescriptive in its intent, describing the policy in terms of 'limits' rather than in terms of the current more relaxed 'guidelines.' The 1,945 characters are taught during the nine years of compulsory education; the first 1,006 – known as the 'Education Kanji' – accounting for 90 per cent of the characters used in newspapers, are taught during the six years of elementary school. The early 21st century situation is very different from that pertaining 100 years ago. It has been necessary to draw up contemporary policies because in the early Meiji Period (1868–1912), when Japan came out of its period of self-imposed feudal isolation and began to modernize in response to both external and internal pressures, the characters in theory available for use numbered in the tens of thousands. Many were much more complex in form than today's somewhat simplified versions.

Major dictionaries list different numbers of characters; the largest, the *Daikanwa Jiten*, records almost 50,000, including those needed to read the classics. A 1933 survey of school readers, newspapers and literary works found a total of 6,478 characters used in those sources (Hayashi, 1977: 112–114). The size of this available character set has not diminished; the characters are still there, but policy priorities have now been set for which ones are of most general use and should therefore be taught in schools.

Quite early in the modern period, it became clear that the writing system needed rationalization, partly as a result of increased contact with European languages and partly as a result of the perception that the many years needed to master the existing writing system hindered the rapid acquisition of knowledge needed for modernization through the national education system established in 1872. A call emerged for a decrease in the number of characters for general use or, indeed, for the complete abolition of characters in favour of one of the phonetic *kana* scripts or the Roman alphabet (Twine, 1991). These early ideas on script reform, however, could not succeed. From the 1870s to the 1890s the still deeply held pre-modern upper-class view of what constituted appropriate writing for public consumption placed great importance on adherence to classical and pseudo-classical Sino-Japanese literary conventions; the men then in power had been educated in this tradition and accepted it as a given. Prior to the modern period, characters had been the preserve of the upper classes (aristocrats and samurai) who had both leisure and sponsored education available to master their use. Education for the lower classes was self-sponsored at temple schools and other places and was marked by a concentration on literacy in *kana* and basic *kanji* rather than by the heavy emphasis on the rote learning of the Chinese classics that was the hallmark of upper class education. Characters were invested with a weighty cultural mystique; despite the fact that they had been imported from China, they had come to be seen as icons of the essence of Japanese culture, an association that they still carry. Suggestions that the number of characters might be rationalized, or that they might be replaced with a different script, were very much frowned upon by the men in power, concerned not only with modernizing the country but also with preserving its cultural heritage in the face of potential Western imperialism. As the modern period wore on, an increasing number of journalists, educators, novelists and civil rights educators, motivated by pragmatic concerns in their own fields to do with literacy and the spreading of ideas, called for some sort of rationalization of the orthography. The writing system was not the only concern; other needs included the development of a written style based on modern spoken Japanese rather than on archaic literary conventions as well as the designation of a standard language understood from one end of the archipelago to the other despite the multiplicity of dialects, thereby helping to unite the nation and foster a sense of national unity and identity (Twine, 1991).

The resolution of these issues was greatly aided by the return in 1894 from study in Germany of Ueda Kazutoshi (1867–1937), the first Western-trained linguist in Japan. Ueda founded the linguistics department of the then Tokyo Imperial University (now Tokyo University) which trained many of the men who were to become influential in Japan's 20th-century language moderni-zation movement. As an undergraduate at the university, Ueda had studied under the British scholar, Basil Hall Chamberlain (1850–1935), and had been influenced by Chamberlain's views on style and script reform for Japanese; he was prepared from the start to join the groundswell of opinion in Japan in the late 1890s calling for language modernization, and his postgraduate study in linguistics had led him to view script as a means to an end rather than as an end in itself. Japan's defeat of China in the Sino-Japanese War of 1894–95 also helped, as the subsequent upsurge of nationalism prompted a re-examination of the national language, which was now to be used outside Japan in the new colony of Taiwan. Ueda established the Linguistics Society in 1898, participated actively in other language-related pressure groups and lobbied a sympathetic Education Minister for a national body to oversee language matters. As a result, the first national body to deal with language issues, the National Language Research Council, was set up within the Ministry of Education in 1902, with a four-fold charge:

- to look into the feasibility of replacing characters with a phonetic script (either *kana* or the alphabet);
- to encourage the widespread use of a written style based on modern speech;
- to examine the phonemic system of Japanese; and
- to select a standard language from among the dialects.

The Council was responsible for many of Japan's first large-scale language surveys, documenting and classifying information that would in time provide the basis for policy decisions by later bodies. Nothing ever came of the first of the tasks, but one result of the Council's work was that the standard language came to be defined as the speech of educated people in the Yamanote district of Tokyo. The government could see the utility of standardization in education and was prepared to support this. With this one exception, however, no lasting policies were formulated before the Council disappeared in an administrative shuffle in 1913. The official view was that to tamper with the existing writing system, even with the commendable aim of improving it, was tantamount to an attack on the nation's cultural heritage. Attempts to arrive at script policies in the first half of the 20th century were characterized by an unevenly weighted struggle between linguists (who regarded script as secondary to language) and ultranationalists (who regarded the orthography as a sacrosanct icon of national spirit). Govern-ment input into language planning was restored when the Interim National Language Research Council was inaugurated in 1921, but the Interim Council was replaced in 1934 by the National Language Council that remained in charge of language policy formulation until 2001. Since the Interim Council was charged with finding solutions to aspects of language use which caused difficulties in daily life and education, its members elected to investigate plans to limit characters, to revise *kana* spellings and to rationalize such conventions as the multiple *on* and *kun* readings a character could have. In 1923 the Interim Council proposed a list of 1,962 characters for general use; in 1924, it proposed a change to *kana* spelling based on modern Tokyo pronunciation; and in 1926, it proposed simplification of character shapes. Despite strong support from major newspapers that were keen to see character limits adopted as policy, the proposals (and particularly the *kana*-related one) resulted in a virulent backlash from conservatives, and the government did not accept the proposals. Several years later, in 1931, a revised version of the *kana* proposal almost succeeded when the Education Ministry of the day decided, in the face of ultranationalist opposition, to implement it in textbooks once it had been passed by the Educational Administration Committee; however, a change of minister occurred before that happened, and the Prime Minister shelved the proposal on the grounds that national unity took precedence over the likely social controversy the change would cause. As long as the military, holding rigid views on the sanctity of tradition, held power nothing could be done about script reform. When the subsequent National Language Council offered another proposal to limit characters in 1942, Japan had already been at war for a long time and the *kotodama* (i.e. the spirit of the Japanese language) ideology (never to be altered) had become even more deeply entrenched. During World War Two, those who openly advocated script reform were vilified by right-wing interests; foreign loanwords such as *beesubooru* (baseball) were dropped in favour of Sino-Japanese equivalents; in one incident in 1939 a group of Waseda University students who advocated Romanization were accused of anti-nationalist sympathies and were arrested by the secret police. In this atmosphere the status quo held; the term *language policy* was perceived to refer only to the spread of the Japanese language in the conquered territories and not to the management of language issues at home. Thus, much remained to be done to allow the written Japanese of the early modern period to develop into contemporary written Japanese, but the potential was impeded by vested intellectual and political interests and a strong ultranationalist philosophy; it took the major cultural and intellectual shift resulting from defeat in World War Two to break this stalemate. The purging of right-wing powerbrokers and the concurrent emphasis during the Allied Occupation on democracy provided an atmosphere for both an ideological and a practical break with the past, including the issue of script reform. Members of the National Language Council trying to proceed with reform wisely tapped into the zeitgeist, arguing that the writing system made it needlessly difficult for all sectors of the populace to participate in the written debate on public life in postwar Japan and was thus not democratic. Since the 1946 Constitution located sovereignty in the people of Japan and not in the Emperor, this proved a particularly effective line of reasoning.

When, after a three-year wartime hiatus, the National Language Council reconvened in 1945, the majority of members decided upon a moderate approach, rejecting radical proposals:

- that characters be dropped altogether,
- that the shapes of the more complex ones be modified,

- that *kana* spelling be brought into line with modern pronunciation, and in general
- that related changes aimed at reducing complexity were appropriate.

The policies presently in operation emerged over the following decade out of this compromise, with proposals being first submitted to the Minister as reports from the Council and then being officially promulgated once accepted by Cabinet. Since these policies were binding on government departments, they were disseminated through school textbooks so that the postwar and subsequent generations of school children grew up under their influence. The policies were subsequently slightly revised during the period from 1965 to 1991 as the result of a request for a re-evaluation from the Education Minister, under pressure from a resurgence of conservative opinion fearing that literacy standards had become inferior to those prewar; these changes were largely cosmetic, involving no substantial reversal of direction. Only a few characters were added to the list for general use in 1981, and the revised *kana* spelling remained unchanged. While it appeared that script policy matters had been settled, they do in fact receive ongoing attention even at present, driven by technological developments. Once the Council had produced the last of the current policies in 1991, it turned its attention to the spoken language, producing reports (but not policies) that discussed the use of honorifics and the influx of loanwords from other languages, in particular English. The development of character-capable word processing technology had brought changes to the way Japanese is written. The size of the character set meant that Japan had not experienced a successful typewriter age; while companies certainly did use Japanese typewriters, they were large, clumsy machines requiring specially trained operators, and they never reached the speeds possible with a conventional keyboard. Later, fax technology made it possible to transmit handwritten documents. Consequently, current script policies were predicated on a culture of handwriting shaped by the need to recognize, remember and accurately reproduce a large number of characters; since the invention of the first character-capable word processor (1978) and the subsequent rapid uptake of this technology and its later extension to the Internet has undermined the pillars which had supported postwar script policy. Word-processing software contains many thousands more characters than the 1,945 on the List of Characters for General Use. For a time, until users became accustomed to viewing the technology as a bonus rather than as a source of exotic effects, documents looked somewhat 'blacker' owing to an increase in the proportion of characters in the text. Some very complex characters – long gone from the official lists – also made an occasional comeback in electronically produced documents. Inexperienced users sometimes made mistakes by using the wrong characters from the list of homophones offered by the memory to fit their typed-in phonetic input. The fact that so many characters had become available on demand led some academics and publishers to suggest that language policy might need to be changed to accommodate the presence of the technology, perhaps by altering the current policy so that fewer are taught for reproduction and more are taught for recognition. The Council, recognizing the challenges, was nevertheless slow to respond, choosing instead to focus mainly on rationalizing the shapes of those characters not on the List of Characters for

General Use to be used in computers. However, the 2005 report of the Council's successor (the National Language Subdivision of the Committee for Cultural Affairs) acknowledged that technology was having an effect on how people wrote and announced that it would soon embark on a thorough reappraisal of the existing policy on characters. This move is timely. The proportion of Japan's population who grew up in the period when handwriting was the norm is rapidly ageing, subsequent generations never having known a time when electronic character input and output were not possible.

Written culture in the 21st century includes a technology-mediated aspect that has definite implications for script policy, and changes in script policy are likely. High rates of accessing the Internet by mobile phone and text messaging make Japan distinctive in the transnational arena; cheap messaging available through Internet-mode (a wireless service launched in Japan by DoCoMo in 1999 which enables e-mails to be exchanged between mobile phones) means that e-mail messaging rather than talk is the major use for those phones in Japan, contributing to a type of innovative use of language not envisaged by those who drew up the current script policies. Not only is the language used in messaging more often free of the formality of other written text, it has the added dimension of variations in script use – i.e. greater use of the *kana* script where characters would normally be used. All these things are the focus of current examination by the National Language Subdivision as the beginning of a major shift in policy outlook at the national level in response to now well-entrenched challenges to former ways of using the orthography.

As noted, the National Language Council, after 1991, turned its attention to spoken aspects of the national language. Along with the previously mentioned change in the status of dialects, other aspects of language use were also addressed. Members of the older generation often feel that language standards are being eroded. The National Language Council's report on *Language Policy for a New Era*, for example, noted, 'Most older people rely on linguistic practices that are traditional and typical, and tend to be critical of or feel alienated from the new ways in which younger people speak.' The term used to express these misgivings is *kotoba no midare* (disorder in the language). Two major foci for such perceptions are the increase in loanwords and the supposedly declining use of honorifics. New technologies, in particular information technology, have led to an increase in the number of foreign loanwords in circulation, many of them replacing perfectly good Japanese equivalents. Furthermore, young people seem not to be able to use the complicated system of honorifics in the way that their parents do, making this matter one of the major issues in intergenerational transmission of the language. Concern about *kotoba no midare* is not a new phenomenon, having been a frequently recurring theme in discourse about the national language since the late 18th century. These perceptions of declining ability across all language skills continued a trend that has been apparent since the surveys began in 1995. Many respondents spoke of their belief in a clear connection between the gaps in today's abilities and the erosion of time available for studying honorifics, proverbs and *kango* since the introduction in recent years of the new Courses of Study aimed at a more relaxed curriculum. The government's response was to announce that, as one arm of a strategic plan to foster Japanese able to speak English well, 200 schools at all three levels of education nationally would be designated flagship Japanese language education providers, with a special emphasis on fostering advanced reading and writing skills, on knowledge of the classics and oral communication skills and on the basis that a good command of students' first language is a prerequisite for successful acquisition of a foreign language. The use of loanwords was to a certain extent unavoidable, given the nature of globalization, and this was bound to be particularly the case in specialist areas such as information technology. In non-specialist areas, however, caution has been urged: to use words not universally understood could impede communication, particularly with older people. Since it is younger people who most enthusiastically adopt loanwords, it was thought intergenerational communication might suffer as a result. The six years of compulsory English study at junior and senior high school no doubt contribute to the high proportion of loanwords from English (Honna, 1995), but the fact of their existence does not guarantee comprehension. In 2002, Prime Minister Koizumi took direct action to counter this problem when he instituted a committee to study the matter under the auspices of the National Institute for Japanese Language, a group that issued four reports between 2003 and 2006 recommending the replacement of certain loanwords with Japanese equivalents.

On the matter of honorifics, it appears that knowing when the use of such language was appropriate in the interests of smooth communication had become more important than the correct forms of the honorifics themselves – a move away from the more prescriptive past attitudes towards a more holistic view of language and communication. Interestingly, whereas a 1952 report on polite speech by the Council had criticized the overuse of honorifics and euphemisms by women, a similar investigation conducted in the early 1990s found no significant difference between the language of men and women in this respect. The less formal language used in text messaging and email has had a definite effect on language use, in areas as diverse as forgetting how to write *kanji* and traditional letter forms, an increase in abbreviations and neologisms, and a loss of nuance. There is a clear tendency to abbreviate characters in online chat and text messaging, including the highly specialized and ludic *gyaru moji* (girl script – qv) that manipulates characters in ways unforeseen by policy makers. The informal text practices used in email chat groups and phone texting are likely to become a subject of discussion in terms of literacy practices in the future. This discussion has highlighted the centrality of the language to concepts of national identity, the central role of the orthography in this, the importance of language policies regulating that orthography and the manner in which they were developed, and the significant challenges now being posed to the current policy stance by electronic media and to concepts of 'proper' writing by mobile phone text messaging. Far from the fossilized and static concept of 'the national language' presented in the monolingual *kokugo* myth, the language itself is a vital organic entity that is constantly evolving, often in ways that provoke controversy among its users.

Taiwan

The island of Taiwan lies some 120 kilometers off the southeastern coast of mainland China, across the Taiwan Strait, and has an area of 35,801 square kilometers (13,823 square miles) (see *Wikipedia*, <http://en.wikipedia.org/wiki/Taiwan>, consulted 4 November 2007.) About 80 per cent of the people in Taiwan (*Minnaruren*) belong to the Hoklo ethnic group and speak both Standard Mandarin (officially recognized by the ROC as the National Dialect) and Taiwanese (a variant of the Min Nan dialect spoken in the costal provinces of Fujian and Guandong). Mandarin is the primary language of instruction in schools and dominates radio and television; however, non-Mandarin dialects have recently undergone a revival in public life in Taiwan. The Hakka, about 15 per cent of the population, speak a distinct Hakka dialect. Aboriginal minority groups – about 1.7 per cent of the population – still speak their native languages, although most also speak Mandarin. English is a common second language, and it is also featured on several of Taiwan's education exams.

Japan and Taiwan fit together more clearly as their histories partially merged from 1895 to 1945 (see the monograph by Gottlieb elsewhere in this volume), but prior to that Taiwan had an extremely complicated linguistic history. Evidence of human settlement in Taiwan dates back 30,000 years, although the first inhabitants of Taiwan may have been genetically distinct from any groups currently on the island. The Austro-Polynesian aboriginal people arrived in Taiwan 6,000 to 8,000 years ago from the southeast coast of the Asian continent. They soon became divided into two groups: the *Pingpu Zu* (plains people), and the *Gaoshan Zu* (mountain people), each group divided into nine tribal configurations. Most aboriginal groups in Taiwan have their own languages that, unlike Taiwanese or Hakka, do not belong to the Chinese language family, but rather belong to the Austronesian language family. The extent of contact with the mainland is not clearly recorded; in 230 CE, during the Three Kingdoms period, Emperor Sun Chuan tried unsuccessfully to conquer the island, and in the 13th century Kublai Khan (1260–1295) made two similarly futile attempts. The Dutch invaded the southern part of the island in 1624, and in 1625 the Spanish invaded the northern part of the island. The Spanish were driven out in 1648 by the Dutch, who ruled the island from 1624 to 1661. In 1662, Zheng Cheng-kong (a.k.a. Koxinga) and his family achieved authority over Taiwan and kept it for 21 years (1662–1683). This period was followed by Ch'ing Dynasty domination from 1683 to 1895; during the early years of this period there was a wave of immigration from the mainland, bringing immigrants from Fujian Province and, slightly later, speakers of Hakka. In 1895, following China's defeat in the first Sino-Japanese war, the island was ceded to Japan, which occupied the island until the end of World War Two in 1945. Over that long period of time (1662 –1945) the aboriginal people were increasingly marginalised, and the Han people achieved great numerical superiority – in 1895 Han inhabitants already outnumbered aboriginal people, and by 1905 there were 2,970,000 Chinese vs. 113,000 aboriginal people – outnumbered by a mass more than 25 times as great.

The influence of Japanese, over a 50-year long occupation, was extensive; Japanese was mandated in all public domains, and Taiwanese was prohibited. Thus, in 1945, most Taiwanese could not use their first language beyond the home registers. And even in those registers, many Japanese loan words were employed. This was completely consistent with larger Japanese policy; i.e.:

- to make the people understand the position of the colonies as members of the East Asian Co-Prosperity Sphere (*Dai Töa Kyöeiken*),
- to make them aware of the true meaning of the New Order in that Sphere, and
- to foster among them a new culture based on the self-awareness of the people as Orientals.

Japanese language policy centred primarily on education. Instruction in *kokugo* and in Japanese ethics 'served to mould the outlook of . . . [the] youth and to instil in them a respect for Japan and its political institutions' (Peattie, 1984: 188). In other words, the policy in the colonies of Japan, amassed over a half century between 1895 and 1945, was assimilation into Japan, Japanese ethics, and Japanese language (Coulmas, 2002: 214–217). People educated during the Japanese period (1900 – 1945) used Japanese as the medium of instruction. Some in the older generations speak only the Japanese they learned at school and the Taiwanese they spoke at home and are unable to communicate with many in the modern generations who speak only Mandarin.

There is a need at this point to look at events on the China mainland as these provide the historical background for post-1945 Taiwan. In this section there is an overlap with materials in the final monograph on Chinese characters. When the Republic of China was established in 1911, the country was composed of more than 50 ethnic groups, each speaking one or more languages representing the Sino-Tibetan, Austronesian, Altaic, and Indo-European language families. The Han group was by far the largest, accounting for more than 90 per cent of the population; however, this population was not in any sense homogeneous – rather it consisted of seven major dialect groups:

Mandarin 70%,	Wu 8.4%,	Xiang 5%,	Cantonese 5%,
Min 4.2%,	Hakka 4% and	Gan 2.4%.	

Clearly, such diversity significantly interfered with national unification and political, economic and social development. As early as the end of the Qing dynasty, China's leaders realized that, in order for China to become a strong nation, it would need a national language. Additionally, they realized that the matter of widespread illiteracy had to be addressed. This matter was not really addressed until the time of the Republic, but as recently as the mid-1950s it was estimated that between half and two-thirds of the adult population were functionally illiterate, and the representation among women and girls was significantly higher than among males. Thus, two enormous language-planning problems faced the national leaders of the new republic:

- Which dialect would be selected to be the national language?
- How could it be written so that the masses could learn it in the shortest possible time?

The government began to address the two issues immediately; on 10 July 1912 a meeting on education was convened at the Offices of the Ministry of

Education (MOE) in Beijing. An important resolution was passed requiring the immediate organization of a Committee for the Unification of Pronunciation (CUP). It was agreed that the Committee would have three major functions:

- to examine and standardize the pronunciation of all the words in the National Language (NL);
- to analyze the phonemes of the NL and to determine their number;
- to adopt phonetic alphabets – one symbol for each phoneme.

The 45-member Committee was convened and empanelled on 13 February 1913 as a subcommittee of the MOE. The issue of determining the NL was discussed at length in that initial meeting; there were two candidates: Mandarin and Cantonese. Even though Mandarin was the most obvious choice, the CUP adopted a compromise – an artificial version of Mandarin with important features from major dialects added. This compromise was perceived to be inappropriate for two primary reasons:

- there were no native speakers of this artificial variety to serve as teachers;
- a majority of Chinese people already spoke some type of Mandarin.

As a result, Peking Mandarin was recognized as the National Language, and the National Language Movement (NLM) was born. In 1932, without any announcement of radical changes, the *Pronouncing Dictionary of the National Language,* authorized by the MOE in 1919 on the basis of CUP recommendations, was quietly revised with the new title *National Pronunciation of Common Vocabulary,* containing 9,920 words and 2,299 synonyms based entirely on the educated speech of Peking, was reauthorized by the MOE and was disseminated.

While all this activity was ongoing, another dispute was working its way through the government; what writing system would be selected for the proclaimed National Language? (The following monograph in this volume – Chinese Character Modernization in the Digital Era: A Historical Perspective – deals with this problem in greater detail.) It had been decided, at the 1912 meeting previously mentioned, that characters were to be kept intact but that an auxiliary system of phonetic alphabets – to be devised by the CUP – was to be adopted for education. It was gradually decided that the traditional transcribing alphabet (rather than the Latin alphabet) should be adopted as the official phonetic (transcribing) device (a device roughly between the Latin alphabet and the Japanese syllabary) supplementing the characters. The effect was that the transcribing alphabet – consisting of 25 consonants, 3 glides, 12 vowels and 4 tones – looked exactly like the simplified Chinese characters. On 23 November 1916, the transcribing alphabets were authorized by the MOE. More or less concurrently, in April 1929 the Committee for the Propagation of a Unified National Language (CPUNL) was founded; the CPUNL was charged with improve the transcribing alphabets by way of a system known as the National Phonetic Symbols. In 1928, the MOE, on the recommendation of the CPUNL, authorized a Romanization system for transcription – known as the second form of the National Phonetic Symbols (NPS2); that system was largely developed by Chao, C.R. and Lin Yu-Tang, and it endured until 1984.

As the preceding remarks suggest, there was much activity during the first third of the 20th century. All of the details of that activity are recounted in the original monograph entitled 'The Language Planning Situation in Taiwan' republished here. While it appears that, during the period, much was happening in the area of language policy development and policy implementation despite the many interruptions due to political turmoil and the Sino-Japanese War, on the contrary not much was happening in the area of language development (except, perhaps, for the work of the Institute for Compilation and Translation, which produced 25 volumes of word lists in such scientific and technical fields as mathematics, physics, chemistry, various medical specialties and several areas of engineering and social science [i.e. economics, education and psychology]). In short:

- the selection process for the NL was quite smooth;
- the NL selection was not entirely satisfactory because the variety chosen constituted a compromise that added a number of features to the NL and thus resulted in the total absence of native speakers of this variety;
- an almost exclusive concern with the pronunciation of the NL developed;
- an almost exclusive concern with language policy matters to the exclusion of language development matters occurred; and
- an absence of systematic evaluation measures in any of the planning and propagation activities was evident.

In 1945, at the end of World War Two, Japan returned Taiwan to China. The unfortunate choice of General Chen Yi as administrator for Taiwan led to two years of confusion and conflict. The language planning activities in China between 1911 and 1949 and in Taiwan between 1949 and the present represent a top-down development, all decisions in Taiwan lying in the hands of the MOE, a body that has acted in accord with a national language policy designed to promulgate the NL at all costs. The success of the spread of the NL has been accomplished (at least in Taiwan) at the cost of aboriginal languages as well as other varieties of Chinese spoken in Taiwan. While the special problems associated with the NL have certainly been addressed over the past century, and while some of those problems have been resolved, the cost has been very great. The cost in fiscal terms cannot be determined, but the cost in the sense of the gradual loss of the aboriginal languages and of Chinese dialects spoken in Taiwan has been substantial. While the NLM was intended not only to promulgate the NL but also to solve a variety of social problems, there is little evidence that the social problems have in fact been resolved; more importantly, there is scant evidence that there is any relationship between language issues and social issues. There is no question that the individual standard of living in Taiwan has improved substantially, but it is unclear that the economic development is a corollary of the NLM.

It will be important over at least the next decade to compare the outcomes of the NLM in mainland China and in Taiwan and to disambiguate language developments from various other changes. It is also important to note that, in both situations (China and Taiwan), language policy decisions were commonly made on political grounds by individuals not particularly cognizant of reasonable linguistic considerations or of outcomes that might have been anticipated on the basis of language planning theory and experience. Nevertheless, the decade intervening between the 2000 monograph and the update published in this volume has been spent largely in correcting the problems created by the initial NLM and in creating new problems springing from a failure to consider the probable consequences of policy changes.

Across the Three Polities

In summary, while language planning has been practiced across the polities represented in this volume and while language-in-education planning is widespread across all three of those polities, it seems clear:

- that the general condition of language policy, and especially of language-in-education policy, is often chaotic and frequently ineffective;
- that, at least initially, language-in-education policy has been oriented toward the rapid spread of literacy among an essentially illiterate and multilingual (or multidialectal) population (see, e.g., Kaplan & Baldauf, 2003, especially that section dealing with North Korea);
- that language-in-education policies are rarely anchored in national language policies – indeed, it is not clear that national language policies in any serious sense of the term have in fact been developed across the three polities reported on in this volume;
- that language-in-education policies are frequently ad hoc and sometimes driven by market forces; the same might be said of language policies, but since such policies are rare, it is hard to characterize those invisible plans; and
- that language-in-education policies are subject to sudden and radical changes in direction in accord with unstable political agendas.

Chinese Character Modernization in the Digital Era: An Historical Perspective

After a century of effort directed at modernizing Chinese script, it is still the case that Chinese characters [henceforth *hanzi*] remain a deficient communication system both for human use and for mechanical application. In some respects, the reform of Chinese *hanzi* has been a very political process, driven ultimately by politicians, yet at the same time influenced by the masses and by historical traditions. Early views of language planning saw the discipline as a clinical linguistic process aimed at solving language problems, while modern-day critical theorists would argue that it is rooted in the social, economic and political agendas of the dominant elites. A similar struggle of ideologies has been played out in *hanzi* reform during the last century, and the history of the process highlights the enormous challenge that Chinese language planners face and have faced. In this monograph, the reform process is examined and explained in light of these struggles. While this process of reform is peculiar to China, it also constitutes a much wider issue with implications for a number of other polities. The focus is on a discussion of the recent developments in the Chinese *hanzi* modernization process, with a historical description designed to provide the necessary background for understanding the origin of the underlying issues and also to provide a prospective view that suggests possible future developments, particularly in light of the impact of technological change.

Polity studies, as they are normally practiced in *Current Issues in Language Planning*, usually undertake to cover the whole range of sociolinguistic developments and changes specific to a particular polity. However, in the case of Chinese and China, issues of language policy and planning loom so large in the social, political and economic scheme of things that a more focused approach to the study of this complex language system seems warranted. Thus the editors of the *CILP* series have chosen to call such studies 'polity studies'; such efforts may not encompass all of the language policy and planning activities of a particular nation state (or they might deal collectively with matters related to several smaller political entities). In the case of China, one polity study on Taiwan (Tsao, 2000) has already been produced; it is reproduced and updated here and immediately precedes this monograph for which it serves as an introduction. This study examines another major set of issues important to Chinese language planning – those related to script reform, examining in some detail recent developments in the People's Republic of China and their implications for future developments in Chinese writing. Additional polity studies relating to China might include language policy and planning in Hong Kong, planning for the oral language use of *Putonghua* and of the other Han regionalects, and planning for the many minority languages spoken in China.

Script reform has been the focus of both formal and informal language planning in China for millennia – characters were shaped and reshaped and developed during the dynastic period, but it has only been since the founding of the Republic of China in 1912 that major reform has occurred. In dynastic China, writing was the tool of the privileged and was available only to the wealthy elites who had the time required to study and learn the complex system of characters. After the revolution, there was seen to be a need to reform the language in parallel with the reforms occurring in society – to simplify the language to deal with the country's large number of illiterates. The first simplification scheme (FSS) proposed a list of 324 characters that were approved for use in 1935 by the nationalist Ministry of Education based on decades of careful deliberation, extensive discussion and patient research on simplified characters in use historically and in the community. Although the FSS was withdrawn in the following year, allegedly due to the outbreak of the Sino-Japanese war, it provided the basis for the script reforms that subsequently occurred in the Peoples' Republic of China (PRC).

While the Chinese were fighting the Japanese, they were also split between fiercely rival Communist and Nationalist camps. The Nationalists had turned their backs on script reform in 1936, but the Communists started to use simplified materials in printed materials in regions they controlled as part of initial literacy efforts and as part of eradicating the feudal roots of the traditional system. When they came to power in 1949 on the mainland, with the nationalists having retreated to Taiwan, script reform constituted part of their radical reforms. In 1956 the Table of Simplified Characters was adopted; it was built on the 1935 FSS, but with an added total of about 2,200 simplified characters and with a halving of the average number of strokes for the most common characters from 18 to 9. One of the major objectives of this reform was to create the basis for universal literacy[6]. A second simplified scheme was drafted during the Great Cultural Revolution of 1966 to 1976 and was decreed for use in 1977 but was withdrawn in 1986. Since 1986, the emphasis has shifted from simplification to developing comprehensive databases of characters. It needs to be noted that the use of simplified characters applies to government documents and other printed documents. Individuals' handwriting, which has always included simplifications for convenience, is exempt from legislated restrictions.

While simplification was initially aimed at providing the basis for universal literacy – an objective that has largely been achieved – a series of new issues have arisen for character use. First, the various reform schemes have been confusing for many people, so handwritten characters used in the PRC are drawn from the various schemes, even from characters that have been withdrawn. Ideally, some rationalization should occur. Second, with the opening up of China to the West, resulting in more contact with traditional character-using societies (e.g. in Taiwan and Hong Kong) and with the need for the current government to stress its historical links with its Chinese heritage, more traditional characters have begun to appear, even in some printed materials. Now that the public is literate and better educated, complex or traditional *hanzi* are easier to learn and are seen as prestigious. Finally, *hanzi* are still not ideally suited to use with technology as many characters are still too complex to display on computer or mobile phone screens. Furthermore, the many different coding and entry schemes make a distant dream of the kinds of interoperability alphabetic language users take for granted on their computers.

These issues suggest that there are needs both for further simplification (for technology), and for a general broadening to include some widely used traditional *hanzi* and *hanzi* from the Second Scheme of Simplified Characters (SSSC). In addition, some of the previous reforms have created malformed or confusing characters that need to be rewritten. The difficulty for language planners is that these competing interests and the weakened ability of the government to dictate reforms have meant that change has been nearly impossible to implement. Yet, if changes are not implemented, more and more Chinese may begin to use English or *pinyin* – the alphabetic script used to represent *hanzi* for initial learning purposes in China – for technological purposes. If this happens, the use of *hanzi* on the internet may gradually decline, reducing the potential of Chinese to serve as an international language.

Discussion

In this volume, conservative forces of almost mythic tradition have been interrupted; consequently, planners are sometimes confronted by periods of 'revolutionary' violence shaping and disrupting the four key issues identified at the beginning of this article (see the first two pages of this introductory article). In this climate it has been difficult for language planners to have much of an impact and to work on languages on an evolutionary basis.

At least in Japan, Taiwan, and China, and perhaps more recently in Nepal, there have been literacy campaigns that have served to move literacy from an elite, limited access skill, to one widely available across the entire population. While the basis for such language planning activity and standardization has been revolutionary, technology has had a major impact on the character-based systems. In some respects, technology has had a revolutionary impact, but English has had, and is having, a revolutionary impact on educational systems and on the understanding of the uses and limits of language in each of the polities. Finally, policies have had revolutionary impacts on the status of indigenous and exogenous minority languages. These four issues are, of course, similar to those in polities in other parts of the world, but they are complicated by the greater complexity of the language systems in the polities represented in this volume.

Notes

1. Eagle, S. (2000) The language situation in Nepal. *Journal of Multilingual and Multicultural Development* 20 (4&5), 269–271; Tsao, F. -f. (2000) The language-planning situation in Taiwan. *Journal of Multilingual and Multicultural Development* 20 (4&5), 272–327; Gottlieb, N. (2008) Japan: Language policy and planning in transition. *Current Issues in Language Planning* 9 (1), 1–68; Zhao Shouhui (2005) Chinese Character Modernization in the Digital Era: A Historical Perspective. *Current Issues in Language Planning* 6 (3), 315–378.
2. The alliance is composed of the seven major political parties, including the two largest parties, the Nepali Congress Party (NC) and the United Marxist-Leninist Party (UML).
3. The foreign population figures can be shown in detail by reference to the findings of the most recent census figures available, those of the 2000 population census, which listed a total of 1,310,545 foreigners in Japan:

   - 970,878 Asians (Bangladesh, Cambodia, China [including Taiwan], India, Indonesia, Iran, Korea, Laos, Malaysia, Myanmar, Nepal, Pakistan, Philippines, Singapore, Sri Lanka, Thailand, Viet Nam and 'others,' of which the Korean, Chinese and Philippine groups were the largest respectively),
   - 47,984 North Americans (Canada, Mexico, USA and 'others,' with the United States group the largest),
   - 230,556 South Americans (Argentina, Bolivia, Brazil, Colombia, Paraguay, Peru and 'others,' with Brazil and Peru by far the largest),
   - 30,417 Europeans (France, Germany, Italy, Romania, Russia, Spain, United Kingdom and 'others,' with the United Kingdom the largest by a wide margin),
   - 5,628 Africans (Ghana, Nigeria and 'others,' with the unspecified 'others' the largest group),
   - 8,878 from Oceania (Australia, New Zealand and 'others,' with Australia as the largest group), and
   - 16,204 stateless or 'not reported' others (Statistics Bureau, Ministry of Internal Affairs and Communication, Japan, no date).

   There are, then, at least 25 languages other than Japanese being spoken as the first or home language of people from these groups, 26 if the Ainu are included since they are not counted in the 'foreigner' figures (see, e.g., Kaplan, 2000).
   The foreign resident population in Japan in 2005 exceeded 2 million or 1.57% of the total population – the largest number ever recorded (The Ministry of Justice, 2006a). Compared with the situation 10 years ago, this is a 47.7% increase, with the greatest proportion coming from other Asian countries; 73.8% from Asia, 18.7% from South America, 3.2% from North America, and 2.9% from Europe. According to the Ministry of Justice (2006b), foreign visitors staying less than three months increased by 33% from 2000 to 2005 to over 5.7 million with 68% coming from other Asian countries, 19% from North America and Oceania, and 12% from Europe. These demographics reflect the increasing interactions between Japan and other Asian countries in recent years.

4. Although Ainu is commonly accepted as a variety spoken by the indigenous people of the Japanese islands, another dialect variety, Luchu, is spoken throughout the Okinawan islands. Central Okinawan, or *Luchu*, has some 900,000 speakers. Other varieties include *Shuri, Naha, Torishima*, and *Kudaka*, spoken across southern Okinawa Island, Kerama Islands, Kume-jima, Tonaki, Aguna Islands, and islands east of Okinawa Island. These dialects are generally not mutually intelligible with Japanese or with other Ryukyuan languages (Shibatani, 2003). These varieties should not be confused with Okinawan dialect, a variety of Japanese spoken in Okinawa. There are a number of regional dialects of Japanese: *Tokyo dialect* has become synonymous with 'standard' Japanese; in addition, at least *Osaka dialect, Kyoto dialect, Tohoku dialect, Kyushu dialect* and *Okinawa dialect* should be mentioned. The use of dialects was officially strongly discouraged during the first half of the 20th century; Children were punished for using their home dialects in the schoolyard. As social mobility meant that employment prospects in other parts of Japan could depend upon being able to speak Standard Japanese, schools were vigilant in policing its use (Carroll, 2001: 183–184).

    Over time, as the standard spread through intergenerational transmission, the degree of fracture between standard and dialect use blurred, though never disappearing completely. This led to a more relaxed official stance some decades into the postwar period. In response to the policy of regionalism – which came to inform government directions from the late 1980s – there emerged a new respect for local dialects, which were now viewed as being valuable in their own right and worthy of maintenance alongside the Standard (Neustupný, 1987: 158–160). The revised policy stressed that dialects should be valued as an important element in the overall picture of 'a rich and beautiful national language,' showcasing the vibrancy of the people and cultures of local areas.

5. Miyagi Prefecture became the first prefecture in Japan to draft bylaws – in January 2007 – (the drafts written in Chinese, English, Japanese, Korean and Portuguese) promoting multiculturalism in that prefecture.

6. In North Korea, in November 1946, the Preliminary Peoples' Committee (later, the North Korean Peoples' Committee) adopted what was called the Winter Illiteracy Eradication Movement in Rural Areas – a four-month program running from December 1947 to March 1948. All persons between 12 and 50 years of age were required to participate. A second campaign was adopted immediately following the close of the first. The entire population was involved either as teachers or as learners; e.g. college students and teachers became literacy teachers through adult schools (specially organized *Sengin hakkyo*) at night and during vacation periods in every workplace; the Youth Organization, the Women's League and the Peasant's League were all involved. Enrolments in the *Sengin hakkyo* jumped from 8,000 in 1945 to 40,000 by 1947. While literacy education was the central feature of these activities, ideological education was an important objective as well. Simultaneous with the literacy program, a second program was implemented – The Movement for Total Ideological Mobilisation for Founding the Nation [*Kenkwuksasang chongtongwen wuntong*]. The government claimed that it had achieved 100 per cent literacy in less than four years after independence – i.e. by 1949 (Kaplan & Baldauf, 2003).

References

Aspect (2006) On WWW at http://www.aspect.co.jp/english/index.html. Accessed 1 November 2007.

Backhouse, A. (1993) *The Japanese Language: An Introduction*. Melbourne: Oxford University Press.

Baldauf, R. B., Jr., Yeo-Chua, S. K. C., Graf, J., Hamid, O., Li, M. L., Nguyen, T. M. H., Ota, K., Sunggingwati, D. and Wu. H.-f. (2007, 2 August) Successes and failures in language planning for European languages in East Asian Nations. Paper Presented at the 5th Nitobe Symposium, Sophia University, Tokyo, Japan. Available at: http://www.info.sophia.ac.jp/ei/nitobe2007.htm

Butler, Y. G. (2007) Foreign language education at elementary schools in Japan: Searching for solutions amidst growing diversification. *Current Issues in Language Planning* 8 (2), 129–147.

Carroll, T. (2001) *Language Planning and Language Change in Japan*. Surrey: Curzon Press.

Coulmas, F. (2002) Language planning in modern Japanese education. In J. W. Tollefson (ed.) *Language Policies in Education: Critical Issues.* (pp. 203– 223). Mahwah, NJ: Lawrence Erlbaum.

Gregson, J. (2002) *Massacre at the Palace: The Doomed Royal Dynasty of Nepal.* New York: Hyperion Press.

Hayashi, Ō. (1977) Kanji no mondai (The question of characters). In Iwanami Kōza *Nihongo 3: Kokugo Kokuji Mondai (Japanese 3: Issues in the National Language and Script)* (pp.101–134). Tokyo: Iwanami Shoten.

Honna, N. (1995) English in Japanese society: Language within language. In J. Maher and K. Yashiro (eds) *Multilingual Japan* (pp. 45–62). Clevedon: Multilingual Matters.

Hogan, J. (2003) The social significance of English usage in Japan. *Japanese Studies* 23 (1), 43–58.

Internet World Statistics (2006) On WWW at http://www.internetworldstats.com/stats.htm. Accessed 1 November 2007.

Kaplan, R. B. (2000) Language planning in Japan. In L. S. Bautista, T. A. Llamzon and B. Sibayan (eds) *Parangalcang Brother Andrew: Festschrift for Andrew Gonzales on his Sixtieth Birthday* (pp. 277–287). Manila: Linguistic Society of the Philippines.

Kaplan, R. B. and Baldauf, R. B., Jr. (2007) An ecological perspective on language planning. In A. Creese, P. Martin and N. H. Hornberger (eds) *Encyclopedia of Language and Education (2nd Edn), Vol. 9, Ecology of Language* (pp. 41–52). Heidelberg: Springer.

Kaplan, R. B. and Baldauf, R. B., Jr. (2003) *Language and Language-in-Education Planning in the Pacific Basin.* Dordrecht: Kluwer Academic.

Kaplan, R. B., Baldauf, R. B., Jr., Liddicoat, A. J., Bryant, P, Barbaux, M.-T. and Pütz, M. (2000) Current issues in language planning. *Current Issues in Language Planning* 1 (2), 135–144.

Katsuno, H. and Yano, C. (2002) Face to face: On-line subjectivity in contemporary Japan. *Asian Studies Review* 26 (2), 205–231.

Kondo, M. and Wakabayashi, J. (1998) Japanese tradition. In M. Baker and K. Malmkjaer (eds) *Routledge Encyclopedia of Translation Studies* (pp. 485–493). London: Routledge.

Li, M. L. (2007) Foreign language education in primary schools in the People's Republic of China. *Current Issues in Language Planning* 8 (2), 148–161.

The Ministry of Education, Culture, Sports, Science and Technology (MEXT), (2006) 2006 White paper on education, culture, sports, science and technology. Retrieved 3 July 2007, from http://www.mext.go.jp/b_menu/hakusho/html/hpab200601/016.pdf

Ministry of Education and Sports. (2007) School Sector Reform: Core Document: Policies and Strategies. (Draft: For Consultation and Dissemination) Nepal. September 2007.

The Ministry of Justice. (2006a). Statistics of registered foreign people in 2005. Retrieved July 1, 2007, from http://www.moj.go.jp/PRESS/060530-1/060530-1.html

The Ministry of Justice. (2006b). Immigration control in recent years. Retrieved July 1, 2007, from http://www.moj.go.jp/NYUKAN/nyukan53-2.pdf

Neustupný, J. (1987) *Communicating with the Japanese.* Tokyo: The Japan Times.

Nishimura, Y. (2004) Establishing a community of practice on the Internet: Linguistic behavior in online Japanese communication. In Berkeley Linguistics Society (eds) *Proceedings of the 29th Annual Meeting of the Berkeley Linguistics Society* (pp. 337–348). Berkeley, CA: University of California Press.

Peattie, M. R. (1984) The *Nan'yō*: Japan in the South Pacific, 1885–1945. In R. H. Myers and M. R. Peattie (eds) *The Japanese Colonial Empire, 1885–1945* (pp. 173–210). Princeton, NJ: Princeton University Press.

Raj, P.A. (2001) *Kay Gardelo?: The Massacre in Nepal.* New Delhi: Rupa & Co.

Seeley, C. (1991) *A History of Writing in Japan.* Leiden: Brill.

Shibatani, M. (1990) *The Languages of Japan.* Cambridge: Cambridge University Press.

Schneer, D. (2007) (Inter)nationalism and English textbooks endorsed by the Ministry of Education in Japan. *TESOL Quarterly* 41 (3), 600 – 607.

Statistics Bureau, Ministry of Internal Affairs and Communication, Japan (no date)

Foreigners by Nationality (44 Groups), Age (Five-year Groups) and Sex. On WWW at http://www.stat.go.jp/English/data/kokusei/2000/gaikoku/00/hyodai.htm. Accessed 4 November 2007.

Twine, N. (1991) *Language and the Modern State: The Modernization of Written Japanese*. London: Rutledge.

Willesee, A. and Whittaker, M. (2004) *Love and Death in Kathmandu*. New York: St. Martin's Press.

Zhao, S. H. and Baldauf, R. B., Jr. (2008) *Planning Chinese Characters: Reaction Evolution, or Revolution*. New York: Springer.

Further Reading

Japan

Butler, Y. G. (2007) Foreign language education in elementary schools in Japan: Searching for solutions amidst growing diversification. *Current Issues in Language Planning* 8 (2), 129–147.

Butler, Y. G. and Iino, M. (2005) Current Japanese reforms in English language education: The 2003 'Action Plan'. *Language Policy* 4 (1), 25–45.

Carroll, T. (1995) NHK and Japanese language policy. *Language Problems & Language Planning* 19 (3), 271–293.

Chen, V. W.-c. (1977) Simplified characters in the People's Republic of China, Japan, Singapore, and Taiwan. *Journal of the Chinese Language Teachers Association* 12 (1), 63–75.

Coulmas, F. (1989) The surge of Japanese. *International Journal of the Sociology of Language* 80, 115–131.

Coulmas, F. (1990) Language adaptation in Meiji Japan. In B. Weinstein (ed.) *Language Policy and Political Development* (pp. 69–86). Norwood, NJ: Ablex.

Coulmas, F. (2000) The nationalization of writing. *Studies in the Linguistic Sciences* 30 (1), 47–60.

Coulmas, F. (2001) Language policy in modern Japanese education. In J. W. Tollefson (ed.) *Language Policies in Education: Critical Issues* (pp. 203–223). Mahwah, NJ: Lawrence Erlbaum.

Coyaud, M. (1983) La Reforme de la langue au Japon. [The reform of the Japanese language.] In I. Fodor and C. Hagégé (eds) *Language Reform: History and Future, Vol. I* (pp. 375–386). Hamburg: Buske.

Daniels, F. J. (1978) Japanese officialdom and the language. *Journal of the Association of Teachers of Japanese* 13 (1), 52–70.

Daulton, F. E. (2004) The creation and comprehension of English loanwords in the Japanese media. *Journal of Multilingual and Multicultural Development* 25 (4), 285–296.

Gates, S. (2003) Inconsistencies in writing within the Japanese Junior High School EFL education system. *JALT Journal* 25 (2), 197–217.

Gottlieb, N. (1994) Language and politics: The reversal of postwar script reform policy in Japan. *Journal of Asian Studies* 53 (4), 1175–1198.

Hara, K. (2005) Regional dialect and cultural development in Japan and Europe. *International Journal of the Sociology of Language* 175–176, 193–211.

Hashimoto, K. (2000) 'Internationalisation' is 'Japanisation': Japan's foreign language education and national identity. *Journal of Intercultural Studies* 21 (1), 39–51.

Hashimoto, K. (2007) Japan's language policy and the 'lost decade'. In A. B. M. Tsui and J. W. Tollefson (eds) *Language Policy, Culture, and Identity in Asian Contexts* (pp. 25–36). Mahwah, NJ: Lawrence Erlbaum.

Honna, N., Tajima, T. H., and Minamoto, K. (2000) Japan. In H. W. Kam and R. Y. L. Wong (eds) *Language Policies and Language Education: The Impact in East Asian Countries in the Next Decade* (pp. 139–172). Singapore: Times Academic Press.

Inoue, F. (2005) Econolinguistic aspects of multilingual signs in Japan. *International Journal of the Sociology of Language* 175–176, 157–177.

Inoue, K. (1982) The making of a Japanese constitution – A linguist's perspective. *Language Problems & Language Planning* 6 (3), 271–285.

Kaiser, S. (2003) Language and script in Japan and other East Asian countries: Between insularity and technology. In J. Maurais and M. A. Morris (eds) *Languages in a Globalising World* (pp. 188–202). Cambridge: Cambridge University Press.

Kam, H. W. (2004) English language education in China, Japan, and Singapore. *Language Policy* 3 (3), 289–292.

Kaplan, R. B. and Baldauf, R. B., Jr. (2003) Language planning in Japan. In R. B. Kaplan and R. B. Baldauf. Jr. (eds) *Language and Language-in-Education Planning in the Pacific Basin* (pp. 17–30). Dordrecht, Netherlands: Kluwer Academic.

Katsuragi, T. (2005) Japanese language policy from the point of view of public philosophy. *International Journal of the Sociology of Language* 175–176, 41–54.

Koike, I. (1993) A comparative view of English-teaching policies in an international world with a focus on Japanese TEFL policy. In *Georgetown University Round Table on Languages and Linguistics* (pp. 275–284). Washington, DC: Georgetown University Press.

Koike, I., and Tanaka, H. (1995) English in foreign language education policy in Japan: Toward the twenty-first century. *World Englishes* 14 (1), 13–25.

Liddicoat, A. J. (2007) Internationalising Japan: Nihonjinron and the intercultural in Japanese language-in-education policy. *Journal of Multicultural Discourses* 2 (1), 32–46.

Maher, J. C. (1984) English language education in Japan: Historical and macro issues in the teaching of English in schools. *Language Learning and Communication* [*Zhongying Yuwen Jiaoxue*] 3 (1), 41–52.

Maher, J. C. (1997) Linguistic minorities and education in Japan. *Educational Review* 49 (2), 115–127.

Majewicz, A. F. (1999) Visiting Japan's southern-most islands (1996): A summary of a report. *Linguistic and Oriental Studies from Poznan* 3, 183–185.

Matsuura, H., Fujieda, M. and Mahoney, S. (2004) The officialization of English and ELT in Japan: 2000. *World Englishes* 23 (3), 471–487.

Moriguchi, K. (1970) The modernization of the Japanese language from the 19th to the 20th century. In S. T. Alisjahbana (ed.) *The Modernization of Languages in Asia* (pp. 47–56). Kuala Lumpur: Malaysian Society of Asian Studies.

Morrow, P. R. (1987) The users and uses of English in Japan. *World Englishes* 6 (1), 49–62.

Nakano, K. (1972) Some problems of Japanese writing system. In A. Q. Perez and A. O. Santiago (eds) *Proceedings of the Conference on Language Policy and Language Development of Asian Countries* (pp. 1–12). Manila: Pambansang Samahan Sa Linggwistikang Pilipino.

Namba, T. (1995). The teaching of writing in Japan. *Journal of Asian Pacific Communication* 6 (1–2), 55–65.

Neustupný, J. V. (1976) Language correction in contemporary Japan. *Language Planning Newsletter* 2 (3), 1, 3–6.

Neustupný, J. V. (1978) *Post-structural Approaches to Language: Language Theory in a Japanese Context*. Tokyo: University of Tokyo Press.

Neustupný, J. V. (1984) Language planning and human rights. In A. Gonzalez (ed.) *Panagani: Essays in Honour of Bonifacio P. Sibayan on his Sixty-Seventh Birthday* (pp. 66–74). Manila: Linguistic Society of the Philippines.

Neustupný, J. V. (1986) A review of Japanese kana spelling. *New Language Planning Newsletter* 1 (1), 2–3.

Nilep, C. (2006) Language and society in Japan. *Journal of Pragmatics* 38 (8), 1313–1318.

Oda, M., and Takada, T. (2005) English language teaching in Japan. In G. Braine (ed.) *Teaching English to the World: History, Curriculum, and Practice* (pp. 93–101). Mahwah, NJ: Lawrence Erlbaum.

Sasaki, T. (1972) The language of instruction of Japan. In A. Q. Perez and A. O. Santiago (eds) *Proceedings of the Conference on Language Policy and Language Development of Asian Countries* (pp. 1–16). Manila: Pambansang Samahan Sa Linggwistikang Pilipino.

Seeley, C. (1995). The 20th century Japanese writing system: Reform and change. *Journal of the Simplified Spelling Society* 2, 27–29.

Stanlaw, J. (2004). *Japanese English: Language and Culture Contact*. Hong Kong: Hong Kong University Press.

Takashi, K. (1992) Language and desired identity in contemporary Japan. *Journal of Asian Pacific Communication* 3, 133–144.

Taki, T. (2005) Labor migration and the language barrier in contemporary Japan: The formation of a domestic language regime of a globalizing state. *International Journal of the Sociology of Language* 175–176, 55–81.

Teplova, N. (2006) Translation and language policy in Japan: From 'opening up to the world' to 'globalization'. *Meta* 51 (4), 758–770.

Watanabe, N. (2002) Language planning in Japan: Standardization, orthography and internationalization. *Geolinguistics* 28, 76–90.

Watanabe, N. (2007) Politics of Japanese naming practice: Language policy and character use. *Current Issues in Language Planning* 8 (3), 344–364.

Wetzel, P. J. (2002) Language planning and language change in Japan. *Language in Society* 31 (5), 800–803.

Yamada, Y. (1972) The national language development of Japan. In A. Q. Perez and A. O. Santiago (eds) *Proceedings of the Conference on Language Policy and Language Development of Asian Countries* (pp. 56–78). Manila: Pambansang Samahan Sa Linggwistikang Pilipino.

Yoshida, K. (2003) Implications of a research on the state of English education in Japan. *Sophia Linguistica* 50, 53–65.

Nepal

Cook, K. and Langdon, M. (1988) An interview with Narendra Suwal. *Linguistic Notes from La Jolla* 14, 3–14.

Kansakar, T. R. (1996) Multilingualism and the language situation in Nepal. *Linguistics of the Tibeto-Burman Area* 19 (2), 17–30.

Sonntag, S. K. (1980) Language planning and policy in Nepal. *ITL: Review of Applied Linguistics* 48, 71–92.

Sonntag, S. K. (2007) Change and permanence in language politics in Nepal. In A. B. M. Tsui and J. W. Tollefson (eds) *Language Policy, Culture, and Identity in Asian Contexts* (pp. 205–217). Mahwah, NJ: Lawrence Erlbaum.

Whelpton, J. (1998) Language policy in Nepal. *New Language Planning Newsletter* 12 (3), 1–3.

Taiwan

Chang, Chiang-chun. (張湘君) (2002) Embracing English and mother tongue, rejecting Mandarin? (英語母語當道，國語閃邊?) *Min Sheng Daily* (民生報) 21 Jul. 2002. p.A8.

Chang, Mau-kuei. (1994) Toward an understanding of the *sheng-chi wen-ti* in Taiwan: Focusing on changes after political liberalization. In Chen Chung-min, Chuang Ying-chang, and Huang Shu-min (eds), *Ethnicity in Taiwan: Social, Historical, and Cultural Perspectives* (pp. 97–150). Taiwan: Institute of Ethnology, Academica Sinica.

Chen, Mei-ying. (2005) Taiwan de Muyu he Guoyu Shuangyu Jiaoyu: Xuanzexing Jinru Shuangxiang Jiaorong Shuangyu Jiaoyu [Taiwan's Mother-tongue and Mandarin Bilingual Education: Dual Language Immersion Program]. Jiaoshi Zhi You [Teachers' Friends], 46, 4, 82–106. Jiayi: Jiayi University.

Chen, P. (1993) Modern written Chinese in development. *Language in Society* 22 (4), 505–537.

Chen, P. (1996) Modern written Chinese, dialects, and regional identity. *Language Problems & Language Planning* 20 (3), 223–243.

Chen, Su-chiao (2003) *The Spread of English in Taiwan: Changing Uses and Shifting Attitudes.* Taipei: Crane Publishing Co.

Chen, Su-chiao (2004) The Spread of English in Taiwan: Sociolinguistic perspectives. In *Proceedings of the Conference on Cross-Strait English Language Teaching.* National Chiayi University, Taiwan.

Chen, V. W.-c. (1977) Simplified characters in the People's Republic of China, Japan, Singapore, and Taiwan. *Journal of the Chinese Language Teachers Association* 12 (1), 63–75.

Chern, C.-L. (2003) English language teaching in Taiwan today. In H. W. Kam and R. Y. L. Wong (eds) *English Language Teaching in East Asia Today: Changing Policies and Practices* (pp. 427–439). Singapore: Times Academic Press.

Chuang, P. F. (2001) The impact of forced language on three-generational relationships among Taiwanese families. *Dissertation Abstracts International, A: The Humanities and Social Sciences* 61(11), 4564-A.

Chun, C.-C. (2006) Language-in-education planning and bilingual education at the elementary school in Taiwan (China). *Dissertation Abstracts International, A: The Humanities and Social Sciences* 67(01), 63.

Ebele, T. F. (2001) Social power and the cultural effects of globalization: Why do Taiwanese learn English? PhD Thesis, Washington State University.

Erbaugh, M. S. (1995) Southern Chinese dialects: A medium for reconciliation within greater China. *Language in Society* 24, 79–94.

GIO (Government Information Office) (2005) *Taiwan Six-Year National Development Plan.* (挑戰2008國家發展重點計畫) Retrieved April 20, 2005 from the World Wide Web at: *http://www.washingtonstate.org.tw/English/taiwan-trade-economy/6-year-plan/index.htm*

GIO (Government Information Office) (2005) *Taiwan Yearbook. http://wwwgio.gov.tw/taiwna-website/5-gp/yearbook/* [accessed 7/2/2006]

Hakkhiam, T. (1998) Writing in two scripts: A case study of digraphia in Taiwanese. *Written Language and Literacy* 1 (2), 225–248.

Heylen, A. (2005) The legacy of literacy practices in colonial Taiwan. Japanese-Taiwanese-Chinese: Language interaction and identity formation. *Journal of Multilingual and Multicultural Development* 26 (6), 496–511.

Huang, C. (2007) LP for naming and its socio-cultural connotations: A case study in Taiwan. *Current Issues in Language Planning* 8 (3), 305–323.

Huang, C. M. (1998) Language education policies and practices in Taiwan: From nationism to nationalism. *Dissertation Abstracts International, A: The Humanities and Social Sciences* 58 (12), 4531-A.

Huang, S. (2000) Language, identity and conflict: A Taiwanese study. *International Journal of the Sociology of Language* 143, 139–149.

Jeon, M. and Lee, J. (2006) Hiring native-speaking English teachers In East Asian countries. *English Today* 22 (4) 53–58.

Jernudd, B. H. (1985). Chinese language contact: An introduction. *Anthropological Linguistics, 27*(2), 119–121.

Jordan, D. K. (1969) The languages of Taiwan. *La Monda Lingvo Problemo* 1, 65–76.

Jordan, D. K. (1973) Language choice and interethnic relations in Taiwan. *La Monda Lingvo Problemo,* 5 (13), 35–44.

Jordan, D. K. (1985) Taiwan's Romanized script for Mandarin Chinese. *Language Problems & Language Planning* 9 (2), 134–136.

Jordan, D. K. (2002) Languages left behind: Keeping Taiwanese off the world wide web. *Language Problems & Language Planning* 26 (2), 111–127.

Kaiser, S. (2003) Language and script in Japan and other east Asian countries: Between insularity and technology. In J. Maurais and M. A. Morris (eds) *Languages in a Globalising World* (pp. 188–202). Cambridge: Cambridge University Press.

Kaplan, R. B. (1976) Current status of the Taiwan English language survey. *English Around the World* 14(May), 3.

Kaplan, R. B. (1987) English in the language policy of the Pacific rim. *World Englishes* 6 (2), 137–148.

Kaplan, R. B. and Baldauf, R. B., Jr. (2003) Language planning in Taiwan. In *Language and Language-in-Education Planning in the Pacific Basin* (pp. 47–62). Dordrecht, Netherlands: Kluwer Academic.

Kaplan, R. B. and Tse, J. K. P. (1982) The language situation in Taiwan (The Republic of China). *Linguistic Reporter* 25 (2), 1–5.

MOE (the Ministry of Education, 教育部). (1998b) *General Guideline of Grade One to Nine Curriculum of Elementary and Junior High Education.* (民教育九年一貫課程總綱) Taipei: Ministry of Education.

MOE (the Ministry of Education, 教育部). (1998c) *The Report of Education Reform.* (教育改

革成果報告) Retrieved August 15, 2001 from the World Wide Web at: *http://www.edu.tw/secretary/publishent.html*

MOE (the Ministry of Education, 教育部). (2000) Guomin Zhongxiaoxue Jiunian Yiguan Kecheng Zanxing Gangyao: Yuwen Xuexi Lingyu. [The Nine-year Joint Curriculum Plan for Primary and Junior High Schools, Temporary Guideline for Language Areas]. Taipei. MOE.

MOE (the Ministry of Education, 教育部). (2003) *Teachers' Manual for English Language Teaching in Elementary and Junior High Schools.* (國民中小學英語教學手冊) Taipei: Ministry of Education.

MOE (the Ministry of Education, 教育部). (2005) *The Six-Year National Plan: Project on Cultivation of Talent for the E-generation.* (挑戰2008國家發展重點計畫：E世代人才培育計畫) Taipei: Ministry of Education.

(MOE) Ministry of Education, Republic of China (Taiwan). (2005). *Challenge 2008: National Development Plan.* Retrieved June 19, 2007, from http://english.moe.gov.tw/ct.asp?xItem = 7043&ctNode = 784&mp = 2

MOE News. (教育部新聞) (25 Mar. 2003) Introducing foreign English teachers and creating a different English learning environment. (引進外籍教師，打; 打造不一樣的英語環境). Retrieved from the World Wide Web at: http: *www.edu.tw/secretary/importance/importance.htm*

MOE News. (教育部新聞) (18 Aug. 2003) The Gradual Unification of the Starting Grade of English Education in Elementary School. (國小英語教學起始年漸趨一致). Retrieved 10 Dec 2003 from the World Wide Web at: *http://www.edu.tw/primary/importance/920818–2.htm*

Nunan, D. (2002) The impact of English as a global language: Policy and planning in greater China. *Hong Kong Journal of Applied Linguistics 7* (1), 1–15.

Saillard, C. (2000) Nommer les langues en situation de plurilinguisme ou la revendication d'un statut: Le Cas de Taiwan. *Langage et Societe* 91, 35–57, 128.

Saillard, C. (2004) Can the Austronesian languages of Taiwan escape from minorization? *Faits de Langues* 23–24, 361–378.

Sandel, T. L. (2003) Linguistic capital in Taiwan: The KMT's Mandarin language policy and its perceived impact on language practices of bilingual Mandarin and Tai-gi speakers. *Language in Society* 32 (4), 523–551.

Shih, C.-F. (2003) Language and ethnic politics in Taiwan. *International Journal of Peace Studies* 8 (2), 89–102.

Tsao, Feng-fu. (1997) *Ethnic Language Policy: A Comparison of the Two Sides of the Taiwan Strait.* Taipei: Crane Publishing Co. [In Chinese]

Tsao, Feng-fu. (2004) Guo xiao ying yu jiao yu de zhan wang [Prospects of English teaching in elementary schools]. Paper presented at the Conference on Cross-Strait English Language Teaching. National Chiayi University, Taiwan.

Tse, J. K. P. (1986) Standardization of Chinese in Taiwan. *International Journal of the Sociology of Language* 59, 25–32.

Tse, J. K. P. (1995) The teaching of writing in Taiwan. *Journal of Asian Pacific Communication* 6 (1–2), 117–123.

United Daily News. (聯合報) (1 May 2002) Prime minister: English to be quasi-official language in six years. (游揆:英語六年後列準官方語), p.6.

United Daily News. (聯合報) (7 July 2004) Worries about English education: Foreign threat to English teachers. (教師有「外患」，英語教育隱憂), p. B2.

van den Berg, M. E. (1986) Language planning and language use in Taiwan: Social identity, language accommodation, and language choice behavior. *International Journal of the Sociology of Language* 59, 97–115.

Wei, J. M. (2006) Language choice and ideology in multicultural Taiwan. *Language and Linguistics* 7 (1), 87–107.

Young, R. L. (1988) Language maintenance and language shift in Taiwan. *Journal of Multilingual and Multicultural Development* 9 (4), 323–338.

Young, R. L., Huang, S. F., Ochoa, A., and Kuhlman, N. (1992) Language attitudes in Taiwan. *International Journal of the Sociology of Language* 98, 5–14.

Chinese Character Modernisation in the Digital Era: A Historical Perspective

Shouhui Zhao
CRPP (Centre for Research in Pedagogy and Practice), Nanyang Technological University, Singapore

After a century of effort, directed at modernising Chinese script, it is still the case that Chinese characters (henceforth *hanzi*) remain a deficient communication system both for human use and for mechanical application. In some respects, the reform of Chinese *hanzi* has been a very political process, driven ultimately by politicians, yet at the same time influenced by the masses and historical traditions. Early views of language planning (henceforth LP) saw the discipline as a clinical linguistic process aimed at solving language problems, while modern-day critical theorists would argue that it is rooted in the social, economic and political agendas of the dominant elites. This struggle of ideologies has been played out in *hanzi* reform during the last century and highlights the enormous challenge that Chinese language planners face. In this monograph, the reform process is examined and explained in light of these struggles. The focus is on a discussion of the recent developments in the Chinese *hanzi* modernisation process, with a historical description provided to create the necessary background for understanding the origin of the underlying issues. It provides a prospective view that suggests possible future developments, particularly in light of the impact of technological change.

Keywords: script reform, *hanzi*, socio-political context, character simplification, technological advances, standardisation.

Introduction

Polity studies, as they are defined in *Current Issues in Language Planning*, usually set out to cover the whole range of sociolinguistic developments and changes specific to a particular polity. However, in the case of Chinese and China, issues of language policy and planning loom so large in the social, political and economic scheme of things that a more focused approach to the study of this complex language system seems warranted. This is why the editors have chosen to call these studies polity studies; they may not encompass all the language policy and planning activities of a particular nation state (or might deal collectively with matters related to several smaller ones). In the case of China, one polity study on Taiwan (Tsao, 2000) has already been produced. This particular study examines another major set of issues important to Chinese language planning, those related to script reform, examining in some detail recent developments in the People's Republic of China and their implications for future developments in Chinese writing. Other polity studies, related to China, might include language policy and planning in Hong Kong, planning for oral language use for *Putonghua* and the other Han regionalects, and planning for the many minority languages in China. The editors would also note that this monograph provides another illustration of language planning for socialist state building (as in North Korea, particularly under Kim Il Sung (Kaplan & Baldauf, 2003)), highlighting both the destructive (the Cultural Revolution) and constructive elements of this approach, and recognising LP as an essentially political activity (Baldauf & Kaplan, 2003). Language planning has often been associated with nation building, but political intrusion has permeated all aspects of LP in China, with early top level LP in the new China being substantially about socialist state building, with language being merely an addendum. While this is certainly an interesting perspective, it only applies to polities that operate through a centralised system with absolute governmental control over all aspects of life.

Indeed, to a certain extent, in the quest for character standardisation, the focus on text may overlook the reality that ultimately language is about communication between human beings – not exclusively between human beings and machines – and this focus tends to dehumanise the processes of language and language-in-education planning. The monograph raises the question of whether, as China opens up, changes in the model of LP will need to be considered if LP is to serve the users of language rather than the bureaucrats seeking to build a perfect computer-applicable model. This is not to disparage the significant and important achievements in LP in China over the past half century or the standardisation efforts needed to improve electronic communication in the Chinese language; rather, it constitutes an appeal to planners in China not to lose sight of the vital human aspects of language use and usage. [The Editors]

Before proceeding to a discussion of script reform, it is necessary to provide an overview of issues concerning language planning in China as a whole. This introductory section provides background information on the linguistic situation in China and gives an overview of the identification of problems concerning LP decision-making processes.

LP and Script Reform in China: Contents and Organisations

Each polity has its own unique way of dealing with language issues. The process is determined by many factors: linguistic and ethnic complexity; the academic tradition; the political system and the administrative structure.

The demographic setting of Chinese language

Almost as large as the whole European continent, the total land area of the People's Republic of China is nearly 10 million square kilometres (3,691,521 sq. miles), and has a varied topography. As the most populous land on earth (1,261,832,482 persons) with a long history, China is rich in terms of her linguistic diversity and complexity.

Languages and group identity

China is a multinational country with many ethnic groups. According to the national census of 1990, besides the Han Chinese, there are 55 national minorities that account for 8.04% of the total population; generally, each has its own traditional culture and language. Chinese minorities are characterised by their uneven geographical distribution. Constituting only a small percentage of the population spreading over more than 60% of the land, the minorities are to be found in every part of the country, with concentrated populations in the remote mountainous regions of the vast outlying areas of China proper. The population of non-Han Chinese is growing more rapidly than the Han majority due to the pro-minority birth control policy. Non-Han minorities are not required to become literate in Chinese by law, although if they show interest they are encouraged by the Government to become bilingual in *putonghua* (Common Speech, or Mandarin) and their own languages.[1] Linguistically, these non-Chinese ethnic languages derived from Sino-Tibetan, Altaic, Indo-European, Tai, Hmong-Mien, Austroasiatic and Austronesian origins (Cheng, 1976: 43; Kaplan & Baldauf, 2003: 48). A number of ethnic groups speak the same language (or dialectal variations of the languages spoken in polities adjacent to the areas where they live in China; e.g. languages such as Korean, Thai, Mongolian and even Russian).

Table 1 Non-Han languages spoken by Chinese minority nationalities with more than 1 million people

Ethnic minority	Population	Language spoken	Major area of distribution
Zhuang	16,178,811	Zhuang	Guangxi
Manchu	10,682,263	Manchu (in both script and spoken language) and Han (Man) (standard Chinese)	Virtually scattered over all of China, the largest group, about 46.2% of the total, live in Liaoning Province, and the rest mostly in Jilin, Heilongjiang, Hebei, Beijing, Gansu, Shandong, Inner Mongolia, Xinjiang and Ningxia, as well as in Chengdu, Xi'an, Guangzhou and other cities.
Hui	9,816,802	Han	Ningxia, Gansu, Henan, Hebei, Qinghai, Shandong, Yunnan, Xinjiang, Anhui, Liaoning, Heilongjiang, Jilin, Shanxi, Beijing, Tianjin
Miao	8,940,116	Miao	Guizhou, Hunan, Yunnan, Guangxi, Sichuan, Hainan and Hubei
Uygur	8,399,393	Uygur	Xinjiang
Tujia	8,028,133	Tujia	Hubei and Hunan
Yi	7,762,286	Yi	Sichuan, Yunnan, Guizhou and Guangxi
Mongolian	5,813,947	Mongolian and Han	Inner Mongolia, Liaoning, Jilin, Heilongjiang, Xinjiang, Henan, Hebei, Gansu, Qinghai, etc.
Tibetan	5,416,021	Tibetan	Tibet, Qinghai, Sichuan, Gansu and Yunnan
Bouyei	2,971,460	Bouyei	Guizhou
Dong	2,960,293	Dong	Guizhou, Hunan and Guangxi
Yao	2,637,421	Yao and Miao	Guangxi, Hunan, Yunnan, Guangdong and Guizhou
Korean	1,923,842	Korean and Han	Jilin, Liaoning and Heilongjiang
Bai	1,858,063	Bai	Yunnan and Guizhou
Hani	1,439,673	Hani	Yunnan
Kazak	1,250,458	Kazak	Xinjiang, Gansu and Qinghai
Li	1,247,814	Li	Hainan
Dai	1,158,989	Dai	Yunnan

Source: http://www.china.org.cn/english/2001/Nov/ 22210.htm

Except Hui and Manchu, two of 18 minorities with over 1 million people, 53 ethnic groups use their own spoken languages[2] and 27 groups have their own written language. (Table 1 lists some major languages still spoken by the non-Han Chinese population.) Four of the non-Han ethnic groups use Chinese characters; two groups (*Hui* and *Man*) have already assimilated to Chinese language use. During the 1950s and 1960s, the Government organised a number of linguistic contingents to launch a nationwide survey among the minorities in more than 1500 survey sites, and to devise writing systems for 16 previously unwritten languages. In a more general sense, these activities amount to a substantial part of the Chinese Government's commitment to carrying out national language planning.

Populace and dialects

According to the latest sample survey of 1% of the total population, the People's Republic of China (PRC), as of January 2005, had a population of approximately 1.3 billion (excluding Hong Kong (6,750,000) and Macau (460,000) which have a total population of more than 7 million). China's population density is relatively high but uneven; the coastal areas in the east are densely populated with more than 400 people per square kilometre, whereas the less habitable plateau areas in the west are sparsely populated, with fewer than 10 people per square

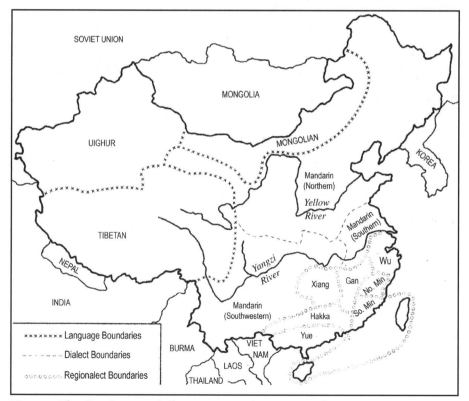

Figure 1 The distribution of Chinese regionalects across Chinese provinces

(*Source*: DeFrancis, 1984: 34)

kilometre. As a developing agricultural country, only 35% of Chinese live in urban areas while 65% are rural.

China is enormous and so is its language in terms of its great dialectal diversity. However, 70% of the Han Chinese speak a variety of standard Chinese, historically called Northern Speech (*Beifang Hua*), or Mandarin, which is a linguistic notion rather than a geographical reference that extends in a southerly direction as far as the region south of the Yangtze River in the south-west. There is little or no mutual intelligibility, even among the four major sub-groups within Northern Speech, but the dialects spoken in this vast zone are enormously cohesive in lexical stock and syntax, forming the basis of modern Chinese. DeFrancis has observed, 'the greatest differences among the regionalects are in the area of phonology, the least in the area of grammar. Vocabulary differences fall in between these extremes' (1984: 63). The rest of the Han Chinese people speak a variety of regional Chinese dialects that are unintelligible to other groups. It is widely believed by international linguists that the differences among these dialects are about the same as those between different languages in Europe, say German and Polish. These dialects are used mainly in the south-central and south-eastern coastal provinces[3] (see Figure 1). Cantonese, plus Min and Hakka, are the mother tongues for most overseas Chinese, estimated at approximately 30 million persons across the five continents of the world.

The four tasks of Chinese language planning

Currently, LP in China includes at least the following four tasks:

- Status planning of languages other than *Guojia Tongyong Yuyan Wenzi*, which refers to the lingua franca for all Chinese regardless of the ethnic background.[4]
- Language planning in education,[5] including adult literacy education, first language education for both Han and non-Han Chinese students, foreign languages education in the school context, and the teaching of Chinese as a second language to foreigners and non-Han Chinese.
- Terminology supervision and the management of proper noun translation.
- Language and script reform for the National General Language; the major activities at present focus on *Putonghua* promotion and script reform, which mainly refers to Chinese character simplification (before the mid-1980s), standardisation and orthographic experiments in Romanisation.

However, these activities are not coordinated by a single body such as the State Commission of Language Work, the state's top body for LP (see below 'Decision Making: Leadership and Research'). Over the past few years there have been suggestions from some scholars to carry out a more fundamental and comprehensive reorganisation of the LP agencies that would include status planning as part of their brief, and that would bring all four LP agendas together under one roof.

Generally speaking, modern China's LP activities, related to script reform, can be grouped into three historical periods: (1) the earliest attempts and the 1935 reform; (2) reforms between 1956 and 1978; and (3) after the 1986 National Language Conference including the latest developments.

As far as the national general language is concerned, it is generally agreed that the main tasks of LP in modern China refer to the following five matters (Fei, 1997: 1):

- the vernacularisation movement (文体口语化);
- modern official language promotion (语言共同化);
- Chinese character simplification and modification (文字简便化);
- romanisation/alphabetisation (表音字母化);
- Chinese language and character computerisation (中文电脑化).

Except for the first task, basically completed in the course of the National Language Movement during the 1920s and 1930s, the other four tasks of Chinese modernisation are still major components for current LP work. In a broader historical perspective, most of the language reform efforts before 1949 concentrated on schemes of alphabetisation, but after that, when the People's Republic of China (PRC) was established, the priority switched to character simplification.

Using terms from Haugen's (1983: 275) 'fourfold problem areas' LP model, graphitisation includes two aspects: devising an orthographic system and reforming the existing scripts. While the former refers specifically to a phonetic orthography, the latter customarily refers mainly to modifying character shapes by reducing the number of strokes. In the 1950s this was seen as the whole basis for modifying *hanzi* for convenience, and two other important factors did not get much attention. The standardisation shift was instituted in the milestone conference of 1986, stemming from the desire to tackle the constant requirements generated by the developments in the IT industry (see the sections, 'Technological Requirements from the IT Industry: A Digital View' and 'Four Fixations: Difficulties and Technological Implications'). From then on, the reform of *hanzi* has moved towards a planned approach to orthographic standardisation. During this same period, there has also been significant work on Chinese characters and writing systems in Taiwan, but this is a vast and divergent literature from the one discussed here and as developments have occurred separately with little interaction, this material is not covered in this monograph (see e.g. Tse 1980, 1982a, 1982b, 1986).

Decision Making: Leadership and Research

From the top to the grassroots: Organisations at various levels

The newly established Communist Party Government of PRC has had a great interest in language issues. The most important initiative for language administration so far has been the establishment of the State Commission of Language Work in 1986 (henceforth SCLW), which replaced the 1956 Commission of Language Reform (henceforth CLR) as the national LP agency promulgating decisions under the leadership of the highest state apparatus, the State Council (Cabinet). Making use of its members' scholarship, the Committee is basically a research institution rather than a decision-making organ. In recent years it has also been concerned with editing and publishing (it owns a specialist press: Language Press). SCLW has been involved in the area of professional training (a national training centre was established within its system), which demonstrates that it has been very quick in taking up the challenge of the complex diversi-fication of LP issues in the modern period. One of the most significant actions that SCLW has taken is its instrumental role in the promulgation of the Law of National General Language and Script, People's Republic of China, which was passed on 31 October 2000, and came into force on 1 January 2001.[6]

As the country's LP authority, the SCLW is not an autonomous permanent institution like an academy or institute, but an appointed committee whose members are drawn from a variety of different academic backgrounds and from relevant bureaucratic ministries. In order to deal with the impact brought about by technology in the latest reform scheme launched in 1998, its affiliation was transferred from the State Council to the Education Ministry. Two special-ist offices, the Department of Language and Information Administration and the Department of Social Use of Language and Script, were added. At the same time, the Research Institute of Applied Linguistics (henceforth RIAL) was also relocated under these two bureaucratic departments. It should be noted that although it was ostensibly relegated to the vice-ministerial level in the Chinese bureaucratic system, it gained more executive power in enforcement and legis-lation, albeit under the tutelage of the Education Ministry, and its jurisdiction and administrative functions are not confined to the education sector. An exam-ination of its structure shows that it includes more members who are currently in positions of power and who have a background in science and engineering. In December 2000, its membership was reduced to 18 experts, who were then called consultants, from its previous 40 members, with an increase of techno-crats (9 members) from IT-related ministries and departments.

The local representatives of SCLW operate at three levels: provincial, municipal and county. The official guidelines (Wei, 2003: 16) state that at provincial and municipal levels full-fledged special units with full-time staff should be estab-lished within the educational administration of the local government; as for county and county-level administrations, LP offices are required to be attached to the relevant bureaucratic departments; alternatively, a highly placed official should be in charge of LP affairs on an everyday basis. Their efficiency very much depends on the local circumstances and individual leadership, with the work ranging from educating the public to monitoring public use of language and script.[7] For the provincial branches of SCLW, when scientific evidence is needed to make decisions concerning local language policy, they would turn to the academic findings specific to the regional situations, where there is close collaboration between the provincial language authorities and the linguistic research institutes and centres located in higher-learning institutions in respec-tive provinces and autonomous regions. The activities of different level LP agencies are largely coordinated through distribution of research funds.

Haugen (1968) categorised the way in which government intervenes in the language choice and in people's specific linguistic behaviour as status planning and corpus planning respectively. The exclusion of terminological development (an aspect of corpus planning) and the minority languages (status planning) from the SCLW's brief are remarkable features of Chinese LP (see below, 'Four Tasks of Chinese Language Planning'). Translation and proper foreign names and the standardisation of technical vocabulary (corpus planning) are carried out by a special office in the official news agency and the commissions under the Ministry of Science and Technology, e.g. the National Approval Commission of Technological Terms and the Examination Commission of Chemical Names. The language affairs of the 53 ethnic groups are left to the nationalities' affairs administration. On 16 December 1985 a decision passed by the State Council clearly stated that 'minority languages affairs are still held under the State National Minority Affairs Commission'[8] (SCLW, 1987: 329), but making and overseeing the standards and norms for national minority languages were listed under the SCLW's responsibilities in the statement of restructuring in 1998 (SCLW, 2005a).

In the past, LP programmes were imposed by coercion, depending solely on official promotion (activities of government). The existing 'top-down' (see e.g. Kaplan, 1989) structure was designated when China was an authoritarian and simple society. Admittedly, this model functioned well with the gullible population, in those credulous years prior to the opening up to the outside world. In an increasingly opening and democratic polity, institutional promotion (activities of agencies) and pressure groups and individual promotion would be deemed necessary for facilitating language change (see Haarmann, 1990: 120–1; Kaplan & Baldauf, 1997: 6).

Advisory units: Research Institute of Applied Linguistics

Set up by the State Council in September 1984, the Research Institute of Applied Linguistics (RIAL) was originally under the dual leadership of SCLW and the China Academy of Social Science, but became a research institute directly responsible to the Education Ministry in 1998. In April 2001, its organisational structure was enlarged as follows:

- three research sections: *Putonghua* and Language Education Research Office; *Hanzi* and *Pinyin* (Chinese Romanisation) Research Office (the Centre of Dictionary and Encyclopaedia Study); Sociolinguistics and Public Media Language Research Office (the Centre of Broadcasting and TV Language Research);
- one editorial office, editing and publishing two journals: *Applied Linguistics* and *Language Construction* (Research Centre of Applied Linguistics);
- two functional sections: *Putonghua* Training Centre and *Putonghua* Testing Centre.

Now chaired by Prof Li Yuming, the RIAL serves as the advisory body of SCLW and aims at providing assistance and reliable data as the base of policy formulation. Its specific work has changed to meet the requirements set by the national economic and social development scheme, which is reformulated every five years. According to the latest agenda, its responsibilities include (SCLW, 2005b)[9]:

- studying the theoretical and practical issues of language application;
- researching language and script codification and standardisation;
- exploring policy for language development and planning;
- carrying out the organisational activities on testing, benchmark evaluation, education and research of the National General Language; and
- providing training and consultative services for the public and society.

The description in this section defines the current general context for everyday language policy and planning in China. The issues of major language reform of Chinese characters lie inside this system, both historically and currently. As it is these issues which are important for understanding the problems of bringing Chinese into the digital world, it is to a description of the three *hanzi* simplification movements that attention is turned.

The Development of *Hanzi* Simplification Movements

In modern history, there have been three major government-sanctioned reforms aimed at simplifying the complex physical structure of Chinese characters. Namely, the First Simplification Scheme (FSS) in 1935, the Second Scheme of Simplified Characters (SSSC) in 1977, and the 1956 reform which is referred to as the Table of Simplified Characters (TSC) in this monograph. Concentrating on the planning process of *hanzi* simplification, this part of the monograph provides an overview of the developing trajectory of script reform. The reflection on history aids the attempt to find the relationships between variables, that is, relationships between external influential factors and *hanzi*'s future development. The focus of the analysis is on the accounts of the multi-dimensional sociopolitical context that led to the successes, failures or undesired results of these reforming activities.

The earliest attempts and First Simplification Scheme (FSS) of 1935

In dynastic China, writing was a privileged tool in the hands of a minority of wealthy elites, who ruled over the illiterate and poor majority. This occurred, to some extent, simply because *hanzi* are too complicated to be acquired effortlessly by the common population. It is in this sense that the early language reformers saw the language reform in parallel with the reform of society. By the beginning of the 20th century, a feeling had been powerfully developing that Chinese characters were responsible for the country's large number of illiterates. In 1935, feeling the pressures from eminent individuals and non-governmental organisations, the nationalist Ministry of Education officially approved the first list of 324 simplified characters. Although this effort was aborted in the following year, it was a precursor of the subsequent reforms.

The formation period: Research and proposal (1908–32)

Simplified characters are a historical phenomenon. Simplification and complication are two countervailing processes that have been evident throughout the evolution of Chinese script (Wang, 1992: 18). The simplified characters, or folk form/unorthodox characters, as they were referred to in the past, go hand in hand with standard, or governmentally sanctioned characters. A substantial number of today's simplified characters can be traced back to the variant forms found in *Jiaguwen* (shell and bone script), the earliest form of Chinese characters that consisted of inscriptions on animal bones and tortoise shells dating from the 13th century BCE. The major function of these inscriptions during the Shang dynasty was to keep records of divination rather than being a means of visual communication for people's everyday use. On the whole, however, in the subsequent 3000 years of development, various different stylistic forms of *hanzi* have come and gone, whereas the unorthodox forms seem to dig in and hang on. '[E]ven during the period of the Ming and Qing dynasties, when the Government imposed a relatively conservative writing standard, simplified characters not only existed among the common users, but they could also be seen in scholars' work' (Zhou, 1979: 320). Zhou notes that the first scholar who proposed and consciously used simplified characters as a matter of preference in his writing was Huang Zongxi (1610–1695), a Confucian philosopher in the Ming Dynasty. Since that time, the use of simplified characters in formal writing no longer has been looked upon as being grotesque.

Thomas (1991: 112) has observed that 'language reform rarely, if ever, begins as a grass-roots, mass movement; it is most often instigated by an individual or a group of like-minded individuals'. The simplification movement, at its earliest stage, was a purely academic enterprise initiated by a group of influential scholars. Wang Li (1938: 621) categorised simplified character proponents into two groups. One group, represented by Qian Xuantong, argued that the Government should select and recognise only the popular and acceptable simplified forms that have circulated since the Song[10] and Yuan Dynasties. Another group insisted that, apart from the existing simplified characters that had been used by the general population, the newly coined simplified characters should also be included if they were based on the principle of being easy to write. Chen Guangyao, a solitary amateur enthusiast in *hanzi* simplification, was the central figure of this group.[11]

At the turn of the 19th century, the last imperial regime was overthrown. With the gradual introduction of a Western-style education system, the traditional 'state public servant examination system' (*keju*, or *jinshi* examinations[12]) was abolished, and the traditional heritage, of which the writing system is an important part, suddenly found itself facing new challenges. For a substantial period after the fall of the imperial regime, significant efforts were devoted to research on character simplification by a number of scholars from a range of academic disciplines.

Period of promulgation and its withdrawal (1933–35)

The first simplification took a relatively long period of time before it was translated into real action. Although there is a general perception that the modern simplification movement was begun by Lu Feikui, Du Zijin (1935: 13) has argued that Zhang Taiyan was the first person to propose simplification.[13] The outcome was that in 1932 some simplified characters were included for the first time in a dictionary accredited by the Government, the *National Standard Phonetic Vocabulary*.

Faced with resistance from the defenders of traditional culture and a significant segment of the general population, many came to the realisation that the first thing to do was to legitimise the notion of simplified characters. Therefore, even though a lot of the time that the reformers had spent was on justifying the handwritten simplified characters as not only being time-saving, but also as having an equal status with their complex counterparts in a modern situation, cultural conservatism persisted and strongly influenced peoples' minds. Therefore, during this period it took great effort to shift general attitudes to character reform from 'cannot', to 'should not', to 'must', but eventually massive individual efforts left the Government with no choice but to follow the historical trend. The blueprint of the FSS was prepared at the beginning of the 1930s by some of the staff working in the Association of Promoting a Unified National Language, under the leadership of the eminent linguist Qian Xuantong. The staff drafted a table of over 2000 characters and submitted it directly to the Education Ministry for approval. The first table was issued by the Education Minister and jointly approved by the Senate Session and the Central Political Conference on 21 August 1935 (Du, 1935: 53). Although the number of characters approved was reduced to the 324 most frequently used characters on a trial basis,[14] as expected, it encountered immediate opposition from traditionalists, and the All China Character Preservation Congress, a nationwide organ of the anti-script-reform alliance, was formed. And, more directly, due to conservative opposition within the then Government and the outbreak of the Sino-Japanese War of 1937–1945, the table was withdrawn in the following year.[15]

No convincing justification can be found as to why a nearly 30-year-old, well-deliberated and extensively discussed reform programme should have been overturned in the short period of less than six months. A widely held view says that a senior official's opposition to the reform was the major reason. The story goes that Mr Dai Jitao, who was then the Minister of Supervisions, knelt down before Chiang Kai-shek, the head of the Nationalist Party and Chairman of the Military Commission, appealing for the life of Chinese characters in a session of Parliament. In response, Chiang ordered the Education Ministry to discontinue its promotion (Zhou, 1979: 325). In Mainland China, this story about the death of the First Scheme has been widely spread and quoted, but no primary historical sources can be found to support the claim.

Simplification activities during the 1950s and 1960s

As indicated in the previous section, the Nationalist Government had turned its back on any language reform by the late 1930s, leaving all further efforts of transforming the writing system to its arch-rival, the Chinese Communist Party (CCP). From 1937 to 1945, during the eight-year war with Japan, the CCP started to use simplified characters in materials printed in the regions and base areas under its control to gain the wartime support of the people for its policies. It also experimented with *Latinxua Sinwenz* (new Latin script) for these same purposes.

An ideological link therefore appears to exist between language reform and the CCP, as language reform was a way to engage with the vast illiterate working population that was the basic source of the CCP's revolutionary endeavour. As a revolutionary party, the communists saw eradicating feudal roots as their main mission. Bearing this in mind, it is not surprising that some of the Communist Party leaders themselves were in the forefront of the script reform movement in the 1930s and 1940s, signalling the Party's firm commitment to language reform long before the establishment of the PRC of China in 1949.

The Table of Simplified Characters (TSC) of 1956

As part of an integrated set of social contexts, language reform took place simultaneously with radical changes in politics. The early 1950s marked a time when Chinese people celebrated the birth of a new country, and their enthusiasm for national construction was at a high. Social reforms were not only considered necessary but even unavoidable, overwhelming strong historical trends at a time when change became the norm. It took nearly 30 years to complete preparations before the first modest reform of 324 characters in 1935 was officially carried out. The much more significant and drastic Table of Simplified Characters, however, happened over a period of just six years.

After the People's Republic of China was established in October 1949, the Government saw the urgent need to eliminate illiteracy as a key agenda to building a new country. The Committee for Language Reform was created in 1954, which resulted in the set up of two tentative schemes of character simplification. Under the first measure, a total of about 2200 simplified characters was introduced from 1956; some of these were further modified in 1964. The TSC of 1956 reduced the average number of strokes from 18 to nine for the most common characters.

Preparatory activities

Before considering the technical aspects of the three lists of simplified characters, an analysis of the sociolinguistic factors inherent in the formation process will be of great help in understanding the accomplishments of the reform.

The Government took considerable precautions before it formally introduced simplified characters as the official standard in 1956. Milsky (cited in Yao, 1976: 85), a French Chinese LP observer, is of the opinion that the preparation work in the beginning period (October 1949 to February 1952) was carried out in a manner that encouraged open discussion and that planning agencies were free of party and government bias. One of the noticeable features of the Table's composition is its well-defined planning and decision-making process that was put in place over a very short period of time. The preparations included three key elements: (1) involvement of a wide spectrum of people, (2) support from the top and (3) propaganda.

Involvement of a wide spectrum of people

After the establishment of the Commission of Chinese Script Reform, one of the first acts of the commission was to draft a plan for character simplification and disseminate it to various groups and agencies for consideration. Before submission to the State Council for final approval, all the characters in the scheme came under close scrutiny by a special team, composed of experts in the field. Having taken the feedback from specialists and the general public into consideration, the team voted on the simplified characters and basic components on a case-by-case basis.

Prior to the promulgation of the General List of Simplified Characters (GLSC) in 1964, members of the commission were mobilised to spend six months collecting responses from the public by organising discussions, investigations and workshops as well as correspondence and on-the-spot inspections. A survey of mass literacy was distributed to 77 departments and bureaux at provincial, municipal and local levels to collect opinions over a more extensive area.

The First National Conference on Writing Reform was held in 1955, resulting in a draft plan that was formally promulgated in February 1956. Negative and positive responses poured forth in the 'Hundred Flowers Blooming and Hundred Schools Contending' campaign.[16] In order to widely solicit sufficient opinions about simplification, Hu Yuzhi, the Party's propaganda official, presided over three forums that year to invite many of the specialists and intellectuals in other fields, mainly critics, to speak freely about the simplification plan. Not without sincerity, opposition from certain aspects of technical, historical and aesthetic viewpoints were collected and documented as a reference for further reform measures.

Support from the top

Three high-level national leaders were committed to script modernisation and showed their overwhelming support. Mao Zedong (Chairman of the Party) had shown great interest in script reform, in spite of his intensive agenda during the first days of the PRC of China. Reading from the documentary records, Fei Jinchang (1997: 115–219) found that Mao Zedong had mentioned script reform matters in speeches, directives and personal letters from 25 August 1948 to 20 January 1956 on 11 different occasions.

Liu Shaoqi, Chairman of the Standing Committee of the People's Congress – the Chinese Parliament – concerned himself with giving concrete instructions five times during the drafting of the tables. To avoid the confusion caused by a large number of new characters, Liu ordered in 1955 a promotion of simplified characters by piecemeal tables over a span of three to four months at a stretch. Once the new table was put in force, the scheme had to be published in major newspapers within seven to 10 days (Fei, 1997: 205). As Premier of the State Council (Senate), Zhou Enlai was actively involved in the whole process; his important speech, delivered to the National Political Consultative Conference in January 1958, has been seen as the most authoritative official document in script reform history; it 'provided a major boost for language reform work' (Seybolt & Chiang, 1979: 5).

Propaganda campaign

Apart from much fanfare and a considerable amount of media publicity, during the period from 5–16 September 1955 the commission held an Exhibition of Script Reform Archival Materials and History at the Exhibition Hall of Beijing Library. Despite the short period of its introduction, the well-defined and effective communist propaganda system helped to ensure that the Scheme very quickly penetrated deep into public life.

The length of this monograph does not allow an examination of the whole simplification movement step by step using the framework set out in Cooper's 'Accounting Scheme' (1989: 97–8), but it is not hard to see from the previous material and following introduction that the formulating process of major simplification programmes during 1950s and 1960s substantially fits into the 'basic language planning model' outlined by Kaplan and Baldauf (1997: 105–6). Figure 2 schematically shows the process of the study, formation and implementation of the simplification tables.

Implementation

The simplification reform of 1956 generally refers to the General List of Simplified Characters (1964). However, this is just the final outcome of a series of tables that preceded it. In broader terms, simplification entails the total reduction of the numbers of forms and rationalisation of variant forms, apart from the structural simplification for each individual character through stroke reduction. Thus, the General List should also include two accompanying lists:

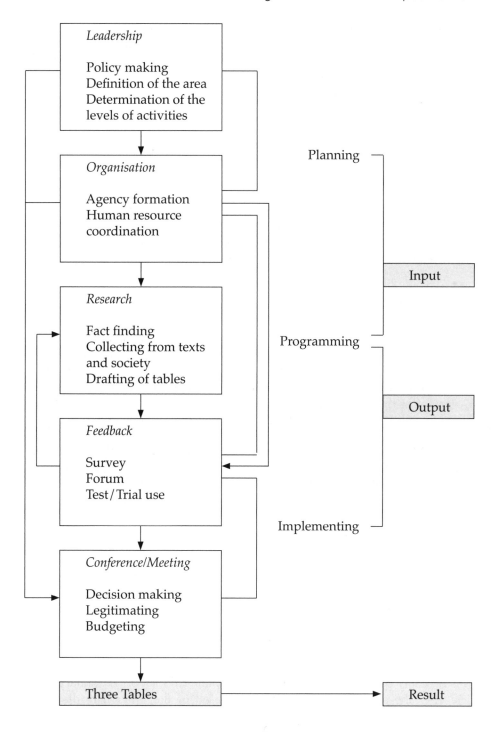

Figure 2 The process of the formulation of the TSC in the 1950s

the First Table of Verified Variant Forms (FTVVF, 1955), and the General List of Printed Forms of Chinese Characters (GLPFCC, 1965). The reduction of the total number of characters is left for discussion in subsequent sections. The whole process unfolded in three steps: the preparation of tables, implementation and final outcomes.

First step: Preparatory tables

In the first meeting concerning *hanzi* simplification, held on 9 August 1950, a draft table of simplified characters, based on four principles, was put forward by the Social Education Department of the Education Ministry. The table was modified in 1951 by the Research Association, and included 555 simplified characters, but failed to get publicised. In February 1952, under the Research Commission of Script Reform, after a two-year intensive study and after having gone through several stages of official and public discussion, the draft sim-plification scheme was completed. It aimed at simplifying three aspects of a character: stroke, number and structure. The Scheme included three tables:

- 798 Simplified Characters;
- 400 Abolished Variant Forms;
- Simplified Handwritten Radicals.

One other important event during this period was reduction of variant form characters. The First Table of Verified Variant Forms was first a part of the sim-plification scheme, and later on it was enlarged and became a separate table, when the draft simplification scheme was amended in September 1955. In December of the same year, prior to the official promulgation of the Table of Simplified Characters (TSC), FTVVF was jointly commissioned by the Cultural Ministry and the CLR in its own right. The table listed 1876 characters in 810 groups, with 2–6 variant forms in each group; a total of 1055 characters were eliminated. The preface of the FTVVF stated that, except for a few special cases, the elimination of these characters should be implemented in all publications starting from 1 February 1956. As a consequence of this reduction in variation, a great unification in *hanzi* use has been achieved in all printed texts ever since, but because of the hastiness of its implementation and the complex nature of the issue, the FTVVF became the table that has had the most problems from among the three lists created in this reform. Three adjustments to the table were made in March 1956, October 1986 and March 1988 respectively. As a result, the total number of characters eliminated in FTVVF was reduced to 795 groups, and 30 eliminated variant characters were resumed in the Table of Common Chinese Characters (1988).

Second step: Implementation

The most significant event in the 1950s was the promulgation of the TSC. It was officially passed by the 23rd session of State Council on 28 January 1956. The TSC, the amended version, containing all of the previously discussed draft tables, excluding the table concerning the variant forms and handwrit-ten radicals, included 515 individual simplified characters and 54 simplified radicals in three tables.

The first table included 230 simplified characters that already had been intro-duced by most print media on a trial basis, so it was effective immediately upon its declaration. The second table had 285 characters and the third concerned 54 simplified radicals that could be generalised to all characters.

Third step: Final outcomes

Because TSC was formulated over a short time and was initially intended for provisional use before *hanzi* were replaced wholesale by Latin letters, there were a lot of problems in sub-tables. Even some contradictions occurred, such as one character being discharged in one table but appearing in another table as a radical. The TSC had too many diverse tables that had been decreed by different institutions over the period of introduction, leaving discrepancies in publications after the tables were officially put in use. These conditions lasted until the TSC, under the guidelines of the State Council, was finalised and republished by the CLR in May 1964 as the General List of Simplified Characters. The General List contained 2238 characters (including characters derived from the 54 simplified radicals) and, because of its inclusiveness and comprehensiveness, it was actually the sum total of all prior simplification tables. Its publication, therefore, served as an anchor that fixed the simplified characters and, at last, put decades of chaos in actual use to an end until 1986, when a minor adjustment was made.

Apart from the simplification and number reduction carried out during the 1950s and 1960s, standardisation was another important part of LP activities concerning *hanzi*. The research work on the General List of Printed Forms of Chinese Characters was started by the CLR in 1955, and the draft list came into being in 1956. It took eight years to formulate the final version. In May 1964 work was declared completed, and notification to put it into formal use was issued to the press and to printers all over the country by the Ministry of Culture and the CLR in January 1965. The list is very significant in that it not only standardised the detailed features of the physical make-up of 6196 Song-style *hanzi* (see Note 10 and the section 'Fixation of the Physical Shape') for printing purposes, as all characters were arranged in fixed positions, this table also covertly specified the stroke number and order, as well the structural composition. In this sense, it actually standardised the all-round dimensions of 6169 characters, and this standardisation was done based on the principles of practicality, convenience and acceptability. Regrettably, its function was confined to printing and publishing circles. It was not made available for public use until the Cultural Revolution came to an end in 1976.

Second Scheme in the 1970s

During the Great Proletarian Cultural Revolution of 1966–1976 (henceforth, the Cultural Revolution), language planning in China, like other economic and cultural activities, came to a virtual halt for nearly a decade. The Second Scheme of Simplified Characters (henceforth SSSC) was drafted during the turmoil of the Cultural Revolution and decreed in 1977, at the end of this period of turbulent circumstances. It was quietly withdrawn by the Government in the following year, but its formal official repeal was not declared until 1986, at the National Conference on Language Work, on the grounds that it had encountered strong opposition from both scholars and the public.

This section attempts to trace the dramatic implementation and demise of the ephemeral SSSC, and provides a critical examination of its formation, promulgation and abandonment. Attempts have been made to shed light on the sociopolitical reasons that led to its failure.

Sociopolitical background and its impact on script reform

Cultural Revolution

In the face of the grim economic reality of the mid-1960s, Mao Zedong eventually realised that most of his long-time colleagues, who increasingly ignored him, were themselves becoming a 'privileged stratum' and had begun taking the capitalist road. He thought that a great majority of national and local party leaders should be replaced by younger, 'redder' successors. Mao regarded the mass movement, which had been tested in revolutionary upheavals and repeatedly used since 1949 in political campaigns, as still the most powerful weapon to win political battles and accomplish great goals. He had decided to take advantage of the citizens' resentment over the leaders' abuses of power to regain control of China's leadership. The Cultural Revolution was thus a double-edged operation: the purging of the older generations and their replacement by a new generation whose revolutionary zeal would be enhanced by the very act of toppling the power holders.

In order to unleash the revolutionary potential of the masses to bring down the power holders, and to make young people believe that nothing was wrong with rebelling and inciting others to rebel, Mao had once said 'all truth of Marxism can be summed up in one sentence, "To Rebel Is Justified (*Zaofan Youli*)"'. The radicals tried to link their opponents as much as possible to the old enemies of the revolution, the landlords and capitalists. Expert bureaucrats, managers and technicians were subjected to beatings and imprisonment. In order to establish their authority, the radicals dismissed all those achievements of the past 17 years on the educational and cultural front. These political opportunists (Gang of Four and its followers) realised that the greatest threat to their power came from people with critical skills. Consequently, there was a general attack on intellectuals, and they were called 'the stinking ninth category'[17] of society.

The cost of this 10-year catastrophe was phenomenal for a relatively backward country trying to modernise its economy: lives lost, students not educated, cultural heritage destroyed and economic growth delayed for years. In broad terms, as a result of a decade of class struggle, China suffered a general breakdown of law and order. Academic quality fell far below pre-1965 levels. Distortions of truth and science in various areas of public life became very common and reached a very high level during and after the Cultural Revolution. In 1976, both Zhou Enlai and Mao Zedong died. Mao's successor, Hua Guofeng, promptly arrested the extreme left-wing Gang of Four,[18] thus paving the way for Deng's economic reforms. At their subsequent trial, the Four were blamed for all the wrongdoings and economic disasters of the 1960s and 1970s.

Language planning politicisation

The Cultural Revolution has affected script reform in three ways:

(1) *Interference from political ideology*: In the name of mass-line principles, experts and academics in LP areas were replaced by 'the masses', which basically meant working-class people, including workers, peasants, and

soldiers. According to Mao's historical materialism theory, the masses, rather than a minority of 'heroes', are the makers of history. (His widely quoted saying is, 'the people, and only the people, are the true driving force of historical development'.) Everyone was supposed to believe that the common people had both the right to avoid being dominated by a few authorities, and the ability to carry out any task of national importance without having to depend on special skills.

(2) *Institutional destruction*: According to the 'two-line' struggle theory, the main target of the Cultural Revolution had been those in power who took the capitalist road against proletarian interests. Therefore, most experienced LP practitioners and senior officials were expelled from the Commission of Language Reform and criticised as 'scholar tyrants', 'revisionists' and 'counter-revolutionary authorities' in academic fields. The CLR was restructured and staffed with non-expert personnel representing the masses. Moreover, in order to convert 'bad elements' from their 'wrongs', many intellectuals and expert administrators were sent to training camps for intensive re-indoctrination in the form of prolonged physical labour. It was reported that, at one time or another, all personnel in the CLR were forced to engage in manual labour in farming or industry.

(3) *Direct impact*: Extreme left-wing leaders, who had risen to power in the Cultural Revolution, feared that if the past was scrutinised, their revolutionary achievement would be challenged, and they adopted a strategy of giving prominence to their own present activities through obliterating others' previous achievements. Viewing past LP achievements as the legacy of 'wrong line' rules and practices, reform programmes were stopped or cancelled and did not resume until the middle of the 1970s.

How political values were incorporated into LP issues

Language problems in China, like art and literature, are components of the superstructure, hence they are generally viewed as political vehicles. The relationships between political ideology and linguistic dimensions began to be established in the mid-1950s, when intellectuals were targeted by the Anti-Rightist Movement. During this period and later during the Cultural Revolution, linguists could not say anything without referring to quotations from Mao's works, which were the rationale for every kind of action.

Political struggle, spurred on by combined internal and international factors, manifested itself as a power clash between various interest factions within the Party and the ideological views of dissident intellectuals. The CCP is a particularly great believer in political campaigns and politicising academic research as the most effective way to get a grip on people's minds. Hence the central tenet of the CCP leadership is to politicise every action, a process that culminated in the Cultural Revolution. In Mao's thought, nothing was free of ideological definition, and he held the belief that society was rent with latent conflict between the proletariat and the bourgeoisie. In such a situation, the traditional belief in the separation of script from politics no longer effectively addresses this complex system of relationships. The fact that only the privileged classes of society have the time and energy to achieve literacy also suggests that *hanzi* might have a class base. It is quite natural to criticise traditional characters as a tool for elitists to perpetuate their power over the people. After all, the knowledge represented by traditional characters was the property of only a few, inaccessible to the masses, and therefore feudalistic and counter-revolutionary. Chinese characters, used by the exploiting class for thousands of years, must be replaced by a new form used by the masses – the new masters in a socialist country.

Formalisation and implementation

After 1964, all activities and publications related to LP were discontinued due to the outbreak of the Cultural Revolution, until 1972, when Guo Moruo published an article in *Hongqi* (*Red Flag*) *Magazine*, explaining how to deal with simplified characters created by the masses. This short two-page answer to a reader's letter is in itself nothing special; what is significant is its author and the place selected for publication.[19] *Hongqi* (*Red Flag*) *Magazine* was the mouthpiece of the CCP and the yardstick that has always served as an accurate indicator of the direction of the power struggle in the Chinese ideological landscape. The author, Guo Moruo, was China's vice-premier and the president of China's Science Academy; he himself was also a recognised authority in a good number of social science fields. The main points in this article are (Guo, 1972: 84–5):

- Character simplification is a transient phase in the broader outline of language reform. Mao's directive of phoneticisation of script reform was reiterated after a temporary lull since it was made public 21 years earlier.
- The underlying principle of language reform is, 'come from the people, back to the people'; while pointing out that the simplified forms of characters that are confined to a particular geographical area are unofficial, it also emphasised that simplified characters created by the masses should get timely recognition.
- Characters are subject to constant simplification; public enthusiasm in simplifying characters should be respected.

The message the article conveyed not only highlighted the necessity for further simplification endeavours with the masses at the centre of this cause, but was, at the same time, tantamount to encouraging, or even urging, the masses to take the initiative in simplifying characters. In compliance with this end, the biweekly Language Reform column in *Guangming Daily* was resumed, and articles dealing with further simplification by peasants, soldiers, and workers were published in this column. A small dictionary of newly simplified characters (*Hanzi Zhengli Xiao Zihui*) was published in 1973, and a book, entitled *The Overhauling and Simplification of Chinese Characters* (*Hanzi de Zhengli he Jianhua*), was published by the Language Reform Press (Beijing) in 1974. In these ways, opinions from non-specialists, workers in particular, were extensively aired through the official press. The consequence was that a large number of newly simplified characters were created by commoners over a short period of time, and these characters provided the basis for the officially recognised simplified characters that subsequently appeared in the SSSC.

When the better-known TSC was published in 1956, the central government issued a directive, announcing that in order to facilitate the acquisition of literacy by schoolchildren and adults, a series of schemes would come out until all characters of common use with over 10 strokes were reduced to 10 or less.

Table 2 Five different characters that were represented by one character after the SSSC

Before SSSC	After SSSC	Pinyin	Gloss
盯	丁	Ding	To stare at
叮	丁	Ding	To sting, bite
钉	丁	Ding	Nail
靪	丁	Ding	To mend shoes
丁	丁	Ding	A small piece

During the peak period of the Cultural Revolution, the leftist mood prevailed; traditional purists no longer posed a threat to the work of character simplification. The situation was, in fact, even more suitable for a more radical reform as the Cultural Revolution was approaching its end.

On 20 July 1977, the CLR and the National Bureau of Standards jointly issued a circular as a prelude to the formal declaration. Half a year after the appearance of the circular, on 20 December 1977, the committee published the major work of character simplification of the SSSC in the two most influential newspapers: *Renmin Ribao* and *Guangming Ribao*. The draft scheme contained 853 simplified characters and 61 simplified radicals. As they had been widely circulated to test the public response, they could be experimented with immediately in the print media. In addition to this, 263 characters were eliminated by making use of the homophone substitution method. Table 2 demonstrates cases where words, written as different *hanzi*, but homophonic in speech, now use the same form. Before simplification, all five characters with the same phonetic radical '丁' (a small piece) were pronounced 'ding', but were not related in meaning, as indicated by the respective semantic radicals for the other four: 目 (eye), 口 (mouth), 钅 (metal), 革 (leather). In the Second Scheme table, all five of these *hanzi*, represented orally by a homophonous syllable, were substituted for, using the simplest character, '丁'. While this character was much easier to write than the original ones, the subtle written semantic distinctions were compromised.

The end of the Second Scheme

As can be seen from the evidence presented, the SSSC was burdened from the very beginning with political involvement. Its announcement engendered a wide debate in society. As expressions of displeasure had been growing in the wake of its release, the pressure to modify and even repeal the SSSC became intense. This can be gleaned from the fact that the Scheme was attacked not only by those diehard conservatives who consistently objected to any thought of alteration made to the traditional characters, but also by those who had been enthusiastic proponents of simplified characters since the 1920s and keen participants in drawing up the TSC during the 1950s.

However, because of its complex background, the SSSC's final official repeal was neither straightforward nor immediate. In terms of the time sequence, three main periods stand out: an initial reaction (1978–1980), re-evaluation (1980–86) and formal withdrawal (1986).

Initial reaction (1978–1980)

During the first few days after the announcement, many signed articles were arranged to hail the publication, and the response from the general public was to a greater or lesser extent positive. Most articles and responses were characterised by having very heavy-handed propaganda themes, on both general and specific aspects of the Scheme. On the other hand, no comment on the Scheme was written by any eminent linguistic researcher or influential LP specialist. Concerning this topic, only three papers were published in 1978, in the first two issues of *Zhongguo Yuwen* (*Chinese Linguistics*), the most widely-read research journal on the Chinese language. The journal itself did not use any of the SSSC characters. This stance was entirely contrary to the linguists' position in the 1950s and the early 1960s.

In 1978, the political pendulum began to swing in the opposite direction, and more pragmatic and powerful leaders began eventually to regain positions of power. It was becoming clearer that it was only a matter of time before the chilling influence of the Leftist faction would fade from educational and cultural affairs. This idea encouraged intellectuals to be more confident and to speak out on a wide range of topics. On 4 March 1978, the annual meetings of China's People's Political Consultative Conference and the National People's Congress were opened; they are the most important yearly events in Chinese political life. During the conferences, some senior LP experts and administrators, Hu Yuzhi, Wang Li, Zhou Youguang and others, who are also deputies of these most powerful state organs, lodged a petition demanding that characters listed in the First Table of the SSSC should not be used to write the key documents of these two meetings (Fei, 1997: 352). This was a very unusual way of dealing with such an issue.

Then, on 7 January 1980, in the insignificant column of 'Answers to Readers' Questions', the *People's Daily* declared: 'the large-scale experiment [of the SSSC] has been accomplished and will enter a revision phase. Therefore, all newspapers have stopped using them.' This quiet withdrawal, without an official announcement, was in stark contrast to the vigorous fanfare after the release two years previously.

Re-evaluation (1980–1986)

In the spring of 1980, after a hiatus of over a decade, China's LP agency CLR officially resumed normal work. One important problem it had to deal with in the committee's first meeting was the SSSC. Unfortunately for historians of LP, there are no references available to document how this revision was proceeding, or to reveal the agreements and disagreements which contributed to the final policy decision. What is known from reports in the news is that most activists involved with the Second Scheme during the Cultural Revolution were excluded from the new CLR. According to Wang Li (1981: 20), after the CLR was reorganised it immediately set up a sub-committee for SSSC Revision, with Zhang Zhigong as director and Wang Li and Ye Laishi as vice directors; all of its 11 members were renowned scholars in linguistics and in other areas. It is also believed that they were the main lobbying group that objected to the Second Scheme.

Between July and December 1980, the revision committee held seven meetings,

and 116 characters from the Scheme were determined by ballot for consideration to be adopted. Later on, these 116 characters were reduced to 111 as a result
of the 1981 opinion poll, and with the hope that it would win a more favourable
reception. However, in August 1981, it failed to get the approval of participants
in a closed-door meeting. Then, in 1986, the crucial National Conference on
Language Work was convened in Beijing. After long internal deliberation, the
Conference decided that from 1986 onward the Second Scheme's trial use was
formally terminated.

Various reasons have been given for the failure of the short-lived SSSC. It
is generally agreed that three factors are accountable for the failure: (1) legal
processes; (2) technical aspects; and (3) sociopolitical reasons.

Reasons for abandonment: Lack of legitimacy

From a legal perspective, as deduced from the First Scheme, it is understood that five procedures, as schematically presented in Figure 3, have to be
gone through before a new language reform scheme is decreed (Zhou, 1982:
7). The feasibility study and the formulation are the first step for any key LP
programme, normally carried out by the staff members of the CLR before the
RIAL was established. Then proposals and schemes were submitted to the
official language authority for examination and re-examination by higher-
level State Council. And usually the proposals/schemes were required to be

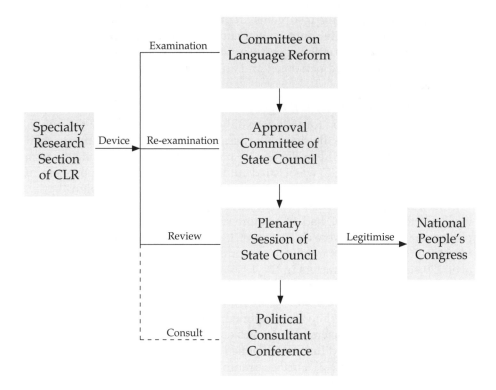

Figure 3 The five-step legal procedure for promulgating language reforms

presented to the Chinese People's Political Consultative Congress[20] for further deliberation.

Official LP in China is the responsibility of the State Council, the top body of the national government, where the framework of a scheme is mapped out. But the National People's Congress (Parliament) has the final say – this is in policy-making as well as in politics. So far, only four major LP schemes have been promulgated by the state legislative apparatus: two by State Council (simplification schemes in 1956 and 1977), and two by the People's Congress (the Phonetic Scheme in 1958 and the Language Law in 2000). The responsibility to put the parliamentary language policy into effect has been the business of the Education Ministry and the CLR. Since the SSSC was technically announced only for trial use, the final step of submitting the Scheme for legislation by the People's Congress was legally not required.

However, a very crucial procedure was omitted before the Scheme was shown to the public. The majority of the academic members of the CLR played no active role during the last stage of the Scheme's formulation and promulgation, so there are contending views on whether procedures four and five were observed (Fei, 1997: 347–8, 368; Zhou, 1986: 21). Zhou (1992: 219) and a number of other senior linguists were particularly unhappy about being by-passed. Lv Shuxiang (1995: 3), a highly respected linguist, says, 'During the Great Cultural Revolution any weird thing could happen. Even an institution like the CLR, which was under the direct administration of the State Council, was forced by the insurgents [21] to release the SSSC'. In fact, the legal considerations are a quite controversial and superficial argument; what these senior CLR members queried was the authenticity of the ad hoc committee, composed of unqualified personnel and appointed by those in power during the Cultural Revolution.

Reasons for abandonment: The great leap forward in LP

One much-cited reason for withdrawal was 'unacceptability' by the public, who were unable to use the characters because of this sudden change in their shape. Just as the Great Leap Forward [22] happened on the economic scene in 1958, the immature SSSC was issued under a similar leftist atmosphere of utopian idealism, hoping for a quick result through a mass campaign.

Chen Ping (1999: 160) noted, when the TSC of 1956 was formulated 65% of the characters in the TSC had 14 or more strokes, but 'the main target of simplification in the SSSC were characters of 13 strokes or fewer, which accounted for 59% of the characters involved'. According to Duan Shennong (1990: 209), over 270 simplified characters in the 1956 scheme were re-simplified in 1977. Generally speaking, a character with more than 10 strokes is viewed as a complex character. Having taken a bold leap forward, the Second Scheme re-simplified the characters that were already simplified, or those in frequent use but with fewer strokes, i.e. characters with 10 strokes or less. In 1956 國 (guo, country) was simplified as 国, and further simplified as 囗 in the 1977 scheme (also, see Zhao & Baldauf, 2007: 82–3). Further examples are provided in Table 3.

Another radical goal projected in the SSSC, at least for some advocates, was movement towards phoneticisation, i.e. Romanisation or alphabetisation.[23] The SSSC has been regarded as being the main platform to fulfil a long-debated

Table 3 Characters simplified in the 1950s that were further simplified in SSSC (1977)

Traditional form	Simplified form in TSC (1950s)	Simplified form in SSSC (1977)	Meaning	Pronunciation
國	国	囗	Country/state	Guo2
費	费	弗	Fee/to waste	Fei4
彈	弹	弓旦	Bullet/to flip	Dan4/Tan2
輸	输	车入	To lose/to transfer	Shu1
齡	龄	令	Order/age	Ling4

double aim: from simplification to phoneticisation through a number of radical simplification schemes like the 1956 reforms. While there was an attempt to minimise the inventory of the most frequently occurring characters for general reading purposes, another important step was to reduce substantially the number of strokes, thereby eventually to create a prototype of a phonetic alphabet. Quite a few politically motivated members were interested in accelerating the progress towards the desired goal of phoneticisation, proposed by Mao Zedong: 'The writing system must be reformed. It should take the phonetic direction common to the languages of the world.' For these Romanisation/Latinisation advocates, simplification was just a temporary measure before the destined embarkation on the road to Romanisation. The SSSC, in a sense, was projected to realise Mao's aspiration by maximising the simplification of the graphic form until the components of Chinese characters became so simplified that the individual strokes themselves functioned as a phonetic alphabet, as has happened in Japanese. For the same purpose, the homophone substitution method was overused, in order to 'eliminate some problems of unnecessary differentiation of characters, and hence, was a step forward in the direction of the phoneticisation of the writing system' (Cheng, 1979: 4). The reduction resulted in a large number of homonyms, which could no longer be disambiguated in written text. Hence, reading speed was slowed as readers tried to guess the meanings.

Sociopolitical reasons: The ill-timed decision

Script reform history shows that timing is crucial if a language reform programme is to be successful. It is widely believed (see e.g. Ball, 1999) that most successful, wide-ranging script reforms are generally accompanied by sociocultural upheavals. Ball (1999: 280) illustrated this point by citing cases; for example, the adoption of the Latin alphabet for Turkish as part of a much wider programme of Westernisation; the modification made to the Russian alphabet after the 1917 Revolution; and the radical simplification of the Japanese writing system after the end of the Second World War. Another kind of successful approach is that, broadly speaking, in a linguistically mature society with a stable government, long and sufficient preparation and a relatively short period of completion make script reform programmes easier to implement. The adoption of the TSC is also a very good example to illustrate these observations. That is, in the discussion of the 1935 Scheme and TSC, it was made clear that simplification had been discussed, prepared and tried since the beginning of the 20th century, so large-scale simplification could be smoothly carried out. It took only five to six years (PRC was founded in 1949 and the TSC was formally commissioned in 1956). This could be done because of (1) long-time deliberations prior to TSC, including the 1935 Scheme; and (2) the people's confidence and revolutionary spirit during the founding days of a fresh new country were at their peak during the early 1950s – this was the necessary social condition that supported implementing the TSC over such a short period.

The Second Scheme was considered ill-timed insofar as the circumstances were concerned. The Cultural Revolution had caused unprecedented upheaval to every aspect of Chinese society, and the population had not recovered from the shock of that social catastrophe, which, after 1977, brought about new values and a social psychology that was opposed to any drastic changes in life. Zhou (1992: 219) says, 'People just settle down to normal life and are still fluttering with lingering fear of the Great Cultural Revolution.' Taylor and Taylor (1995: 188) have made a similar argument in discussing the Scheme's withdrawal in 1978: ' . . . So soon after the traumatic Cultural Revolution, the population yearned for stability'. These comments show that the political atmosphere was turning in the opposite direction. During the Cultural Revolution, in order to establish their positions, the Gang of Four or ultra-leftists did their best to revolutionise all the accomplishments achieved in areas of culture and the arts in the 17 years before their ascendancy. After the demise of the Gang of Four, national sentiment was ready to reassess what had been done and undone under their influence. This sentiment had become stronger after 1979, when Hua Guofeng, Mao's successor, who vigorously resisted any reassessment and correction of previous policies, was removed by the political clout of reformers led by Deng Xiaoping.

Script Reform in Transformation

Having examined the historical context of two unsuccessful simplification schemes in the 1930s and 1970s, as well as the technical aspects of the TSC in the 1950s, this section discusses the recent developments in China's language planning in relation to the changes in the political arena and the impact from technological advances.

At the National Conference on Language Work in 1986, further simplification of Chinese characters was dropped from the agenda of the revised policy and the possibility of phoneticisation was also implicitly ruled out. Emphasis was given to the standardisation and consolidation of what had been achieved. But shortly after these decisions were taken, a debate on the future of *hanzi* took place between conservatives and reformers, although, when this debate threatened to undo several decades of solid progress made in LP, the polemic was brought to a close by political intervention. Many underlying and disputed issues that were brought up during the debate had existed for some time and were waiting for their chance to emerge.

Technology as a catalyst: IT-oriented policy after 1986

Adjustment to suit a new society – National Conference on Language Work in 1986

As previously indicated, the national LP work was completely paralysed during the Great Cultural Revolution. Nearly a decade after that chaotic situation came to an end, the National Conference on Language Work, organised by the State Council, was held in Beijing from 6–13 January 1986. It compares with the first national language conference, held in October 1955, as a milestone in Chinese LP history in terms of its far-reaching impact on the Chinese language landscape.

A series of events, happening in the wake of this grand meeting, which can be termed 'LP Vision in the New Era', marked not only a significant shift but also a new era in respect of changing the setting of sociopolitical objectives. Promoting *Putonghua* and standardising modern Chinese were given equal priority in LP; Romanisation was not supported; simplification was deliberately diluted without publicly announcing any radical change. This marks a pivotal turn in government policy in three particular ways: an evaluation of the past, institutional change, and a reorientation of the LP agendas.

Evaluation of the past

An analysis of the situation found at the conference suggests that the emphasis was placed on stability, rather than on simplification, let alone phoneticisation. Worse than this for the reformists was the understanding that the conference fell short of a determined resolution to fight against the increasing revival of the cancelled traditional characters (*fanti zi*)[24]. Worse still, official speeches employed equivocal attitudes and inexplicit wording in summing up what had been achieved by the past script reform programmes, blurring any directions for the future. Furthermore, the way the Government handled the tough problem of priority and policy choice in the subsequent years suggests that the picture of script reform was no clearer even at the highest administrative level, than among the scholars.

Notwithstanding the fact that script reform was at the centre of interest, as it had been three decades earlier, in order to clear up confusion greater weight is devoted in this monograph to the interpretation of why there was a shift in the focus of LP at the conference. The detailed accounts of the official conference, documented by Yu (1996: 157–76), show how the policy makers tried to hedge the simplification issue by using evasive and noncommittal wording in the final conference statement. This usage signals that the simplification problem was too difficult for the participants at the meeting to resolve, and that recognition explains the authority's hesitation in making a policy decision on this matter. It also gave people the impression that a major reversal in policy was going to occur on script reform.

Institutional change: Restructuring the LP body

At the conference, China's highest language legislative organ unavoidably had to undertake steps to reform itself by addressing new changes that had been put in place. The CLR was formally changed to the State Commission of Language Work. The newly founded SCLW consisted of some 18 consultative members.

The inclusion of higher-ranking official members such as vice-ministers of the concerned ministries indicates the emphasis on the commission's bureaucratic function. Since the national language administration came into being in 1949, this was the third landmark reform that had been made to the official LP body. One key issue that SCLW had yet to address properly was a clearly defined working agenda.

However, the lack of a much-needed vision for both the immediate and more distant problems at the highest level left SCLW officials foundering. This lack of an agenda might be one important reason why SCLW presented an invisible face to the public during much of the more aggressive *hanzi* cultural movement debate that had occurred around the mid-1980s. Hu Qiaomu, the top decision maker with respect to the national language policy, also acknowledged in 1982 that the national language policy was in great need of stability and consistency. When talking with the five major LP academics on script reform work, he said:

> The current work on LP is now at its low ebb, and the credibility of CLR is very low. Not only are the central leaders too busy to care about the LP work, there are even fewer leaders at the provincial level concerned with script reform. (Editing Team, 1999: 301)

Reorientation of the LP agenda

One of the main tasks of the 1986 conference was to draw up the goals for the future. The issues of greatest concern, further simplification and phoneticisation, were the focus of the conference. However, Liu Daosheng (1987: 24), the first director of SCLW, declared that these two responsibilities were 'future topics and not current concerns'. At the same time, to promote the spread of *Putonghua*, to optimise current characters, to create standards for diversified purposes, and to research Chinese Information Processing (CIP)-oriented language and character issues, were presented as the core tasks of the SCLW conference. By the time the conference was held, China was engaged in devising the first generation of character input schemes and character-capable computers. Given that the IT industry is the pillar for all aspects of science and technology development, creating various suitable standards of *hanzi* began to stand out as the paramount concern.

Technological requirements from the IT industry: A digital view

Stroke simplification was the sole basis of the script reform in the 1950s, accompanied by the slogan 'The Less, The Better', which contrarily resulted in complexity in *hanzi* composition and encouraged the conservatives to complain about the modernisers' 'getting the sesame, but losing the melon', i.e. losing the greater good for a lesser result. Now, to keep abreast in the information age, computerisation has become of increasing concern. Structural simplification, which has proved to be critical for computer input optimisation through reducing the number of components, and the total number of characters, has attracted substantial attention from scholars.

In order to facilitate computer processing of *hanzi*, the IT industry has three special requirements about the physical makeup of characters: minimising the composing parts, improving the internal consistency of the *hanzi* system, and disambiguating the graphic vision.

Minimising the composing parts

The majority of *hanzi* can be composed with a fixed and relatively small number of frequently used components. This requires deleting rarely used components, or at least reducing them to a minimum, because rarely used components need equal amounts of computer space, in both software and hardware, as those that are regularly used.

To save typing time, the character is ideally composed of no more than three components; preferably, by just one independent whole or by two components. However, after simplification, about 20 new components were created. Most of them were not frequently used; some rarely used components were not merged. Furthermore, a large number of frequently used characters remaining to be simplified are characters with more than three components. For instance, in the dictionary, under the entry of *ying*, there are 贏 (to win), 影 (film), 鷹 (eagle), 櫻 (cherry).

On the other hand, a number of new radicals have been created to replace their complex counterparts for some characters, but the same replaced complex radicals are still used in some other characters, so that the total number of radicals has in fact been increased. Some characters are composed of different existing components and have been simplified as independent characters; new elements that came into the *hanzi* component system are not used productively for creating more characters. For example, 習 was simplified as 习, but the original components (羽, 白) are still used as radicals for other characters. There are also other instances of this failure to use components productively, such as 農 (曲, 辰) → 农, 頭 (豆, 頁) → 头, 個 (人, 固) → 个, 書 (聿, 日) → 书.

The greatest difficulty for input-scheme designers is the large number of radicals and components. Simplified characters have not overcome this problem, but have instead created more variation and therefore more rather than fewer problems.

Improving the internal consistency of the Hanzi system

Component Optimisation refers to making the composing parts transferable, moveable and suitable to be reassembled. Thus there is a need to create a stock of interchangeable and disposable components, so that they can be freely disassembled just like basic building blocks. In other words, they should be easy to dismantle and be reproducible on a computer. Ma Xiwen (1987: 104), a renowned AI (Artificial Intelligence) expert at Beijing University, made this proposal:

> [T]he only thing IT workers require linguistic circles to do is to make changes to some characters' structure, so as to compose them with a few independent basic units. This is a very minor assignment for linguists, but the social benefit is unlimited.

The components of characters in his examples consist of unassembled parts. After optimisation, all parts of these two characters are transferable and movable:

我 (wo, me/I) → 禾 (he, plant) + 戈 (ge, an ancient weapon/axe) = 禾戈
拜 (bai, to pray) → 手 (shou, hand) + 手 = 手手.

Disambiguating the graphic vision

In the digital era, reading has become the central concern for *hanzi* users, more so than writing. A good, reasonably legible vision of a character is more desirable than ease of writing. Unfortunately, the visible distinctness of some complex characters was blurred by their simplified counterparts. This is illustrated by the following examples.

设有: 没有; 风 : 凤; 沪 : 泸; 获 : 获; 誉 : 誊; 拔 : 拨; 抢 : 抢;
压 : 庄; 庆 : 庆; 备 : 奋.

The paradox is that characters that are effortlessly written come into inevitable conflict with the demand of being easy to recognise. How to strike a balance between these two demands remains a major factor for a further script reform programme: not to compromise their distinctiveness, while making them simple enough for handwriting.

Complex factors in simplification: A systems view

The TSC in the 1950s was guided by the dominant theory of 'more simple [is] more efficient'. Since the policy change in 1986, and in the light of the latest studies, script reformers have come to realise that the predominant approach in script reform theory has moved from an emphasis on simplification to frameworks based on a system view. Today, while simplified characters have won the approval of the majority of scholars with objective minds, it has become clear to those scholars that systematic rationalisation is more important than the pure quantitative reduction of stroke complexity. The systems view here provides a useful concept in understanding the complex nature of simplifying characters.

Throughout its several thousand years of uninterrupted growth, *hanzi* has become a well-developed system. Any minor change of its parts may risk altering the internal energy of the whole consistent operating chain. The character must be viewed as a whole, taking into consideration the interrelationships and interdependence among its parts and its relationship within the system. From the systems view, it is apparent that if any element acting on the system is modified, the wholeness of the system at large is going to change in some ways. On the basis of Cooper's statement (1989: 177), the interrelatedness of all parts is the most striking feature of the system. Change in one dimension of the language development is likely to ripple throughout the system, causing changes in other parts. 'Giving a pull at the hair makes the whole body sway,' a Chinese saying declares – the whole is more important than its parts is the central point of a systems view (see, Zhao & Baldauf, 2007: 76–9).

Externally, the systems view is also consistent with what is known about the impact on script simplification from the sociopolitical dimension. Internally, applying the linguistic implications of the systematic view to LP, the factors that should be taken into consideration in reforming *hanzi* include:

- ambiguity;
- lexical productive ability;
- misunderstanding;
- consistency within the system;
- classification; and

- pronunciation.

Take ambiguity for example. Most commonly used characters should be simplified first. This assumption is consistent with the natural development trend. But, when too large a number of most-used characters are simplified, semantic differentiation of the text is sacrificed. There is a threshold for the maximum of frequently used characters as well as a maximum for the number of stroke reductions. The number of frequently used characters is inversely proportional to that of stroke reductions; the relationship can be expressed as:

$$\text{Disambiguation} = \frac{\text{The number of frequently used characters}}{\text{The number of strokes reduced}}$$

The bigger the number of frequently used characters, the larger is the text that is covered. The stroke reduction of individual frequently used characters is much more limited where disambiguation is concerned. On the other hand, if the number of simplified characters is small, even when the differentiating information is lost; the number of non-simplified characters is great enough to offset graphic ambiguities in the text. The problem becomes apparent if too many units look similar in the running text, and oversimplification tends to contribute to the opacity and ambiguity in everyday language with which the average readers have to cope.

A Debate about *Hanzi's* Future and its Sociopolitical Implications

Character use after the abandonment of the SSSC

China in the 1980s was, sociopolitically, a very homogenous country in every respect, yet in contrast to the highly centrally-controlled nature of Chinese society, character use was in a chaotic state. When the Second Scheme began, China still had a very stable standard that was virtually consistent with the prescription set by the Government. However, in comparison with the character use prior to the 1980s, China today has witnessed more deviation from the official standard in its script. The 'regulations on language issues are beginning to lose the authority or binding force they used to enjoy in the 1960s and 1970s' (Chen, 1999: 192).

In informal writing and private correspondence, many people invent their own shorthand-style characters that are simplified and time saving; i.e. a very large number of variant forms have been coined, using the analogy of the methods of previous simplification schemes, and a good many of these have taken root more widely. On the other hand, the intrusion of traditional characters back into the Mainland had been progressing rapidly, and some bureaucrats were alarmed by the influx of such characters in a wide range of official or semi-official publications.[25] The changes effected have not been revolutionary in scope, but they have been parallel with the changes under way in the political, economic and social fields, and they have even caught the attention of the highest authorities. The 'severe situation of the disorder in character use' was emphatically documented in SCLW's submission to the State Council in the application requesting the official withdrawal of the SSSC (The Office of Standard Work, 1997: 20).

The genesis of the debate

Since the 1980s, discussion about character complexity/simplification and orthographic phoneticisation has long disappeared from consideration in Chinese LP. However, the conservatives who had been shattered by the vicissitudes of the anti-rightist campaign and the Cultural Revolution during the 1960s and 1970s have not disappeared as a force opposing script reform. Right after these decisions of ruling out the further simplification of Chinese characters were taken at the 1986 Conference, a decade-long debate commenced on these two issues between conservatives and reformists, triggered by a wave of new cultural traditionalism. A relatively close scrutiny of sociolinguistic conditions has revealed that political shift, institutional policy and technological changes were the most important contributing factors to the renewed interest in the script issue, leading to a lengthy nationwide debate. These controversies are still on-going, without having reached an authoritative conclusion.

Political background: Neo-traditionalism

Discussion of script reform has never been purely a 'language matter' in China; it has always been part of a much broader debate with obvious political overtones. The halting, or reversal, of the language reform programme in 1986 is an indication of the waning of the overall governmental grip on society, and thus can only be understood as the result of the abolition of the ideology with which this reform is linked. Communist Party rule is characterised by consolidating its position not just through the state apparatus, but also through strict control of the cultural life of the general population.

After a series of student protests in the late 1980s, especially the June 4 Democracy Movement in the spring of 1989, the ideological edifice in China rapidly eroded. A major ideological shift that diverged from the dated politics of the early years was becoming irreversible. The largest cultural-ideological quandary facing the new generation of political elites was how to use a variety of cultural activities as weapons against total Westernisation. Thus, 'neo-traditionalism', or Cultural Renaissance, was formulated as a result of searching for an alternative propaganda strategy.

It is known that one of the purposes of the disastrous Cultural Revolution was to revolutionise the past, but, under the new context, overcorrecting the historical mistakes led to the opposite outcome: the traditional heritage exorcised by Communists in the past was now being glorified by this emerging Cultural Renaissance movement. Traditionalism always manifests itself in extreme nationalism and chauvinism. The enthusiastic revival of various forms of traditional heritage in the mid-1990s resulted in the development of a worship of its own culture in native forms, clearly boosting the renewed awareness of self-identity and a rediscovery of the merits of *hanzi*.

In contrast to the Gang of Four's disdain for traditional culture, in the new CCP leaders' ideological strategy, all traditional forms of literacy are exploited as potential vehicles to convey the Party's propaganda. A 'Back to the Ancients' sentiment has been a new trend in popular culture, with a large number of classic works being reintroduced into school education, which is a sharp contrast to the textbooks replete with political slogans that were used before 1977. This change has strongly influenced ordinary people's perception about old and traditional things, and it accounts for the reappearance everywhere of a certain amount of classical writing during this period. Accordingly, the masses' nostalgic feeling for the *fanti zi* in the 1990s is in essence a reflection of a political shift. While it was unintentionally and only obliquely encouraged through the authority's favouring of traditional culture, those in power were increasingly nervous about a growing dissatisfaction with the limitations of freedom in cultural life, and wanted to avoid being seen as being unnecessarily heavy-handed in relation to such matters. Thus looser control of the ideological realm created for the general population an environment of more choice in character use and an opportunity to influence the official standard.

Technology: Characters in the domain of hi-tech

A primary justification given for script reform, be it Romanisation or simplification, is the cumbersome and time-consuming procedure needed to gain access to reading. Since the 1970s, interest and concern about using Chinese characters with computer systems has been widespread. Researchers have conducted painstaking experiments to find the best means for computerised character input, and to a certain degree characters were finally successfully computerised, thus creating the basis for computerisation in the mid-1970s.

However, there is a good deal of disagreement about whether *hanzi* is still an obstacle for script modernisation. The various rosy accounts in newspapers, reporting the success of Chinese computer input and the display of *hanzi* on the screen or from printed output, have been at variance with public experience. The technological development in the information age challenges all conventions of society, and LP is no exception to this rule. Therefore, in the face of a rapidly increasing computer-literate population, the technological implication is more than ever bound to be a crucial issue for the debate about the advantage and disadvantage of *hanzi*.

The traditionalists have argued that the labourious process needed to master the characters has been greatly reduced. Therefore, not only is the effort to further reform *hanzi* deemed unnecessary, the completed reform programmes, given their harmful effect on China's cultural heritage, should be reviewed. The reformers, on the other hand, have argued that the current resolutions to input characters are far from satisfactory. In spite of the exponential need for human resources and the tragic waste of creativity in inventing the thousands upon thousands of input schemes in the past couple of decades, machine processing of written Chinese is so sophisticated that it has remained the privilege of a few. Moreover, character input and word processing do not encompass the whole of Chinese computerisation. Insofar as the Internet is concerned, it appears that there is a long way to go to ensure effective and efficient transmission. Then there are the higher level applications for artificial intelligence and Chinese information processing, which are seen as very critical for China's competitiveness in the areas of science and technology.

Diffusion of liberal thought

Seen in retrospective, the language struggle has provided abundant evidence of the way in which politics works. In the three decades since 1956, when Mao launched the anti-rightist campaign in which a large number of democracy-minded intellectuals were criticised and prosecuted to the point of committing suicide, there were few who dared to challenge the official policy on script reform by having their opposing opinions openly published. Since the 1980s, however, this situation has changed. China entered an ideologically liberal period in which many doctrines were challenged. With the opening-up policy proceeding well on the economic front, Chinese academics enjoyed more liberty in expressing their views on government policy. Comments or suggestions on the nation's language policy began to appear in journals and newspapers, and dissident voices against simplification were often publicised and presented to society; this could not have been imagined when the ultra-left forces were in power. By mid-1980, with the cessation of strong-arm tactics that had been used to silence critics, it was perceived by the public that the excessive control of language affairs was a minority's interference in the majority's will. Given this hostile resistance from a wide sector of the general public, it is not surprising that the effectiveness of restrictions and prescriptions for character use were questioned and attacked in various quarters. Under such conditions, the overturning of past accepted practices was not proscribed for many ideological participants, and the vigorous debate in the LP area was unquestionably fostered by the moderate tone of official conference statements, which fell short of reaffirming phoneticisation or further simplification. On the other hand, disillusioned SCLW members, having had their fingers burnt by the SSSC, were perplexed by the opaque policy that the central government took to deal with the emerging neo-traditionalism; unsure of the line to take, many ultimately adopted an ultra-cautious line. They never appeared so weak and indecisive as when responding to the challenge from an aggressive Chinese Character Culture Faction.

The formation of the Chinese Character Culture Faction (CCCF)

All these factors taken together created fertile ground for the CCCF, which shrouded itself in a cloak of patriotism. In contrast to the ever less visible activities of the weak LP agency, the CCCF quickly gained momentum in this unprecedentedly favourable political and social environment. The *Hanzi* Culture Faction took shape around 1986. Its birth was marked by the formal establishment of the International Research Institute of Chinese Characters, including its flagship journal *Chinese Character Culture* in Beijing, under the sponsorship of Yuan Xiaoyuan, a returned Chinese-American. Although few participants in the *hanzi* culture faction were professionally trained experts in the field of linguistics, a handful of towering scholars in various disciplines gave a lot of credit to the *hanzi* culture camp. At the time, the central concern in the Party's work was to play the traditionalism card to keep unwanted 'pollution' from the Western world at bay. The *hanzi* cultural theories on the relationship between *hanzi*'s superiority and patriotism became tools that the Party propaganda workers could use to get their message across to a wider audience. Early indications of the renewed interest in complex characters did not draw much attention from the linguistic community until the beginning of the 1990s, when the fully functioning CCCF launched a series of attacks aimed at invalidating what language reformers had done to *hanzi*.

Their theories on the advantages of the Chinese writing system, most of them 'new wine in old bottles', were packaged for modern interpretation, appealing to both the ordinary population and politicians. According to the official line, anything that was promoted as indigenous through either official or non-official channels was worth encouraging. Although most of the disputes focused on linguistic principles rather than on nationalistic feelings, *hanzi* was presented as an indigenous creation in opposition to Western influence. For the general public, *traditional culture* was a relatively neutral term, lending some respectability to cultural practices due to its link with 5000 years of Chinese history. Consequently, it did not cause resistance from the population, which had been recovering from the devastating consequences of the Cultural Revolution.

However, there was some evidence of resentment from some experts who had been previous participants in drawing up the national language policy. Finally, they became impatient with the squabbling, as heated controversies erupted, and they started vigorously criticising the CCCF's unprofessionalism. An avalanche of treatises firmly and extensively denouncing the pro-*hanzi* proponents and their linguistic suggestions were produced in a short time. Articles appeared in both elite journals and the popular press, and even in mass-market magazines. Over a period of one decade, both sides engaged in a series of charges and countercharges in discussions across the country that eventually moved into the public arena. In China, factional opponents of the ideological extreme have been all too ready to use Party-style language, infected by a type of sectarian narrowness and virulence. Some attacks were by no means just articles based on linguistic arguments, but were rather framed as emotional accusations enriched by personal vituperation. A good illustration of the point is a legal case between the two key figures of this debate that caught the intellectuals' attention across the country (Collective Editors, 2004). Xu's radical and unorthodox argument was castigated as claptrap by the reformers, earning him the criticism that he lacked any depth of understanding of quality in linguistics. Being dubbed a counterfeit scholar and opportunist by Prof Wu Tieping, Xu brought the case to court.

The inability to free themselves from personal attack and stay above political squabbles haunts Chinese linguists to this day. As mentioned previously, instrumentalising cultural and literary issues to serve politics has been a traditional aspect of Chinese history. It is not hard to understand that the members of the CCCF were seen as a group of people using any means to achieve personal profit of some kind, in the name of patriotism, linguistic science and technology, rather than through strength of character alone. Both opposing camps entered into a debate about these issues, which quickly revealed a style of political rhetoric typical of extreme radicals. The language of both sides was full of scathing words and derogatory accusations, reminding one of the terms used in the days of political persecution during the Cultural Revolution.

A love of characters is patriotic

Seeing themselves as elitists deciding the country's future and posing as the guardians of the soul of the nation, most of the contending intellectual groups in modern China have, despite ideological clashes and heated debates, essentially pursued nationalistic goals. As far as the language issues are concerned, a number of them have risen to national importance tending to revolve around questions that touch sensitive political issues. The articulation of patriotism through character use becomes apparent. Revitalising the traditional culture is the theme of the CCP's Patriotism Education propaganda[26] and of the 'Real State of the Country' education campaign, launched after the 1989 Democracy Movement. The relatedness between patriotism and the preference for a particular writing form is always the most convenient weapon for script conservatives of any language, as Coulmas (1991: 227) notes: '[W]riting is a cultural tool which defines the cultural sphere more clearly than many other societal features and techniques'. A nationalistic bias for *hanzi* is deeply embedded in the Chinese psyche and poses a deterrent to any reform attempt. Patriotism manifests itself in passion for indigenous culture, and indigenous Chinese culture can be represented best by traditional characters.

At its initial stage, as long as its impact was confined to the academic area, the debate did not draw much serious concern from language authorities and it was dismissed as demagogic misbehaviour by the media. When the re-evaluation of the simplification implementation and the rediscoveries of the advantages of *hanzi*, proposed by those supporting *hanzi* superiority, gained momentum and created a significant stir, it clashed directly with the Government's language policy.

Rediscovering the merits of Chinese characters

Superficially, what the new traditionalists claimed they wanted to do with *hanzi* was to use it as a tool or means to revitalise the country. Such an aim is, of course, laudable, but this newer approach is possible only when the claims are not too far-fetched. The CCCF holds that Chinese characters are not only artistically elegant and culturally rich (qualities that were praised by the previous traditional character promoters), but also logically meaningful and intelligently sound.

Specifically, they 'discovered' six superiorities of Chinese characters:

- information orientation;
- intelligent script;
- transferability and internationality;
- permanent perspicuity – unifying force;
- ease of acquisition; and
- cultural heritage and historicity.

They go even further in overemphasising the characters' advantages, most of which were previously virtually unknown but were heralded by their promoters as 'rediscoveries' of the legacy of the national script by using rhetorical language and a journalistic style of writing replete with turgidity. These articles, written by the CCCF to promote *hanzi* culture, often showed glaring errors or misunderstandings, presenting some extreme arguments that highlight the necessity of adhering to objectivity in research. Other superior qualities they claimed for *hanzi* were as follows.

The monosyllabism of Chinese is a strength rather than a weakness; association is the mother of all inventions and, as the Chinese language encourages and facilitates association, it stands the Chinese in good stead; Chinese grammar is the closest to the rules of mathematics, musical notation, chemical symbols; all leading to the conclusion that Chinese has the potential to become the best international language (Guo, 2004: 96–7).

The CCCF claims that *hanzi* is China's fifth invention of great significance for world civilisation. The economic miracle, achieved in most East Asian countries, has occurred under the centuries-long influence of the peripheral *hanzi* culture. Chinese characters are being rejuvenated in the information era, and the 21st century is the century of Chinese characters, which will replace all other scripts as the sole writing system for all human beings. This type of rhetoric is illustrative of why the CCCF came into conflict with language officials and LP scholars.

Political interpretation: Political hand behind the scene?

In the mid-1980s, during the initial contact regarding unifying characters across the Taiwan Strait, a proposal of *Shifan Xiejian* (read the complex and write the simplified) came forward from Taiwanese scholars. Although serious discussions were carried out about the possibility, *Shifan Xiejian* did not last long before it was rejected by LP administrators from the Mainland side for its potential to undermine the country's language policy. An added complication was that *Shifan Xiejian* was using the same basic arguments that the CCCF advocated, which were launched by Yuan Xiaoyuan on the Mainland in 1988, so they were also referred to as the *Shifan Xiejian* faction. The new prevailing opinion in the 1980s–1990s was that the computer's arrival in ordinary people's lives gave them the choice of using either *jianti zi* or *fanti zi*. So *Shifan Xiejian* was propagated by the CCCF as the solution to overcome the disorderly circumstances where simplified characters were everywhere interspersed with traditional ones, with the latter posing as increasing threat to the former. To make the problem more complex, *Shifan Xiejian* is the official language policy that has been practised in Taiwan since 1976.[27] A series of articles, titled 'Unveiling the Puzzle of Chinese Characters', some of them amateurish, some written using reasonable linguistic argumentation, started to appear in CCCF's institutional journal and in the national media. Ostensibly, these articles were about the advantages of *hanzi*, but because character superiority is closely related with *fanti zi*, the so-called notion of 'character superiority' is essentially linked to the advantages of using traditional characters. The natural result of *Shifan Xiejian* was a shift back to the traditional system and an attempt to force those in authority to withdraw the simplified characters. Wu (1994: 87) remarks, 'Character superiority naturally leads to the conclusion that both character simplification and the phoneticisation efforts are a policy of disaster'.

In the highly politicised atmosphere of China, the debate inevitably caused a more complex interpretation. At one stage, the ultimate motive of the *Hanzi* Culture faction was labelled a cultural conspiracy to undermine the foundation of the Chinese Government's cultural policy. Summarising their further explanations, the CCCF strategy is perceived to 'kill three birds with one stone'. Their stone is *hanzi*'s superiority and *Shifan Xiejian*; the three birds are:

- resuming traditional characters, thereby hindering technological development through sabotaging the national language policy;
- putting the country at risk of being seen as degenerating into chauvinism and what Bianco (1971: 3) called 'Sinocentrism', thereby undermining the relationship between the Han majority and ethnic minorities; and
- isolating emerging China from the world by encouraging an excessively nationalistic fervour.

Although official propaganda is much less pervasive now than during the Maoist era, the Party's ideological machine is still at work at all levels, controlling the whole cultural life of the people and permeating into the superstructure. Whenever a political attack occurred or an academic dispute arose, 'orchestrated from across the Strait' was a ready accusation for both competing sides in the language arena. The CCCF's financial strength and political influence grew quickly, enabling them to carve out their own niche in the cultural hierarchy, and making a great impact over a relatively short period of time. At the same time, their strong financial support of the advocates of the wholesale shift back to traditional characters was invariably interpreted as being politically motivated and manipulated by foreign powers, aiming strategically to undermine the foundations of the Government's language policy by promoting traditional characters under the banner of patriotism.

The 1980s were a very critical transitional period for Chinese LP. Alongside the politically saturated debate about *hanzi*'s future was an even more significant change, driven largely by advances in communications technology. The following section describes this change of LP focus from reform for human use to standardisation for computer convenience, and seeks to explain these changes as being underpinned by changes in epistemology and views of how to plan a writing system.

Standardisation: New Reform Agenda in New Contexts

As previously seen in 1986, urgent technological demand pushed the Government to reassess its LP agenda, and IT-oriented standardisation was identified as one priority in the new context. It may not be an exaggeration to say that it has come to a stage now where no major advance in *hanzi* computerisation can be expected until the infrastructure for LP is improved. Standardisation is the key for enhancing all types of language software products, particularly *hanzi*'s input and output methods.

Four fixations: Difficulties and technological implications

Although standardisation is a clear historical trend and the basis of LP, until the 1990s few efforts at standardising the language, with the goal of *hanzi* computerisation, had been made. Language standardisation has lagged far behind the demands of the IT industry, and full-fledged participation in the IT industry will inevitably involve working out a series of national official standards for use on computers, as Shi (1987: 115), a renowned Chinese computer scientist, has pointed out. The central tasks of standardisation have been the so-called 'four fixations', which aim at settling the four most unstable attributes of *hanzi*, namely the number of *hanzi*, their ordering, shape and pronunciation. The 'four fixations' has been repeatedly confirmed as the SCLW's foremost task, but each fixation has been confronted by a variety of difficulties thus far.

In comparison with first language standardisation movement in the 1950s, which focused on pronunciation, grammatical and lexical codification, the ongoing standardisation effort has involved developing standards for character processing, with the single clear aim to better serve the IT industry and to counter the *laissez-faire* state of the language-related software market.

Fixation of pronunciation

It is well known that there are two streams of keyboard inputting schemes to enter Chinese characters on a computer – the ideographic method and the phonetic method. After nearly three decades of chaos and market competition, an increasing number of people have come to recognise that the phonetics-based software has been gradually gaining the upper hand in the competitive marketplace. This makes standard pronunciation a prerequisite for the Chinese citizen to communicate with computers. Regional variation in pronunciation poses a paramount difficulty for computerisation as 70% of Chinese speak various dialects (Hannas, 1997: 373–4). Other factors that influence these pronunciation problems include age, education and misleading information in the *hanzi* radical.

The common speech movement, which started at the end of the 19th century, has remained a central theme of LP in the 1950s. But, pronunciation has remained one of the most confusing areas and needs to be addressed urgently; yet it may take more time and energy for the regulators to standardise pronunciation than it will take to unify the writing system. The difficulty of achieving standard pronunciation can be understood from a statement by Su (2001: 227–8): 'if we select a text from the school language textbook, few people can correctly read every character. Even in public education, little has been achieved' (cf Liu, 2003: 58).

The pluricentric (Clyne, 1992) – more than one standard – nature of Chinese makes this problem more complex, and the ultimate solution for unifying pronunciation requires extensive involvement from all Chinese-speaking polities (e.g. Taiwan, Hong Kong, Singapore). Although, broadly speaking, the general populace in these societies would turn to the Mainland for standard usage (Coulmas, 1989: 252; Shepherd, 2003: 68), each Government has developed its own norms for pronunciation. The Government of the Mainland has enacted two tables of unifying pronunciation, in 1962 and 1985 respectively, but the pronunciation issue still appears to be more in disarray than that for character use.

More problematic are characters with multiple pronunciations. Ideally, users would produce the desired character by typing the actual sound of the character; but some characters' pronunciation can only be determined in context, and in such cases users are very often forced to type the wrong spelling (pronunciation), in order to get the correct character.[28]

Fixation of the physical shape

In terms of increasing stringency, there have been three types of *hanzi* standardisation work. Before typographic printing was invented in the Song Dynasty (960–1279), printing was very much an individual affair and there were no major differences between printed shapes and handwriting. What the standard could control was only the basic structure through official model characters (stone tablet inscriptions) and well-accepted calligraphic works. Typographic printing provided conditions for a higher-level standard as the fixed cases for each character in the same printery were stable, so stylistic shapes were determined and have been used up to the present. But large discrepancies exist not only in different style categories, but often with even the same stroke having several style forms in the same dictionary. For example, 俞-兪 (yu, a surname), 并-幷 (bing, together), 即-卽 (ji, namely / at once), 真-眞 (zhen, true / real), and the compound characters that are created from these components are all included in *Kanxi Zidian* (1767) (Deng & Zhang, 1997: 114). It should be noted that this is the very dictionary that has been used as the generic source of standards by China, Taiwan and Japan to encode characters for information interchange purposes. The negative effects on character processing include adding an unnecessary burden to ideographic input schemes and making *hanzi* order sequencing (which depends on stroke sequence) more difficult and confusing.

Traditional understanding of the physical shape of characters is a rough concept, basically referring to the approximate make-up of characters and their structural differences such as simplicity, complexity and variant forms. IT-oriented standards require a higher level of consistency and precision. In 1965, the shapes of 6196 characters were fixed in the *General List of Printing Fonts of Chinese Characters*, which brought to an end the chaotic situation that had plagued publication. However, the characters standardised in this table had many defects from the technological point of view: some irregularities in composing elements, i.e. stroke length and thickness or structural balance, which are minuscule differences undetectable to the human eye; or differences which are irrelevant in recognition thanks to contextual tolerance. Nevertheless, graphic uniformity and stability in dealing with these shapes are essential for the computer, as machines are very sensitive to stroke variation. This factor causes problems in applications, as these differences either may result in the failure of Optical Character Recognition (OCR) identification, or create an unnecessary burden for the amount of storage needed to develop input schemes.

Basically, there are two broad types of such characters. The first type, when used as a compound to form another character, is not consistent with its form when it stands as a character by itself. The second type is always used as a composing part, but manifests itself in two different forms while there are no grounds within the *hanzi* system to treat it as two different things. For whichever reason, the overriding desire is to get rid of illogical corruption that has resulted from character evolution or reform. It is necessary to make minimum alterations to original shapes in order to make them consistent and systematic. Various reasons may account for the non-standard composing units. Fei Jinchang argues that one of the major disturbing challenges for Chinese OCR development is the emerging non-standard characters that come into China along with imported printing equipment and software. Another source of difficulty relates to character designers and producers, who, out of eccentricity or in pursuance of their own neologism, have created a number of unorthodox shapes for software developers. According to a statistical analysis, done on a short passage of 349 characters, 78 (22%) of the characters were characters with self-defined shapes, and there was more than one form for the same radical produced by the same software (Fei, 1996: 266).

Fixation of the order

Western scripts have a small, stable and unchanging number of letters in a universal and fixed order, thus not only making alphabetical ordering of vocabulary easy to do and understand, but also giving alphabetic script a great advantage in data management and information retrieval systems (IR). As Hannas (1997: 259) has put it, 'delays of the sort that plague character-based programs are unconscionable to someone accustomed to the luxury of alphanumeric word processing'. Without ordering, classification is impossible. Fixed ordering and regular units are the most basic requirements for some higher-level computer application, such as database retrieval and stroke-based input schemes. For Chinese script computerisation, this is almost an insoluble problem and, after decades of intensive effort, the current situation is that each software program has its own sorting rule for arranging the characters, and as a result, 'the failure to sequence Chinese *hanzi* order by a unifying standard has impeded the compatibility of different software and their wider application' (Peng & Huang, 1994: 26). In order to facilitate information interchange between different systems, what is urgently needed is a unification of interchange character coding on a wider scale and a standardisation of internal character coding for each individual system. However, at the present time, 'there are a number of coding systems spread around within and outside the country, and what's more, none of these systems successfully resolves the problem of sequencing character order' (Feng, 1995: 17).

Before the computer, order standardisation referred to activities intended to unify dictionary indexing and classifying systems, the ostensible aim of which was sequencing character order to facilitate dictionary making and cataloguing in libraries, but the birth of the IT industry has widened the context. In a wider sense, standardisation of ordering should include standardisation of:

- the characters at different levels by different domains;
- the ordering of strokes; and
- the structural component.

Each of these issues is now briefly examined under these three headings.

Sequencing character order

Hanzi can be described as being a great welter of units; there is no efficient way to arrange and categorise such a large number of different graphic signs. Mair and Liu (1991: 5) consider that this deficiency disadvantages the Chinese computer character input operation economically:

> [P]erhaps the single greatest barrier to economical information processing in East Asian scripts is that there exists no rational, recursive method for ordering the sinographs. Not only does this make sorting and listing of verbal data a major challenge to the programmer, inputting – usually the simplest step in the information processing for alphabetic scripts – becomes a nightmare.

It also should be noted that, as words are arranged under head characters, character order sorting rules are also a precondition for making various kinds of linguistic corpora. The potential of these computer corpora that have been developed over decades cannot be fully utilised, due to the lack of a unifying way to do the data processing. Ideally, the character position in the corpus of different domains or internalised vocabulary bank should be fixed, so it can be identified without too much trouble. Users of inputting programs find it very annoying to search for the intended *hanzi* in a panel of candidates listed in a box popping up on the screen. When one gets familiar with the order of these choices, at least for a number of the most commonly used characters, one can choose the right character without bothering to look at the screen when using a different input scheme (changing schemes is very common). A unified standard would require the same character to be placed in a permanent fixed order; this is also very significant for library information processing, indexing and retrieval. The problem of how to arrange the character ordering used in the traditional dictionary in conformity with the ordering used for computer software is another eminent task before experts. In other words, there is a need to unify classification systems across genres of dictionaries, libraries and computer database systems.

Fixing the stroke order

Characters are composed by using specified strokes according to traditional conventions. There are 24 distinct strokes, with five or six basic major strokes accounting for the overwhelming majority of occurrences. Although teachers are compelled to teach beginning learners to follow some conventions for writing strokes, based on nine commonly acknowledged writing rules, there are too many exceptions and conflicts, making the general rules almost invalid (Chen, 1999: 173–8). This situation also causes endless troubles in *hanzi* input and automatic handwriting recognition. Gu Xiaofeng (1997: 116) identifies the yet unstandardised handwriting as one of the most important factors preventing OCR software products from being commercialised.

The most important operating principle of the simultaneous writing OCR method (also known as Pen Input) is that the machine has to collect sufficient information from the trace of a special light pen designed for this purpose. Such information includes not only the writing trace, but also information such as stroke order, the stroke direction, the time gap between writing two strokes, and the locus of where the pen is lifted and reapplied, and even the whole orbit between the two linking or breaking strokes. By constantly gauging such abundant graphic aids and moving signals, the simultaneous OCR gains a higher quality than the scanning OCR method, thus upgrading the recognition speed. Each scheme has its own specific requirement on how *hanzi* should be written in running text. At present, the working quality of Chinese OCR is much compromised by factors such as graphic shape, writing style, stroke order, and so on.

The advent of character input through handwriting actually transforms the computational part of the input problem from physical pattern recognition to linguistics, and the industry has turned to the language authorities with the hope that they can do something to regulate people's writing habits, predominant handwritten styles and the ordering of strokes, with the latter being seen as the key to the former. The Government needs to take a hand in imposing a uniform mode of stroke ordering. In pursuance of this aim, as well as for educational purposes, the SCLA has proposed its own standard in 1997 (Working Committee, 1997); unfortunately, it has had little influence on public writing behaviour.

The proposition that handwriting should be standardised and that people should be trained in only one style has been argued and debated for quite some time, as has its desirability and the time it might take to accomplish. It has been the IT industry that has been demanding language administrators to work out standards. The industry reasoning is as follows:

(1)   Ideally, it would greatly facilitate mechanical processing of information wrapped in *hanzi*. The first beneficiary would be simultaneous OCR system vendors and ideography-based input system developers.

(2)   It is better to have an official standard than a chaotic situation without any management at all. At least, we can have an agreed upon standard for everyone to comply with. Such a standard may be a guideline only for the general population, but it is the yardstick for software developers, although the relevant authorities seldom push through such standards by force, like the implementation of the standard code set for Chinese characters GB 18030 in 2000 and 2001. The *Official Guidelines for Handwritten Characters* that was put in place in 1976 in Taiwan is frequently mentioned as a good example to follow; Japanese education authorities have tried to impose stringent standards on students' handwriting behaviour, but gave up after confronting strong resistance (He, 2001: 135).

(3)   School education urgently needs such a standard. There are over 200 million school students in China and Chinese language education, along with mathematics and foreign languages, constitutes the so-called 'Three Big Major Subject Knowledges'.

Fixing the structural component

Another issue related to the ordering problem is how to deal with the unstable number of component classifications adopted by different dictionaries. *Hanzi* uses a limited number of components to generate unlimited characters; the difficulty is how to classify *hanzi*'s composing units. Historically, three dictionaries were very influential in shaping the *hanzi* classification system. *Shuowen Jiezi* (Xu Shen, 197 CE) is the first dictionary that has creatively classified all characters (9353) under 540 composing units, traditionally known as *bushou*, which were reduced to 214 in *Zihui* (1615) by Mei Yongzuo in the Ming Dynasty. These 214 *bushou* have become the *de facto* standard followed by most dictionaries. *Kangxi* Dictionary (collectively compiled, 1767), which uses 240 *bushou* to control 47,043 characters, reinforced the official status of Xu and Mei's classification methodologies, thereby basically laying the foundation for the compilation of modern dictionaries. Huang Peirong (1992: 73–7) looked into the classification systems employed by the dictionaries published in Taiwan, the Mainland and Hong Kong, and found that, out of 20 highly popular dictionaries in Taiwan, 18 classify *hanzi* under either 213 or 214 *bushou*. Huang's findings also show that the issue has actually become alarmingly chaotic, particularly in mainland China, where at least 16 different *bushou* systems exist in the 21 most important dictionaries. The main reason for the great diversity is that, unlike Taiwan scholars who are relatively conservative and stick to traditional conventions (Fei, 1993: 35–6; Xu, 2004: 262), their Mainland counterparts are rather more pragmatic in dealing with the traditional heritage, in the hope of providing expediency for both human users and machines. In the 1960s, the Government launched a standardisation movement to unify the index systems, offering four standardised dictionary classification systems, including one radical-based system, and the Government recommended all of them to the whole society. But it turned out that the recommendations were only embraced by official dictionaries, and almost all individual dictionary compilers and input scheme designers have developed their own systems.

The tendency appears to be that there is a gradual reduction insofar as the input systems are concerned. Too many categories will make a system too complex to operate for both humans and machines but, if the number of categories is too small, then a number of characters with special components would drop out of the system. The ideal system will be able to reconstruct the largest possible number of characters with the smallest number of components. How to strike a balance and develop a well-accepted and efficient method has been a major concern. In a certain sense, every ideography-based input scheme can be seen as an experiment exploring the issue of component optimisation.

Fixing the total number

It is generally held that *hanzi* is an open system, so the total number increases over time. After developing for over 3 millennia without a thorough streamlining, the total number of *hanzi* has increased through the voluminous classics (approximately 80,000 titles), preserved and handed down from remote antiquity, growing ever larger and larger, and the trend is ongoing, if not speeding up. Wang Fengyang's calculation shows that, since the Qin Dynasty, the total number of *hanzi* has grown annually by an average of 20 to 30 (1989: 532). In a broader sense, a widespread estimate is that the ultimate number is well beyond 100,000, if all Chinese characters and derived forms that have ever existed, including variant forms and non-Chinese *hanzi* and dialect *hanzi*, were added up. For instance, 85,568 characters were included in the *Ocean of Chinese Characters* (1992), so far the most inclusive dictionary published.

Total quantity reduction has long been regarded as a hard nut to crack in modern *hanzi* study. It has been talked about long enough – to put an upper limit on the number of *hanzi* – because any further delay is unthinkable if *hanzi* are to survive in the future digital world. It is necessary to analyse, categorise and encode every character used in the ancient texts in order to process classics automatically, which inevitably involves a thorough investigation of ancient publications. Given the fact that *hanzi* is the only ancient writing system that has survived thousands of years of uninterrupted civilisation, to overhaul the total number of *hanzi* is inordinately difficult.[29] Presently, the number of standard encoded characters in the largest IT-oriented Character Sets, issued by the Government, are 20,902 in GB13000.1 or ISO 10646 (1993), and 27,484 characters in

GB18030 (2000).[30] This number, obviously, is far from being sufficient to process all the character forms that ever existed.

Admittedly, it is relatively easy to control the number of characters for common daily use, but not for the infrequently used characters, which have been created for special purposes, for example, for newly discovered chemical elements. Variant forms, obsolete characters and rarely used characters (RCs) constitute three major reasons contributing to making the number of total *hanzi* misleadingly large. Some experience has been gained and progress is being made on how to manage special characters, so that the total number of *hanzi* can be brought under control. There are research projects for standardised character use for personal and geographical names, technological terms and translations, which makes up a substantial part of the Applied Linguistics Research Scheme and Project Guidelines for the Tenth Five-Year National Social and Economic Development Plan.

Standardisation has often meant amalgamation, which mainly refers to the reduction of RC. Although it is usually acknowledged that the most common 2400–3000 characters cover 99% of the total number used in modern writing, the number of the RCs increases by 20 times the number of common characters. They differ greatly in frequency of usage, and act like submerged rocks in an ocean of characters. Being a potent obstacle and appearing only occasionally, but with unpredictable frequency, RCs include two major categories of characters: literary and specialty characters. The former are used most often for writing in a highly literary style, contain a large number of classical Chinese expressions, and are the most difficult to control. Technological RCs, despite their very small number, can create endless difficulties in social use and mechanical processing.

The instability of the total number of characters has caused great confusion in the IT industry. In 1986, the Xinhua News Agency, the biggest news provider in China, investigated its 90,672 news reports, and 395 characters were found beyond the BSSECII, which has 6763 characters based on some of the best known household dictionaries, such as the *Dictionary of Modern Chinese* (Yang, 2000: 195–6). This means the agency had to create characters by using a software package that can generate new *hanzi* upon demand. However, that small number of characters accounted for over 15% of the total number of characters that the agency used in 1986.

At present, this problem is only felt in a limited way in technologically advanced areas: e.g. a client's name cannot be transmitted through the Internet banking system, or a college entrant's name cannot be found on a website. But these problems are only the tip of the iceberg; seriously harmful consequences may be caused by the unavailability of some characters in other areas, when more social services go online in the future (e.g. Wang, 2002: 59).

Standardisation as a Linguistic Solution to the Technological Impact

The digital era provides greater impetus for the development of many languages, and this impetus is more important for some languages than for others. Given that the lion's share of Chinese LP work from 1986 onwards has revolved around serving IT development, it would be appropriate to say that in today's China, standardisation is the main focus for LP. *Hanzi* is a writing system that has enormous variations, a complex structure and an unstable number. From a technological point of view, Chinese language planners are hypnotised by the fact that a non-standardised language is not an advanced language, and it will be increasingly marginalised in the modern world unless it is optimised through persistent and vigorous standardisation.

It can be argued that one of the most notable phenomena in modern life has been that governments impose ever more regulations to standardise various practices of social activities. Modern society becomes more standardised every day, and the standards are increasingly ubiquitous. Many industry standards are now well accepted by people in their daily lives. In an attempt to enhance the linguistic environment for computer-mediated language to serve society better, standardisation has been proposed by the Government as a viable option to adapt script development to the demands of the new age. Standardisation is a set of rules enabling a member of a given community to transpose his written utterances into the corresponding encoding/decoding process on the machine. The way language functions as a communication medium has changed from being an oral/aural medium to writing and then to typesetting. Communication has become less human and more mechanical, developing from interaction between humans and machines and then from machine to machine; in this continuum, the dependency on standardisation in communications between computers has increased. When thinking about IT-related communication, standardisation ensures that everything runs in a simple and effective way; there is hardly any doubt that there is a need to impose IT-oriented standards to regulate language use. There used to be a time when each computer company employed its own encoding system to represent *hanzi*, which resulted in incompatibility and meant that information/software could not be shared by different platforms. 'The implementation of the Basic Set of Standard Chinese Characters for Information Exchange-GB 2312.80 has made Chinese information communication between computers in China possible' (Shi, 1987: 111). Every input scheme designer uses his own method or system to reproduce *hanzi*, either ideographically or phonetically. The absence of a shared standard on how to read and write a *hanzi* has a pernicious effect on *hanzi* computer input. A number of frequently used characters are written and pronounced in many ways, for reasons that may be regional or educational, economical or psychological. This situation, however, has caused great confusion among both consumers and students.

The influence of globalisation of information exchange on international communication networks has had a growing homogenising effect on orthographic repertories (cf. mobile phone text messaging). Standardisers believe that the inherent defects in the mechanic application of Chinese script can be partly counteracted by standardisation. International communication networking is more effective if there is a certain degree of writing homogeneity among Chinese character-using polities. Standardisation means quicker and more reliable exchange of digital messages, but such a regional unification can only be accomplished on the basic premise of an international standard. China undoubtedly has the commitment to play a leading role in such multinational cooperation.

Standardisation and codification are prerequisites for the development of a new industry. The new link between the detailed standards of *hanzi* use and IT advancement has gained an increasing degree of recognition; it has never before been as pivotal to the success of digital survival. A report from the American Embassy in Beijing (US Embassy, 1997) observes that:

> Poor technical standard compliance resulted in inferior character alignment and display of the wrong character. . . . Greater compliance with PRC national technical standards will improve the Chinese-language information product quality and make these products much easier for people to use.

The sociolinguistic consequence from the IT impact presents an unprecedented opportunity for LP workers to have a thorough look into what should be done to overhaul the stock of all characters.

An overhaul of *hanzi*'s repertoire: Current government undertakings

Chinese character computerisation has reached a level where it is moving away from being a single-country endeavour, and is increasingly becoming a remarkably multinational activity. In the digitally designed linguistic environment, computer-mediated language knows no borders. Quality assurance and system stability in viewing online information, wrapped in Chinese characters (or sinographs, to use Mair's term), has become a key issue for easy web browsing in all sinographic countries/regions. Those using characters are not able to communicate effectively because of a lack of versatility among internalised code labelling systems. Versatility requires that the code used in the shared document must always be identified, so the machine can recognise and process those identical codes. Over 20 Chinese character standard sets for information exchange were released by government authorities and the major computer industries around the Eastern Asia region, but no single encoding system was versatile enough to allow for the reliable representation of all sinographic signs encoded in even a few of the finite number of these standard sets and thus guarantee trouble-free inflow of online information.

Unicode was born out of the need to employ a single set of numerical codes to accommodate digitally all the world's scripts, allowing them to be identified, processed and displayed on all future computers regardless of any given script's physical complexity. Over the last couple of years, seeing the dangers of each polity going down its own road without policy coordination in formulating the standard sets, there have been increasing discussions about the possibility of unifying all code set standards for sinographs, so that an agreement on a universal standard within the region can be achieved. But to unify these encoding standards calls for input from each individual government. The Unicode requirements, concerning computer-designated standards, have spurred a flurry of activities in formulating Chinese character encoding sets from different governments in adjacent countries in East Asia. In this context, Chinese language authorities have started to set their long-delayed standardisation programmes in motion and have, consequently, embarked on the road of overhauling the Chinese *hanzi* repertoire.

During the past 47 years, Chinese LP workers and IT experts have performed important work and used the power vested in government to fix some problems. Starting in November 1954, with the Directive on Discussing the Chinese Character Simplification Scheme issued by the Centre of CCP, through to October 2001, when the Law of the PR China for General Chinese Language was promulgated, various government agencies at the state level have issued 101 laws, regulations, directives, decisions and guidance on the use of language and *hanzi* (SCLW, 2004). By 2001, 18 laws had provisions about language use. In May 1981 the first IT-oriented standard, BSSCCII-GB2312-80, was formu-lated, and by December 2001 *The Chinese Character Turning Stroke Standard of GB 13000.1 Character Set* came into effect. In these 20 years, 81 IT-oriented technical standards have been promulgated. (A few of these standards concern non-*hanzi* scripts such as Mongolian and the Uygur orthography.) Seventy 'Class GB Standards' were issued by the State Bureau of Technology Supervision, or by the Chief Bureau of National Standards, eight 'Class GF Standards' by the SCLW and two ISO standards.

Latest development: Two ongoing standardisation projects

For the past few years, motivated mainly by IT industry pressure, the author-ities have dramatically increased the pace of rationalising *hanzi*, which would otherwise have been a decade-long protracted matter. The most significant governmental endeavours for standardisation currently proceeding are the composition of the Comprehensive Table of Standardised Characters (CTSC) and the building of a database platform for all characters found in China proper, the Corpus of China's Whole Character Set (CCWCS). The former is already being implemented according to well-defined research objectives, an overall framework and operational principles. Starting in 2002, intense preparation has begun, with consecutive conferences having been sponsored since the end of 2001.

The Comprehensive Table of Standardised Characters (CTSC): Its conditions and implications

The activities of composing a complete table of *hanzi* can be said to have begun as early as the 1960s. Wang T.K. (2003) concludes: 'In the past two decades, the project was included in the national LP agenda from time to time; this is the third time that it has been formally established as the key LP research project at national level'.[31]

It should be noted that the prelude to this work was The Table of Standard Modern Characters, issued in 1988. On 20 May 1980, in the first plenary session of the reconstructed CLR, Wang Li, Ye Laishi, Ni Haishu, Zhou Youguang, the four prime members, first proposed a plan to produce The Table of Standard Modern Characters (Chen, 1981: 33). This laid the foundation for the subse-quent tables that eventually led to the birth of a series of standard character tables, and finally to the CTSC. Consequently, the current project should be seen as the conclusion of all these cumulative efforts. The following analysis is based on three paramount research papers, written by Zhang Shuyan (2003), the executive convener of the research team of CTSC, Wang Tiekun (2003) and Li Yuming (2004b), respectively the vice-director and the director of the Depart-ment of Language and Information Management in the Education Ministry.

Since the First Table of Verified Variant Forms was published by the Government in 1955, a number of specialist standard tables about *hanzi* have been enacted by the central Government. However, as repeatedly pointed out by scholars, not only did these tables contradict each other in many ways, but some standards have become outdated and increasingly incompatible with modern society, because social life itself has changed over nearly half a century. The focus of the *hanzi* reform during the last two decades has shifted from handwriting to computer processing. Now it has moved to the international medium of telecommunications, a form of globalisation which requires that *hanzi* should not only be effectively input and processed for local applications within the polity borders, but should also be able to be read and processed anywhere in the world.

Whilst being a kind of very basic work of language codification, it has been exploratory and thus must eventually influence the national linguistic work to a larger degree. For instance, Standard *Hanzi*, one of the most talked-about notions in LP in recent years, will remain a vague concept until the CTSC table is completed and enforced.

Unquestionably, the publication of CTSC would be one of the most significant LP events in the history of Chinese LP. Not only has the resumption of use of some of the discarded variant forms of the 1950s been openly speculated on by the government agency, but also the formulation by CTSC constitutes the first time that there has been the potential for a partial roll-back to the use of some traditional characters. Whereas these kinds of corrections would have appeared impossible in the past, there is now reason to expect that a number of old taboos in LP work will be questioned, and in this sense, the CTSC can be seen as an indicator that testifies to the maturity of LP policy in the new historical context. During the process of creating the CTSC, many mistakes and problems found in the tables promulgated by the Government in the past will get corrected, including the reintroduction of some traditional characters and abolished variant forms, and the adoption of some character forms from tables endorsed in Taiwan. This implies unlearning or partially officially acknowledging past incorrect practices. Furthermore, the policies and principles adhered to by LP professionals will be reviewed and corrected. Reducing the political presence to a minimum and correcting the past testifies that Chinese LP is becoming more forward looking. From a wider perspective, Li Yuming (2004b: 68) argues that the formulation of CTSC is one of the most important events that 'concerns the cultural life of all Chinese people around the world'.

Another noticeable change is the total number of *hanzi* the CTSC will include. The new tendency, regarding the number of both character tables and dictionaries in the information age, is 'the more, the better'. This tendency to pursue a large set of characters also applies to the character databank, because the ability of data processing to handle a larger number of *hanzi* creates a selling point in the software marketplace. The attempt to include as many characters as possible in the encoding set has been partially triggered by competition from Taiwan, which has the lead in covering the maximum number of *hanzi* since the introduction of the CCCII (Chinese Character Code for Information Interchange) with over 40,000 characters, the first *hanzi* encoding standard for computer information processing published in 1980.

Contending for the largest size leads inevitably to the inclusion of rare *hanzi*, which add little value in practical terms. The *hanzi* in the CTSC are arranged in four hierarchic levels, totalling 30,000 characters:

- Grade I 3500 characters, roughly commensurate with the Table of Most Used Modern Chinese Characters (1988);
- Grade II 4500 characters, roughly commensurate with the *Table of Common Chinese Characters* (1988), excluding the characters covered under Grade I;
- Grade III 4000 specialty characters, for special domains including proper nouns (geographical and personal names), science and technology;
- Grade IV 18,000 characters, including rare archaic characters and dialect characters.

The inclusion of traditional and variant forms of characters would make the total number between 45,000 and 50,000. This was the number that was released in the *Tentative Plan* by Zhang Shuyan (2003), but was later lowered to 12,000 in Wang Tiekun (2003). It is difficult to know how to deal with Grade IV characters. Wang considers they should be put in a separate 'Table of Verified Characters', numbering between 20,000 and 30,000. In the latest paper by Li Yuming (2004b: 66), the total number was readjusted to a more conservative limit and a Table of Speciality Characters was proposed.

LP decision makers hope the full-fledged enforcement of the table is going to push *hanzi* standards to a higher level, due to its emphasis on the precision and consistency in unifying and standardising unofficial characters and its influence on a wider range of characters. The official publication of CTSC will have a major impact on linguistic life, including language education, diction-ary making, the media, and most importantly, computer software. Consecutive new information media products, equipped with new standards, are expected to come into use following the completion of the table, thereby greatly facili-tating Chinese IT development. Some separate tables, such as *hanzi* for name giving, have already started to invite comments and opinions from the public. More integral sub-tables are expected to be completed in the next few years. The final result of the project will be a complete table composed of these individual sub-tables, in which the fixed standard of sequencing order, graphic shape, pronunciation, stroke number and order will be defined and listed under each character, either overtly or covertly, eventually forming the basis for dictionar-ies and other lexicographic products. As the most significant LP undertaking since the 1950s, the CTSC is to be formally promulgated by the State Council. Presumably, all previous tables of various standards in conflict with this master table will automatically become invalid.

Corpus of China's Whole Character Set (CCWCS): An overhaul of all graphic codes in Chinese script

It is clear that society is moving from being paper-based to being computer-based. The gradual emergence of Unicode on the Internet means that increasingly people are living in a world where most varieties of written language, in use (such as minority scripts, e.g. Limbu, Tai Le, Osmanya) or historical scripts (e.g. Cypriot and Ugaritic), are being encoded and can be found online; those that lack Unicode standardisation are being locked out. The objective of initiating the CCWCS project was to give all Chinese ideographic signs digital recognition and global transferability when they are unicoded.

Although the total number of Chinese characters encoded in extended versions of ISO/IEC CJK 10646 (Chinese, Japanese and Korean ideographic characters) has already reached the stunning figure of 70,205, and the Chinese-speaking world has begun to establish a siseable presence on the Internet, ancient Chinese civilisation and the rich information of colourful modern Chinese culture are almost nowhere to be found. The issue of online transmission of the Chinese cultural heritage in its original forms has frequently been raised in the process of constructing digital libraries, museums and archives. Traditional heritage digitalisation includes ancient texts and ancient scripts. Throughout its history, China's written culture has been recorded in different distinct shapes of *hanzi*, and sometimes these graphic features carry important valuable cultural information in their own right. The *hanzi* form we are using today took shape around 220 CE. The various forms before this date, starting from Oracle Bones (1711–1066 BCE), or even earlier, had developed over nearly 2000 years. These embryonic forms of ancient script, archaeological significance aside, still have an extensive presence in modern life for their artistic value. With the gradual adoption of ISO 10646–1:93 and its A., B. and C. extensions, the Chinese world has achieved a great deal in converting ancient classics into software media. Hong Kong and Taiwan have established a sizeable presence on the Internet in the field of ancient Chinese civilisation and the colourful Chinese culture (for additional information see http://www.chant.org/info default_jiaguwen.asp, and http://www.sinica.edu.tw/~cdp/ paper/1999/19990615_1.htm).

The question arises of how to keep ancient forms of *hanzi*, *hanzi*-derived script and various graphic signs alive and readable over the long term, in a computer-based medium, in their *original faces*.[32] There are two ways of addressing the problem in computerising Chinese ancient scripts: either by scanning or by encoding. The scanning method skips the problem of encoding the data by turning all characters into pictures, and it does not require a special browser to view it on a web page. But there are two major disadvantages to this approach: it can be extremely difficult to make any changes that might be necessary; and it is very time consuming for users to upload and download pictures. Considering the goal of data preservation and user convenience, the scanning and loading of data in hard disc memory simply functions to restore, copy/paste and display/ view the information in plain photocopying form, whereas an encoding scheme provides a manipulative solution that would enable computers to reproduce, edit and digitally process the restored graphic information. Alternatively, in more technological terms, only the documentation of all culturally visual properties in the form of bits and bytes can ensure that the behaviour of characters in different software programs and digital environments is correct.

The broad range of different sinographs is not confined to the historically diversified shapes of *hanzi* per se; the entire set of Chinese graphic code also includes numerous kinds of pictographic signs that are derived from *hanzi* and used by other ethnic groups to record their own languages – some of which are genetically different from the Chinese language. These *hanzi*-derived characters aside, the Chinese mainstream culture of the Han nationality has brought into modern times a gigantic volume of material. Different shapes of characters are recorded, many unique to certain original sources, such as *jiaguwen* and *jin wen* (metal utensil inscriptions on ancient bronze objects). These ancient scripts are an inextricable component of Chinese culture, some perhaps being real icons of Chineseness, i.e. ones which can be seen to carry the essential message of Chinese traditional heritage. For example, the *hanzi* on China Seal (logo of 2008 Olympic Games) is *Zhuanshu* instead of modern standard characters. If these distinct features of ancient scripts are glossed over by a one-size-fits-all standard character set, such irreplaceable cultural treasures will consequently be lost to cyberspace. All of the above-mentioned efforts, either dealing with ancient texts or with ancient scripts, were accomplished through their own proprietary platform encodings short of Unicode support and were, therefore, not readily transmittable across worldwide networks and systems for end users. To spread these electronic products in an unrestricted way, Unicode, which is rapidly becoming the Internet standard, will provide the ultimate solution. Standardisation is the passport to enter Unicode, so the aim of CCWCS is to assemble all signs and symbols that have ever existed, and then to standardise them in a systematic framework. It is hoped that one day, through the overhaul and integration into an international standard, scholars will be able to turn all characters from oracle bones, bronzes, silk and bamboo, into a magnetic and optical format of a Unicode system.

Organisationally, unlike the CTSC which has been well coordinated by a centralised leadership and carried out by an ad hoc research team, CCWCS, although launched in 2004 as one of the working agendas of SCLW, seems to be too ambitious to produce any concrete outcome in the near future. The relevant projects have been spread over a number of universities and research institutions across the country, and are being carried out in a piecemeal manner by researchers in different academic areas. From the framework provided by Li Yuming (2004a), the major portion of the proposed characters, in addition to the above-mentioned existing corpus of *hanzi* sets, in quantitative terms are: (1) ancient Chinese scripts; (2) the obsolete *hanzi*-derived scripts of all the non-Chinese minorities that have ever existed in Chinese history, but are no longer in active use today; and (3) Chinese dialectal scripts.

The grand plan, characterised by its wholeness and inclusiveness, has been conceived on the assumption of large enough or unlimited space provided by Unicode.[33] The new version (4.0) has been expanded to provide a greater coverage of minority scripts and has encoded characters for ancient alphabets and historical heritage characters. Future considerations have already indicated the willingness to make extensive additions of Chinese, Japanese and Korean characters to cover dictionaries and historical use. According to Mark Davis (2003), the President of the Unicode Consortium, the two latest developments of the Unicode are 'a significant step towards the digital preservation of world heritage'.

The significance of the CTSC and CCWCS for Chinese LP has an impact on the three following issues.

Annotating an IT-driven LP policy

Until the mid-1990s, Chinese language authorities were mistaken in expecting that character computerisation would significantly alleviate the bottleneck effect on the country's creation of an information access infrastructure. Computerised word processors and character input software, for instance, were too hastily seen as the new writing technology that would finally resolve technical difficulties related to the inherent problems of the Chinese writing system, without realising that putting characters into a computer is just the first step to process Chinese information. The problematic nature of *hanzi* is most felt when it is used for e-mailing and Internet transmission, which is predicted to be the main area where computers contribute most to the future information society.

Only gradually have the national language policy makers fully realised what the implications of LP work are for IT development. At the 1986 Conference, although it was acknowledged that Chinese Information Processing (CIP) is a newly emerging science with broad prospects, the working agenda failed to identify CIP as the core of the future LP venture. Instead, it merely stated 'today's language work should include it [CIP] as a part of it'. It took over 10 years to create a specialist department of language and information management under the Education Ministry.

The significance of CIP in spreading Chinese traditions has started to catch the attention of LP and IT circles, and some high-profile advocates are playing a vital role in reorienting Chinese LP. Xu Jialu, one of a few national-level officials who are acutely aware of the role of CIP in preserving Chinese cultural heritage, points out that LP's cultural importance is not as evident as its importance in the economic sphere. He goes further (2003):

> [S]piritual culture also has to face digitalisation. The recording, storing and transmitting of our unrivalled rich culture, whether it is recorded by script, through the medium of stone, wood or painting, or expressed by action and gesture, is increasingly dependent on digital technology. . . . the processing of Chinese traditional culture should also be treated as an integral part of CIP.

Xu's exposition reveals that the implications of CCWCS go beyond its technical significance. The government-initiated action plan to address the technological threat to cultural maintenance and transmission clearly demonstrates that *hanzi* modernisation is taking an important step forward; Chinese LP will be increasingly organised around IT-driven development in the future. Because the Internet is ubiquitous, the language issue has never before been so relevant to people's cultural lives and the fate of the nation. Operating on the theory of 'go online or be left out' induces the idea that the people are living in an epoch of lingual and cultural imperialism. As a result of the impact of computerised global communication, the aim of Chinese LP activities has developed from serving essentially nation building to serving culture preservation.

Laying the groundwork for future script reform

The ultimate aim of CCWCS is to create a compendium of all signs and symbols that have ever existed. Technically, the implementation of CCWCS will present many unprecedented challenges to LP practitioners, the first of which might be how to develop a set of sorting rules that could be applied to put such a large mass of unorganised aggregate signs and symbols into a meaningful framework. Clearly, this is necessary to analyse and categorise every character by application of typology, which inevitably involves an in-depth investigation of all stocks of ancient texts.

The CCWCS is indisputably the most important infrastructure construct that has ever been developed to deal with the Chinese writing system – the completion of CCWCS will give China a competitive advantage in spreading Chinese culture to the world through the international electronic media. On the other hand, some less desirable outcomes of the plan can be predicted. First, it will undermine support for the argument that the *hanzi* is incompatible with modern technology, and ostensibly weakens the theory that *hanzi* modernisation is needed in the information age. Secondly, the sudden explosion of so many sources of non-standard characters will cause many problems for script management. The ancient scripts, whether they consist of *hanzi* or archaic *hanzi*, can be confined to scholars' work, but once the huge number of dialectal *hanzi* find their way onto the Internet, they will proliferate in an unrestricted fashion around the world along with the influx of information, becoming worrisome for some scholars (Gu, 2004: 101). What makes the problem more complex is the question of how to deal with dialects that have political ramifications. The first notable intricate issue is the inclusion of Hokkien, a Chinese 'dialect' known as Minnan Speech on the Mainland and Taiyu in Taiwan, which is the native tongue of about 50 million people. At least for the time being, as noted by Jordan (2002: 120), 'both the PRC and the ROC governments oppose recognition of written colloquial Hokkien as a legitimate written standard'. Thus, the prospective inclusion of Hokkien-only characters in the official *hanzi* corpus that is ready to apply for Unicode encoding space appears to be tantamount to encouraging the independence forces in Taiwan. Given the knotty nature and unpredictable future of the relationship between the two Chinas, it is a topic worthy of appropriate attention. Another practical and urgent thorny issue is the treatment of Cantonese characters (Meyer, 1998: 35–6). Cantonese is the only dialect that has a relatively well-developed writing system and its own publications in Hong Kong, but the Basic Law, the Hong Kong constitution, does not specify the language status of Cantonese in the special administrative region, leaving this issue open to debate.

Highlighting the sociopolitical consequences of technological development

In contemporary China, little work can be done in LP without strong support from the political system and coordination from the bureaucratic sector. LP in China is basically a matter of governmental decision-making, but to what extent and under what conditions LP activities come under government control depends primarily on two factors: the political system and the sociocultural context. The role of the CCWCS emphasises the decisive nature of official policy and party politics in LP decision-making.

The publication of GB 2312–80, and a series of other subsequent tables of standardised characters in the 1980s and 1990s, signifies that China has already completed the task of encoding basic parts of the massive *hanzi* system. As stated earlier, a substantial part of the CCWCS includes the standard forms for either local folk dialects or historical *hanzi*, the majority of which are obsolete and extinct or are dying out. Although having a significant history of use, at present they are only relevant for special purposes, and are academically or culturally significant rather than of practical value. Language, particularly in its script form, is undoubtedly the most visible and tangible symbol of a culture, and because of this, the launch of the CCWCS as a platform to deliver Chinese culture online has become a governmentally determined target. The importance of having a project like the CCWCS has found a resonant response in a wide range of academic disciplines, and has increasingly become a hot topic for discussion over the past few years. Given *hanzi*'s valuational and emotive nature, this phenomenon should also be best understood via its significance for national pride and political sensitivity. If China wants to integrate into the international mainstream the various ancient forms of non-Han culture, represented by various forms of *hanzi*, it must make sure that none will be ignored or missed in its continuous efforts to secure more space in the Unicode. The implications for national unification are self-evident. Furthermore, there is an especially serious real-life challenge for a number of endangered Chinese languages. The only way to combat the increasing obsolescence is to deal with the standard, i.e. to store them in electronic records through a standard-oriented overhaul.

Unicode's growing impact on the development of IT has also brought a new dimension to the relationship between politics and language. Finding ways in which this new technology could be used to empower Chinese culture to survive the English-dominated Internet is a strategic consideration of some insightful LP policy makers. This new direction has happened to coincide with the culture renaissance movement, spurred on by CCP propaganda departments in the 1990s. Unicode will not only offer a more convenient way for producing characters on screen through the use of the keyboard, but will also preserve the ancient culture and carry it into the remote future through a globally available medium. That will undoubtedly inspire Chinese people to take a renewed interest in their cultural treasures.

Conclusion

As the introduction to this monograph suggests, language planning in China is a complex topic and thus too large a task to describe in depth in a paper of this length. The scale of this monograph had to be confined to just one aspect of corpus planning with a focus on the latest development in official efforts to align script reform with technological requirements. The path of modern script reform runs parallel with modern history and is closely intermingled with political circumstances. Undoubtedly, all language plan types occur in a political and socioeconomic context, and every revolution or social transformation brings about major changes in social and productive relations. Such a robust change sends a tremor through culture, creating the social conditions that make script reform possible. China's case is typical of state intervention and political influence, or in Schiffman's (2002: 89) term, 'the linguistic dirigisme'. In China, in contrast to the general direction in other countries, politics has a determining role with a strong influence played by the traditional heritage. The economic and sociocultural factors play a role only where they are in line with the political need, or in other words, they do not contradict the Party's ideology, which is the superstructure and determines the economic foundations. Therefore, there are two main themes that run through the monograph. The first is power and control, which are well understood at the system level but can also be used as analytical devices at the level of implementation. The second is the technological impact on Chinese script as a visual communications system.

The close connection between economic development and LP in the post-modern age calls for more investigation, particularly from multiple perspectives. On the one hand, as an aspect of a large economic transformation, script reform in a rapidly changing digital age demonstrates some new features, invariably challenging the concepts and paradigms based on past practices. On the other hand, the ideology of the ruling party is also undergoing a radical transformation, which will have an unavoidable impact on official policy that guides the future reform of *hanzi* (as noted above in 'A Debate about *Hanzi*'s Future and its Sociopolitical Implications'). Script reform policy must be interpreted within a framework that emphasises power and competing interests. This requires that policy must be seen within the context of its role in serving the interests of the group that dominates it. The emerging standardisation movement reflects the political and economic imperatives of particular elite groups. As Luke *et al.* (1990: 35) trenchantly point out in discussing the rationales for language elaboration in other polities, 'the call for language standardisation and change under the auspices of "technological development" may serve an economic and ultimately political agenda'. In the past, people in the LP domain were chiefly referred to as character learners and users with little education, excluding the social groups who had already become the owners of characters. Now the entire country is in rapid transition from a socialist ideology to an increasingly elite-dominated society. Language planners are more concerned with a literate population, or it is perhaps truer to say, a steadily expanding computer-literate population.

To enhance the computability of Chinese characters, China's language administration authorities have been battling with *hanzi* standardisation issues since the mid-1980s. The 'four fixations' have been a major argument for advocating an instrumental role for language planning (as discussed above in 'Four Fixations: Difficulties and Technological Implications'). This implies that the focus of Chinese LP activities has shifted from serving the masses to becoming elite-oriented. The change in social strata and political ideology has provided the external enabling conditions to make this radical policy modification in LP possible. The elitist nature of the ruling party has taken shape in the course of embarking on a market and opening-up economy. This has been indubitably so after the Three Representations Theory[34] was epitomised as the revised doctrine under the so-called new historical conditions. The Party was no longer representing the sole interest of the working classes. During Mao's time, the grassroots masses were the base for communist revolution and the *raison d'être* of language reform – simplification and alphabetisation; two of the Three Tasks of LP were masses-oriented. But they were dropped from the main official agenda after 1986. Currently, the SCLW tends to concern itself largely with regulating the language use, which is the basic requirement in a digital society, but is far from being a real-life issue for the majority of China's population, as even today the computer is still basically a professional tool for a minority of urban Chinese.

In the future, Chinese script reformers face a dual task: simplification for humans and standardisation for machines. As a result, simplification is giving way to standardisation. From the economic and technological perspective, a shift of focus from a human orientation to a computer orientation is inevitable. However, to plan language is to plan society; any prediction of success would be invalid without a sound analysis of the sociopolitical context. In order to predict future development and to propose reform programmes for *hanzi*, one must look into internal and external interacting forces, or, in other words, implicating sociolinguistic dimensions (or extra-linguistic factors) and linguistic possibilities. Most of the time, these two factors are intermingled in determining the developmental direction for *hanzi*. When drawing up the current configuration, LP success tends to occur when the Government acts where the two factors – external pressures and the linguistic rationale – are in balance.

China's script reform work is entering a new era. Social factors that have always influenced character use are now substantially changing the orthographic situation in China as it faces a new environment and new tasks. The ongoing drastic changes in the social use of language and characters, especially the growing importance of character use in technological areas, makes standardisation an unprecedentedly urgent and important task, and IT-oriented LP activities will remain a fundamental feature of most of the ensuing script reform activity. Standardisation mainly involves the choice between existing variants, discarding the less viable ones and keeping the more prestigious ones. But, before it is possible to formulate and codify new standard sets, it is necessary to rid the system of undesirable outcomes that have been carried over from the previous simplification efforts (discussed above in 'Technological Requirements from the IT Industry: A Digital View' and 'Fixation of the Physical Shape') and to make adjustments to the previous standards to comply with new circumstances. On the other hand, although *hanzi* are still much in need of further reform, the clinical treatments such as stroke simplification or structural modification should be kept to a minimum, as these have become many times more difficult to implement – compared to previous undertakings – as a result of the ever more complex external conditions in a new historical context.

Correspondence

Any correspondence should be directed to Shouhui Zhao, CRPP (Centre for Research in Pedagogy and Practice), NIE. Nanyang Technological University, Singapore, 637616.

Notes

1. According to the Chinese Constitution (Constitution, 2000), as adopted in December 1982. Although 'the state promotes the nationwide use of *Putonghua*' (Article 19), 'the people of all nationalities have the freedom to use and develop their own spoken and written languages, and to preserve or reform their own ways and customs' (Article 4.3). Article 121 and Article 134 (1) and (2) in the 1982 Constitution further specify the language rights of minorities.
2. This is the official figure that has consistently been given by Chinese governments since the late 1950s. But a leading Chinese linguist listed 120 languages spoken by ethnic groups in Mainland China, and in a recent article that comprehensively assessed the state and status of non-Han Chinese languages, Bradley (2005: 12–3) argues that even 200 is too small an estimate.
3. The major Chinese regionalects are: the *Xiang* dialect in Hunan Province in central

China; to the east in Jiangxi, the locals speak *Gan* dialect, which can be subdivided further into Northern Gan and Southern Gan. The same can be done with the *Min* dialect (Northern Min and Southern Min) spoken in Fujian province. Southern Min dialect is the first language of the Taiwanese people, which is now being politically promoted as Taiwanese language by the current DPP Party Government (Xu, 2003). The *Wu* dialect is spoken south of the lower Yangtze in Jiangsu and Zhejiang, of which Shanghai speech is a sub-dialect. Another important dialect is *Kejia*, or Hakka, which can be heard in several widely scattered Southern China provinces. Finally *Yueyu*, or Cantonese, is the local dialect for the people in Guangdong and Hong Kong.

4. *Guojia Tongyong Yuyan Wenzi*, National General Language and Script, is a new essential term coined during the discussion of the Law of National General Language and Script, People's Republic of China, which was passed on 31 October 2000 and came into force from 1 January 2001. The term is used as a substitute for Chinese language or Mandarin in the context where a distinction between the language for the entire population and languages for ethnic groups needs to be made.

5. Language planning in education is a broader term which is very specific to the Chinese situation. It is used here deliberately to differentiate it from Baldauf's (1990) language-in-education planning, or acquisition planning, as preferred by Cooper. Cooper (1989: 31, 33) argues that acquisition planning, as one of 12 definitions of LP, is an additional third focus paralleled to Haugen's Status-Corpus Planning distinction, while some other LP paradigm developers, such as Kaplan and Baldauf, prefer to use the term language-in-education planning to expand Haugen's dichotomy. For additional relevant discussion about this issue, see Kaplan (1990: 9), Baldauf (1990: 16–20) and Kaplan and Baldauf (1997: 122–7).

6. An unofficial translation of this law is available in Kirkpatrick and Xu (2001) as well as Rohsenow (2004: 40–3).

7. Monitoring and administrating language use are two of its main functions; otherwise, it is not essentially different from LP agencies in any other country. LP agencies in China are supposed to direct, encourage and persuade people to use language/script under the relevant laws, regulations or guidelines, but they do not have legitimate power to force anyone or any institution through the use of state force, e.g. police or penalties. Although there have been some occasions in which the language policy has been implemented in a very 'Chinese way', and the public have called LP practitioners 'Language Police', these are pretty rare and exceptional cases.

8. In this monograph, unless otherwise specified, quotations from various Chinese scholars and bureaucrats are wholly translated by the author. If quotations are from references for which there are only Chinese titles, these are annotated in Pinyin Romanisation in the reference list.

9. RIAL also maintains an online service on national language modernisation; runs the Department of Applied Linguistics in collaboration with the Linguistics Institute of the China Academy of Social Science; and conducts masters degree and doctorate programmes jointly with other research and higher learning institutions.

10. The Song Dynasty was founded in 960 CE in a period that had experienced large-scale publication due to a new printing technology invented by the Song scientist, Bi Sheng. Therefore, the *hanzi*'s physical shape was at last stabilised, and Song Style characters are one of three major typographic font styles for the *hanzi* repertoire.

11. The simplified characters in his book, *Table of Highly Used Simplified Characters*, were selected from 25 sources, including shop receipts, private letters, price bulletins at the markets, bills, invitations, public posters and notices in companies. Chen made an outstanding contribution in the initial stage of the 1935 reform, yet he has long been neglected by Chinese LP historians because of his youth and junior position. Fortunately, Barnes' (1988) case study has provided a relatively detailed description of Chen's effort in simplifying Chinese characters.

12. The merit-based civil servant recruiting system was practised from the Sui Dynasty (589–618) up to 1905. As it was a flexible and sophisticated centralised public examination system and the major means of entry into officialdom, it was

the most important form of education before modern education was introduced in China.

13. As early as 1908, Zhang proposed adopting handwritten simplified characters as a remedial measure, to offset the difficulty of writing characters, in his paper '*To Rebut the Advocacy of Replacing Chinese with Esperanto*', which was actively supported by Chinese students studying in France. Lu's landmark paper, 'Popular Characters Should be Used in Public Education', appeared in the first volume of *Education Journal* in 1909, when he was lecturing in Tokyo (Zhou, 1979: 321).

14. It is widely believed that the education minister personally circled these 324 characters with a red pen out of the 2340 characters proposed by Qian (Du, 1935: 35; Zhang *et al.*, 1997: 15).

15. In one account, Sun Jince (2000: 63), a witness of the historical event, revealed that the table was originally scheduled to be launched in 1931, but the launching was postponed because of the Japanese invasion of north-eastern China in that year.

16. Launched by Mao Zedong in early 1957 to encourage intellectuals to voice their criticism of the Communist Party's policies. Unfortunately, this process misfired after one year, and many of the critics suffered political persecution.

17. The 'stinking ninth category' (Chou Laojiu): A derogatory term referring to teachers and scientists during the Cultural Revolution, notorious for its large-scale persecution of intellectuals. The term actually emerged during the Yuan Dynasty (1279–1368 CE), when, in order to eliminate national consciousness from the minds of the Han (Chinese) people, the Mongol rulers reduced Confucian scholars to the lowest stratum of society. There were 10 professional ranks, and the Han literati were deliberately ranked at ninth position, which was only followed by the beggars.

18. The four members of the 'Gang of Four' were Wang Hongwen, Zhang Chunqiao, Jiang Qing (Mao's wife) and Yao Wenyuan. By the end of the Cultural Revolution, they had ascended to key positions in the central government, but were suddenly ousted from power by a bloodless coup, plotted by Deng Xiaoping in October 1976.

19. The *Hongqi Magazine* is one of the so-called 'Two Newspapers and One Magazine' (liangbao yikan), referring to *Renmin Ribao* (*People's Daily*) and *Guangming Ribao* (*Guangming Daily*). They were tightly controlled by the highest propaganda apparatus and served as the tone-setter for political movements during the Cultural Revolution period.

20. The Chinese People's Consultative Conference (CPCC) is a political coalition consisting of the so-called eight democratic parties. The CPCC takes part in consultations and decision-making regarding issues that are of national importance.

21. 'Insurgents', or *Zaofan Pai*, literally means 'rebellious force' in Chinese, referring to a group of revolutionary zealots at various institutions during the Cultural Revolution. At one stage, they usurped the leadership and seized power in their working places.

22. Great Leap Forward: Discontent with the method and result of the first socialist Five Year Plan, and in an attempt to speed up the development, Mao Zedong called for a High Tide of Socialism and a radical alternative to an orthodox organisation of production and investment in 1958. The result of extreme socialist measures led to a swift collectivisation of agriculture, including the creation of the People's Communes by coercion. Such unrealistic expectations of a rapid revolution and vast democratic movement brought China's economy to the verge of collapse at the end of 1958.

23. Before 1986, all simplification schemes were done as a temporary measure, before the ultimate goal of Romanisation; this was both official policy and the agenda of some radical language reformers. Therefore, one of the purposes of releasing the Second Scheme was, through gradual reduction of *hanzi* strokes, to one day have a number of characters that would be simplified to the degree that these characters could be used as an alphabetic system to spell phonetically, or represent all Chinese characters.

24. The comeback of traditional characters in the early 1980s was a spontaneous social phenomenon; there was no conscious 'effort', at least in Mainland China, to reintroduce them as no one in authority dared to promote traditional characters without risking being accused of sabotaging the national language policy.

25. On 26 April 1993, in order to examine the implementation of the 'Regulation on Character Use in Publications', jointly issued by the Media and Publication Department and SCLW, the two authorities organised an investigation into the character use in 14 central and local newspapers published on 4 February, and 526 characters were found to be against the regulations. The worst case was one local evening newspaper, in which 1173 unofficial characters were found during that month (Fei, 1997: 560).

26. Three Loves Campaign: Love our country, love our people and love our Party.

27. Taiwan has two official tables of standard characters: one for publication (1979) and the other for handwriting (1976). In the Official Guidelines for Handwritten Characters, 1580 Mainland simplified characters were included, accounting for 40% of the total (Fei J.C., 1993: 37).

28. Some inputting schemes list only the most common pronunciation. For example, in Chinese Star–2.5, one cannot get 得 (have/has to) by keying in the correct pronunciation 'dei 3', but it will appear instantly as the first candidate on the screen if you type 'de2', which is the wrong pronunciation in the former context when it means 'have/has to', but correct in 得到 (de2dao4, to gain). By using such schemes, the user is required to work against the official pronunciation standard, and the thinking process is also disturbed.

29. To exemplify the difficulty of this task, one may look at classical encyclopaedias written during various Chinese dynasties. The *Complete Book by Four Categories* (《四库全书》) is the last encyclopaedia issued under royal patronage, compiled in 1773. This 79,309-volume book contains 3,461 titles with nearly 1 billion characters. The total number of characters in the 'History of Twenty-Five Dynasties', a small part of this encyclopaedia, has 13,966 characters recurring 31,409,450 times (Ding, 1990).

30. GB18030 (2000) includes both simplified (excluding the SSSC characters) and complex characters, as well as variant forms and all characters used in Japanese and Korean.

31. According to Wang Tiekun (2003), CTSC was projected to complete and pass the final examination around mid-2004, but the project seems to be running behind schedule as the Draft Table 'for public perusal and comments' has not yet been published, as promised by Wang. Instead, a tentative plan, detailing the working principles and some difficulties encountered by the research team after three and a half years of field work were presented to academics for nationwide comment (Zhang, 2003).

32. The emphasis here is to stress the importance of the original appearance, or features. For example, Oracle Bone Script (*jiaguwen*) has over 200,000 pieces, and about 3500 distinct forms of *hanzi*. Metal Script (*Jinwen*), the subsequent forms of *Jiaguwen*, used about 3000 years ago, has over 120,200 characters so far. One of the main purposes of CCWCS is to sort out and standardise these archaic and antiquated forms (*Jiaguwen*, *Jinwen*, *Zhuanshu*, *Lishu*, and so on), then to encode these character forerunners in order to computerise them.

33. According to Jordan (2002), 'the Unicode scheme provides a portal to a larger, 32-bit world with room to encode vastly more characters than human ingenuity has yet imagined: 4,294,967,298 (= 2^{32})'. But Li Yuming (2004a) has offered a different number: ($128 \times 256 \times 65,536$), equal to 2,147,483,648 according to my calculations.

34. Three Representations was designated as core political ideology of the current CCP leadership. The first representation holds that what we are undertaking should represent the forward direction of the productive forces and the progress of the social development. Its manifestation in LP is to directly associate the outcome of LP with this representation, as the language issue is seen as an important contribution to facilitating economic activities.

References

Baldauf, Jr. R.B., (1990) Language planning and education. In R.B. Baldauf, Jr. and A. Luke (eds) *Language Planning and Education in Australasia and the South Pacific* (pp. 14–22). Clevedon: Multilingual Matters.

Baldauf, Jr. R.B., and Kaplan, R.B. (2003) Language policy decisions and power: Who are the actors? In P.M. Ryan and R. Terborg (eds) *Language: Issues of Inequity* (pp. 19–40). Ciudad Universitaria, Mexico: Universidad Nacional Autónoma de Mexico, CELE.

Ball, R. (1999) Spelling reform in France and Germany: Attitudes and reactions. *Current Issues in Language and Society* 6 (3/4), 276–80.

Barnes, D. (1988) A continuity or constraints on orthographic change: Chen Guangyao and character simplification. *Journal of Oriental Studies* (Monumenta Serica, 1988–1989), Vol. XXXVIII, 135–166.

Bianco, L. (1971) *Origins of the Chinese Revolution, 1915–1949*. Stanford: Stanford University Press.

Bradley, D. (2005) Language policy and language endangerment in China. *International Journal of the Sociology of Language* 173, 1–21.

Chen, M.Y. (1981) Biaozhun xiandai *Hanzi* biao de dingliang gongzuo [The work of fixing the numbers of the Table of Standard Modern Chinese Characters]. *Language Modernization* 5, 32–59.

Chen, P. (1999) *Modern Chinese: History and Sociolinguistics*. Cambridge: Cambridge University Press.

Cheng, C.C. (1976) Chauvinism, egalitarianism, and multilingualism: China's linguistics experience. *Studies in Language Learning* 1, 41–58.

Cheng, C.C. (1979) Language reform in China in the seventies. *Word* 30 (1/2), 45–57.

Clyne, M. (1992) *Pluricentric Language: Differing Norms in Different Nations*. Berlin: Mouton de Gruyter.

Collective Editors (2004) *Kexue Bian Wei Ji* [*Critique of Pseudo-science*]. Beijing: Zhongguo Gongren Chubanshe.

Constitution (2000) On WWW at http://www.unesco.org/most/Inchina.htm.

Cooper, R.L. (1989) *Language Planning and Social Change*. Cambridge: Cambridge University Press.

Coulmas, F. (1989) *The Writing Systems of the World*. Oxford: Blackwell.

Coulmas, F. (1991) The future of Chinese characters. In R.L. Cooper and B. Spolsky (eds) *The Influence of Language on Culture and Thought – Essays in Honor of Joshua A. Fishman's Sixty-Fifth Birthday* (pp. 227–43). Berlin: Mouton de Gruyter.

Davis, M. (2003) What's new in Unicode 4.0. *MultiLingual Computing & Technology* 14 (6). On WWW at http://www.multilingual.com/FMPro?-db=archives& -format=ourpublication%2 ffeaturedarticlesdetail.htm&-lay=cgi&-sortfield=Magazin e%20Number&-sortorder=descend&-op=cn&Author=Mark%20Davis&intro=yes&- recid=33516&-find=

DeFrancis, J. (1984) *The Chinese Language – Fact and Fantasy*. Honolulu: University of Hawaii Press.

Deng, C.Q. and Zhang, P. (1997) Kaishu *Hanzi* zixing biaozhunhua yu Zhongwen xinxi chuli [The standardization of *Kaishu* style characters and Chinese information processing]. In P. Zhang *A Collection of Essays on the Keyboard Input Method of Chinese Characters* (pp. 113–22). Beijing: Zhongguo Biaozhun Chubanshe.

Ding, F.H. (1990) *Xiandai Hanzi Zaozifa* [*The Methodology of the Creation of Modern Characters*]. Beijing: Zhishi Chubanshe.

Du, Z.J. (1935) *Jianti Hanzi* [*Simplified Characters*]. Kaifeng: Kaifeng Nvzi Zhongxue.

Duan, S.N. (1990) *Guanyu Wenzi Gaige de Fansi* [*Reflection on Character Reform*]. Beijing: Jiaoyu Kexue Chubanshe.

Editing Team of Hu Qiaomu Biography (eds) (1999) *Hu Qiaomu Tan Yuyan Wenzi* [*Hu Qiaomu's Talk on Language and Script*]. Beijing: Renmin Chubanshe.

Fei J.C. (1993) Haixia liang an xianxing *Hanzi* zixing de bijiao fenxi [Comparative analysis of the current shape of Chinese characters across the Strait]. *Yuyan Wenzi Yingyong* 2, 33–44.

Fei J.C. (1996) Xinxi shehui dui yuyan wenzi yingyong guifanhua de yaoqiu [The demand for language and script standardization from the information age]. In J. Wang, Y.M. Yan and P.C. Su (eds) *Yuwen Xiandaihua Luncong* (di er ji) [*Forum on Language Modernization* 2] (pp. 258–74). Beijing: Yuwen Chubanshe.

Fei J.C. (1997) *Yuwen Xiandaihua Bainian Jishi* [*Records of Chinese Language Modernization in 100 Years*]. Beijing: Yuwen Chubanshe.

Feng, W.J. (1995) *Hanzi Xinxi Chuli Jiaocheng* [*Chinese Character Information Processing Readers*]. Dalian: Dalian Haishi Daxue Chubanshe.

Gu, X.F. (1997) Shouxieti *hanzi* shibie [Optical recognition of handwritten Chinese characters]. In Y. Chen (ed.) *Hanyu Yuyan Wenzi Xinxi Chuli* [*Information Processing of Chinese Language and Script*] (pp. 88–109). Shanghai: Shanghai Jiaoyu Chubanshe.

Gu, X.F. (2004) Jisuanji yingyong zhong de *hanzi* guifan wenti [The issues of *Hanzi* standardization in computer application]. In Y.M. Li and J.C. Fei (eds) *Hanzi Guifan Bai Jia Tan* [*Various Views on Hanzi Standardization*] (pp. 99–106). Beijing: Shangwu Yinshuguan.

Guo, M.R. (1972) Zenyang kandai qunzhong zhong de xin liuxing jianhuazi [How to deal with the new popular simplified characters circulated among the masses]. *Hongqi* 4, 84–85.

Guo, Y.J. (2004) *Cultural Nationalism in Contemporary China – The Search for National Identity under Reform.* London / New York: Routledge Curzon.

Haarmann, H. (1990) Language planning in the light of a general theory of language: A methodological framework. *International Journal of the Sociology of Language* 86, 103–26.

Hannas, W.C. (1997) *Asia's Orthographic Dilemma.* Hawai'i: University of Hawai'i Press.

Haugen, E. (1968) Dialect, language and nation. *American Anthropologist* 68, 922–35.

Haugen, E. (1983) The implementation of corpus planning: Theory and practice. In J. Cobarrubias and J.A. Fishman (eds) *Progress in Language Planning* (pp. 269–90). Berlin: Mouton.

He, Q.X. (2001) *Hanzi zai Riben* [*Chinese Characters in Japan*]. Hong Kong: Commercial.

Huang, P.R. (1992) *Hanzi de Zhengli yu Tonghe* [*Unification and Rationalization of Hanzi – A Research Report Sponsored by the Foundation of the Cross Strait Exchange*]. Taipei: Foundation of the Cross Strait Exchange.

Jordan, D.K. (2002) Language left behind: Keeping Taiwanese off the World Wide Web. *Language Problems and Language Planning* 26 (2), 111–27.

Kaplan, R.B. (1989) Language planning vs. planning language. In C.H. Candlin and T.F. McNamara (eds) *Language, Planning and Community* (pp. 193–203). Sydney: NCELTR.

Kaplan, R.B. (1990) Introduction: Language planning in theory and practice. In R.B. Baldauf, Jr. and A. Luke (eds) *Language Planning and Education in Australasia and the South Pacific* (pp. 3–13). Clevedon: Multilingual Matters.

Kaplan, R.B. and Baldauf, Jr R.B., (1997) *Language Planning from Practice to Theory.* Clevedon: Multilingual Matters.

Kaplan, R.B. and Baldauf, Jr R.B., (2003) *Language and Language-in-Education Planning in the Pacific Basin* (pp. 31–46). Dordrecht: Kluwer Academic.

Kirkpatrick, A. and Xu, Z.C. (2001) The new language law of the People's Republic of China. *Australia Language Matters* 9 (2), 14–15.

Li, Y.M. (2004a) Dajian zhonghua zifu da pingtai [Building the big platform of China Character Set (Original English)]. *Journal of Oriental Languages Processing.* On WWW at http://cslp.comp.nus.edu.sg/cgi-bin/journal/paper.exe/abstract?paper.

Li, Y.M. (2004b) Guifan *Hanzi* he 'Guifan *Hanzi* Biao' [Standard Chinese characters and the Table of Standardized Characters]. *Zhongguo Yuwen* 298, 61–9.

Liu, D.S. (1987) Xin shiqi de yuyan wenzi gongzuo [Language and script work in the new era]. In SCLW (ed.) Xin Shiqi Yuyan Wenzi Gongzuo – Quanguo Yuyan Wenzi Gongzuo Wenjian Huibian [*Language and Script Works in the New Era – Collection of Documents of the National Conference on Language and Script Works*] (pp. 16–34). Beijing: Yuwen Chubanshe.

Liu, X.W. (2003) Chongfen fahui 'Zhu qudao', 'zhu zhendi' de zuoyong [Making the most of 'key channels' and 'key fronts']. In P.C. Su (ed.) Yuwen Xiandaihua Luncong (di wu ji) [*Forum on Language Modernization (5)*] (pp. 55–60). Beijing: Yuwen Chubanshe.

Luke, A., McHoul, A. and Mey, J.L. (1990) On the limits of language planning: Class, state and power. In R.B. Baldauf, Jr. and A. Luke (eds) *Language Planning and Education in Australasia and the South Pacific* (pp. 25–44). Clevedon: Multilingual Matters.

Lv, S.X. (1999/1995) Jian bu duan, li huan luan-*Hanzi* Hanwen li de hutu zhang, [Confusion in Chinese characters and language]. In P.C. Su and B.Y. Yin (eds) *Issues of Modern Character Standardization* (pp. 1–5). Beijing: Yuwen Chubanshe.

Ma, X. (1987) Yuyan gongzuo yu texue jishu [Language works and science and technology]. In SCLW (ed.) *Xin Shiqi De Yuyan Wenzi Gongzuo – Quanguo Yuyan Wenzi Gongzuo Wenjian Huibian* [*Language and Script Works in the New Era – Collection of Documents of the National Conference on Language & Script Works*] (pp. 103–10). Beijing: Yuwen Chubanshe.

Mair, V.H. and Liu Y.Q. (eds) (1991) *Characters and Computers*. Amsterdam: IOS.

Meyer, D. (1998) Dealing with Hong Kong specific characters. *Multilingual Communication and Technology* 9 (3), 35–8.

Peng, S.J. and Huang K. (1994) *Hanzi Xinxi Chuli* [*Chinese Character Information Processing*]. Chengdu: Chengdu Dianzi Keji Daxue Chubanshe.

Rohsenow, J.S. (2004) Fifty years of script and language reform in the P.R.C. In M.L. Zhou (ed.) *Language Policy in the People's Republic of China: Theory and Practice since 1949* (pp. 21–43). Kluwer Academic.

Schiffman, H.F. (2002) French language policy: Centrism, dirigisme, or economic determinism. In W. Li *et al.* (eds) *Opportunities and Challenges of Bilingualism* (pp: 89–104). Berlin. New York: Mouton de Gruyter.

SCLW (2004) Zhengce Fagui he Guifan Biazhun [Language Policies, Guidelines, Regulations and Standards]. On WWW at http://www.china-language.gov.cn/weblaw/index.asp

SCLW (ed.) (1987) *Xin Shiqi De Yuyan Wenzi Gongzuo – Quanguo Yuyan Wenzi Gongzuo Wenjian Huibian* [*Language and Script Works in the New Era – Collection of Documents of the National Conference on Language & Script Works*]. Beijing: Yuwen Chubanshe.

SCLW (2005a) Guojia Yuyan Wenzi Gongzuo Weiyuanhui Zhize [The responsibilities of the State Commission of Language Work] On WWW at http://www.china-language.gov.cn/jgsz/ content6. asp#1.

SCLW (2005b) Yuyan Wenzi Yingyong Yanjiusuo Jianjie [The introduction about Research Institute of Applied Linguistics] On WWW at http://www.china-language.gov.cn/jgsz/ index1.asp.

Seybolt, P.J. and Chiang, G.K. (trans 1979) *Language Reform in China – Documents and Commentary*. New York: M.E. Sharpe.

Shepherd, J. (2003) *Striking a Balance: The Management of Languages in Singapore*. Frankfurt am Main: Peter Lang.

Shi, Y.C. (1987) Yuyan xinxi chuli de xin renwu [The new task of language information processing] In SCLW Xin Shiqi Yuyan Wenzi Gongzuo – Quanguo Yuyan Wenzi Gongzuo Wenjian Huibian [*Language and Script Works in the New Era – Collection of Documents of the National Conference on Language and Script Works*] (pp. 111–20). Beijing: Yuwen Chubanshe.

Su, P.C. (2001) *Xiandai Hanzi Xue Gangyao* [*The Outline of Modern Hanziology*]. Beijing: Beijing Daxue Chubanshe.

Sun, J.C. (2000) Huiyi guofu jianti zi [Memoirs of the publication of simplified characters by the Nationalist Government]. *Chinese Language Review* 63, 26–27.

Taylor, I. and Taylor, M. (1995) *Writing and Literacy in Chinese, Korean and Japanese*. Amsterdam: John Benjamins.

The Office of Standard Work Commission, the State Commission of Language Work (ed.) (1997) *Guojia Yuyan Wenzi Guifan Biaozhun Xuanbian* [*Collections of the State Standards and Norms of Language and Script*]. Beijing: Zhongguo Biaozhun Chubanshe

Thomas, G. (1991) *Linguistic Purism*. London: Longman.

Tsao, F-F. (2000) The language planning situation in Taiwan. In R.B. Baldauf, Jr. and R.B. Kaplan (eds) *Language Planning in Nepal, Taiwan and Sweden* (pp. 60–106). Clevedon: Multilingual Matters.

Tse, K-P. (1980) Language planning and English as a foreign language in middle school education in the Republic of China (Taiwan). Unpublished PhD Dissertation, University of Southern California.

Tse, K-P. (1982a) Language policy in the Republic of China. In R.B. Kaplan *et al.* (eds) *Annual Review of Applied Linguistics* 2 (pp. 33–47). Rowley, MA: Newbury House.

Tse, K-P. (1982b) Some advantages of sociolinguistic surveys for language planning purposes. *Ying Yu Yen Chiu Chi K'an* [Studies in English Literature and Linguistics] 8 (April), 157–67.

Tse, K-P. (1986) Standardization of Chinese in Taiwan. *International Journal of the Sociology of Language* 59, 25–3.

US Embassy, Beijing (1997) To make the Net speak Chinese: Emerging Chinese-language information services. On WWW at http://www.usembassy-china.gov.cn/sandt/chinfca.htm.

Wang, F.Y. (1989) *Hanzi* Xue [*Chinese Hanziology*]. Changchun: Jilin Wenshi Chubanshe.

Wang, F.Y. (1992) Wenzi de Yanjin yu Guifan [Evolution and standardization of Chinese characters]. Yuwen Jianshe 4, 14–20.

Wang, L. (1938) *Longchong Bingdiao Ji* [*Collection of Essays from Longchong Bingdiao Studio*]. Beijing: Zhonghua Shuju.

Wang, L. (1981) Guanyu 'Erjian' de xiuding gongzuo [Works about the Revision of the Second Scheme of Simplified Characters]. *Yuwen Xiandaihua* 5, 20–22.

Wang, T.K. (2003) 'Guifan *Hanzi* Biao' yanzhi de ji ge wenti [Some issues regarding research of the comprehensive table of standardized Chinese characters]. On WWW at http://www. china-language.gov.cn/webinfopub/ list.asp?id=1271&columnid=164 &columnlayer=01380164.

Wang, Y.W. (2002) Dangdai *hanzi* yong zi ding liang de jige wenti [On some issues of fixing numbers of modern *hanzi*]. *Nanyang Technological University (Singapore) Journal of Language and Culture* 5 (2), 55–76.

Wei, D. (2003) Guanyu difang zhiding '"Guojia Tongyong Yuyan Wenzi Fa" Shishi Banfa' de youguan wenti [The various issues on making 'Local Policy of Complementing "*Law of National General Language and Script*"']. In P.C. Su (ed.) *Yuwen Xiandaihua Luncong* (di wu ji) [*Forum on Language Modernization* 5] (pp. 6–21). Beijing: Yuwen Chubanshe.

Working Committee of the Standardization, State Commission of Language Affairs (1997) *Xiandai Hanyu Tongyong Bishun Guifan* [*The Stroke Ordering Standard of Modern Chinese Characters*]. Beijing: Yuwen Chubanshe.

Wu, Z.G. (1994) Ping *hanzi* youyue lun [On the superiority of Chinese characters]. In B.Y. Yin and P.C. Su (eds) *Kexue de Yanjiu Hanyu he Hanzi* [*Scientifically Study Chinese Language and Characters*] (pp. 87–95). Beijing: Sinolingua.

Xu. C.A. (2003) Taiwan 'Yuwen Taidu' shuping [Summary of 'Linguistic Independence' movement in Taiwan]. In P.C. Su (ed.) *Yuwen Xiandaihua Luncong* (di wu ji) [*Forum on Language Modernization* 5] (pp. 344–57). Beijing: Yuwen Chubanshe.

Xu. C.A. (2004) Taiwan zhengli *hanzi* gaishu [Summary of *hanzi* overhaul in Taiwan]. In Y.M. Li and J.C. Fei (eds) *Hanzi Guifan Baijia Tan* [Various Views on *Hanzi* Standardization] (pp. 249–64) Beijing: Shangwu Yinshuguan.

Xu, J.L. (2003) 'Zhongwen Xinxi Chuli Ruogan Zhongyao Wenti Xu' – *Zhongwen Xinxi Chuli de Yanjiu Yinggai Zouxiang Gaochao* [Chinese information processing has to be approaching to its peak. Preface to *Key Issues for Chinese Information Processing*]. On WWW at http://www.china-language.gov.cn/webinfopub/list.asp?id=1126&colum nid=143& columnlayer=00860143.

Yang, R.L. (2000) *Xiandai Hanzi Xue Tonglun* [*General Introduction to Modern Hanziology*]. Beijing: Changcheng Chubanshe.

Yao, D.H. (1976) Constantin Milsky he ta de guanyu Zhongguo wenzi gaige de jinzuo [Constantin Milsky and his latest work on the development of the Chinese language reform.] *Dousou* 3, 85.

Yu, G.Y. (1996) *Ershiyi Shiji de Zhongguo Yingyong Yuyanxue Yanjiu* [*Research of Chinese Applied Linguistics in the 20th Century*]. Taiyuan: Shuhai Chubanshe.

Zhang, S.Y. (2003) 'Guifan *Hanzi* Biao' de Yanzhi [The tentative plan for the formulation of the Comprehensive Table of Standardized Characters]. On WWW at http://www.china-language. gov.cn /webinfopub/list.asp?id=1054&columnid=164&columnlayer=01380164.

Zhang, S.Y., Wang, T.K. Li, Q.H. and An, N. (1997) *Jianhuazi Suyuan* [*Tracing the Sources of Simplified Characters*]. Beijing: Yuwen Chubnashe.

Zhao, S.H. and Baldauf, R.B. Jr. (2007) *Planning Chinese Characters: Evolution, Revolution and Reaction*. Dordrecht, The Netherlands: Springer.

Zhou, Y.G. (1979) *Wenzi Gailai Gailun* [*An Introduction to Chinese Character Reform*]. Beijing: Wenzi Gaige Chubanshe.

Zhou, Y.G. (1982) Guanyu wenzi gaige de wujie he lijie [The understanding and misunderstanding about the script reform]. *Wenzi Gaige* 2, 5–7.

Zhou, Y.G. (1986) *Zhongguo Yuwen de XianDaihua* [*Chinese Language Modernization*]. Shanghai: Shanghai Jiaoyu Chubanshe).

Zhou, Y.G. (1992) *Xin Yuwen de Jianshe* [*Reconstruction of the New Language*]. Beijing: Yuwen Chubanshe.

Japan: Language Policy and Planning in Transition

Nanette Gottlieb
Japan Program, School of Languages and Comparative
Cultural Studies, University of Queensland, Queensland,
Australia

This monograph discusses the language situation in Japan, with an emphasis on language planning and policy. Japan has long considered itself to be a monoethnic and therefore monolingual society, despite the existence of substantial old-comer ethnic minorities, and this – with the instrumental exception of English – has been reflected in its language planning and policy until quite recently. Increasing immigration (and hence emergent new-comer multilingualism), technological advances affecting the way people write and a perceived need to improve the teaching of English, however, mean that policies have begun to undergo a rethink. This monograph is divided into three main sections. Under the language profile of Japan I discuss in detail the national language and minority languages; the next section discusses language spread and maintenance through the education system and other means; and I conclude with some thoughts on how language planning and policy might develop in the future. My aim is to give readers a sense of how major language issues in Japan are evolving in such a manner that many of the policies developed during the 20th century may no longer be totally relevant.

Keywords: Japan, language policy, minority languages, language spread, language maintenance, future trends

Introduction

Throughout its modern period, which began with the overthrow of the Tokugawa military Shogunate and the restoration of the Emperor Meiji to the throne in 1868, Japan has consistently represented itself in both internal and external discourse as a monolingual nation. As recently as October 2005, for example, Internal Affairs and Communications Minister Aso Taro referred to Japan in a speech at the opening of the Kyushu National Museum as the only country in the world having 'one nation, one civilisation, one language, one culture and one race' (*The Japan Times*, 18 October 2005). Official policies and a highly influential essentialist literary genre called 'Nihonjinron' (theories of what it means to be Japanese) have both reflected and shored up this view.

'Nihonjinron' theories and their forerunners have in the past constituted a key influence on much of the government, academic and cultural discourse on Japanese society, including ideas about language. Although they have been directly challenged by a large body of academic research over the last two decades, they remain influential in some circles today, as the Minister's comment related above shows. In this discourse, the Japanese language is portrayed as somehow uniquely different from all other languages; at the same time, Japan is resolutely viewed as linguistically homogeneous despite all evidence to the contrary. The Japanese language is seen as too difficult for any but Japanese themselves to master by virtue of its orthography and its much-touted preference for ambiguity over directness. Race, language and culture are inextricably tied together, so that issues surrounding language carry a heavy freight of sensitive historical, political and cultural significance. This has informed language policy to date, explaining in part the slow pace at which planning and policy at the national level have responded to demographic change.

In Japan, as elsewhere, the national language has been used as a key part of Japanese nation- and empire-building, and diversity has not been encouraged. The early modern period saw use of minority languages on both northern and southern borders of the archipelago suppressed under a policy of assimilation designed to foster and reinforce the ideology of one whole and unified nation. In the colonies of Taiwan (1895–1945) and Korea (1905–1945) and later in the occupied territories during World War Two, inculcating use of the Japanese language became a key element in the formation of good subjects of the Emperor. During much of this period, efforts were made – not without substantial resistance from educated supporters of entrenched language ideologies – to transform the language in both its spoken and written forms into something able to function as a modern standard that would be an effective instrument in the service of national unity. By the 1920s, several major steps in this process had been achieved: a standard language had been designated and was being disseminated through the education system and the national broadcaster, and the classical-oriented written styles which had previously been the language of public life were well on the way to being replaced by a modern written Japanese based on contemporary speech rather than on centuries-old literary conventions. The one sticking point remained script reform, which had to wait until after World War Two.

I will discuss these issues at length later in this monograph. For the moment my purpose is simply to draw attention to the intellectual and ideological framework – the monolingual myth – within which discussions of language in Japan have been situated, before beginning to examine the details of the reality of Japan's language profile. Monolingualism is certainly a myth, built upon an equally shaky foundation of monoethnicity, but it has been an enduring and strongly entrenched pillar of what we might call the foundation myths of modern Japan, and the following discussion of the language situation in Japan must be understood within that context. It is certainly true that nearly everybody in Japan does speak Japanese, that the language used for official purposes is Japanese and that the bulk of the population is Japanese. To insist that Japan is therefore monolingual, however, disregards the existence of large ethnic communities from Korea, China, Brazil and other parts of the world, of the language of the indigenous Ainu people and of the fact that Japanese students must study English for at least six years.

An important part of the following discussion will deal with language planning and language policy activities in Japan, which I argue are now entering a period of transition in response to significant changes in the social fabric. It has been suggested in the past that language planning is of concern only to developing nations and not to a highly developed nation like Japan

(Miller, 1982: 180–181). Language planning and policy formulation (LPP), however, have been features of Japan's linguistic activities since the early 20th century and continue to be undertaken today by a range of agencies. I utilise here Kaplan and Baldauf's definition (1997: 3) of language planning as the means through which change in language use in communities is achieved, involving '*deliberate*, although not always overt, *future oriented* change in systems of language code and/or speaking in a societal context'. Other useful definitions include:

- 'the organised pursuit of solutions to language problems, typically at the national level' (Fishman, 1974: 79);
- 'the activity of manipulating language as a social resource in order to reach objectives set out by planning agencies which, in general, are an area's governmental, educational, economic and linguistic authorities' (Eastman, 1983: 29), giving explicit recognition to the nature of language as social capital;
- 'deliberate efforts to influence the behaviors of others with respect to the acquisition, structure, or functional allocation of their language code' (Cooper, 1989: 45);
- 'the formulation and proclamation of an explicit plan or policy, usually but not necessarily written in a formal document, about language use' (Spolsky, 2004: 11), although Spolsky prefers the term 'language management' to 'language planning'.

Common to all these definitions is the recognition that language planning is consciously engineered change in the way language is used, that is, not natural evolution but human intervention working to achieve specific desired purposes. Language planning of this sort aimed at achieving particular linguistic and social outcomes in Japan has covered many areas, among them standardisation, script reform, language spread through the teaching of Japanese both as the national language and as a foreign language, the revival of the Ainu language and the teaching of English and other foreign languages. It is only relatively recently, except in the case of English, that language policy has included recognition of a language other than Japanese.

This is likely to change over the coming years. One of the most pressing issues for language planning and policy making in Japan today is the growing awareness of emergent multilingualism arising from increasing immigration over the last 20 years. The fact that this is occurring within the lingering framework of the monolingual myth accounts for the slow pace at which the national government has responded to these developments, as opposed to the greater responsiveness of local governments. Change at the national level of language policy involves many years of discussion and consultation on issues that affect the nation as a whole. Local governments, however, enjoy greater freedom to respond as area-specific challenges arise, and what we are seeing in Japan today is a more proactive stance in bottom-up than in top-down language planning initiatives. Local governments and NGOs are working to assist increasing numbers of immigrants living in their areas, moving towards a greater recognition of the actual ecology of language in Japan. In January 2007, Miyagi Prefecture became the first prefecture in Japan to draft bylaws (the drafts are written in

Japanese, English, Chinese, Korean and Portuguese) promoting multiculturalism in that prefecture.

I begin by examining the language profile of Japan today, starting with the Japanese language and moving on to other languages. This section will show that many languages are spoken in addition to Japanese, some of them as a result of recent immigration, others as the legacy of colonial-period population flows and of historical alliances.

The Language Profile of Japan

The national language

Japan is what Fishman (1968) described as a Cluster B nation, or an old developing nation: one in which the attributes of both nation and sociocultural identity have long coincided. In 1968 Japan was yet to achieve the economic ascendancy of the 1970s and 1980s which has since taken it far beyond the stage where it could be described as a developing nation, old or not. As Fishman's definition makes clear, however, Japan began its modern period with both a venerable literary tradition and a relatively high literacy rate already in place. It has, moreover, never been colonised by another power; the closest it came to anything resembling colonisation was the post-World War Two Allied Occupation from 1945 to 1951, and no move was made during that period to give official status to the language of the occupying powers. In the case of the national language, then, language planning has focused not on the selection of a national language from a range of competing contenders but on modifying and promoting an existing asset.

As is the case with English in Australia, Japan's constitution makes no mention of any official language; it is simply taken for granted that the dominant (indeed only) historical contender is the national language. The language is referred to by native speakers in two ways: when it is used by native speakers it is called *kokugo* (lit: the language of our country), but when it is taught to foreigners, it is called *nihongo* (lit: the language of Japan, a more neutral term devoid of the affective nuances of *kokugo*). Language classes in Japanese schools, for example, are called *kokugo* classes; remedial language classes for non-native speakers of Japanese in the same school would incorporate the word *nihongo*, and education in Japanese as a foreign language both in Japan and in other parts of the world is referred to as *nihongo kyōiku* (Japanese-language education).

This distinction reflects an enduring belief that the Japanese language is a cultural property specific to, and a crucial part of, being Japanese: *kokugo* is 'our language, for us,' while *nihongo* is 'the Japanese language for others'. Linguist Kindaichi Haruhiko (1978: 154) has described this as a reflection of a very strong Japanese propensity to mark the difference between what is Japanese and what is not, as also exemplified by the visual differentiation of foreign loanwords by writing them in the katakana syllabary used primarily for that purpose. McVeigh (2004: 215–216) puts it in terms of in-group and out-group relationships:

> This linguistic nationalism dichotomizes the Japanese language into 'ordinary Japanese' (*nihongo*) and 'very Japanese Japanese' (*kokugo*). The

former is what non-Japanese learn in order to communicate with Japanese, while the latter is what Japanese learn in school. *Kokugo* (literally, 'national language') is *our own* language, the language of the in-group, as opposed to the Japanese language for the out-group (*nihongo*).

Small moves to challenge this ideology have recently been observed, in that a number of university departments and professional societies have changed *kokugo* to *nihongo* in their names. The Society of Japanese Linguistics, for example, changed its Japanese name in 2004 from Kokugo Gakkai to Nihongo Gakkai, while the College of Japanese Language and Culture at Tsukuba University near Tokyo calls its curriculum Nihongo, Nihon Bunkagaku.

Nearly all of Japan's 128 million people speak and write Japanese, most as *kokugo*, some as *nihongo*. Standard Japanese, based on the speech of the Yamanote area of Tokyo, is spoken and understood throughout the country. The standard form was designated as such in 1916 by one of the earliest language policy bodies, the Kokugo Chōsa Iinkai (National Language Research Council), and was then disseminated through the national education system and through the state broadcaster, NHK (Japan Broadcasting Corporation). The 'ideal' form of the standard, known as *hyōjungo* (lit: standard language), is used in writing and in formal speech. In casual interactions, people use a variant called *kyōtsūgo* (lit: common language), close to Standard Japanese in all its main features but less formal: it includes contractions, for example, and, in regional areas, expressions from the local dialect (Neustupný, 1987: 158–160). While regional dialects do of course remain, some exhibiting quite marked differences from those of other areas (see subsequent discussion), any potential communication difficulties are overcome by the universal use of the Standard.

Japanese is an agglutinative SOV language characterised by the use of postpositions signifying grammatical relations and by a complex system of honorifics indicating through lexicon and verb forms the relative status differences between participants in an interaction. It is believed to be either a language isolate[1] or a member (together with the Ryukyuan languages in Okinawa) of the Japonic language family. No clear explanation of its origins exists, although theories have been advanced linking it variously with Altaic and Austronesian languages, Tamil and Korean (see Shibatani, 1990: 94 for a detailed list). The lexicon consists of approximately two-thirds loanwords and one-third words of Japanese origin (*wago*). Of the loanwords, the majority consists of *kango* (words of Chinese origin), borrowed from Chinese over centuries of linguistic and cultural contact and absorbed into the lexicon to such a degree that most Japanese do not think of them as loanwords. *Kango* are perceived as being more formal in tone than words of Japanese origin, reflecting the centuries during which Sino-Japanese, a literary style heavily influenced by Chinese, was the major formal written variant used by the upper classes. The remainder of the lexicon consists of *gairaigo*, loanwords from languages other than Chinese (predominantly English), reflecting the historical specificities of Japan's contact with speakers of European languages. Estimates of the exact percentage of *gairaigo* differ: Backhouse (1993: 74, 76) suggests around 6%, whereas Honna (1995: 45) puts it higher, at around 10% of the contents of a standard dictionary. English loanwords make up 60–70% of the new words added to Japanese dictionaries each year (Hogan, 2003: 43).

Japanese is not a language of diaspora to the same extent as are English, Chinese and other languages that are widely spoken throughout the world. Outside the Japanese archipelago itself, it has a position in some countries as a heritage language stemming from earlier, limited waves of migration (the west coast of North America, Hawaii, parts of South America, notably Peru and Brazil and to a lesser extent Mexico) and in others as a now-fading relic of the Japanese colonial period (Taiwan, Korea) and occupation leading up to and during World War Two (e.g. China, parts of South East Asia). It is also, of course, spoken by Japanese expatriates, many of them academics in universities around the world or business people on overseas postings. During Japan's economic boom in the 1980s, Japanese came to be widely studied as a foreign language by people looking for an advantage in employment-oriented skills. The number of overseas learners doubled between 1988 and 1993 as a result of the activities of the Japan Foundation (set up within the Ministry of Foreign Affairs in 1972 to promote Japan's language and culture overseas) and of policies and funding decisions adopted by governments such as the state and federal governments of Australia.

The majority of newspapers and magazines are published in Japanese, although some may be found in other languages as well, in particular English (see subsequent discussion). In 2003, total newspaper circulation was over 70 million, compared with over 55 million in the United States and over 18 million in Britain. A comparison of circulation figures for major business dailies – the *Nihon Keizai Shimbun* (*Nikkei*) (Japan), the *Wall Street Journal* (United States) and the *Financial Times* (United Kingdom) – in the first half of 2004 showed the *Nikkei*, at over three million, to be far ahead of the *Wall Street Journal*, at nearly two million, and the *Financial Times*, at under half a million (*Nikkei*, 2005). The *Nikkei* is not alone in numbering its readers in the millions. The *Yomiuri Shimbun*, for example, has the largest circulation of any newspaper in the world (14,067,000 in 2005); of the top 10 of the world's most widely circulated newspapers, seven are Japanese (World Association of Newspapers, 2005). The six major newspapers – the *Yomiuri*, the *Asahi Shimbun*, the *Mainichi Shimbun*, the *Nihon Keizai Shimbun*, the *Chūnichi Shimbun* and the *Sankei Shimbun* – issue both morning and evening editions, as do others. They are also available both online and through mobile news services which allow mobile phone users to check news through their phones. Given that Japan leads the world in the development and uptake of the mobile internet, more people access news services through their cell phones than through computers.

Japanese is of course also the major language of broadcasting on Japan's large network of radio and television stations. At the end of 2005 there were 1057 commercial broadcasters, of whom 386 were terrestrial (including 189 community FM broadcasters), 136 satellite and 530 cable (Ministry of Public Management, Home Affairs, Posts and Telecommunications, 2006). Major cities (Tokyo, Nagoya, Fukuoka, Osaka) do have foreign-language FM stations: Radio Co-co-lo in Osaka, for instance, staffed by volunteers, has been broadcasting in 14 languages for the last 10 years. There are five main national television networks, all of them affiliated with major newspaper corporations: TV Asahi [Asahi], TBS [Mainichi], Fuji Television Network [Sankei], NTV [Yomiuri] and TV Tokyo [Nikkei]. The Nippon Hōsō Kyōkai (Japan Broadcasting Corporation), widely known as NHK, is the country's public broadcaster on both radio and television. In addition to Japanese-language broadcasting, NHK offers weekly radio language-learning programmes in English, Chinese, French, Italian, Korean, German, Spanish, Russian and Arabic for domestic listeners, and its overseas 'Radio Japan' programmes are broadcast in more than 20 languages.

Dialects

Leaving aside the Ryukyuan dialects in Okinawa Prefecture, which are not dialects of Japanese, the major categorisation of dialects is into those of eastern Japan, western Japan and the southern island of Kyushu, although Kyushu may be subsumed into western Japan (Shibatani, 1990: 196). Dialects vary in terms of lexical items, verbal inflections and sentence-ending particles. In the Miyagi dialect, for instance, 'frog' is *bikki*; in the Chikura dialect of Chiba Prefecture, it is *ango*; and in standard Japanese, *kaeru*. In Osaka dialect, the negative verbal inflection is mahen instead of the standard masen; in Nagoya *janyaa* replaces the standard *de wa arimasen* for the negative copula, and in Fukuoka *n* is used instead of *nai* for negative verbs, for example, *taben* for 'don't eat', instead of the Standard's *tabenai*. Sentence ending particles vary too: in Miyagi dialect, for example, *–ccha* is used to add emphasis, in Nagoya dialect an elongated *yō* (this would be yō in standard Japanese).

As commonly happens when the standard form of a language is being promoted, the use of dialects was officially strongly discouraged during the first half of the 20th century. Children were punished for using their home dialects in the schoolyard and in Okinawa were made to wear the hated *hōgen fuda* (dialect placard, a shaming placard worn round the neck to indicate that the wearer had been heard to use language other than Standard Japanese). As social mobility meant that employment prospects in other parts of Japan could depend upon being able to speak Standard Japanese, schools were vigilant in policing its use (Carroll, 2001: 183–184).

Over time, as the standard spread through intergenerational transmission, the degree of fracture between standard and dialect use blurred, though never disappearing completely. This led to a more relaxed official stance some decades into the postwar period. In response to the policy of regionalism which came to inform government directions from the late 1980s, for example, reports from the Kokugo Shingikai (National Language Council, the body then charged with overseeing language policy) during the 1990s urged a new respect for local dialects, which were now viewed as being valuable in their own right and worthy of maintenance alongside the Standard. The Council's 1995 report, while restating the centrality of the standard for purposes of communication, stressed that dialects should be valued as an important element in the overall picture of 'a rich and beautiful national language', showcasing the vibrancy of the people and cultures of local areas. It stressed the importance of ongoing research into the dialects, citing the series of dialect surveys and atlases produced by the National Institute for Japanese Language[2] and various university research centres as important contributions to this area of national language research (Kokugo Shingikai, 1995: 432). The 1998 national curriculum guidelines for *kokugo* in schools reflected that shift, specifying that students in the latter years of elementary school should be able to distinguish between dialect and Standard Japanese, with those at middle school expected to develop an understanding of the different roles of the standard and the dialects in sociolinguistic terms.

Dialects are particularly noticeable in certain areas of the media. Although the standard version of Japanese is of course the major variant used on radio and television, local dialects, in particular that of the Osaka region (known as Kansai), are also used, most often to inject a note of humour. The Kansai dialects, of which Osaka-ben (Osaka dialect, the dialect of Japan's second largest city) is the most widely spoken, are considered by other Japanese to sound bumbling, rough and rustic, thereby providing fertile ground for laughter. The *manzai* form of stand-up comedy, popular on television, for instance, is closely associated with Osaka. The Kansai dialects are thus widely linked to comedy in Japan and feature in such contexts on television. When programmes featuring dialogue in a local dialect are screened on national networks, they are usually subtitled to ensure that viewers throughout Japan will be able to understand.

The writing system

In the absence of any native writing system, ideographic characters (kanji) were adopted from China (via Korea) around the sixth century CE. As the characters had developed to fit the requirements of the Chinese language and not those of the very different Japanese language, they were initially used to write Chinese as a foreign language in Japan. Over time, however, characters were adapted to form two phonetic scripts (hiragana and katakana) in order to provide a means of representing the sounds and grammatical features of Japanese on paper. The phonetic scripts were developed in different parts of Japan for different purposes. Hiragana, a flowing and rounded script used in everyday letters and poems and in the literature written by the noblewomen of the Heian Period (794–1192), abbreviated the whole of a Chinese character until it was intelligible only to Japanese; katakana, more angular and used in Buddhist scriptures, extracted only one part of the relevant character. Originally there were several hundred symbols in each; today, however, they have been standardised to only 46 basic symbols, and each represents the same syllables: in hiragana, for example, the sound 'a' is represented by the symbol あ、in katakana by ア; 'su' is す (hiragana) and ス (katakana). Diacritics are added to some of the symbols to indicate syllables beginning with voiced consonants: 'ka' (か in hiragana, カ in katakana), for example, becomes 'ga' (が and ガ respectively), while 'ha' (は,ハ) becomes 'ba' (ば,バ) or 'pa' (ぱ,パ).

The prestige of Chinese characters as a mark of erudition was such that they did not fall out of use once the phonetic scripts were available, with the result that Japanese today is written with a combination of several scripts: characters for nouns and the stems of inflected words; hiragana to show Japanese pronunciation where required and for the copula, pronouns and grammatical features such as inflections and postpositions; katakana for non-Chinese loanwords and for emphasis; and Arabic numerals in phone numbers and other situations. The Roman alphabet, though not an official script, nevertheless features prominently as a design feature in advertising and commerce. Of the many thousands of characters available, current script policy recommends 1945 of the most commonly occurring for general use, and these are taught in schools during the nine years of compulsory education. In practice, however, as many as 3000–3500 characters are needed in order to read the multiplicity of texts found in newspapers and advertisements (Seeley, 1991: 2).

To take an example sentence to show how the orthography works:
オーストラリアは広い国です。Oosutoraria wa hiroi kuni desu. (Australia is a big country)

The word *oosutoraria* (Australia), being a foreign word, is written in katakana. Hiragana symbols are used for the topic marker postposition *wa* which follows *oosutoraria*, for the inflection *-i* at the end of the adjective *hiro* (big) and for the sentence-ending copula *desu* which is never written in kanji. The two kanji in the sentence are used for the stems of the adjective *hiro* and the noun *kuni* (country).

Combining the three scripts in this manner poses no particular problem once the basic principles are mastered. The two phonetic syllabaries are easy to learn. Characters require more time, not just because they are so much more numerous and complex in form but because the pronunciation of each character may vary depending on the context in which it occurs, that is, most will have at least one each of what are known as *kun* and *on* readings. The *kun* reading is the word's pronunciation in Japanese, the *on* reading represents an earlier Japanese attempt to approximate the pronunciation of the character in Chinese. *On* readings will usually be found in character compounds. The character 人 (person), for example, has a *kun* reading of ひと (*hito*) when used alone or in certain specific compounds to represent the word 'person', and at least two *on* readings when used in compounds: じん (*jin*) when it is used after the name of a country to indicate a person of that nationality (e.g. オーストラリア人, *oosutorariajin*, Australian person) and にん (*nin*) when it is used after a numeral greater than three to indicate the number of people (e.g. 人 or 五人, *gonin*, five people). Character shapes themselves range from the very simple (e.g. 人, person; 木 tree) to the quite complex (e.g. 鼻 nose; 曜 day of the week) from the current list in general use. It is also often necessary to differentiate between which of several similar characters is used for a particular word.

A great advantage deriving from this complex system is that it allows a high degree of ludicity in writing. 'To play with speech or writing is to be artful in formulating a message' (Danet, 2001: 10). In English, we might do this by using varying fonts in the same message. In Japanese, it can also be achieved simply by varying the way in which one of the scripts is normally used (by using katakana, e.g. instead of kanji) to create a novel and interesting impression. This is a frequent practice in advertisements and invitations and on web pages, creating (usually) pleasant variations through the unexpected. To give an example: on a recent visit to Japan, I saw a sign outside a used-car business announcing that it had on offer ４００車, キス**なし (400 cars without 'kizu', defects, where the word 'kizu', usually written in kanji, is here written not in hiragana as might be expected if it were written phonetically but in katakana as if it were a foreign word, and the two little diacritics marking the 'su' as voiced 'zu', normally ズ, are rendered as asterisks). As with other languages, emoticons (*kaomoji*) are also used in both handwriting and in online communication, whether by computer or mobile phone, to convey attitudinal information without words: (^-^), for instance, is one variation of a smiling face, in contrast to the western :) or ☺. A study by Katsuno and Yano (2002: 211) found that at least 20 dictionaries (hard copy and online) of *kaomoji* have been published since 1993. Mobile phones come with them already built in.

A second area of text manipulation is the innovative and well documented *gyaru moji* (girl talk), in which users – usually young women, hence the name – manipulate text messages in a series of maneuvers which include, for example, arranging the disarticulated component sections of characters in a vertical line. They may also include Roman letters, typographic or mathematical symbols, Greek letters and so on in their messages. To give an example from a website which converts user input into *gyaru moji* which can then be sent directly to a friend's mobile phone: if I input 八時に会いましょう (*hachiji ni aimashō*, let's meet at eight), and click on the 'mild scramble' option, the programme returns 八時に会いま∪ょう, that is, the only difference is that one of the phonetic symbols has been replaced with a capital U and two of the others have been made smaller. The same phrase given the 'all-out' option returns 八時レ=会レヽ мa U ょぅ: the first phonetic symbol, formerly hiragana 'ni' に, is now レ= (a combination of the two katakana symbols pronounced 're' and 'ni'); the hiragana 'i' い in 'aimashō' has likewise been scrambled into レ; the hiragana 'ma' ま has been romanised to MA; again the 'shi' し hiragana symbol has been replaced with a capital U; and the final hiragana symbol has been made smaller.[3] This sort of orthographic play functions both for privacy (to protect the content of text messages from being understood by fellow passengers on crowded public transport) and as a kind of subcultural identity marker for this particular group of young women. Similar 'in-group' language play has been documented in postings to Channel 2, a well known unmoderated website (see Nishimura, 2004).

Languages used on the Internet in Japan

Talk of online language practices leads us to the broader issue of what languages are used on the Internet in Japan. The Japanese language has established a strong online presence, as the list of the top ten languages used on the web for 2006 shows: the top six, in descending order, are English, Chinese, Japanese, Spanish, German and French (Internet World Statistics, 2006). Chinese and Japanese have risen to the position of second (13.3%) and third (7.9%) respectively, despite early views that their character-based orthographies were not suited for electronic use. An enabling factor in Japan's web presence is of course the capacity to access large amounts of information in the national language, an aspect usually linked with economic power. Japan is an economically advanced nation with a standard national written language which in the 1980s developed the technological capacity to reproduce that written language electronically. It has a high literacy rate; does not recognise community languages in its language policies; exhibits no perceived pressing need to teach and use foreign languages other than English as a language of international communication; and is an island country secure in its borders. Its minority groups have been forcibly assimilated over time to speak Japanese. Japan has one of the world's largest domestic publishing industries, and a thriving translation industry means that most information is readily available in Japanese not long after it has appeared in other languages. In other words, it is self-sufficient when it comes to developing a web presence and does not need to rely on another language to access information. This means that the Internet, and particularly the web, in Japan is likely to remain largely monolingual, except for the instrumental use of English and of other languages where required at local government level to facilitate the settlement of foreign residents or where used by speakers of other languages themselves. As discussed previously, Japanese is not used worldwide as a language of diaspora or a legacy of colonialism to the extent that other languages are. Its profile in the global picture of language use on the Internet therefore conforms largely to the national borders of Japan.

Within Japan, other languages are of course used on the Internet in personal emails and messaging by their speakers, web-based language teaching sites, and major business and cultural websites. Apart from these, the most proactive official use of other languages is found at local government level, where foreign-language web pages offer instrumental benefits in facilitating the integration of non-Japanese residents into the community. Of the entry-level web sites of the 23 special wards of central Tokyo, for example, 20 offer web pages in English in addition to Japanese and 11 supplement that with Chinese and Korean. Katsushika Ward offers Chinese only (no Korean), and Taito-ku (home of several major national museums) adds information pages in French and German to the other four options. Shinjuku Ward offers an online video in English, Chinese and Korean on living in the area; Suginami and Edogawa Wards both offer multilingual online handbooks (English, Chinese and Korean) of the same kind. The website of the Tokyo Metropolitan Government itself provides for Japanese, English, Chinese and Korean. We find the same thing in other parts of Japan, and not just in the other major cities of Osaka and Nagoya. Niigata, for example, in western Japan, has Japanese, English and Chinese pages on its website; Fukuoka, in the southern island of Kyushu, adds Korean to that list.

Sendai, a city of just over a million people north of Tokyo, is a good example of a city making efforts to incorporate foreign-language information into its web page (http://www.city.sendai.jp/), which offers pages in Japanese, English, Chinese (both simplified and traditional characters to take account of usage in the PRC and Taiwan), Korean, Italian, Spanish, German and French. As of 1 November 2006, Sendai was home to over 10,000 registered foreign students, many of them international students at the city's universities (City of Sendai, 2006). The top page of the municipal websites contains links to a list of hard-copy guides to living in Japan, published by the Council of Local Authorities for International Relations (CLAIR)[4] in Japanese (including an easy kana-only version), English, Chinese, Portuguese, Korean, German, Spanish, French, Vietnamese, Indonesian, Tagalog, Thai and Russian. It also has a link to English-language information for foreign residents provided by the Sendai International Relations Association, dealing with emergencies, transportation, children, health and other issues likely to be of concern. Like many other municipalities, Sendai provides a multilingual DVD and manual on what to do in the event of an earthquake; at present only the English version is available online, but Chinese, Korean, Portuguese, Russian, Bengali, Thai, Spanish, Tagalog, Mongolian and 'simple Japanese' editions are available for perusal at the Sendai International Centre. Information on the Sendai Child and Family Information Station is provided on the web page in Japanese, English, Chinese and Korean, as is information on how to separate residential garbage into the correct categories for recycling.

It is true that the web in Japan is largely monolingual in terms of language content of pages and that this is unlikely to change. As the above discussion shows, however, we do find pockets, particularly at local government level, where foreign languages are used to achieve strategic objectives of integration. It seems certain that the web in Japan will feature increased use of other languages as time goes on and multilingualism becomes more accepted as a feature of daily life.

Publishing and reading

Publishing and printing are major industries in Japan. In 2004 there were 4431 publishing companies, with 7778 bookstores and 2759 libraries. Despite the stature of the publishing industry in comparative international terms, the industry recently suffered a seven-year slump in sales figures from which it emerged only in 2004 thanks to the publication in that year of several very widely selling books, first among them the translation of *Harry Potter and the Order of the Phoenix*. Traditional means of expanding sales have been undermined by the appearance of 'new-used' bookstores, discount bookstores at which almost new books are sold cheaply; there are around 2000 of these across Japan. The emergence of the Internet has also led to new forms of publishing and of distribution which threaten the circulation figures not only of books but also of magazines, although new periodicals continue to appear (JETRO, 2005). Sales of the ever-popular manga (cartoons) and the associated sub-genres doubled between 1979 and 1999 (Kinsella, 2000: 21); they flattened out after 1997, however, as new computer-centred pursuits emerged. More recently the popularity of *manga* cafes (where customers sit and read *manga* without buying them) and the 'new-used' stores has posed a challenge for sales figures.

The postwar self-image of Japanese as avid readers of print-based publications, though still strong, has begun to falter slightly in recent years in the face of competition from handheld games and cell phones. During the pre-Internet years, sales of the small *bunkobon* and *shinsho* (small pocket-sized paperbacks) boomed; casual observation of public transport passengers these days, however, reveals that more people are texting with their mobile phones than reading something in print form, with the possible exception of newspapers. While literacy and reading rates remain high, Japan, like other countries, may be experiencing a decline in the more traditional forms of reading as other activities encroach upon available time. Numerous surveys of reading habits and the drop in book sales in recent years would seem to confirm this. The Agency of Cultural Affairs' 2002 survey on language issues, for example, included a question on reading habits over a month which found that 37.6% of respondents did not read at all during that period (Agency for Cultural Affairs, 2003).

One area continuing to show lively sales activity is that of books relating to the Japanese language itself, in particular guides to correct usage. Number seven on the list of ranked best sellers for 2004, for example, was a book called Professor Kawashima Ryūtarō's *Reading Drills for Adults to Sharpen the Mind: 60 Days of Reading Masterpieces and Transcribing Kanji* (JETRO, 2005). Major bookstore Kinokuniya's list of best-selling books on the Japanese language for April 2006 included *Nihongo o shikaru*! (Taking Japanese to task!) by Kaganoi Shūichi, which bemoans what the author perceives as the increasing disorder in the language, attributing it to an influx of foreign loanwords, the rough speech of young people, and the influence of text messaging among other things. Other top sellers that month included *Mondai na Nihongo: Doko ga Okashii? Nani ga Okashii?* (Problematic Japanese: Where and What is Peculiar?) edited by Kitahara Yasuo, which points out common errors and discusses their origins, and Anno Mitsumasa's *Yonimo Utsukushii Nihongo Nyūmon* (Introduction to Truly Beautiful Japanese), which discusses the beauty of the language to be found in the classics and the importance of enjoying it from an early age. Tokyo University's Komori Yōichi has noted that this trend towards reading about language is common during times of recession, perhaps because, during such periods, readers substitute pride in the cultural heritage of their language for pride in national economic prowess which fuels sales of different sorts of books in more prosperous times. Given that many of the books on language are compilations of quotations from famous literary and other works, nostalgia clearly plays a part in boosting sales figures for these offerings (Komori, 2002: 1–2). A recent best-seller has been *Empitsu de Oku no Hosomichi* (Oku no Hosomichi in Pencil), aimed at adults, where readers trace over the words of the classic *Oku no Hosomichi*,[5] thereby achieving the twin aims of improving handwriting and inculcating a deeper appreciation of this classic work at the same time. By mid-2006 this had sold over 800,000 copies (Kiyota, 2006), and other classics have since been issued in the same series.

The translation industry in Japan plays a major part in the book trade, with many Japanese-language versions of foreign books available in any bookstore. Aspect publishing house, for example, specialises in translating foreign publications into Japanese, mostly English-language bestsellers with some titles from Europe, South America and Asia. About 5000 translated works, most originally in English, are published every year in Japan (Aspect, 2006). Translation has always been important in Japan, from the early translations of the Chinese classics to the modern period's influx of translations of western books. It has provided one of Japan's major sources of information from other parts of the world. Translations of both fiction (most recently the huge success of the translated *Harry Potter*) and non-fiction are widely read. Around 10% of the books published each year are translations, mostly from English (Kondo & Wakabayashi, 1998: 492).

Books in other languages are also widely sold. In 2004 Japan spent over 44 billion yen on importing books and magazines and almost 15 billion yen on exports of books and magazines to other countries (PACE, 2005).[6] Imports came from a wide range of countries in the west and Asia, predominantly from the United States and the United Kingdom. Most are academic books and magazines, language-learning textbooks, popular foreign books, magazines and dictionaries and encyclopedias, in English, French, Dutch, Chinese, Korean, Italian, Spanish and other languages. Most foreign-language literature is imported from abroad by distribution agencies specialising in this area (JETRO, 2005). Yohan Inc., the largest distributor of foreign books and magazines in Japan, for example, imports 1300 popular magazines from around the world (Yohan Inc., 2006). There are also small domestic companies publishing in Chinese or Korean. The major English-language publishers in Japan are Tuttle Publishing, Kodansha International and The Japan Times.

Publication exports in the main are Japanese-language publications and translations (particularly of literature and *manga*) to be sold by Japanese bookstores overseas, predominantly in the United States and South East Asia, where customers comprise expatriate communities, students of the Japanese language and more generally people interested in Japan.[7]

What emerges here is a picture of a highly literate population reading widely both domestic and translated books. Clearly the intricate writing system, although it may pose problems for children with learning difficulties or for recent migrants, is no barrier in broad terms to the reading habits of the general public. Those habits are presently undergoing some degree of change, in part owing to changes in the nature of publishing outlets, in part owing to the influence of electronic media and in part – as surveys show – simply owing to the pressures of everyday life. Nevertheless, publishing and reading remain strong elements in Japan's language profile.

Language policy: History and issues

Japan has a diverse range of language policies in place at national level, administered by an equally diverse body of ministries and other government organisations. Policies relating to the national language and to the teaching of English in schools are administered by the Ministry of Education, Culture, Sports, Science and Technology (MEXT).[8] Policies relating to other languages and to the teaching of Japanese overseas are implemented by the following bodies:

- Ainu maintenance (The Foundation for Research and Promotion of Ainu Culture, set up by the Hokkaido Development Agency and the Ministry of Education in September 1997).
- Teaching of Japanese as a foreign language overseas (The Japan Foundation, within the Ministry of Foreign Affairs).
- Foreign language teaching in schools, while under the control of MEXT in terms of curriculum, is supported by the Japan Exchange and Teaching (JET) programme for foreign language teaching (under the Council of Local Authorities for International Relations [CLAIR], administered by three ministries, set up in 1987).

In addition to the official policies, informal language policies of a sort are exercised by the print and visual media, which have strict regulations about the kinds of language which cannot be used in print or on screen because of the likely offence it would give to readers/viewers (see Gottlieb, 2006). Other informal language promotion agencies active in Japan include the British Council (English), three Confucius Institutes at different universities (Chinese), the Cervantes Institute (Spanish), the Alliance Française (French) and the Goethe Institute (German).

In this section, I will concentrate on those policies administered by MEXT which relate to the national language. Of the current cluster of policies relating to the Japanese language itself, all deal with the written language, specifically the orthography. This is hardly surprising when we consider the complexity of that orthography. As Haugen (1966: 53) has asserted, language planning attempts primarily to shape the formal written manifestation of language. In the case of Japanese, although the writing system already existed and had done so for well over 1000 years, there was much to be done in the 20th century in order to shape it to modern needs. Contemporary policies are the result of almost a century of deliberation on how best to rationalise what was formerly a much more unwieldy system of writing.

The major policies in force today are:

- *Jōyō Kanji Hyō* (List of Characters for General Use, 1981).
- *Gendai Kanazukai* (Modern Kana Usage, 1946, revised in 1986).
- *Okurigana no Tsukekata* (Guide to the Use of Okurigana, 1959, revised in 1973).
- *Gairaigo no Hyōki* (Notation of Foreign Loanwords, 1991).

The current List of Characters for General Use is the outcome of a revision of an earlier list, the *Tōyō Kanji Hyō* (List of Characters for Interim Use, 1946), and also incorporates two earlier policies, one on the *on* and *kun* readings for characters (1948) and another on character shapes (1949). These policies were adopted by Cabinet on the basis of reports from the Kokugo Shingikai (National Language Council), the body responsible for investigating language matters and formulating recommendations for policy between 1934 and 2001, located within the then Ministry of Education. In 2001, as a result of administrative restructures, the Council was reorganised into the Kokugo Bunkakai (National Language Subdivision) of the Agency for Cultural Affairs' Bunka Shingikai (Committee for Cultural Affairs), within the new MEXT super-ministry. This subdivision remains the body in charge of language policy relation to *kokugo*.

The status of the above policies setting out guidelines for orthography is that they are binding on government (which includes, of course, the education system and all government publications) but not on anyone else. The press largely adopted them voluntarily from the beginning and was indeed instrumental in pushing for them, since rationalisation of the orthography was clearly in the media's interest both in terms of printing technology and of boosting circulation figures. Private usage, however, is entirely up to the individual, although most people, having been socialised into writing in accordance with the policies through their years in the education system, will write accordingly.

In order to understand why such policies are necessary, we need first of all to know their parameters and then to understand why those parameters were developed. The contemporary List of Characters for General Use, as we saw, recommends a total of 1945 characters for use in general everyday writing, while recognising that writing in specialist fields may require many more. The earlier List of Characters for Interim Use (1946) was slightly trimmer, at 1850 characters, and more prescriptive in its intent, describing the policy in terms of '*seigen*' (limit) rather than the current more relaxed '*meyasu*' (guidelines). The 1945 characters are taught, as we saw, during the nine years of compulsory education. The first 1006 are known as the *Kyōiku Kanji* (Education Kanji) and are taught during the six years of elementary school; they account for 90% of the characters used in newspapers.

The current early 21st century situation vis-à-vis characters is very different from that pertaining 100 years ago. It has been necessary to draw up contemporary policies because in the early Meiji Period (1868–1912), when Japan came out of its period of self-imposed feudal isolation and began to modernise in response to both external and internal pressures, the characters in theory available for use numbered in the tens of thousands. Many were much more complex in form than today's somewhat simplified versions. The old form of *kuni* (country), for example, today written as 国, was formerly written as 國. Major dictionaries list different numbers of characters; the largest, the *Daikanwa Jiten*, records almost 50,000, including those needed to read the classics. A 1933 survey of school readers, newspapers and literary works found a total of 6478 characters used in those sources (Hayashi, 1977: 112–114). The size of this available character set has not diminished today; the characters are still there, but policy priorities have now been set for which ones are of most general use and should therefore be taught in schools.

Quite early in the modern period, it became clear to a few would-be reformers that the writing system was in need of rationalisation. This came about partly as a result of increased contact with European languages and partly as a result of the perception in some quarters that the many years needed to master the existing writing system hindered the rapid acquisition of knowledge needed for modernisation through the national education system established in 1872. Some began to call for a decrease in the number of characters for general use or, indeed, for the complete abolition of characters in favour of one of the phonetic kana scripts or the Roman alphabet (for details, see Twine, 1991). Had the first of these alternatives been a realistic alternative, modernisation of the kana spelling conventions would also have been needed, as they were based on classical pronunciations long out of date.

These early ideas on script reform, however, were not destined to succeed. To understand why not, since with hindsight they seem eminently sensible, we need to understand that, from the 1870s to the 1890s the pre-modern upper class view of what constituted appropriate writing for public consumption, which placed great importance on adherence to classical and pseudo-classical Sino-Japanese literary conventions and use of characters, was still strong. Most of the men then in power had been educated in this tradition and accepted it as a given. Prior to the modern period, characters had been in the main the preserve of the upper classes (aristocrats and samurai), who had both the time and the sponsored education available to master their use. Education for the lower classes was self-sponsored at temple schools and other places and was marked by a concentration on literacy in kana and basic kanji rather than by the heavy emphasis on the rote learning of the Chinese classics that was the hallmark of upper class education. In addition, characters were invested with a weighty cultural mystique. Despite the fact that they had originally been imported from China, they had come to be seen as icons of the essence of Japanese culture, an association that they still carry today. Suggestions that their numbers might be rationalised, therefore, or that they might be replaced with a different script, were very much frowned upon by the men in power, who were concerned not only with modernising the country but also with preserving its cultural heritage in the face of potential Western imperialism. Hence, early suggestions for script reform were ignored.

Nevertheless, as the modern period wore on, an increasing number of journalists, educators, novelists and civil rights educators, motivated by pragmatic concerns in their own fields to do with literacy and the spreading of ideas, began to call for some sort of rationalisation of the orthography. The writing system was not their only concern; other perceived imperatives were the development of a written style based on modern spoken Japanese rather than on archaic literary conventions and the designation of an official standard language which would be understood from one end of the archipelago to the other despite the multiplicity of dialects, thereby helping to unite the nation and foster a sense of national unity and identity (see Twine, 1991).

The resolution of these issues was greatly aided by the return in 1894 from study in Germany of Ueda Kazutoshi (1867–1937), the first Western-trained linguist in Japan. Ueda founded the linguistics department of the then Tokyo Imperial University (today's Tokyo University) which trained many of the men who were to become influential in Japan's 20th-century language modernisation movement. As an undergraduate at the university, Ueda had studied under the British scholar and romanisation advocate Basil Hall Chamberlain (1850–1935) and had been strongly influenced by Chamberlain's views on style and script reform for Japanese. He was thus well disposed from the start towards the groundswell of opinion in Japan in the late 1890s calling for language modernisation, and his postgraduate study in linguistics had led him to view script as a means to an end rather than as an end in itself. Japan's defeat of China in the Sino-Japanese War of 1894–1895 also helped: the subsequent upsurge of nationalism prompted a re-examination of the national language, which was now to be used outside Japan in the new colony of Taiwan. Ueda took full advantage of this, establishing the Linguistics Society in 1898, participating actively in other language-related pressure groups set up around this time and lobbying a sympathetic Education Minister for a national body to oversee language matters.

As a result, the first national body to deal with language issues, the Kokugo Chōsa Iinkai (National Language Research Council), was set up within the Ministry of Education in 1902, with a four-fold brief: to look into the feasibility of replacing characters with a phonetic script (either kana or the alphabet); to encourage the widespread use of a written style based on modern speech; to examine the phonemic system of Japanese; and to settle upon a standard language from among the dialects. This body was responsible for many of Japan's first large-scale language surveys, documenting and classifying information which would in time provide the basis for policy decisions by later bodies. Nothing ever came of the first of the tasks listed above, but one result of the Council's work was that the standard language came to be defined as the speech of educated people in the Yamanote district of Tokyo. The government could see the utility of standardisation in education and was prepared to support this. With this one exception, however, no lasting policies were formulated before the Council disappeared in an administrative shuffle in 1913, largely owing to the still very influential political and intellectual opposition to language reform of any kind. The official view was that to tamper with the existing writing system, even with the commendable aim of improving it, was tantamount to an attack on the nation's cultural heritage.

Attempts to arrive at script policies in the first half of the 20th century were thus characterised by an unevenly weighted tussle between linguists who regarded script as secondary to language itself and ultranationalists who regarded the orthography as a sacrosanct icon of national spirit. While the former participated actively in formulating proposals aimed at streamlining the writing system, the latter held power and were able to frustrate any attempt to have those proposals officially adopted by the government of the day. Such attempts were certainly made. Government input into language planning was restored when the Rinji Kokugo Chōsa Iinkai (Interim National Language Research Council) was inaugurated in 1921. This body was subsequently replaced in 1934 by the Kokugo Shingikai (National Language Council), which remained in charge of language policy formulation until 2001.

As the Interim Council was tasked with finding solutions to aspects of language use which caused difficulties in daily life and education, its members settled on investigating plans to limit characters, revise kana spellings and rationalize associated conventions such as the multiple *on* and *kun* readings a character could have. In 1923 it proposed a list of 1962 characters for general use; in 1924, a change to kana spelling based on modern Tokyo pronunciation; and in 1926, simplification of character shapes. Despite strong support from major newspapers which were keen to see character limits adopted as policy, the proposals (and particularly the kana-related one) resulted in a virulent backlash from conservatives and the government did not accept them. Several years later, in 1931, a revised version of the kana proposal almost succeeded when the Education Ministry of the day decided in the face of ultranationalist opposition to implement it in textbooks once it had been passed by the Educational Administration Committee. A change of minister occurred before that happened, however, and the Prime Minister shelved the proposal on the grounds that national unity took precedence over the likely social controversy it would cause. As long as the military with its rigid views on the sanctity of tradition held power, then, nothing could be done about script reform.

When the subsequent National Language Council put up another proposal to limit characters in 1942, Japan had already been at war for a long time and the *kotodama* ideology had become even more deeply entrenched. *Kotodama* (the spirit of the Japanese language) was a term used to encapsulate the belief that the national language (by which was usually meant characters and historical kana usage), bound up as it was with the essence of the national spirit, was sacrosanct, never to be altered. During World War Two, people who openly advocated script reform were subject to campaigns of vilification organised by right-wing interests; foreign loanwords such as *beesubooru* (baseball) were dropped in favour of Sino-Japanese equivalents; and in one incident in 1939 a group of students from Waseda University who advocated romanisation were accused of anti-nationalist sympathies and arrested by the secret police. In this atmosphere, domestic language management languished and the status quo remained unchanged. A study of the literature of the period indicates that many people understood the words 'language policy' at the time to refer only to the spread of the Japanese language in the conquered territories overseas and not to the management of language issues at home (see Gottlieb, 1995).

As this brief summary shows, there was much to be done in terms of language and primarily script reform in order to allow the written Japanese of the early modern period to develop into the written Japanese of the present, but vested intellectual and political interests and a very strong ultranationalist philosophy stood in the way. It took the major cultural and intellectual shift brought about by defeat in World War Two to break this stalemate. The purging of the right-wing powerbrokers and the concurrent emphasis during the Allied Occupation on democracy provided a fertile atmosphere for both an ideological and practical break with the past, and this included the contentious issue of script reform. Members of the National Language Council who wanted to proceed with reform cannily tapped in to the zeitgeist, arguing persuasively that the writing system made it needlessly difficult for all sections of the populace to participate in the written debate on public life in postwar Japan and was thus not democratic. Since the new 1946 Constitution located sovereignty in the people of Japan and not, as previously, in the Emperor, this proved a particularly effective line of reasoning.

When the National Language Council reconvened in 1945 after a three-year wartime hiatus, the majority of its members decided upon a moderate approach, rejecting radical proposals from some members that characters be dropped altogether in favour of limiting the number of characters for general use, modifying the shapes of the more complex ones, bringing kana spelling into line with modern pronunciation, and in general implementing related changes aimed at reducing complexity. It was from this background that the policies presently in operation emerged over the following decade, being first submitted to the Minister as reports from the Council and then officially promulgated once accepted by Cabinet. As they were binding on government departments, they were naturally disseminated through school textbooks so that the postwar and subsequent generations of school children grew up under their influence. The policies were subsequently slightly revised during the period 1965–1991 as the result of a request for a re-evaluation from the Education Minister, under pressure from a resurgence of conservative opinion from people fearing that literacy standards were now inferior to those prewar. The changes were largely cosmetic, however, with no substantial reversal of direction; only a few characters were added to the list for general use in 1981, and the revised kana spelling remained unchanged (see Gottlieb, 1995 for full details). The much-contested involvement of government in language matters, seen by some as an unwarranted intrusion by the state into private practices, was not overturned.

While it might have seemed that script policy matters were thus settled, they do in fact receive ongoing attention even at present, driven now by technological developments. Once the Council had produced the last of the current policies in 1991, it turned its attention to the spoken language, producing reports (but not policies) which discussed the use of honorifics and the influx of loanwords from other languages, in particular English. The development of character-capable word processing technology, however, had by that time brought changes to the way in which Japanese is written. The current script policies were formulated in an era when most documents were written by hand; the size of the character set meant that Japan did not experience a successful typewriter age as happened in other countries. While companies certainly did use Japanese typewriters, these were clumsy, large machines requiring specially trained operators and never reached the speeds possible on a QWERTY keyboard. Later, fax technology made it possible to send handwritten documents. The current script policies were therefore predicated on a culture of handwriting shaped by the need to recognise, remember and accurately reproduce a large number of characters. Since 1978, however, the invention of the first character-capable word processor and the subsequent rapid uptake of this technology and its later extension to the Internet has undermined this and other pillars which had supported postwar script policy (newspaper requirements and office automation difficulties).

Word processing software contains many thousands more characters than the 1945 on the List of Characters for General Use. For a time, until users became accustomed to viewing the technology as a quotidian helpmeet rather than as a source of exotic effects, documents looked somewhat 'blacker' than usual owing to an increase in the proportion of characters in the text. Some very complex characters long gone from the official lists, such as 綺麗 *kirei* (beautiful), normally written in hiragana as きれい, also made an occasional comeback in electronically produced documents. Inexperienced users sometimes made mistakes by using the wrong characters from the list of homophones offered by the memory to fit their typed-in phonetic input. The fact that so many characters are available on demand led some academics and publishers to suggest that language policy might need to change to accommodate the presence of the technology, perhaps by changing the current policy on characters so that fewer are taught for reproduction and more for recognition.

The Council, while recognising the challenges, was slow to respond, choosing instead in its deliberations during the 1990s to focus mainly on rationalising the shapes of those characters used in computers which are not on the List of Characters for General Use (see Gottlieb, 2000 for details). The 2005 report of the Council's successor, the National Language Subdivision of the Committee for Cultural Affairs, however, acknowledged that technology was having an effect on how people wrote and announced that it would soon embark on a thorough reappraisal of the existing policy on characters. This move is timely. The proportion of Japan's population who grew up in the period when handwriting was the norm is rapidly ageing; even someone born at the beginning of the word processing boom would be in their early to mid-20s now, with subsequent generations never having known a time when electronic character input and output were not possible.

Written culture in the 21st century, then, includes a technology-mediated aspect which has definite implications for script policy, and changes in script policy are likely before too long. High rates of accessing the Internet by mobile phone and text messaging make Japan distinctive in the transnational arena (see Ito *et al.*, 2005). Cheap messaging available through I-mode (Internet-mode, a wireless service launched in Japan by DoCoMo in 1999 which enables emails to be exchanged between mobile phones) means that email messaging rather than talk is the major use for those phones in Japan. This is contributing to a type of innovative use of language not envisaged by those who drew up the current script policies. Not only is the language used in messaging more often free of the formality of other written text, as in other countries, but in Japan it has the added dimension of variations in script use: greater use of the *kana* script, for example, where characters would normally be used. All these things are the focus of current examination by the National Language Subdivision. What we are seeing now appears to be the beginning of a major shift in policy outlook at the national level in response to now well entrenched challenges to former ways of using the orthography.

Intergenerational transmission issues

As observed in the previous section, the National Language Council turned its attention to spoken aspects of the national language after 1991. Along with the previously mentioned change in the status of dialects, other aspects of language use were also addressed, often in response to a public perception that the language was in decline, as expressed in surveys and in letters to the editor of major newspapers. As is common in other countries as well, members of the older generation often feel that language standards are being eroded. The National Language Council's report on *Language Policy for a New Era*, for example, picked up on this when it noted that 'most older people rely on linguistic practices that are traditional and typical, and tend to be critical of or feel alienated from the new ways in which younger people speak'. The usual term used to express these misgivings is kotoba no midare (disorder in the language).

The two major foci for such perceptions today are the increase in loanwords and the supposedly declining use of honorifics. New technologies, in particular information technology, have led to an increase in the number of foreign loanwords in circulation, many of them replacing perfectly good Japanese equivalents. Furthermore, young people seem not to be able to use the complicated system of honorifics in the way that their parents do; this has become one of the major issues in intergenerational transmission of the language. Bookstores throughout Japan carry many manuals promising to help readers achieve correct use of honorifics; academics discuss *keigo* on television programmes and publish how-to guides for a wide public readership (Wetzel, 2004: 69–70).

Concern about *kotoba no midare* is not a new phenomenon, having been a frequently recurring theme in discourse about the national language since the late eighteenth century. Looking at the last 30 years: NHK surveys on public attitudes to language in 1979 and 1986 revealed concerns about spoken language, honorifics and greetings among other things; later, in 1992, newspaper articles by readers of the *Asahi Shimbun* focused on disorder in spoken language, and, as we have seen, the National Language Council's discussions of *kotoba no midare* also zeroed in on this area (Carroll, 2001: 81–85). More recently, a 2002 Agency for Cultural Affairs survey reported that 80.4% of the 2200 respondents believed that the language was either 'very disordered' or 'disordered to a certain extent', with perceptions of disorder extending to the written as well as spoken word. Close to 90% of respondents believed that the ability to write good Japanese had declined either 'very much' or 'somewhat', compared to a 69% belief in a decline in reading ability, a 59% decline in speaking ability and a 57% decline in listening ability (Agency for Cultural Affairs, 2003).

These perceptions of declining ability across all categories continued a trend which has been apparent since the surveys began in 1995. Many respondents spoke of their belief in a clear connection between the gaps in today's abilities and the erosion of time available for studying honorifics, proverbs and *kango* since the introduction in recent years of the new Courses of Study aimed at a more relaxed curriculum in schools. The government's response was to announce that, as one arm of a strategic plan to foster Japanese able to speak English well, 200 schools at all three levels of education nationally would be designated flagship Japanese language education providers, with a special emphasis on fostering advanced reading and writing skills, knowledge of the classics and oral communication skills, on the basis that a good command of students' first language is a prerequisite for successful acquisition of a foreign language.

The Council addressed the loanwords issue in the mid-1990s, concluding in its 1995 report that the use of loanwords was to a certain extent unavoidable, given the nature of globalisation, and that this was bound to be particularly the case in specialist areas such as information technology. In non-specialist areas, however, it advised caution: to use words not universally understood could impede communication, particularly with older people (Kokugo Shingikai, 1995: 449–450). Since it is younger people who most enthusiastically adopt loanwords, it was thought intergenerational communication might suffer as a result. When the Ministry of Health and Welfare attempted to replace loanwords with Japanese equivalents in medical care programmes for elderly people, however, it ran into difficulties with finding appropriate equivalents and had to put the initiative on hold (Honna, 1995: 46). However, the most recent Agency of Cultural Affairs survey on attitudes to loanwords in 2001 found that, while 91.8% of respondents had heard the word *toriitomento* (treatment), only 81.8% actually understood what it meant (Agency for Cultural Affairs, 2002).

The six years of compulsory English study at junior and senior high school no doubt contribute to the high proportion of loanwords from English, as Honna (1995) has suggested, but the fact of their existence does not guarantee comprehension. A 1999 survey found that nearly half of all respondents reported times when they had not understood loanwords used in everyday conversation (Agency for Cultural Affairs, 2000). In 2002 Prime Minister Koizumi took direct action to counter this and related problems when he instituted a committee to study the matter under the auspices of the National Institute for Japanese Language. This group issued four reports between 2003 and 2006 recommending the replacement of certain loanwords with Japanese equivalents (for full details, see Kokuritsu Kokugo Kenkyūjo, 2006).

On the matter of honorifics, the view expressed in the 1995 National Language Council report was that knowing when the use of such language was appropriate in the interests of smooth communication had become more important than the correct forms of the honorifics themselves (Kokugo Shingikai, 1995: 432–433). This represented a clear move away from the more prescriptive attitudes of the past towards a more holistic view of language and communication, a view which was repeated in the Council's final report on the subject (Kokugo Shingikai, 2000) before it was replaced by the National Language Subdivision. Interestingly, whereas a 1952 report on polite speech by the Council had criticised the overuse of honorifics and euphemisms by women, a similar investigation conducted in the early 1990s found almost no difference between the language of men and women in this respect.

One area bound to become an increasing target for *midare* complaints is the language used in text messaging and email, which is less formal than other written text. Nearly 80% of respondents to a 2003 survey indicated that they thought these media had a definite effect on language use, in areas as diverse as forgetting how to write kanji and traditional letter forms, an increase in abbreviations and neologisms, and a loss of nuance (Agency for Cultural Affairs, 2004). There is a clear tendency to abbreviate characters in online chat and text messaging, including the highly specialised and ludic *gyaru moji* (girl script) mentioned earlier which manipulates characters in ways unforeseen by policy makers. The informal text practices used in email, chat groups and phone texting are likely to become a subject of discussion in terms of literacy practices in the future.

When intergenerational transmission issues create a sufficient amount of public attention, they usually attract mention in the periodic reports of Japan's language policy body, as has been the case with honorifics and loanwords in the past. The National Language Subdivision's 2005 report discussing the impact of technology on writing is also a timely recognition that this concern, like the others, is here to stay.

In the preceding discussion of the national language, I have highlighted some of the main issues: namely, the centrality of the language to concepts of national identity, the central role of the orthography in this, the importance of language policies regulating that orthography and the manner in which they were developed, and the significant challenges now being posed to the current policy stance by electronic media and to concepts of 'proper' writing by mobile phone text messaging. What all this shows is that, far from the fossilised and static concept of 'the national language' presented in the monolingual *kokugo* myth, the language itself, like all other languages, is a vital organic entity which is constantly evolving, often in ways which provoke controversy among its users. We turn now to a discussion of other languages spoken in Japan which will show that Japan has in fact long been a multilingual society even if official recognition of that fact has been withheld.

Minority Languages
Introduction

I turn now from attention to the national language to a discussion of other languages spoken in Japan, several of which are spoken by substantial minority communities in the country. They include Okinawan; Korean and Chinese, spoken by both old-comers (people brought to Japan from its colonies prior to and during World War Two) and newcomers (more recent migrants); Portuguese, Spanish, Tagalog and Vietnamese, spoken mainly by communities of newcomers, including refugees; and English, spoken by expatriate communities of people from English-speaking countries. Since the passing of the Ainu Cultural Promotion Act in 1997, the indigenous Ainu language has also enjoyed a change in status after decades of suppression, although, as we shall see, the number of native speakers remains small.

Language policy in Japan is piecemeal in the sense that there is no overarching document which takes into consideration the national language, minority or community languages, the indigenous Ainu language and the nature of strategically important foreign language learning within the same policy framework. Rather, as we saw in the previous section, policy is formulated and administered within separate areas with defined briefs, none of them devoted to community languages. Given that language policy thinking centres around the belief that mastery of the Japanese language in both its spoken and written forms is a key marker of national identity, the concept of community languages has not yet been seriously addressed.

The term 'community languages' replaced 'foreign languages' in Australia when it became clear that those 'foreign languages' were in fact important in the lives of many Australians; it has since spread to Britain and New Zealand and other countries (Clyne, 2005: 5). This term does not resonate in Japan, however, where the mono-ethnic monolingual ideology is still sufficiently strong to prevent according formal recognition at national level to the fact that large sections of the community speak another language. Japan is not yet used to thinking of itself as a country with immigrants, despite the historical influxes of people from China and Korea during its colonial period and the more recent increases in immigration since the 1980s. Therefore, I have called this section 'minority languages'. Since the national education system is not a major player in the spread and maintenance of such languages, I will also deal briefly in this section with the avenues through which speakers of minority language read, watch television and have web pages available for native-language maintenance. In some but not all cases, this extends to private ethnic schools.

The Japanese government does not collect data on language use by its citizens; census forms contain no question on ethnicity, although there is a 'nationality' category for foreign residents. Listed under the category of 'Japanese' are the Ainu population, Okinawans and any foreigner who has taken Japanese citizenship.[9] It is therefore difficult to estimate how many of those with Japanese citizenship speak another language as their first language at home. Of the non-citizens, many of those listed as resident foreigners in the Korean and Chinese figures are old-comers, that is, people whose families came to Japan three or even four generations ago, so that a considerable number of them now speak only Japanese.

The makeup of the 1,974,000 registered foreigners (including both old-comers and newcomers) at the end of 2004 looked like this: some 607,000 Koreans, 488,000 Chinese, 287,000 Brazilians, 199,000 from the Philippines, 56,000 from Peru, and 49,000 from the United States (Statistical Research and Training Institute, Ministry of Internal Affairs and Communication, Japan, 2006). We can break down the foreign population figures into more detail by reference to the findings of the most recent census figures available, those of the 2000 population census, which listed a total of 1,310,545 foreigners in Japan:

- 970,878 Asians (Bangladesh, Cambodia, China (including Taiwan), India, Indonesia, Iran, Korea, Laos, Malaysia, Myanmar, Nepal, Pakistan, Philippines, Singapore, Sri Lanka, Thailand, Viet Nam and 'others', of which the Korean, Chinese and Philippine groups were the largest respectively).
- 47,984 North Americans (Canada, Mexico, USA and 'others', with the United States group the largest).
- 230,556 South Americans (Argentina, Bolivia, Brazil, Colombia, Paraguay, Peru and 'others', with Brazil and Peru by far the largest).
- 30,417 Europeans (France, Germany, Italy, Romania, Russia, Spain, United Kingdom and 'others', with the United Kingdom the largest by a wide margin).
- 5628 Africans (Ghana, Nigeria and 'others', with the unspecified others the largest group).

- 8878 from Oceania (Australia, New Zealand and 'others', with Australia as the largest group).
- 16,204 stateless or 'not reported' others (Statistics Bureau, Ministry of Internal Affairs and Communication, Japan, no date).

From this we can extrapolate that there are at least 25 languages other than Japanese being spoken as the first or home language of people from these groups, possibly 26 if we include Ainu which does not appear in the 'foreigner' figures.

Immigration, though still small in comparison with other countries, has increased significantly since the 1980s. In 2004, in addition to the registered foreigners described above, there were an estimated 200,000+ undocumented foreign residents (overstayers) in Japan (SMJ, 2004). Officially registered foreigners accounted for only around 1.5% of the total population. However, the birth rate, for many years a source of concern, dropped in 2004 to a record low. Declining birth rates and the consequent demand for labour met by foreign immigrants have led to a dramatic reshaping of many nation-states into formal or *de facto* multicultural and multilingual societies (Guiraudon & Joppke, 2001; Lo Bianco, 2004), with Japan now among them. If immigration numbers continue to rise, as Japan's Third Basic Plan for Immigration Control (2005) indicates will happen, the demographic mix will change markedly over time: a United Nations population projection scenario posits that Japan would need 17 million net immigrants up to the year 2050 to keep the population at its 2005 level; by 2050, these immigrants and their descendants would comprise 17.7% of the total population. Other scenarios took the proportion even higher (United Nations Population Division, 2001).

While such figures are of course only projections, subject to changing variables over the years, it does appear certain that Japan will need to continue to rely upon immigration to fill labour shortages. A society which has resolutely considered itself monolingual for purposes of nation-building rhetoric can therefore no longer afford to brush aside engagement with the reality of its own growing multilingualism, which in turn has implications for the way in which the nation is henceforth imagined. It will be important to understand how the challenge to entrenched views of national homogeneity (both racial and linguistic) posed by the presence of migrant communities in Japan manifests itself in language expectations and to what extent the state itself can develop to meet those expectations through language practices in Japanese government offices, schools, the private sector and the community at large.

Language policies have a direct impact on the classrooms where migrant children are educated; the task facing Japan now is therefore to develop a policy stance which recognises diversity while still maintaining the importance of the national language and which enables migrant children to keep up with education content while they are still mastering Japanese, in particular written Japanese. In the long term, this means a reconceptualising of the place of language in national identity; in the short term, it means a review of language-in-education policies to take account of emerging needs in this area.

A key conceptual dichotomy in Japan has always been 'Japanese vs. foreigner'; we have seen that this division is evident even in reference to the *kokugo/nihongo* divide. Hashimoto (2002: 69) refers to this as 'the emotional struggles with foreignness'. But this struggle, rather than remaining as an influential subtext, is now foregrounded by population flows. Canagarajah spells out succinctly the ramifications of globalisation for language planning: the nation-state can no longer be the sole defining norm in this regard.

> [Language] policies have to be mindful of the porous borders that open up each country to people, goods and ideas that shuttle across communities. On the other hand, we are now increasingly sensitive to pockets of language groups – immigrants, minorities, and 'virtual communities' of cyberspace – who were previously swept under the carpet of national unity and homogeneous community. (Canagarajah, 2005: xx)

It will take some time to unpick these issues, but progress in this area is essential for Japan's evolving identity if it is not to remain bound by the practices of the past: national identity must be seen as dynamic and open to change rather than fixed and immobile. In the area of immigration, government thinking is having now to encompass concerns about the future of language education for migrant children in schools, adult migrants in the wider community, and the relationship of these things to citizenship requirements.

Bearing in mind this broad framework, we move now to a discussion of minority languages in Japan, beginning with the Ainu language.

Ainu

The Ainu people are the indigenous people of Japan, living today primarily in the northern island of Hokkaido. While the officially registered Ainu population is only about 25,000, the actual number of people with Ainu heritage is believed to be much larger. Exact population figures are difficult to ascertain, as intermarriage with Japanese and a history of anti-Ainu discrimination mean that many may not wish to identify themselves as being of Ainu descent.

The Ainu language is a language isolate. Within Ainu itself, there are regional variations, as detailed in linguist Hattori Shiro's 1964 dictionary of Ainu dialects. These may be broadly classified as the dialects of Hokkaido, Sakhalin (the southern part of Russia's Sakhalin peninsula) and the Kurile islands (still the subject of an ongoing border dispute with Russia). Ainu speakers originally lived in all three locations but were later forcibly settled in Hokkaido. Ethnologue records the last speaker of the Sakhalin dialect as having died in 1994 (Gordon, 2005). Since the language had no written form until it was recorded by linguists, its preservation was dependent on oral transmission of songs and stories in non-official settings.

Today, Ainu speakers fall into four main categories: archival Ainu speakers (most no longer living, but their speech is preserved in recordings), old Ainu-Japanese bilinguals (older members of the community who grew up speaking both Ainu and Japanese), token Ainu speakers (those who normally speak Japanese but occasionally insert a few stock words and expressions of Ainu into their conversation) and second language learners of Ainu, motivated either by heritage or personal interest (DeChicchis, 1995: 110). The last of these study Ainu in classes held at various university, community education and other venues. Audio and video recordings are available for self-study, as are Internet sources,[10] and the Foundation for Research and Promotion of Ainu Culture (FRPAC), established in 1997, broadcasts Ainu-language radio courses for beginners.

The language has suffered reversals of fortune during its history of contact with Japan because of differing political expediencies which dictated whether its speakers were to be perceived as non-Japanese or Japanese. For two centuries before the modern period began, it was forbidden for Ainu people living in or operating from trading posts run by Japanese under the auspices of the Matsumae clan to speak or write Japanese, in order to preserve an image of them as alien, Other and subject to control. The upside to this was that use of the Ainu language remained the norm.

After 1868, however, this changed dramatically when it became essential to define the borders of the modern nation state under a central government. It was particularly important to define the northern border in relation to nearby Russia; the Ainu people were therefore to be re-badged, this time as citizens of Japan, in order to maintain a claim on Hokkaido as Japanese territory rather than as a peripheral trading post. Everyone living in Hokkaido had to be shown to be a Japanese citizen who, by extension, spoke Japanese: one unified nation with one national language. Language and national spirit thus became inseparable. The major legal document pertaining to Ainu people was the *Hokkaido Former Aborigines Protection Act* of 1899 which stipulated a policy of total assimilation, including mandatory education of Ainu children in the Japanese language. This proved an effective instrument of cultural destabilisation. Such a policy allowed for no linguistic variation, regardless of geographic location, racial difference or historical and cultural differentiation. Use of the Ainu language and the practice of Ainu customs were forbidden.

As a result of the enforced use of Japanese, Ainu declined over time to the point where it was no longer in daily use but was preserved in an oral tradition of epics, songs and stories. The dominant academic discourse on Ainu throughout the 20th century stressed its impending demise; indeed, the Ethnologue website even at the present time says of Ainu that it is 'nearly extinct' (Gordon, 2005). Maher, however, reminds us that while Ainu may not be widely spoken, it remains

> a language of archival and literary study, recitation, speech contests and song – from traditional to jazz – with a radio program, newsletters and Ainu festivals that feature the language and scores of small language classes throughout Hokkaido. (Maher, 2002: 172)

The radio programme and other classes are largely due to a recent improvement in the profile of Ainu brought about by the enactment in 1997 of the Ainu Cultural Promotion Act (CPA), commonly referred to as the Ainu New Law, which replaced the earlier assimilation Act of 1899. The 1980s were a decade of increased international attention to indigenous minorities. Following an inflammatory remark by then Prime Minister Nakasone Yasuhiro in 1986 to the effect that Japan was a mono-ethnic nation as the Ainu had been completely assimilated and no longer retained their own language and culture, Ainu activists became increasingly vocal. A report produced following a 1995 'Round Table on a Policy for the Ainu People', which found that only an extremely limited number of people were still able to speak the language, recommended legislative and other measures to conserve and promote Ainu language and culture. In 1997, when the Sapporo District Court ruled on a case brought by two Ainu men over the construction of a dam on ancestral lands, it found that – Prime Minister Nakasone's claim to mono-ethnicity notwithstanding – the Ainu did in fact constitute a minority under the terms of Article 27 of the International Covenant on Civil and Political Rights, which Japan had ratified in 1979. This minority status entailed recognition of the rights of separate culture and language.

Soon after, in May 1997, the CPA replaced the disputed Protection Act. The new law stipulated that prefectures develop programmes to foster Ainu culture; this included taking steps to see that the Ainu language did not die out. Consequently, the 1997 budget papers for the Ministry of Education made provision for setting aside subsidies jointly with the Hokkaido Development Agency located in the then Prime Minister's Office in order to implement the new law (Ministry of Education, 1997: 19). This resulted in the setting up of the jointly run FRPAC a month after the new law was passed. As part of its activities, the Foundation trains Ainu-language instructors through three intensive courses each year and conducts Ainu language classes, both through classroom instruction at more than a dozen places around Hokkaido and through radio broadcasts. Weekly Ainu language lessons are broadcast on radio by Sapporo TV and can also be accessed online at http://www.stv.ne.jp/radio/ainugo/index.html. FM-Nibutani, also known as FM-Pipaushi, a community FM radio station staffed by volunteers in Biratori, Hokkaido, has been broadcasting in Ainu since 2001 and can now also be heard on the Internet at http://www.aa.alpha-net.ne.jp/skayano/menu.html.

The first Ainu language schools in Japan actually predated the new law: the Nibutani Ainu Language School was opened in 1983 by prominent activist and politician Kayano Shigeru, and another opened in Asahikawa in 1987 (Hanazaki, 1996: 125). These were private operations, however; it was the CPA that led to government-sponsored teaching of the language. While it is probably still too early for any meaningful evaluation of how successful these policy-supported measures have been in revitalising the study and spread of Ainu, the Foundation's work represents an about-face from the government's earlier neglect of this language.

Ainu is thus the only language other than Japanese and English for which top-level policy has been developed. That policy, formulated in response to both international and domestic pressures, is only a decade old and is perforce narrowly focused. The four main activities of FRPAC are the promotion of research on the Ainu, the revival of the Ainu language, the revival of Ainu culture and the dissemination of and education about Ainu traditions: in other words, a complete reversal of the former policy which led to the suppression of those things. Not everyone has been happy with the outcomes regarding increased teaching of Ainu: Siddle, for instance, notes that

> most Ainu pour their creative energies into dance and handicrafts rather than Ainu-language cultural production and ... in fact most of the Ainu language classes in Hokkaido are attended by Japanese. (Siddle, 2002: 14)

Nevertheless, official recognition and promotion of the language is a considerable improvement on the earlier situation in which its existence was virtually ignored other than as a topic for academic research.

Okinawan

The largest ethnic minority group in Japan today is the Okinawan people who live in the southernmost prefecture of Okinawa, a Pacific Ocean island chain with a population of approximately 1.3 million located between Amami-Ōshima near Kyushu in the north and Yonaguni-jima near Taiwan in the south. Around 300,000 Okinawans also live in other parts of Japan and a similar number in overseas communities such as that in Hawaii (Taira, 1997: 142). As Okinawa is a prefecture of Japan, Standard Japanese is spoken and taught in schools. Older people speak Okinawan languages as well, although younger people show a tendency to monolingualism in the dominant standard as they shift away from areas in which older bilinguals live (Matsumori, 1995: 40). Natural intergenerational transmission is thought to have ceased after 1950 (Heinrich, 2004: 153).

Okinawan, unintelligible to speakers of Standard Japanese, is not a dialect of Japanese as has been claimed in the past for political purposes of nation-building, but is an independent language believed to have diverged from Japanese before the eighth century CE. Okinawan (also referred to as Ryukyuan) encompasses many different dialects spoken throughout the chain of islands. The central Shuri dialect has functioned as the standard form since the fifteenth century, when it was used as the official and literary language of the then Ryukyuan Kingdom.

As with Hokkaido and the Ainu in the north, an assimilation policy was applied to the people of Okinawa in the south when the islands were annexed to become the new prefecture of Okinawa in 1897. Ethnicity was again transformed to serve state interests: the Okinawans were said to be Japanese now and must speak Japanese. Okinawan children were educated in Japanese using Japanese-language textbooks, and, as we saw earlier, those found using their own dialect at school instead of the standard were ridiculed and shamed by being made to wear the *hōgen fuda*. So unwavering was the prefectural emphasis on the inculcation of the standard in Okinawa that when in 1940 visiting philosopher and founder of the folk art movement Yanagi Sōetsu suggested that the standard language campaign was harmful to the preservation of regional linguistic traditions, he was roundly rebuffed by the Okinawans themselves, who supported the use of Standard Japanese in the name of economic advancement and a liberation from the prejudice incurred by their economically backward condition (Clarke, 1997).

During the 1990s, not only on the mainland but also in Okinawa itself, an 'Okinawa boom', led to a large extent by popular bands combining elements of traditional Okinawan music with modern genres, contributed to a new view of Okinawa as having a rich and varied local culture. As with speakers of Japanese dialects, comedians use Okinawan language for dramatic effect on television. While Standard Japanese remains the norm and is increasingly the only language spoken by younger Okinawans, in limited quarters there is a renewed sense of the importance of the Okinawan language. One website offering

Okinawan language lessons, for instance, opens with the uncompromising declaration that 'Japanese IS NOT the native language of Okinawa'.[11] As with Ainu and indeed Japanese itself, the Internet is a useful source of online introductions to the language, usually offering basic phrases and vocabulary.

Korean

Korean is spoken by many of the large ethnic minority of permanent-resident Koreans (*zainichi kankokujin*) and more recently arrived migrants and international students in Japan. The most recent figures available show a total of 607,419 Korean residents at the end of 2004 (Japan Statistical Yearbook, 2006); some of these are newcomers, but the majority are old-comers, the largest such community in Japan. Of the latter, however, it cannot be assumed that all speak Korean: many are third- or fourth-generation residents who speak only Japanese. Only around 20% of young resident Koreans are estimated to be able to speak Korean (Fukuoka, 2000: 27). Also not included in the 2004 figures are those Korean residents who have taken Japanese citizenship, some of whom do speak Korean. The Korean population is mainly clustered in large urban centres such as Tokyo and Osaka. Many of Japan's international students (12.8% of the total in 2005; 15,506 people) are from South Korea (Japan Student Services Organization, 2006).

Although resident Koreans, like Okinawans and Ainu people, have long experienced discrimination of various kinds, a 'Korea boom' in recent years, based on popular culture and helped along by the co-hosting of the soccer World Cup in 2002, resulted in what Maher (2002: 176) has called 'Korean cool', that is, an interest in Korea-related travel, body products, rock music, films and television drama (in particular a Korean soap opera called 'Winter Sonata' in 2004) and food. *Zainichi* authors (writing in Japanese, not Korean) have won prestigious Japanese literary awards. In theory, this surge of interest could perhaps bring about a change in mindset about the Korean language, in that hearing Korean spoken or sung in certain contexts could result in a realisation that Korean is being spoken *in Japan* by people who live there, rather than by visitors. In practice, however, passing enthusiasms for another culture usually do little to result in more generalised exposure to its language outside communities of heritage speakers.

While most of the children of the postwar wave of immigrants attend Japanese schools, ethnic community schools also offer curricula in both Korean and Japanese and their 1000 or so annual graduates can now sit the entrance examinations for national universities. Until 2004, this had not been possible for graduates of Korean schools (and other ethnic schools in Japan),[12] although they could and did apply to private and prefectural/municipal universities (Fukuoka, 2000: 26). Since 1997, students have been able to choose Chinese as a foreign language for university entrance exams, along with English, German and French; Korean was added in 2002 (Izumi *et al.*, 2003). Both Mindan (the Korean Residents Union, pro-South Korea) and Sōren (General Association of Korean Residents in Japan, pro-North Korea, also known as Chongryun) run school systems teaching curricula both in Korean and Japanese. Chongryun has many more schools than Mindan and also runs the four-year Korea University in Tokyo (see Ryang, 1997 for details of structures and curriculum). A 2005 comparison of the curriculum at Chongryun and Japanese primary and middle schools shows the major difference to be the time spent on teaching Korean at the former, which takes time away from the hours spent teaching Japanese; in other curriculum areas the differences are small (Chongryun, 2005). Other avenues through which Korean is taught include community education classes, private language schools and weekly classes on NHK, the national broadcaster.

Ethnic newspapers such as the Chongryun-affiliated *Choson Sinbo*, Mindan's weekly *Mindan Shimbun* (in Korean and Japanese) and others are available in both print and online versions. The Choson Sinbo company publishes the daily *Choson Sinbo* in Korean, *Chōsen Shimpō* in Japanese, and *The People's Korea* in English (Chongryun, 1997). Chongryun's other output includes regional guides (in Japanese) for Korean residents' activities, available too from its website. Korean papers published by ethnic media meant for Koreans encompass 'new-comer media' (aimed at recently arrived international students and migrant workers and published in Korean) and 'old-timer media' (meant for the second- and third-generation resident Korean population and published in Japanese). There are several Korean bookstores in Tokyo and Osaka. SKY PerfecTV broadcasts a Korean-language channel, KN Television. The Tokyo-based Korean News website (http://www.kcna.co.jp/), provides news in Korean and English from the Korean Central News Agency owned by the government of North Korea. Domestic websites providing information in Korean, Japanese and sometimes English include Korea Info (http://www.korea.co.jp/), Han World (www.han.org), the websites of the major groups such as Chongryun and Mindan, and many others, including individual sites.[13]

The breadth of what is available to Korean residents in terms of schooling and both print and visual media highlights the length of time this community has formed part of Japanese society. The same is true of another major ethnic group, the Chinese community.

Chinese

At the end of 2004, 487,570 Chinese people (including those from Taiwan, Macao and Hong Kong) were registered as foreign residents with Japan's Ministry of Justice (Japan Statistical Yearbook, 2006), including among their number Japan's second-largest old-comer community. Early immigrants settled along the east coast in the port cities of Yokohama, Nagasaki and Kobe. A comment in a short story by one of Japan's best known writers of contemporary fiction, Murakami Haruki, illustrates this: 'the town where I went to high school was a port town, so there were quite a few Chinese around' (Murakami, 2003: 225). Today, most of Japan's Chinese community lives in populous urban areas, such as the Tokyo-Yokohama strip, the Kansai area of western Japan and parts of Southern Kyushu outside the Chinatown areas in which they were originally settled in the early modern period. Most of the postwar immigrants speak Mandarin, unlike the majority of prewar immigrants who spoke Cantonese (Maher, 1995: 126, 127). Patterns of residence tend to reflect province of origin in China (Vasishth, 1997: 134). International students from China accounted for 66.2% of all international students in Japan in 2005, by far the biggest group at over 80,000 people, with another 3.4% from Taiwan (Japan Student Services Organization, 2006).

In 2003 there were five Chinese ethnic schools remaining in Japan, two in the port city of Yokohama and one each in Tokyo, Osaka and Kobe. The Tokyo Chinese School, for example, teaches Chinese, English and Japanese languages in addition to other curricula. Around a third of its students are Japanese; the remainder are from China and Taiwan. The 2003 student body numbered 352 across all levels. This school is accredited as a comprehensive school by MEXT, with 80% of its graduates being admitted to universities and colleges, mostly in Japan but also in Taiwan and other countries. The Yokohama Overseas Chinese School is the oldest in Japan; like the others, it teaches three languages; 15% of its students are Japanese, among them ethnic Chinese with Japanese nationality. Students in this latter category also make up 40% of the student body of the Kobe Chinese School. Depending on the school, the same textbooks found in Japanese schools are used in various subjects, supplemented by other textbooks from Taiwan (Center of Overseas Chinese Studies, Takushoku University, 2003).

At least 30 Chinese-language newspapers and newspapers are in circulation: they include Tokyo's weekly *Zhongwen Daobao* and *Chūbun*, the monthly *Kansai Kabun Jihō* in the Osaka area and the biweekly *Chūnichi Shinpō* (both the latter are also published in Japanese). Web-based news sites such as RakuRaku China (http://www.rakuraku.co.jp/club/), China Forum (http://www.cf.net/) and China Online Magazines (http://www.come.or.jp/) provide other outlets for use of Chinese in Japan. The *Zainichi Kakyō* (Chinese living in Japan) website at http://www.cnjp.net/ provides Chinese-language information, bulletin-board services and chat rooms. Small publishing firms such as Nihon Kyohosha (http://duan.jp/) sell Chinese-language books online, while others such as Kyoto's Chuban Shuppansha have their own bookstore. Major bookshops in Tokyo and Osaka include Chinese-language books in their foreign language sections, as do some of the larger prefectural and municipal libraries. As we saw earlier, FM Cocolo, Japan's first multilingual radio station, offers programmes in 14 languages, among them Chinese, Indonesian, Portuguese, Spanish, Tagalog, Thai and Vietnamese. Radio Japan Online broadcasts overseas news in 22 languages, again including Chinese, over the Internet; other languages offered that are relevant to large foreign communities within Japan include English, Korean, Portuguese, Spanish and Vietnamese. Podcasting is also available in those languages. NHK includes Chinese in its list of weekly language learning broadcasts and of course Chinese is offered at many private language schools, as are the other languages discussed in this section.

Extending language planning to proactively fostering and targeting the use and study of regional languages such as Korean and Chinese could prove a strategy which would help Japan not only in its domestic but also in its external foreign relations. In addition to the large resident communities, the majority of the foreign students and trainees studying or working in Japan are from South Korea, China and other areas of East and South East Asia (MEXT, 2006a). Positive recognition and uptake of this existing linguistic resource in regional languages could conceivably play a part in helping to ease current tensions between Japan and its Asian neighbours over lingering wartime hostilities. This was recognised in 2000 in a report commissioned by then Prime Minister Obuchi on Japan's goals for the new century, which recommended that the teaching of Chinese and Korean be dramatically expanded as a strategy for improving neighbourly relations with those two countries (Prime Minister's Commission, 2000). While it is true that English is used as a lingua franca in communication throughout the region, the affective benefits of placing increased importance on communicating in the local languages rather than relying on English could be considerable, particularly in terms of reciprocity: China and Korea had the world's largest numbers of students of Japanese outside Japan at the time of the Japan Foundation's most recent survey in 2003 (Japan Foundation, 2003).

Turning now to the languages spoken by more recent immigrants to Japan, we find further evidence of flourishing linguistic diversity.

Portuguese

Portuguese is spoken by the large numbers of immigrants from Brazil, most of whom are descendants of early 20th-century Japanese immigrants to that country who have come back to Japan to work (see Hirataka *et al.*, 2000). In 1990, the Immigration Control and Refugee Recognition Act was amended to make it easier for *nikkei* (people of Japanese descent living in other countries) to work in Japan by allowing them access to residential visas with no work restrictions. At around 286,557 people in 2004 (Ministry of Justice Japan, 2004), Portuguese speakers are the largest ethnic group after resident Koreans and Chinese. They cluster mainly in the prefectures stretching between Tokyo and Osaka. In all 15 cities covered by the Council for Cities with High Concentrations of Foreign Residents (hereafter CCHCFR), a body formed in 2001, Brazilians accounted for the highest concentrations in April 2004 (CCHCFR, 2004). Most work as manual labourers in the automobile, electronics and food-manufacturing sectors (Higuchi, 2006).

Portuguese-language community schools have been set up in areas with large numbers of Brazilian immigrants;[14] some children attend for three days a week after their Japanese school day finishes, others do not go to Japanese schools at all but rather attend community schools only. Brazilian schools began to appear around 1995. The Japan Association of Brazilian Schools (JABS), which holds monthly meetings to discuss issues faced by Brazilian children, was set up in March 2002, by which time there were 20 authorised schools in existence: most concentrated in nine prefectures including Shizuoka and Aichi, with another 12 seeking accreditation from Brazil's Ministry of Education that year (Nikkei Shakai, 2002). JABS figures for 2005 show 75 schools, a marked increase over the intervening three years (Burajiru Gakkō Kyōgikai, 2005).

Following a visit by the Brazilian president to Japan in 2005, the 'Japan-Brazil Council for the Twenty-first Century' was established. In 2006, this body issued a report on future Japan-Brazil initiatives which included the recommendation that both governments provide support for Brazilian schools in Japan as well as providing funds for scholarships, Portuguese-language teaching materials and the development of distance education in Portuguese (Nippaku 21 Seiki Kyōgikai, 2006). No details are as yet available of what form this support will take, but it would seem to ensure a stronger future for the education of Portuguese-speaking children in Japan.

The Portuguese community is well served by a large number of Portuguese-language media. Weekly magazine *International Press*, founded in 1991 to serve the Brazilian community, had already achieved a putative circulation of 55,000 by 1996 (Trends in Japan, 1996), not much below its current circulation of 60,000 which makes it the most widely sold weekly ethnic newspaper in Japan.[15] Since 1999, the paper has been available online at http://www.ipcdigital.com/br/. Other newspapers include *Tudo Bem* and *Nova Visao* (Hamamatsu). Portuguese-language television is available through satellite channel SKY PerfecTV, and some FM stations offer Portuguese-language programs (Shiramizu, 2004a, 2004b). Websites such as <http://www.brazil.ne.jp/> provide information promoting Brazil in Japanese and a wide range of information such as the location of ethnic schools teaching in Portuguese for migrants living in Japan.

Spanish

Nikkei and other immigrants from Peru and other Spanish-speaking parts of South America account for most of the Spanish spoken in Japan. The 2000 census figures showed 41,309 Spanish-speaking foreigners from South America, 1222 from Mexico and only 1183 from Spain (compared to 188,355 Portuguese speakers from Brazil). Like the Brazilian immigrants, many work on production lines in the automobile, electronics and other manufacturing industries in large urban centres. Four of the cities overseen by the Council for Cities with High Concentrations of Foreign Residents mentioned above listed people from Peru as their second highest concentration of foreign residents in 2004. Ethnic schools are not as much a feature as they are in the Brazilian community, given the comparatively small size of this group, although some do operate.

The International Press publishes a Spanish-language edition; other Spanish-language print media include free monthlies *Wakaranai* (Tokyo), *Hyogo Latino* (Kobe) and *Mercado Latino* (Osaka). Spanish radio and television programmes are available, and websites such as Japan en Espanol (http://www.japonenespanol. com/) provide topical news and other information about Japan in Spanish for Japan's Spanish-speaking Latin American community. Spanish speakers also work in and/or run ethnic restaurants, as is true for most of the other ethnicities named here.

Tagalog

Migrants from the Philippines numbered 93,662 in the 2000 census figures. In 2004, residents from the Philippines made up the second largest concentration of foreign residents in the cities of Hamamatsu, Fuji (both in Shizuoka Prefecture), Kani and Minokamo (both in Gifu Prefecture), and the third largest concentration in Oizumi (Gunma Prefecture), Toyohashi (Aichi), Iida (Nagano), Iwata and Kosai (both in Shizuoka) (CCHCFR, 2004). A Filipino television channel has been available by satellite through SKY PerfecTV since 2000, and a Philippines-Japan portal is maintained at <http://www.winsphil.co.jp/>. Newspapers such as the monthly *Kaibigan* (published in English, Japanese and Tagalog) and *Philippines Today* (in English) serve this community.

Vietnamese

The 2000 census figures showed 12,965 Vietnamese residents, many of them either refugees or workers under the technical intern trainee program (which since 1993 has allowed people to remain in Japan for 'on the job' training after their training is completed). They work largely in Tokyo and in nearby Kanagawa, in the textile, service, construction and printing industries. Online services such as those provided by the Vietnamese Youths and Students

Association in Japan (http://www.vysa.jp/index.php) provide information and chat services under the banner of keeping the community connected. Like things Korean and Okinawan, things Vietnamese have been the subject of a cultural 'craze' in recent years; the number of Vietnamese restaurants has mushroomed, as has that of Vietnamese market and clothing stores, and tourism to Vietnam has boomed (Carruthers, 2004: 407). Vietnam was one of Japan's five top source countries for international students in 2005, with 1745 students (Japan Student Services Organization, 2006).

English

The English-speaking community in Japan (i.e. those who speak English as their first language) includes long-term residents, international students, business professionals, diplomats, journalists, the many teachers of English as a Foreign Language and a wide range of others from English-speaking countries. English is incontestably the most widely spoken and promoted foreign language in Japan: while the numbers of native English speakers are small compared to the larger ethnic communities, Japanese students are required to study English at middle and high school for six years (see subsequent discussion). Most native-speaker children are educated at one of the many international schools where the curriculum is taught in English.

English speakers are well served by the press and other media in Japan. The *Yomiuri*, *Asahi* and *Mainichi* newspapers publish English-language editions, although the *Mainichi*'s English version is now available only online; the others remain available in both print and online form. The *Asahi* also publishes the English-language *Asahi Weekly*, the *Mainichi* the English-and-Japanese *Mainichi Weekly* and the *Nikkei* the English-language *Nikkei Weekly*. The major English-only newspaper is *The Japan Times*, which publishes both a daily and a weekly version. Many English-language magazines such as *Weekender*, *Tokyo Journal*, *Metropolis*, *Kansai Now* and *Kansai Time-Out* provide lifestyle and entertainment information, and the *Japan Echo* journal publishes English translations of topical articles from Japanese magazines and newspapers. Many local English-language websites are available for information of various kinds: as noted earlier, 20 of the top-level web pages of the 23 special wards of central Tokyo, for example, offer web pages in English. Most English-language western films are subtitled rather than dubbed into Japanese, and bilingual television and radio broadcasting means that access to English programmes is relatively freely available across a range of broadcasters.

Education of minority-language children

The preceding discussion of language use in Japan highlights the fact that Japan, despite its mainstream discourse, is far from being a monolingual or ethnically homogeneous polity: it has an indigenous minority, large communities of Brazilian, Chinese and Korean residents and many other smaller ethnic groups. At present, immigration levels have increased to an extent not dreamed of in the postwar years when existing language policies were formulated. The general environment both inside and outside the country is very different from the earlier more insular era, with increasing global interaction encompassing tourism, educational exchange, job seeking, migration and business ventures.

Many of the foreign workers in Japan return to their own countries after a few years; others decide to stay longer, some become permanent residents. Even those who stay only a few years, however, may have children of school age who need education. Some choose to send their children to ethnic schools where those are available; the great advantage of an ethnic school run by the community concerned is, of course, that it 'can create an environment where [its] language and culture are the *central* concern' (Kanno, 2003: 139) rather than peripheral. Others send their children to Japanese schools; still others choose a combination of the two. The most recent available MEXT data show the number of children of immigrants in the school system to be rising each year: in 2005, there were 20,692 students reported as needing instruction in Japanese as a second language (JSL) in the education system, a 5.2% increase over the previous year, 93.5% of them in primary and middle schools. Of the total, only 85% were actually receiving such instruction in school. Of the students' first languages, seven – Portuguese (36.5%), Chinese (21.6%), Spanish (15.3%), Filipino (10.5%), Korean (4.2%), Vietnamese (3.6%) and English (2.4%) – accounted for 94%, with a total of 54 first languages being reported (MEXT, 2006b).[16] The remedial JSL classes offered in schools, however, are often on a rather ad hoc basis. Language classes for adult immigrants are offered through local government and community outlets.

The educational prospects for the rising numbers of immigrant children in Japanese schools are slowly being addressed at national level, although much more remains to be done: in 2005, of the 5281 schools with foreign students, just under half had only one person teaching Japanese as a second language (*The Japan Times*, 27 April 2006). The Agency for Cultural Affairs within MEXT coordinates the training of volunteer JSL teachers and of JSL volunteer coordinators. In 2005, for example, courses for coordinators were carried out in six prefectures and volunteer induction courses in eight (Agency for Cultural Affairs, 2007). At local government level, some schools work directly with the local community to meet language needs: in the city of Ota in Gunma prefecture, home to many Brazilian immigrants working in the automobile industry, for example, the board of education has published for the 226 Portuguese-speaking students currently in primary schools there supplementary readers in Portuguese which translate material from the third- to sixth-grade social studies texts containing Japanese terms students find hard to understand (*The Japan Times*, 18 April 2006). A wide range of Japanese classes taught by volunteers is also available in Ota, as is the case in other cities. In Tsukuba, near Tokyo, for example, volunteers teach JSL classes in some elementary and middle schools as well as in the wider community.

Immigrants themselves are active in carving out new identities in Japan. Language issues are important both in their daily lives and those of their children as well as to their long-term prospects. Local networks such as Solidarity Network with Migrants Japan (SMJ) and Rights of Immigrants Network in Kansai (RINK) have been set up to assist new arrivals. Some local governments in areas where migrants cluster have also set up foreign residents' assemblies which enable migrants a greater degree of participation in public life (Kashiwazaki, 2002, 2003). Clearly, the acceptance of growing multiculturalism and its attendant language implications is proceeding at a much more rapid pace at grassroots level than at the national level.

Language Spread Through the Education System

Introduction

Language spread is defined by Cooper (1989: 33) simply as 'an increase in the users or the uses of a language or language variety'. The main channel of language maintenance and spread in Japan outside of the media and ethnic schools described earlier is of course the national education system, supplemented by a booming private sector teaching languages for commercial profit. As noted previously, the two major foci for the national education system in terms of language spread are the national language and English. Although other foreign languages are taught in schools, their profile is not large.

As Eastman (1983: 103) notes, the role of the education system is pivotal in the dissemination of language policy, and language planning is an aspect of all education in the form of literacy training. The United Nations Development Office Human Development Report for 2003 assigned Japan an adult literacy rate of 99%, where adult literacy was defined as 'the percentage of people aged 15 and above who can, with understanding, both read and write a short, simple statement related to their everyday life' (United Nations Development Programme, 2003). This figure is problematic, of course, since a certain percentage of any population – usually more than 1% – will have learning or other disabilities that inhibit reading and/or writing or will be recent migrants not yet familiar with the language. The definition of literacy itself is also problematic: it represents only a base level and does not take cognisance of the sophisticated operations needed for full literacy in Japanese, given the nature of the orthography. The 99% figure would only begin to approach reality if it referred to writing in the phonetic hiragana script alone, but even children at the end of the first year of elementary schooling are expected to have begun to learn to use characters, and character use escalates over the next eight years until all of the Characters for General Use have been taught. Achievement levels in reading in Japan are partly judged by the degree of script acquisition (Tamaoka, 1996). To attain functional literacy in the language involves many years of hard work in school.

This is not to imply, of course, that literacy rates in Japan are not high. Japan is a highly educated, highly literate society, as exemplified by its large publishing industry, extensive holdings in public libraries and circulation figures for newspapers and magazines. The 99% figure, however, is unrealistic both in its assessment of the makeup of the population and, in Japan's case, in its requirements for functional literacy. It ignores those parts of the population whose existence makes clear that the real figure is very different, and those surveys and research studies that have shown that university students have not always reached the levels of literacy expected at the end of high school. The literacy debate also subsumes the link between literacy and citizenship for migrants: given that access to written language – and thus to information – is a key factor in a citizen's full participation in society, an important emerging issue is whether the nature of the Japanese writing system and the time it takes migrants to master it will play a determining role in access to citizenship (Galan, 2005).

This section will discuss first the education system, explaining the details of how Japanese is taught, how and why English is taught, and the situation with regard to the teaching of other foreign languages. It will then move on to a brief discussion of the promotion and teaching of Japanese as a foreign language and of private sector language schools.

Japanese

Japanese is taught in *kokugo* classes to all students enrolled in Japanese schools at all levels: elementary (six years), middle (three years) and secondary (three years). Compulsory education, which begins at the age of six, finishes at the end of middle school, that is, nine years. National curriculum guidelines for all subjects, including Japanese language, are set by MEXT.

Although teaching children to read and write officially begins in the first year of elementary school, many children have exposure to hiragana through participating in unstructured kindergarten activities and through looking at books bought for them by their parents, so that by the time they enter the compulsory education years they are familiar with this syllabary. A large-scale survey by the then National Language Research Institute in Tokyo between 1967 and 1970 found that 95% of five-year-olds could read hiragana five months before they started school (Sakamoto, 1981), and that a month before school started they knew the meanings and at least one pronunciation of 53 of the kanji taught in Years One and Two (Taylor & Taylor, 1995: 342).

Japanese is not written with a phonetic syllabary alone but with a combination of the two phonetic kana scripts and a very large number of kanji. Hiragana thus represent only the first step on the ladder to literacy. The 1006 Education Kanji taught by the end of elementary school were selected by the policy makers on the basis of relative simplicity, relevance to daily-life functioning and ability to form compounds. By the end of Year One, children have been introduced to all three scripts in their *kokugo* class and have mastered about 80 kanji. Table 1 indicates the number of characters taught at each year level. All 1945 of the Kanji for General Use are to be learned by the end of the period of compulsory education, which leaves 939 to be learned during the three years of middle school.

The kanji for Year One[17] are simple in form and relevant to the lives of six-year-olds; they include, for example, numbers, colours and the first characters of the days of the week. Instruction begins gently in the first year, with only one

Table 1 Number of kanji taught per year at elementary school

Year	*Number of kanji taught*
One	80
Two	160
Three	200
Four	200
Five	185
Six	181

Source: *Gakushū Shidō Yōryō: Kokugo* (Ministry of Education, 1998)

reading (pronunciation) taught for each kanji, usually the *kun* reading, for example, *yama* and not *san* or the other possible *on* readings for 山 'mountain' (Taylor & Taylor, 1995: 347–348). Both the number and complexity of character shapes increase in the following years. In their fourth year students are also introduced to the Roman alphabet. Methods by which the characters are taught include writing in the air, color charts showing radicals (the common elements under which characters are grouped), rote practice on squared sheets of paper, build-up methods and a range of other techniques (Bourke, 1996: 167–174). The whole-class method observed by Mason *et al.* (1989) remains normal practice, with an emphasis on both oral and silent reading and on teacher-centred practices. Much as children whose first language is English achieve variable results in spelling, the ideal of perfect retention of characters and their readings may not always be reached: a 1988 survey report on children in three of Japan's 47 prefectures, for example, showed that at both elementary and high school levels students were better able to recognize than to reproduce kanji by hand, and that knowledge of *on* and *kun* readings fluctuated (Kokuritsu Kokugo Kenkyūjo, 1988: 389–391).

Assessment is internal by teacher rather than through any national scheme, at least until students wish to progress beyond the compulsory period of schooling, at which time they sit the entrance examinations for their high school of choice. Middle school assessment in *kokugo* classes is therefore largely focused on preparing students for the high school entrance examinations in language. In 2007, a national system of testing students in language and mathematics in the final years of both elementary and middle school was implemented, with the first test day scheduled for 24 April. Questions will focus on both core knowledge and application of that knowledge. In the case of *kokugo*, this means among other things ability to read and write kanji and know what they mean, understand the meaning of a text and compose effective texts, collect and order information, and evaluate the content of written information (MEXT, 2007).

Students in the first year of elementary school study *kokugo* for a total of 272 hours, a much greater allocation that the number of hours set aside for other curriculum areas such as mathematics (114 hours). This reflects prioritisation of the time needed to learn to read and to write. At each year level in elementary school, *kokugo* hours account for the largest share of the curriculum. By the sixth and final year, by which time students are familiar with the manner in which the scripts interact and are concentrating on accelerated kanji acquisition, the allocation drops to 175 hours, with 55 of these spent on writing (as opposed to 90 in the earlier years). In middle school, a first-year student spends 140 hours on Japanese classes (again, much more than the 105 allocated to math, science, society and foreign languages), and a student in the third year (the final year of compulsory education) spends 105 hours. Class hours have seen an across-the-board reduction in recent years, reflecting the decision to phase out Saturday-morning school attendance in 2002.

The objectives for the language curriculum, which of course include more than just character acquisition, are set out in the Ministry's *Gakushū Shidō Yōryo* (Course of Study Guidelines) for Japanese language. These are the main instrument of language-in-education policy and all teachers are expected to adhere to them. The Guidelines, set at the national level by the Ministry, have been revised seven times since 1947, approximately once each decade. The last substantial revision occurred in late 1998, for implementation from 2002.[18] The overall contemporary objectives for *kokugo* classes reflect a post-1998 shift from language as skill to language for communication. They are: to teach children to express themselves appropriately and to understand others accurately; to facilitate the ability to communicate with others; to foster thinking, imagination and language awareness; and to nurture an attitude of respect for and interest in language. Specific objectives are set for different year levels in two-year bands. Teachers develop their own materials and approaches within the framework of the guidelines; the only centrally designated specific item that must be followed to the letter is the list of characters to be learned at each level (Lee *et al.,* 1996: 163).

Years One and Two objectives focus on speaking about, listening to, writing and reading about things children have experienced or imagined. Strategies to achieve each objective are specified: with regard to writing, for example, students are asked to collect material in order to fulfill a particular writing task, to keep the reader and purpose of their writing in mind, to pay attention to making sequence clear and so on. During this phase they encounter such basic knowledge as the relationship between subject and predicate and how to use punctuation. They are also introduced to the difference, very important in Japan, between ordinary language and honorific language; most children will already have some understanding of this through parental instruction in how to behave when addressing others, particularly older people. By the time students reach Years Five and Six, the objectives have advanced to include inculcating an awareness of the diversity of language use found within Japanese itself; they are taught to read simple *bungochō* (older literary style) passages, to be familiar with different types of sentence construction and to understand the difference between dialects and Standard Japanese, while still of course speaking in the latter (Ministry of Education, 1998).

The middle school *kokugo* objectives are almost identical to those for the primary school curriculum but at a higher level, with communication and reception of ideas through the four skills again emphasised. Students at first-year level, for example, are asked to research topics and present their own ideas on the issues clearly and accurately; to edit their own writing for expression, orthography and description in order to ensure that their work is easy to read and understand; and to read each other's written work to promote cross-fertilisation of ideas about research. During the following two years, the focus on expressing opinions is sharpened and the purpose of reading classmates' work is expanded to include checking for logical development of ideas. Students at this level are expected to be able to differentiate accurately between dialects and standard language and to grasp the role of each in society, and to be able to use honorifics appropriately in their daily lives. They are taught different genres of writing, including essays, letters and reports, with the time allocated to writing accounting for 'around 20–30%' of the total (Ministry of Education, 1998).

At high school level, the earlier objectives are expanded to include polishing language awareness and deepening interest in the culture of language, maintaining a strong focus on expression. The curriculum at this level is divided into

Japanese Expression I and II, which stress personal expression and language awareness through speaking, listening and writing skills; Integrated Japanese, which adds a focus on reading skills and textual appreciation; Modern Literature (post-1868 texts); Classical Literature, where students are taught Sino-Japanese and other older styles necessary for reading classical texts, which are then contrasted with modern Japanese in order to develop an awareness of language change; and finally, Translating the Classics, in which the classics themselves are read.

In theory, then, those students who leave at the end of middle school (i.e. the end of the period of compulsory education) have mastered all 1945 characters on the List of Characters for General Use and may be assumed to be equipped to read and write fluently. The more than 90% who go on to complete a further three years of high school education are taught a further list of characters used in personal names and receive expanded education in language use and appreciation. In practice, though, as we saw earlier, surveys have shown that not all students – for a variety of reasons, including disability, non-attendance or less than diligent application to study – do in fact reach these levels. College professors have been bemoaning students' less than perfect ability to write characters for at least 20 years (see e.g. Katō, 1985). A 1999 survey into the nature of *kokugo* literacy instruction in high schools found that students were doing insufficient in-class writing to prepare them for the level of academic literacy required for study at university, to the extent that many final-year students were receiving private tutoring to prepare them for the essay-writing component of university entrance examinations (Kobayashi, 2002). At a lower level, adult education classes in Japan often contain people struggling to achieve levels of functional literacy. In some areas, as Maher and Kawanishi (1995: 93) found, such classes are populated by older ethnic Korean residents who, although they speak Japanese, have never learned to read and write it.

School refusers, children with learning difficulties and minority language children are not the only ones who may struggle with language education in Japanese schools. Returnee children (*kikokushijo*), that is, children who have spent time abroad – often several years – during their parents' overseas postings, may also experience difficulty achieving full literacy in Japanese if they have not attended Japanese Saturday schools where they were living overseas to keep up with the Japanese school curriculum. Kanno (2003: 15) found in one such Saturday school in Toronto 'an extraordinary range of Japanese literacy levels' among the students of her Grade 12 class; while some were reading and writing at the expected Year 12 levels, others were struggling at Year Two or Three levels. In 2004, there were a total of 10,068 returnee children in Japanese schools,[19] almost 6000 of them at elementary school and the rest at middle and high school. Such students, depending on their individual experiences, may return to Japan with advanced language skills in the language of the country in which they had been living, but with Japanese literacy skills fossilised at or a little above the level at which they last attended school in Japan.

Much has been written about *kikokushijo* in both academic and mass media circles. A huge literature exists detailing the problems returnees face when they attempt to integrate back into the Japanese education system and the strategies that have been adopted to deal with this (see e.g. Pang, 2000). Before the 1980s emphasis on internationalisation, their experience upon return to Japan was often not positive. They attracted criticism for behaviour considered too brash for Japanese students, and for poor language skills – in line with the Nihonjinron tenets linking language and nation, 'deficiency in Japanese language was considered synonymous with deficiency in being Japanese' (Kanno, 2003: 18). More recently, however, their intercultural experience and skills in other languages have come to be viewed as offering benefits to their home society, and many universities offer a special quota for such students. It is now possible to take a special *kikokushijo* entrance examination instead of the standard university entrance examination. This enhancement of stature may be partly due to the increased government emphasis on the promotion of English since 1987. Rather than being viewed as in some way lacking, bilingual returnees today are often seen as exemplifying what the policies are trying to achieve.

The nature of language spread through the school system previously discussed displays the profile one would expect to find for a country fitting Fishman's Cluster B description, that is, a nation in which the attributes of both nation and sociocultural identity have long coincided, with an old and well established literary tradition and a relatively high existing literacy rate. One might conjecture that in such a society, the teaching of other languages will display a purely instrumental aspect. This is certainly the case when it comes to the teaching of English. In the case of other languages, however, as we shall see later, the motivation is less easy to discern.

English

By contrast with the small-scale focus of the policy on Ainu, the teaching of English has attracted both policy attention and large amounts of funding. Japanese secondary school students, as previously noted, study English for six years as a compulsory subject and often follow this with further study at university level: at most universities, students must study English for the first two years (Honna & Takeshita, 1999).

It is important to understand how English functions in relation to other languages in Japan. Put simply, as reflected in the relevant policy documents and the current specifics of language teaching in Japanese schools and universities, 'English education' is virtually synonymous with the term 'foreign language education'. The most recent Course of Study for Foreign Languages guidelines, available on the MEXT website (MEXT, 2003d), make this abundantly clear: although the 'Overall Objectives' introductory section speaks of 'foreign languages', the only one referred to by name in the rest of the document is English. Schools are enjoined that 'for compulsory foreign language instruction, English should be selected in principle', and the only nod given to other languages is a brief paragraph indicating that where they are offered as elective subjects, schools should adapt the curriculum guidelines for English. This situation has obtained for a long time: the 1951 Course of Study guidelines for the English language curriculum made it clear that no guidelines would be issued by the Ministry for the teaching of other foreign languages, as the study of such languages was minuscule in scale. Teachers of other languages, in 1951 as presently, were exhorted to refer to the Course of Study for English.

In terms of its relationship to the national language, English is understood to function pragmatically as a language of international communication, and only that, as shown by the controversy following a suggestion in 2000 that English might become an official second language of Japan at some unspecified time in the future. Although the policy documents and surrounding discourse feature the term *gaikokugo* (foreign language), the study of English is understood in Japan in the very specific sense of English as an International Language (EIL) rather than as a second or merely a foreign language, and the focus is external.

That focus was clearly articulated in the report of the Prime Minister's Commission:

> Achieving world-class excellence demands that, in addition to mastering information technology, all Japanese acquire a working knowledge of English-*not as simply a foreign language but as the international lingua franca*. English in this sense is a prerequisite for obtaining global information, expressing intentions, and sharing values. Of course the Japanese language, our mother tongue, is the basis for perpetuating Japan's culture and traditions, and study of foreign languages other than English should be actively encouraged. *Nevertheless, knowledge of English as the international lingua franca equips one with a key skill for knowing and accessing the world* (my italics). (Prime Minister's Commission, 2000)

This report on national goals for the new century, submitted by a private advisory body to then Prime Minister Obuchi in January 2000, addressed among other things the issue of 'global literacy', suggesting that to qualify as possessing this attribute people would need mastery both of information technology and of English as the international lingua franca. The report recommended that all government departments and public institutions at both national and local levels adopt a policy of producing web pages and publications in both English and Japanese and flagged the possibility of future long-term discussion on the feasibility of designating English as an official second language. Public antipathy to this latter item was strong, however, and the matter was shelved. Hashimoto (2002) reports on published reactions as variously encompassing a view that a 'second official language' really only means an official language for international communication along with fears that a can-and-cannot social divide with regard to English proficiency would emerge and that Japanese cultural identity would be threatened. One less pessimistic view, however, was that an English-driven change in communication styles would make Japan more competitive internationally.

If Japan today views the study of English as a survival skill, a competence to be acquired to assist in communication outside Japan rather than to play any substantial role within it (Torikai, 2005: 254), this is nothing new. English has always been seen in that light within this particular polity: we are inside and self-sufficient with our own language, but in order to look outside, we need English. English was first brought into middle schools as an elective subject in 1947, when it was promoted as a 'window to the world' following Japan's defeat in World War Two and the subsequent Occupation. Since 2002, when the revised Courses of Study were implemented following the introduction of the five-day school week, it has been a required subject for middle and high school students (MEXT, 2003c). Prior to that time, English was not compulsory (except at certain schools) but was studied by most students because many university degrees have a foreign language requirement, which led to an emphasis in high school and university entrance exams on English (Kitao *et al.*, 1994).

Academic analyses of Japan's relationship with English encompass a range of views. For McVeigh (2004), for example, it is a love-hate relationship: he argues that foreign language learning (predominantly English) has been seriously impaired by nationalist elements in both state and corporate culture which dismiss the humanistic value of language learning in favor of a cultural nationalism strongly influenced by the Nihonjinron nexus of language and identity (linguistic nationalism). Motivation, in his view, is the primary weakness of foreign language learning, because students of English are serving goals which focus on passing examinations, achieving the aims of corporate culture, or even contributing to 'a vague sense of the national collective' rather than developing a sense of themselves as human beings able to speak more than one language. Linguistic nationalism is responsible for a bifurcated view of English depending on its purpose:

> The Japanese version of English, or 'Japan-oriented English' (*eigo*) is 'English for Japanese,' i.e. for nationalist utilitarian purposes. In other words, it is English for climbing the examination-education ladder (actually, *eigo* is a sort of non-communicative, artificial language designed for testing purposes). The non-Japanese version of English, or 'non-Japan-oriented English' (*eikaiwa*) is 'English for communication'. (McVeigh, 2004: 215)

In this view, not being able to speak English well signifies that one is Japanese and is the real underlying explanation for the poor quality of English teaching in Japan, a view with which Hashimoto (2002) concurs. Motivation for McVeigh is key.

Aspinall (2006), on the other hand, sees motivation as present among all actors in the process (students, teachers, parents and policy-makers); it is not a lack of will to learn or an opposition to policies that impedes improvement, he suggests, but rather a failure at the implementation stage. He locates the difficulty in national norms and values relating to teaching and learning and suggests that one solution may lie in a 'small culture' paradigm focusing on group dynamics within a small culture such as a classroom.

The two studies just mentioned are just the tip of a very large iceberg of discussion of English in Japan. The debate about the how, why and when of teaching English is naturally multifaceted and likely to be the subject of continued argument as policy initiatives are evaluated over the next few years. The kinds of questions canvassed in public debate, mostly to do with requisite levels of language competence, reflect those commonly found in other countries in the face of a language policy important to national interests, as English is to Japan. Discussion commonly focuses on the kind of linguistic identity with regard to another language which will best fit the needs of the country concerned. In Japan today, it is the fit between the Japanese and the English language in terms of the broad spectrum of international relations, including their economic aspect, and of cultural flows.

Policies on teaching English have thus been driven by a commitment to internationalisation since the late 1980s. The major policy developments in this area have been the institution of the JET programme in 1987 – motivated by Japan's poor performance in international comparisons of TOEFL (Test of English as a Foreign Language) ratings – and the current 'Action Plan to Cultivate Japanese with English Abilities', announced in 2003. As a deliberate attempt by government to improve the teaching of foreign languages, in particular the strategically significant English, the JET programme clearly comes under the umbrella of language planning. So, too does the Action Plan, with its emphasis on goals – that all Japanese citizens will be able to communicate in English upon graduation from middle and high school, and that university graduates will further be able to use English in their work – and enabling strategies.

Emphasis on a shift to a communicative teaching methodology has been a major element underpinning both these initiatives. The teaching method traditionally used has strongly emphasised reading and writing skills with a heavy focus on grammar aimed at achieving success in university entrance examinations. Extensive classroom practice time based on written multi-choice tests is required for these examinations, which only included a listening test component for the first time in 2006.[20] With large classes all being taught in this way, Japanese proficiency in spoken English has historically been poor. Since 1987, the Japan Exchange and Teaching (JET) programme has aimed to change this through promoting a shift towards a more communicative teaching approach by providing native-speaker Assistant Language Teachers (ALT) to assist Japanese teachers with more communicatively oriented activities in middle and high school classrooms.[21] The ALTs come predominantly from English-speaking countries. In 1991, the Central Deliberative Committee on Education (Chūō Kyōiku Shingikai) recommended that the number of ALTs be increased and that the Course of Study guidelines be revised to promote a greater emphasis on communication (Ministry of Education, 1991).

Japan has not in fact succeeded in improving its performance in the TOEFL ratings. It continues to show low mean scores: 29th out of the 29 countries with data available in 2002–2003 ranked by total TOEFL score (Economic and Social Dataranking, 2006); 180th among the 189 countries in the United Nations in 1998 (Inoguchi, 1999: 1). It may be, as Coulmas (2003: 25) has suggested, that the communicative approach may not work as well in Japan as elsewhere given the lack of opportunities for meaningful language use outside the classroom. It is certainly true that the communicative approach does work better in such circumstances. Nevertheless, any advance in the direction of improved communication skills is to be welcomed, and it is likely to take some time to effect a change in the pedagogical culture of teaching English in schools.

Despite the lack of TOEFL improvement, when the JET programme's effectiveness was evaluated in 2001, primary, junior and senior high schools taking part reported high degrees of satisfaction with the outcomes. Primary students were reported as showing increased interest in foreign languages and cultures, ease in mixing with foreigners and willingness to try communicating in English; high schools reported an increase in the number of students attempting the Step Test in Practical English Proficiency (Eiken), officially accredited by the Ministry of Education in 2000 (MEXT, 2001). An academic study of the programme published in 2000, however, based on interviews with programme participants, suggests that the communicative focus may have been better received in less academically oriented schools than in top academic schools which remain focused more on the largely writing-based preparation for university entrance examinations and may view communicative activities as a distraction from this main goal (McConnell, 2000).

The initiatives begun with the JET programme were reinforced and extended in July 2002 when MEXT announced a strategic plan for improving English abilities. Progress in this area was linked with Japan's ability to participate on the world stage in the policy rhetoric:

> With the progress of globalization in the economy and in society, it is essential that our children acquire communication skills in English, which has become a common international language, in order for living in the twenty-first century. This has become an extremely important issue both in terms of the future of our children and the further development of Japan as a nation. At present, though, the English-speaking abilities of a large percentage of the population are inadequate, and this imposes restrictions on exchanges with foreigners and creates occasions when the ideas and opinions of Japanese people are not appropriately evaluated. (MEXT, 2002)

It is not just a one-way information exchange envisaged this time: not only is English important in terms of understanding foreigners, it is also needed in order for Japanese opinions to be properly heard.

Funding for the strategic plan was for the first time incorporated into the national budget. Given that budgets in other areas were being cut at the time, this may be taken to reflect the importance accorded to English education (Aspinall, 2006: 258). A five-year action plan subsequently made public in March 2003 set out specific proficiency targets for junior and senior high school graduates and advised universities to set their own targets such that graduates would be able to use English in their work. Specific steps detailed the strategies to be used to achieve these targets, including upgrading of teacher proficiency and of pedagogical methods and also improving motivation for learning English through study abroad and other means (MEXT, 2003a). Among the strategies to be adopted were that English would be the medium of communication for most of each class, that students would be streamed according to proficiency and that small-group teaching would be promoted. By the end of 2005 a total of 100 high schools were to be designated as Super English Language High Schools (SELHIs), with immersion or semi-immersion English classes with strong overseas links.[22] Increases in teacher numbers, professional development and further development of curriculum materials were also flagged.

The number of SELHi schools in operation in the 2005 academic year reached 101; 16 of them concluded three-year experimental programmes in March that year. A study by Yoshida (2005), which compared the English proficiency of high school students in Japan, China and South Korea, split the Japanese contingent into those at regular Japanese high schools and those at SELHi schools. The results showed:

(1) That SELHi teachers engaged in more communicative activities than did those at regular high schools.

(2) That whereas students in English classes at regular schools felt they were being taught the forms of the language, SELHi students felt that in addition to the forms they were receiving 'a balanced regimen of meaningful, cognitive activities (and) use of interactive communicative English' (p. 5) incorporating real-world activities.

(3) That SELHi students scored significantly better than students at regular schools on the Benesse Corporation's General Test of English Communication for Students.[23]

In recent years, English conversation has been available in public elementary schools as an elective activity – to be offered or not at the discretion of each school – during the Period of Integrated Study in which all students in Years Three to Six participate three times a week. The content of the activities undertaken during these periods is decided by the school itself. In 2002, when the revised Course of Study guidelines were implemented, approximately 50% of public elementary schools availed themselves of this opportunity. In the financial year 2005–2006, this proportion had risen to 93.6% (MEXT, 2006c). Many private schools had been offering English from much earlier. Support for elementary school English activities is provided under the Action Plan to Cultivate 'Japanese with English abilities' in the form of publication of activity books, placement of ALTs and local-community English speakers in primary schools, designation of pilot schools for research purposes, teacher training and other measures (MEXT, 2003a).

Students, parents and teachers have for the most part responded positively to this development. Whether the next step should be taken to make English a compulsory subject in the elementary school curriculum rather than an elective 'activity' is without doubt the hottest topic in language policy discussions in Japan today. The October 2005 summary of the Central Council for Education's report on 'Redesigning Compulsory Education' (MEXT, 2005b) lists 'enhance English instruction in elementary school' as one of its dot points under strategies for improving educational content, but gives no details. The Council's Foreign Language Division was due to make recommendations on this subject by the end of 2004 but was delayed in doing so, owing perhaps to a backlash against the reduction in teaching hours following the introduction of the five-day school week which led Japan to perform less well than usual on international tests of student abilities. On 27 March 2006, the Division finally put out a report recommending that a mandatory English subject be introduced from Year Five in elementary school; if the report is adopted, it would be implemented from 2010, when the next incarnation of the Course of Study guidelines is due (Yomiuri Online, 28 March, 2006a).

The plan is not without its critics, among them the present Minister for Education, who advance the argument (often heard in other countries as well) that the teaching of a mandatory foreign language at this level will take away hours needed to master the national language, and that teacher qualifications will have to be dramatically upgraded (an issue which the Division's report acknowledges). Supporters, however, in addition to stressing the benefits of beginning language study at an early age, point out that Japan is only following regional trends: South Korea made English compulsory in elementary schools in 1997, and China has been gradually implementing this since 2001.

Turning now to a closer examination of the Course of Study curriculum guidelines for English: these have undergone various changes in emphasis over the years, but the position of English as the language of choice, as previously mentioned, has always been predominant. The joint middle and high school subject guidelines in 1947 were headed 'English', not 'Foreign Languages'. By 1951 this had changed to 'Foreign Language Curriculum: English Section', with other languages enjoined to follow the English curriculum guidelines. Subsequent revisions of the guidelines in 1958, 1969 and later treated middle and high school separately. After 1958 English, German and French received specific mention in the middle school guidelines, now titled 'Foreign Languages', with year-level goals for each set out in separate sections, but year-level goals for the four macro-skills were not separated out until 1989 (previously listening and speaking had been treated together). By 1998, the changes which had been occurring since the education reforms of the previous decade were reflected in the middle school guideline revisions. 'Foreign language' was now a compulsory subject, with English to be selected and other languages to be offered as electives. The objectives now referred specifically to communication, with listening and speaking singled out as essential to communicative competence, and the Course of Study was laid out in terms of functions rather than structures.

For high schools, the 1956 guidelines allowed for a second foreign-language elective in schools with a large cohort of potential students, and differentiated between the objectives for English, French and German when taught as the first foreign language, and again when taught as the second foreign language (with greater emphasis on the four macro-skills in the former). In 1960, 'foreign language' was listed as a compulsory subject but this changed again in 1970. By 1989, seven English-related skills-based subjects were offered in the foreign-language curriculum, three of them in oral communication; the guidelines now placed emphasis on a student-centred approach to teaching involving greater participation by students and fewer lectures. The English subjects were restructured in 1999, and one was made compulsory.

Today's Course of Study for Foreign Languages guidelines in middle schools set out as their overall objectives 'to develop students' basic practical communication abilities such as listening and speaking, deepening the understanding of language and culture, and fostering a positive attitude toward communication through foreign languages' (MEXT, 2003d). Language activities for the four macro-skills are listed, along with instructions on how they are to be implemented at each year level, what language elements are appropriate for doing so and how teachers are to design the syllabus. In the high school guidelines, the primary objective is almost the same, with a more explicit emphasis on depth of communication:

> To develop students' practical communication abilities such as understanding information and the speaker's or writer's intentions, and expressing their own ideas, deepening the understanding of language and culture, and fostering a positive attitude toward communication through foreign languages.

For these years the language activities, their treatment and the language elements are set out by subject: Aural/Oral Communication I and II, English I and II, Reading and Writing.

The JET programme, now 20 years old, continues to underpin the communicative thrust of the syllabus in the classroom through its annual intake of native-speaker Assistant Language Teachers from around the world: the 2006–2007 intake from 44 countries, for example, included 340 from Australia, 655 from Canada, 112 from Ireland, 254 from New Zealand, 699 from the United Kingdom and 2759 ALTs from the United States, all major English-speaking countries. Much smaller intakes were accepted from China (11), France (10), Germany (7), Korea (3) and a long list of other countries (JET Programme, 2006). The Action Plan to Cultivate 'Japanese with English Abilities' aims to build on this by having at least one third of classes led in student-centred activities by native English speakers or junior high school English teachers and to support the undertaking with research and materials development.

Tertiary study of English is not neglected in the Action Plan: that is, one of its goals is that university graduates should be able to use English in their specialised fields of work. Universities have been exhorted to develop attainment targets that would enable this. The University Center Examination was to include a listening comprehension segment from 2006 for students taking entrance examinations, and external evaluation of proficiency, such as TOEIC (Test of English for International Communication) and TOEFL scores would also be considered.

Organisational changes in Japanese universities since the 1991 revision of the Standards for Establishing a University have had an impact on the teaching of English at tertiary level. Prior to that year, a student at a four-year university needed 124 credits to graduate; 48 of these had to come from general education and were allocated as 12 each in the humanities, social sciences and natural sciences plus eight in two foreign languages and four in health and physical education. This US-inspired concept of liberal arts education preceding specialist education, introduced after World War Two in Japanese universities, did not really take root in Japan in philosophical terms. Consequently, the distinction between general and specialised education, which had seen general education subjects taught only in the first two years before proceeding to the final two years of specialised education, was abolished when the Standards were overhauled. Many general education courses were relabeled as basic courses; staff from the former General Education Divisions, many of them English teachers, were redistributed among other existing faculties or in some universities to newly created general education faculties or centres. The previous criticism of English-language teaching as too reading-centred was addressed by incorporating use of language laboratories and videos into teaching (all national universities and 90% of private universities), employing native speakers as instructors (more than half of all universities), introducing special purpose classes for, for example, conversation and speed reading, and in some cases allowing university credit for external achievement in TOEIC or TOEFL scores (Yoshida, 2002).

These positive pedagogical changes notwithstanding, many university teachers of English feel that much remains to be done, in particular in terms of a holistic rather than fragmented approach to the sector. A survey conducted by the Japan Association of College English Teachers (JACET) in 2004 asked members to nominate their current top issues of professional concern. In first place, nominated by 74.7% of respondents, was the need to draw up a firm policy on foreign language education. The JACET president speculated on two reasons for this, one being the influence of the 1991 reorganisation discussed above,[24] the other the ineffectiveness of English-language education in general which had led to a poor public perception of English teachers. Since the 1991 changes, the number of English classes had continued to decline; the study of English was found in departments of English and American literature or linguistics, but not in stand-alone departments of English-language study. Overall, the sector lacks a comprehensive policy to address these issues (Tanabe, 2004).

While general education divisions as part of a two-tier four-year structure were abolished after 1991, general education per se was still recognised as being valuable: it was a matter of reorganising the manner in which it was offered. Some universities drew up plans to do so on a university-wide basis; others, among them 21% of private universities, shaped their offerings to meet the needs of specific faculties (Yoshida, 2002). One example is the Faculty of Science and Technology at one of Japan's top private universities, Keio University, which contains a Department of Foreign Languages and General Education in addition to 12 other academic departments and three graduate schools. Undergraduate students in this department must study required courses in English and one other foreign language. The rationale given for studying languages other than English is that '[a] s part of their preparation for taking on leadership responsibilities in the twenty-first century, students clearly need to acquire skills in more than one foreign language'. The educational goals given for learning English, building on the base of six years study of English at school, are (for the required courses) 'the nurturing of practical English skills' and (for the electives) 'the nurturing of a broad command of English'. For the required courses in a third language, students must choose from Chinese, French, German, Korean and Russian; electives are also available in Arabic, Italian and Spanish. Here the educational goals are listed as 'learning regional languages' and 'improving overall linguistic capacity and sharpening thinking skills'. For both English and the third language, 'developing effective communicators' is an overarching goal (Keio University Science and Technology, 2006).

A report in 2000 from the Round-table Committee for the Improvement of English Teaching Methods (Eigo Shidō Hōhōnado Kaizen no Suishin ni kansuru Kondankai) advocated a different angle on English education in universities when it suggested that a curriculum shift from 'learning English' to 'learning in English' would henceforth be necessary under the influence of globalisation. A number of Japanese universities were in fact already teaching both under-graduate and postgraduate programmes in English for international students who might otherwise have been deterred by the difficulty of achieving the level of proficiency in Japanese required to study at a Japanese university. A Ministry of Education conference in 1995 had recommended an increase in short-term programmes taught in English as a strategy for achieving the government's target of having 100,000 foreign students studying in Japan (surpassed in 2004 with 117,000 such students enrolled). The Ministry's 2005 report on student exchange in Japan listed 31 such courses at private universities and 28 at national universities (Student Services Division, 2005). Some private universities had been offering such courses from much earlier; those taught at national universities began after 1995. Under the terms of the 2003 Action Plan, Japanese students too were to be encouraged to participate in these courses taught in English for foreign students. In addition to undergraduate English offerings of this kind, national universities have begun to offer graduate programmes taught in English: in 2002 there were 33 such programmes across Japan, 10 of them established in 1999 (Horie, 2002: 71).

A lot of money and effort, then, is being invested to improve the teaching of English. How effective this has been will become apparent when specific initiatives are reviewed for the first time, but initial results from the SELHis, at least, are encouraging. As we shall see presently, these government-funded activities are supplemented by personal investment in the private language sector, where *eikaiwa* schools provide English conversation lessons for a clientele with a varied spectrum of reasons for learning the language. Before I examine language spread opportunities through the private sector, however, I want to talk about the teaching of other foreign languages through the education system.

Other foreign languages

Foreign languages other than English are taught quite widely at Japanese universities, but not in schools, where the decision on whether to offer these is up to each individual school. In the absence of any comprehensive national language policy encompassing community languages and/or any position on which languages should be strategically introduced with a view to Japan's regional and international linkages, English has become the pragmatic solution to engagement with the rest of the world. A 2005 report on the activities of a specialist committee on foreign languages in the curriculum, for example, devoted all its space to matters relating to English, with only one line relating to other languages: 'we need a discussion on the aims and content of classes in foreign languages other than English' (MEXT, 2004). Other foreign languages have thus taken something of a back seat, at least at school level, with French and German the preferred European languages where they are offered.

In the last decade, however, the teaching of Chinese and Korean, both major regional languages, has shown signs of growth, following several administrative and bureaucratic developments. In 1987, the Ad-Hoc Council on Educational Reform, established in 1984 in response to public concern over the capacity of the education system to respond to social change, released its final report and recommended *inter alia* that the range of elective subjects in the high school curriculum be expanded. In 1993, a group of Schools for Collaborative Research on the Diversification of Foreign Language Education put out two reports on foreign languages other than English, the first of which suggested that the languages of neighbouring Asian countries be introduced into the curriculum of middle and high schools (The Japan Forum, 1998). Several years later, as previously noted, the 2000 report commissioned by then Prime Minister Obuchi on Japan's goals for the new century also recommended that the teaching of Chinese and Korean be dramatically expanded as a strategy for improving neighborly relations with those two countries (Prime Minister's Commission, 2000). These two languages are also spoken, of course, by large ethnic minorities within Japan. The 2005 White Paper on Education acknowledged the need to teach languages other than English, in particular regional languages, and announced plans to tackle this proactively. Certain prefectures have been given the responsibility in this context, with schools designated as centers for teaching other languages in collaboration with community organizations likely to be useful in this regard for an exploratory period of two years. Kanagawa, Wakayama and Nagasaki Prefectures as well as Osaka City are in charge of Chinese, and Kagoshima Prefecture and Osaka City of Korean (MEXT, 2005a). Things are looking positive, then, for the growth of education in these two languages.

Table 2 shows that in 2005 the top four foreign languages other than English taught in both government and private high schools were Chinese, Korean, French and German. The 'other' languages taught, most of them to very small numbers, include Spanish (2784 students, 84 schools), Russian (478, 21 schools), Italian (159, 10 schools), Portuguese (102, nine schools), Indonesian (40, three schools), Vietnamese (15, three schools), Malay (14, two schools), Tagalog (seven, two schools) and Arabic (six, two schools). Korean has increased its position since 1998, when it was third after Chinese and French (Gottlieb, 2005: 33). The table makes clear how small a part of the educational profile is allotted to foreign languages other than English.

Foreign languages are much more widely taught in universities than in schools. Japan has a total of around 690 universities. Table 3 shows that English is taught almost universally. In second place is Chinese, followed by German (an important language in higher education in Japan since the beginning of its modern period), French, Korean and others. While it is certainly true in schools that foreign-language education means English, the picture at tertiary level looks slightly different, with many more universities teaching other languages as shown in Table 3. This reflects in part Japan's history of engagement with western countries and their languages during its modernisation.

A strong national policy position on the importance of English shored up with targeted funding underlies the dominance of that language in the school system, but the importance of studying other languages will most likely never be recognised on the same scale, even at tertiary level. In particular, there is no consciousness of any domestic need to use foreign languages; other languages are seen predominantly as being pertinent only to the outside world. This, of course, affects motivation to a large extent, as Yoshida Kensaku points out:

> In Japan ... foreign languages are learned predominantly to fulfill an external need. People feel there is very little need to use foreign languages internally, and, therefore, are not very motivated to learn them. (Yoshida K., 2002)

In addition to orientation, a second factor probably relates to the old and well entrenched belief, particularly strong among older people, that Japanese people cannot learn other languages. Evidence to the contrary has been provided in the form of the *kikokushijo* students discussed above, some of whom return from study abroad virtually bilingual, depending on the amount of time spent in the other country, the quality of their immersion experience there and the extent to which they have developed in their own language. These students have achieved their second-language proficiency through immersion conditions overseas rather than through study in Japan, of course, but their very achievements do

Table 2 Top four foreign languages other than English in Japanese high schools 2005

	No. of schools	No. of languages	Chinese	French	Korean	German	Others	Total
Public	504	14	12,737 students (412 schools)	3970 (146)	6349 (209)	1266 (58)	2319 (119)	26,641 (944)
Private	244	11	9424 (141 schools)	5457 (102)	2542 (77)	2932 (47)	1360 (44)	21,715 (411)
Total	748	16	22,161 (553 schools)	9427 (248)	8891 (286)	4198 (105)	3679 (163)	48,356 (1355)

Source: Monbu Kagakushō Shotō Chūtō Kyōiku-kyoku Kokusai Kyōiku-ka (2005). Figures given for schools in parentheses are for 2003

Table 3 Foreign language education in Japanese universities 2004

Language	National universities	Public universities	Private universities	Total
English	83	75	531	689
French	79	52	407	538
German	83	58	421	562
Spanish	40	25	178	243
Chinese	78	63	450	591
Russian	53	21	110	184
Latin	31	7	63	101
Korean	58	36	275	369
Arabic	9	4	35	48
Italian	22	9	86	117
Others	36	12	119	167

Source: Monbu Kagakushō Kōtō Kyōiku-kyoku Daigaku Shinkō-ka (2006)

much to dispel the myth that being Japanese is somehow inherently inimical to being able to speak another language. There are, however, reported cases of returnee students who speak English very well pretending not to be able to do so in order to blend in with their class groups in Japan (Aspinall, 2006: 264). Returnees who are genuinely bilingual may be faulted for their ability in any language other than Japanese; they are accused of being 'less Japanese', and consequently not to be trusted.

Japan might discover several benefits in adopting a policy of increased attention to learning foreign languages other than English. Such a policy would openly recognise its already existing linguistic diversity, strengthen the concept of community languages and accelerate internal cultural internationalisation. Teachers could be trained who could support the education of migrant children by offering supplemental mother-tongue instruction while the students are still in the lengthy process of mastering written Japanese, so that such students do not lose out on content. And finally, as I speculated earlier, this could provide serious evidence of goodwill to regional neighbours where residual wartime memories of bad past relations with Japan create ongoing tensions today, already recognised by Japan as a source of friction.

Other Means of Language Spread

Private language learning

By 2000, Japan had the largest commercial English language education market in the world, valued at US$ 20 billion (Dolan, 2001). Language teaching is big business in the private sector, which since 1991 has had its own version of a quality assurance body, the Japan Association for the Promotion of Foreign Language Education, an association of private language schools which attempts to regulate the industry through a code of practice. Member schools advertise their affiliation with this body to assure clients of their credibility. In addition to English, private language schools offer courses in Chinese, Classical Greek, French, German, Italian, Korean, Latin and Spanish; several of the larger schools, such as DILA (http://www.dila.co.jp/) offer a much wider range. The big drawcard is English: train carriages are festooned with advertisements for the latest or the most scientifically proven method of learning English at particular academies. Many school students attend cram schools specialising in English or take English courses at general cram schools to prepare them for the university entrance examinations. But attendance at private language schools is not limited to people of school age and up: in 2005, 1600 Yamaha Eigo Kyōshitsu cram schools across Japan taught English to 63,000 Japanese children, up 35% on the previous year, with classes for two and three-year-olds being popular (Yomiuri Online, 28 March 2006b).

Attending language schools is not, of course, the only means of learning English in the private sector. A poll conducted in October 2006 by EigoTown. com, a web site devoted to the study of English in Japan, asked respondents about their primary means of learning English and found that new media are now taking their place in the field. While 25% of respondents listed going to an English language school as their main means of learning the language, almost as many (24%) learned from books, followed in third place by 14% who learned from radio shows. New media podcasting held fourth place at 13%, outdoing old media television (11%). Respondents liked learning through podcasting because it was free, could be listened to in the train on the way to and from work, allowed much more individual input than a traditional English class and allowed the user to listen to downloaded conversations between native speakers (Eigotown.com, 2006). This trend, allowing individualised instruction at a time of the user's choosing, is likely to grow as the technology and what is available for download continue to improve and expand.

In the business sector, large Japanese companies provide employees with English-language lessons, and advanced proficiency is increasingly required for certain levels of appointment. Electronics firm Fujitsu, for example, requires all its employees to learn English and to take a national proficiency test to demonstrate achievement (Honna & Takeshita, 1999). More and more companies and local governments are now using performance on English tests such as TOEIC as a criterion for both employment and promotion (Torikai, 2005: 253). Since March 2001, for example, employees at IBM Japan seeking promotion to section chief have required a minimum score of 600 points (useable business English) on the TOEIC test; Assistant General Manager positions require a score of at least 730 (able to communicate in any situation). The company provided subsidised English classes to enable employees to take the test (ELT News, 7 March 2000). Other large companies using TOEIC levels of English ability to differentiate position descriptions include Nissan and Marubeni.

Private sector language schools, employer-sponsored classes for employees of large corporations and a range of other means such as private tuition on a one-on-one basis, language classes on NHK or online and individual study using the many excellent books available at any good bookstore are thus a major means of language spread, in addition to the national education system itself. In private sector language schools, as with the education system, English dominates. The picture which emerges at ground level, through surveys of parental preferences such as Ito (2005), sales figures for English textbooks and other sources, is of a vibrant community interest in learning English which underpins the belated but nonetheless fervent current profile of support for English at national language policy level.

Teaching Japanese as a foreign language

And finally, any discussion of language spread must include a section on promotion of the teaching of that language as a foreign language where applicable. An important externally oriented aspect of Japan's current language policy concerns the efforts that have been made since the early 1970s to promote teaching Japanese as a foreign language (TJFL) both outside and inside Japan. Policies relating to the spread of the Japanese language, which Hirataka (1992: 93–108) calls Language Spread Policies (LSP), while not openly articulated as such in practice, were an outcome of economic development and are implemented by different ministries. Earlier attempts at large-scale teaching of Japanese outside Japan were undertaken in the context of Japanese colonialism in Korea and Taiwan, or in the wartime context of occupation of other parts of Asia. In the 1970s it was not imperialism but Japan's increasing economic power which provided the trigger: the Japanese economy was by that time so strong that not just the Japanese government but other governments as well responded eagerly to the idea of increasing the number of foreign learners of the language. Language proficiency in Japanese was widely promoted as a key to increased employment opportunities, economic benefits, internationalisation and grassroots cultural exchange.

The Ministry of Foreign Affairs is the key enabling agency in this context and fosters international knowledge of Japan and its language through the activities of the Japan Foundation, established within the Ministry in 1972. A great deal of money has been spent since then on promoting Japanese language and culture overseas. The first Japan Foundation Survey in 1979 identified 127,000 learners engaged in formal instruction worldwide; by the time of the latest survey in 2003, this number had grown to 2.3 million. Taken together with those who have graduated from such courses earlier and those who are studying informally, estimates Katō Hidetoshi, former Director of the Japan Foundation's Urawa Language Institute, the total number of learners of Japanese worldwide is likely to be around 10 million (Katō, 2000: 3). The Foundation runs a major language institute in Urawa that holds training programmes for teachers of Japanese, develops and provides educational materials, and acts as a clearing house for information. Other such language institutes perform similar educational functions in Kansai and overseas.

Japanese is not just taught overseas as a foreign language; it is also widely taught as a foreign language within Japan itself, again with an eye to internationalisation. The flip side of teaching English to Japanese citizens is teaching Japanese to non-Japanese students or workers resident in Japan. MEXT, and not the Ministry of Foreign Affairs, administers programmes teaching Japanese to refugees and to returnees from mainland China, and sends Japanese high school teachers to teach the language in other countries under the Regional and Educational Exchanges for Mutual Understanding (REX) programme. In many countries, too, MEXT-approved schools that also hold local accreditation teach the children of Japanese assigned overseas on short-term postings so that these children may fit back into the Japanese educational system upon their return: Japanese high school English teachers are recruited to teach in these schools. Other Ministries which have run TJFL programmes in the past have included the then Posts and Telecommunications (MPT), International Trade and Industry (MITI) and Health and Welfare (Hirataka, 1992: 102–103). In line with the push to increase the numbers of foreign students studying in Japan, many national universities have set up Japanese language education units of their own, either in *ryūgakusei sentaa* (international student centres) or in faculties charged with TJFL. Sixty four-year universities and seven two-year junior colleges in 2006 offered special courses for foreign students; while a few have been doing so for some years, most are of recent origin (MEXT, 2006d). Private language schools also flourish: in 2005, there were 391 such institutions accredited by the Association for the Promotion of Japanese Language Education (MEXT, 2005a).

A 1995 report from the National Language Council outlined several strategies it considered important for TJFL in Japan: these included collaboration between TJFL institutions both in Japan and abroad in developing long-term strategies, promoting TJFL at regional level in areas where many foreign residents live, developing a TJFL database and promotion of multimedia teaching methods (Kokugo Shingikai, 1995: 449–450). Interestingly, another of the strategies was to educate the public about the value of teaching Japanese to others, presumably to break down the belief that the language is too difficult for non-Japanese to master. Katō (2000) also sought to address this when he warned that Japanese people needed to start thinking about their language in international terms: just as native speakers of English must accept that non-native speakers of their widely spoken language will make 'mistakes', so native speakers of Japanese need to accept that the language is now used by non-Japanese and learn to overlook mistakes for the sake of communication. Such a warning seems almost laughably trite in the globalised 21st century; that it is deemed necessary in Japan by a prominent figure in Japanese language education speaks to the tenacity of Nihonjinron cultural beliefs which no amount of experience as an economic superpower – with concomitant implications of cultural influence – has yet been able to undo to any significant degree.

Despite the recession of the 1990s, which might have been expected to lead to a decreased interest in commercially motivated language study, *nihongo kyōiku* remains a flourishing industry in both government and private sectors. Japan remains an economic magnet, even if not on the same scale as the overblown 1980s, and language study continues to open doors to those wishing to avail themselves of opportunities to work there.

Future Directions for Language Policy

Japan is now entering what Ricento (2000) describes as the third stage in the development of language policy in which the focus is on global flows and identity interactions, while its current language policies are largely derived from the first stage, when language was viewed as a tool for nation building (though never as a neutral resource). Emergent multilingualism on the domestic front, together with international population flows and political and cultural relationships in the region, mean that language policy now needs to move away from the nation-building imperatives which shaped it during the modernisation period and again in the aftermath of defeat in World War Two towards a wider, more inclusive remit. To a certain extent this is already happening at national level in relation to external environments, as the evolution of the policies relating to English and Ainu show.

Language planning and policy in Japan have predominantly been top-down, which has contributed to a certain slowness in responding to change. A prime example of this 'lethargy' is the time that it took to adapt the list of characters for general use to its current form from the 1945 version. The Minister of Education requested the reappraisal of the postwar script reforms in 1965, but it was not until 1981 that the character list assumed its present form, having undergone several drafts and a great deal of public consultation after the National Language Council began work on it in 1972. It is only to be expected, then, that the response to multilingualism, which strikes just as deeply to the heart of entrenched ideas of what it means to be Japanese as script reform did, will take time. On the ground and in charge of practical realities, however, local governments and NGOs are not waiting for instruction from above but are implementing a bottom-up approach in response to the language needs of foreign residents in their areas.

Ongoing overarching discussion of language policy needs to accommodate several aspects: the international (the study of English, modes of Internet use, the study of other foreign languages, the promotion of TJFL both overseas and in Japan), the regional (increased promotion of the study of neighboring languages) and the local (national language issues, effect of technology on language, community languages and increased multilingualism among the population, support for the continuing teaching and use of Ainu in order to avoid language death). Whether the current fragmented approach, with different Ministries and Agencies undertaking different language-related responsibilities, will continue remains to be seen, although it appears unlikely that anything will change in this respect. Within MEXT, a coordinated stance on language-in-education policies which takes account of the reality of new social constituencies is clearly required as the number of migrant children in the school system continues to increase: language difficulties may lead to failure to thrive in the education system, resulting in feelings of alienation and a section of the community feeling excluded from full participation in public life. There are encouraging signs that this situation is already being addressed, through the training of volunteer JFL teachers mentioned above, support for language instruction for returnees from China, support for the training of JFL teachers and other means. Much, however, remains to be done.

Katsuragi (2004: 326) has questioned 'whether "planning" is not too strong a word for what the Japanese authorities are doing these days'. From within a framework of public philosophy, he has recently proposed a forward-looking overarching 'language policy framework' for Japan within which individual language policies would be located, that is, an overarching set of policies which complements language policies and sets out the guiding ethos for language issues within the society (Katsuragi, 2005). This argument sits well with the theoretical orientation espoused by Spolsky (2004) and others, namely that language policy, far from being merely a collection of documents supplemented by government practice, is informed by and encapsulates the entire linguistic culture of a society, that is, its specific beliefs about language. Katsuragi's language policy framework would be the framework within which the overarching beliefs about the role of language in Japan today are articulated, which would then guide and shape the formation of specific language policies themselves. Those beliefs, long comfortably accepted and cherished as evidence of a monolingual and monoethnic Japan, are now under challenge from demographic changes and (in the area of written Japanese) from technological developments which are changing the way people relate to and think about writing. Current indications are that the debate on what the new face of language planning and policy in Japan should look like is now under way at several levels as language planning moves away from its central locus in the education system into the broader context of local government and community initiatives.

Correspondence

Any correspondence should be directed to Professor Nanette Gottlieb, Japan Program, School of Languages and Comparative Cultural Studies, University of Queensland, Brisbane, Queensland 4072, Australia (nanette.gottlieb@uq.edu.au).

Notes

1. That is, 'a language which has no known structural or historical relationship to any other language' (Crystal, 1987: 326).
2. A Tokyo-based government institute set up in 1948 to provide empirical survey data on which the National Language Council could base policy decisions and to conduct language-related research projects. It changed its English name to the National Institute for Japanese Language in 2001, having originally been called the National Language Research Institute. The Japanese name is Kokuritsu Kokugo Kenkyūjo.
3. Gyaru Moji Henkan (Gal Talk Conversion), http://mizz.lolipop.jp/galmoji/v2.cgi. Accessed 1 February 2007.
4. A body established in 1988 to deal with matters relating to internationalization, among them the joint running of the Japan Exchange and Teaching program with MEXT, the Ministry of Internal Affairs and Communications (MIC) and the Ministry of Foreign Affairs (MOFA). CLAIR is responsible for local-level internationalization initiatives, in particular grass-roots international exchange of personnel at local government level (see www.clair.or.jp).
5. A famous travelogue written by poet Matsuo Bashō (1644–1694).
6. By comparison, the 2004 estimated value of domestic publication sales was 2.243 trillion yen (943 billion for books and 1300 billion for magazines) for books and magazines published in Japan (JETRO, 2005).
7. Manga sales have been particularly profitable at the New York branch of Kinokuniya, one of Japan's major bookstore chains. See 'Manga sales revive NY's Kinokuniya', *PW Comics Week*, 21 March 2006. On WWW at http://www.publishersweekly.com/article/CA6317282.html. Accessed 7 November 2006.
8. Prior to the formation of MEXT in 2001, the ministry was known as the Ministry of Education. References in this text reflect that chronology.
9. Ainu, Okinawans and foreigners who have taken Japanese citizenship amounted to 15,251 in 2005 (which is roughly the average for the years since 1995). Of these, 9689 were Korean, 4427 Chinese and 1135 'other' (Ministry of Justice Japan, 2006).

10. See, for example, http://ramat.ram.ne.jp/ainu/. Accessed 7 September 2006.
11. http://www.okinawan-shorinryu.com/okinawa/uchina.html. Accessed 7 September 2006.
12. Because they had not gone through the standard Japanese education system offered in government schools.
13. A comprehensive list of links may be found at http://www.han.org/a/link_korea. html. Accessed 6 November 2006.
14. For example, Mundo de Alegria school in Hamamatsu city and Escola Centro Nipo-Brasileiro in Oizumi.
15. 'International Press: The Portuguese Edition'. On WWW at http://www.ipcjapan. com/ptedition_en.html. Accessed 8 September 2006. International Press Japan Co. also publishes Japan's only Spanish-language paper.
16. These numbers refer only to those students in the Japanese education system. Foreign children are also educated at international and ethnic schools in Japan.
17. A full chart of the kanji introduced for each year level may be found online at http:// www.mext.go.jp/b_menu/shuppan/sonota/990301b/990301d.htm, or reproduced in Gottlieb (2005), 84–86.
18. Some curricula were revised slightly in 2001, but not the *kokugo* curriculum.
19. This number also includes a small number of children who have returned from areas in, e.g. China where Japanese settlers lived before the end of World War Two.
20. This has been done at the University of Tokyo since 1988 (Torikai, 2005: 250).
21. This programme is run jointly by the Ministry of Foreign Affairs, the Ministry of Education, Culture, Sports, Science and Technology and the Council of Local Authorities for International Relations, in collaboration with local authorities.
22. For example, in 2004 Matsuyama Technical High School became a SELHi and remained the only technical high school of the 101 SELHi in 2006. Second-year Information Technology students at this school combine English, environmental studies and IT as their SELHi project and have regular email contact with students at a sister school in the US (Mizui, 2006).
23. A test of English proficiency created for the Benesse Corporation of Japan and designed to measure proficiency in authentic communication, first administered in 1998.
24. When the earlier system of general education gave way to a focus on specialization. English was one of the previous basic education courses; many EFL instructors had to reinvent themselves in order to teach English in departments of literature, linguistics or intercultural communication among others.

References

Agency for Cultural Affairs (2000) *Heisei 11 Nendo "Kokugo ni kansuru Seron Chōsa" no Kekka ni tsuite* (*Results of the 1999 Survey on the Japanese Language*). On WWW at http:// www.bunka.go.jp/kokugo_nihongo/yoronchousa/h11/kekka.html. Accessed 14 November 2007.

Agency for Cultural Affairs (2002) *Heisei 13 Nendo "Kokugo ni kansuru Seron Chōsa" no Kekka ni tsuite* (*Results of the 2001 Survey on the Japanese Language*). On WWW at http://www. bunka.go.jp/kokugo_nihongo/yoronchousa/h13/kekka.html. Accessed 14 November 2007.

Agency for Cultural Affairs (2003) *Heisei 14 Nendo "Kokugo ni kansuru Seron Chōsa" no Kekka ni tsuite* (*Results of the 2002 Survey on the Japanese Language*). On WWW at http://www.bunka.go.jp/kokugo_nihongo/yoronchousa/h14/kekka.html. Accessed 14 November 2007.

Agency for Cultural Affairs (2004) *Heisei 15 Nendo "Kokugo ni kansuru Seron Chōsa" no Kekka ni tsuite* (*Results of the 2003 Survey on the Japanese Language*). On WWW at http://www. bunka.go.jp/kokugo_nihongo/yoronchousa/h15/kekka.html. Accessed 14 November 2007.

Agency for Cultural Affairs (2007) *Chi-iki Nihongo Shien Kōdeineeta nado Kenshū Jisshi Chi-iki (Heisei 17 Nendo)* (*Regions Implementing Local Japanese Language Support Coordination Etc 2005*). On WWW at http://www.bunka.go.jp/1kokugo/chiiki_cordi_17.html. Accessed 7 February 2007.

Aspect (2006) On WWW at http://www.aspect.co.jp/english/index.html. Accessed 7 November 2006.

Aspinall, R. (2006) Using the paradigm of "small cultures" to explain policy failure in the case of foreign language education in Japan. *Japan Forum* 18 (2), 255–274.

Backhouse, A. (1993) *The Japanese Language: An Introduction*. Melbourne: Oxford University Press.

Bourke, B. (1996) Maximising efficiency in the kanji learning task. Unpublished PhD dissertation, University of Queensland.

Burajiru Gakkō Kyōgikai (2005) Burajiru Gakkō Ichiran (Overview of Brazilian Schools). On WWW at http://www5d.biglobe.ne.jp/~mingakko/barsilgakko2.mht. Accessed 3 November 2006.

CCHCFR (Gaikokujin Shūju Toshi Kaigi, Council for Cities with High Concentrations of Foreign Residents, 2004). On WWW at http://www.city.hamamatsu.shizuoka.jp/admin/plan/policy/kokusai/conferenceindex.html. Accessed 12 September 2006.

Canagarajah, A.S. (2005) Introduction. In A.S. Canagarajah (ed.) *Reclaiming the Local in Language Policy and Practice* (pp. ix–xxx). Mahwah, NJ: Lawrence Erlbaum Associates.

Carroll, T. (2001) *Language Planning and Language Change in Japan*. Surrey: Curzon Press.

Carruthers, A. (2004) Cute logics of the multicultural and the consumption of the Vietnamese exotic in Japan. *Positions* 12 (2), 401–429.

Center of Overseas Chinese Studies, Takushoku University (2003) *Chinese schools in Japan*. On WWW at http://www.cnc.takushoku-u.ac.jp/~kakyonet/public_old_html/japanese/school/s_c_english_ver1/s_c_english1.html. Accessed 3 November 2006.

Chongryun (2005) *Chōsen Gakkō Shochūbu to Nihon Gakkō Shochū Gakkō – Jugyō Jisū Haibun no Hikaku (Comparison of the distribution of hours in Korean school elementary and middle school curricula and Japanese elementary and middle schools)*. On WWW at http://www.chongryon.com/j/edu/index7.html. Accessed 3 November 2006.

Chongryun (1997) *Major tasks*. On WWW at http://www1.korea-np.co.jp/pk/003rd_issue/chongryun/tasks.htm. Accessed 2 November 2006.

City of Sendai (2006) *Population*. On WWW at http://www.city.sendai.jp/kikaku/seisaku/toukei/jinkou/graph3-e.html. Accessed 10 November 2006.

Clarke, H. (1997) The great dialect debate: The state and language policy in Okinawa. In E. Tipton (ed.) *Society and the State in Interwar Japan* (pp. 193–217). London: Routledge.

Clyne, M. (2005) *Australia's Language Potential*. Sydney: University of New South Wales Press.

Cooper, R. (1989) *Language Planning and Social Change*. Cambridge and New York: Cambridge University Press.

Coulmas, F. (2003) Language planning in Japan. In R. Kaplan and R. Baldauf Jr. (eds) *Language and Language-in-Education Planning in the Pacific Basin* (pp. 17–29). Dordrecht: Kluwer.

Crystal, D. (1987) *The Cambridge Encyclopedia of Language*. Cambridge: Cambridge University Press.

Danet, B. (2001) *Cyberpl@y: Communicating Online*. Oxford, New York: Berg.

DeChicchis, J. (1995) The current state of the Ainu language. In J. Maher and K.Yashiro (eds) *Multilingual Japan* (pp. 103–124). Clevedon: Multilingual Matters.

Dolan, D. (2001) *Re-thinking English language education for professionals in Japan*. On WWW at http://www.glocom.org/special_topics/colloquium/200104_dan_re_thinking/. Accessed 4 October 2006.

Eastman, C. (1983) *Language Planning: An Introduction*. San Francisco, CA: Chandler and Sharpe.

Economic and Social Dataranking (2006) *[Education] English (TOEFL): TOEFL total score*. On WWW at http://dataranking.com/table.cgi?LG = e&TP = ed03–1. Accessed 26 September 2006.

Eigotown.com (2006) *Anata no omo na eigo gakushūhō wa? (What is your main method of learning English?)*. On WWW at http://www.eigotown.com/poll/200607/index.shtml. Accessed 16 November 2006.

ELT News, 7 March 2000. On WWW at http://www.eltnews.com/eltnews.shtml. Accessed 7 March 2004.

Fishman, J. (1974) Language modernization and planning in comparison with other types of national modernization and planning. In J. Fishman (ed.) *Advances in Language Planning* (pp. 79–102). The Hague: Mouton.

Fishman, J. (ed.) (1968) Language problems and types of political and sociocultural integration: a conceptual postscript. In J. Fishman *et al.* (eds) *Language Problems of Developing Nations* (pp. 491–498). New York: Wiley.

Fukuoka, Y. (2000) *Lives of Young Koreans in Japan*, (T. Gill, trans.) Melbourne: Trans Pacific Press.

Galan, C. (2005) Learning to read and write in Japanese (*kokugo* and *nihongo*): A barrier to multilingualism? *International Journal of the Sociology of Language* 175/176, 249–269.

Gordon, R. G., Jr (ed.) (2005) *Ethnologue: Languages of the World* (15th edn). Dallas, TX: SIL International. On WWW at http://www.ethnologue.com/. Accessed 6 December 2006.

Gottlieb, N. (2006) *Linguistic Stereotyping and Minorities in Japan*. London: Routledge.

Gottlieb, N. (2005) *Language and Society in Japan*. Cambridge: Cambridge University Press.

Gottlieb, N. (2000) *Word-Processing Technology in Japan: Kanji and the Keyboard*, Surrey: Curzon Press.

Gottlieb, N. (1995) *Kanji Politics: Language Policy and Japanese Script*. London: Kegan Paul.

Guiraudon, V. and Joppke, C. (eds) (2001) *Controlling a New Migration World*. London: Routledge.

Hanazaki, K. (1996) Ainu Moshir and Yaponesia: Ainu and Okinawan identities in contemporary Japan. In D. Denoon, M. Hudson, G. McCormack and T. Morris-Suzuki (eds) *Multicultural Japan: Paleolithic to Postmodern* (pp. 117–131). Cambridge: Cambridge University Press.

Hashimoto, K. (2002) Implications of the recommendation that English become the second official language in Japan. In A. Kirkpatrick (ed.) *Englishes in Asia: Communication, Identity, Power and Education* (pp. 63–73). Melbourne: Language Australia.

Hattori, S. (ed.) (1964) *Ainugo Hōgen Jiten (A Dictionary of Ainu Dialects)*. Tokyo: Iwanami Shoten.

Haugen, E. (1966) Linguistics and language planning. In W. Bright (ed.) *Sociolinguistics: Proceedings of the UCLA Sociolinguistics Conference 1964* (pp. 50–71). The Hague: Mouton.

Hayashi Ō. (1977) Kanji no mondai (The question of characters). In Iwanami Kōza *Nihongo 3: Kokugo Kokuji Mondai (Japanese 3: Issues in the national language and script)* (pp. 101–134). Tokyo: Iwanami Shoten.

Heinrich, P. (2004) Language planning and language ideology in the Ryūkyū Islands. *Language Policy* 3, 153–179.

Higuchi, N. (2006) *Brazilian Migration to Japan: Trends, Modalities and Impact* UN/POP/ EGM-MIG/2005/11. On WWW at http://www.un.org/esa/population/publications/IttMigLAC/P11_Higuchi.pdf. Accessed 8 September 2006.

Hirataka, F. (1992) Language-spread policy of Japan. *International Journal of the Sociology of Language* 95, 93–108.

Hirataka, F., Koishi, A. and Kato, Y. (2000) Language Environment of Brazilian Immigrants. In M. Noguchi and S. Fotos (eds) *Studies in Japanese Bilingualism* (pp. 164–183). Clevedon: Multilingual Matters.

Hogan, J. (2003) The social significance of English usage in Japan. *Japanese Studies* 23 (1), 43–58.

Honna, N. and Takeshita, Y. (1999) On Japan's propensity for native speaker English: A change in sight. *Asian Englishes* 1 (1). On WWW at www.alc.co.jp/asian-e/honna. html. Accessed 4 October 2006.

Honna, N. (1995) English in Japanese society: Language within language. In J. Maher and K. Yashiro (eds) *Multilingual Japan* (pp. 45–62). Clevedon: Multilingual Matters.

Horie, M. (2002) The internationalization of higher education in Japan in the 1990s: A reconsideration. *Higher Education* 43, 65–84.

Inoguchi, T. (1999) "Eigo shippai kokka o dō tatenaosu?" *Chūo Kōron* (August). Translated as Japan's failing grade in English. *Japan Echo* 26 (5). Summary available on WWW at http://www.japanecho.co.jp/sum/1999/b2605.html. Accessed 28 November 2006.

Internet World Statistics (2006) On WWW at http://www.internetworldstats.com/stats7.htm. Accessed 6 November 2006.

Ito, Y. (2005) English education for elementary school students: Issues viewed from parent hopes, cram school attendance. *JCER Researcher Report No. 60*. On WWW at http://www.jcer.or.jp/eng/pdf/kenrep050517e.pdf. Accessed 22 February 2007.

Ito, M., Okabe, D., Matsuda, M. (eds) (2005) *Personal, Portable, Pedestrian: Mobile Phones in Japanese Life*. Cambridge, MA: MIT Press.

Izumi, K. *et al.* (2003) *An Appeal to the Ministry of Education against the Discriminatory Treatment of Ethnic Schools in Japan*. On WWW at http://www.jca.apc.org/~komagome/english.html. Accessed 6 December 2006.

Japan Foundation (2003) *2003 Survey Report on Japanese-Language Education Abroad 2003: Present Condition of Overseas Japanese-Language Education-Summary*. On WWW at http://www.jpf.go.jp/e/japan/oversea/survey.html. Accessed 10 November 2006.

Japan Statistical Yearbook (2006) *Registered Foreigners by Nationality (1985–2004)*. On WWW at http://www.stat.go.jp/data/nenkan/zuhyou/y0214000.xls. Accessed 5 September 2006.

Japan Student Services Organization (2006) *International Students in Japan 2005*. On WWW at http://www.jasso.go.jp/statistics/intl_student/data05_e.html#no3. Accessed 13 September 2006.

Jet Programme (2006) *2006–2007 Participant Totals by Country*. On WWW at http://www.jetprogramme.org/e/outline/2006-2007%20participants_country.pdf. Accessed 28 September 2006.

JETRO (2005) Japanese Publishing Industry. *Japan Economic Monthly* (July). On WWW at www.jetro.go.jp/en/market/trend/industrial/pdf/jem0507-2e.pdf. Accessed 6 November 2006.

Kanno, Y. (2003) *Negotiating Bilingual and Bicultural Identities: Japanese Returnees Betwixt Two Worlds*. Mahwah, NJ: Lawrence Erlbaum.

Kaplan, R.B. and Baldauf Jr., R.B. (1997) *Language Planning from Practice to Theory*. Clevedon: Multilingual Matters.

Kashiwazaki, C. (2003) Local government and resident foreigners: A changing relationship. On WWW at http://www.jcie.or.jp/thinknet/pdfs/plu_kashiwazaki.pdf. Accessed 9 November 2006.

Kashiwazaki, C. (2002) Japan: from immigration control to immigration policy. *Migration Information Source*. On WWW at http://www.migrationinformation.org/Profiles/display.cfm?ID = 39. Accessed 8 November 2006.

Katō, H. (2000) *Nihongo no Kaikoku (The Globalization of Japanese)* Tokyo: TBS Brittanica.

Katō, J. (1985) Wapuro to kanji nōryoku (Word processors and kanji ability). *Kyōiku Kenkyū* 1005, 84–86.

Katsuno, H. and Yano, C. (2002) Face to face: On-line subjectivity in contemporary Japan. *Asian Studies Review* 26 (2), 205–231.

Katsuragi, T. (2005) Japanese language policy from the point of view of public philosophy. *International Journal of the Sociology of Language* 175/176, 41–54.

Katsuragi, T. (2004) Review of *Language Planning and Language Change in Japan* by Tessa Carroll. *Social Science Japan Journal* 7 (1), 324–326.

Keio University Science and Technology (2006) *Department of Foreign Languages and General Education*. On WWW at http://www.st.keio.ac.jp/english/class_lang/index.html. Accessed 17 October 2006.

Kindaichi, H. (1978) *The Japanese Language*. Tokyo: Tuttle.

Kinsella, S. (2000) *Adult Manga: Culture & Power in Contemporary Japanese Society*. Surrey: Curzon Press.

Kitao, K, Kitao, K, Nozawa, K and Yamamoto, M. (1994) *Teaching English in Japan*. On WWW at http://www1.doshisha.ac.jp/~kkitao/library/article/tejk.htm. Accessed 15 December 2006.

Kiyota, Y. (2006) *New trend: Books to be worked on*. On WWW at http://www.accu.or.jp/appreb/02/02-02/02-02country/02jap.html#29. Accessed 1 February 2007.

Kobayashi, H. (2002) L1 Japanese High School Literacy Training: Student and Teacher Perspectives. *Hiroshima Daigaku Sōgō Kagakubu Kiyō: Gengo Bunka Kenkyū* 28. On WWW at http://home.hiroshima-u.ac.jp/souka/h_database/h-5kiyou/h-5-5gengo/index28.html. Accessed 8 February 2007.

Kokugo Shingikai (2000) *Kokusai Shakai ni okeru Nihongo no Arikata (The Ideal State of Japanese in International Society)*. On WWW at http://www.mext.go.jp/b_menu/shingi/12/kokugo/toushin/001217.htm. Accessed 29 November 2006.

Kokugo Shingikai (1995) Atarashii jidai ni ōjita kokugo shisaku ni tsuite (Towards a language policy for a new era). In Kokuritsu Kokugo Kenkyūjo (eds) *Kokugo Nenkan 1995 (Japanese Language Yearbook 1995)* (pp. 427–451). Tokyo: Shūei Shuppan.

Kokuritsu Kokugo Kenkyūjo (eds) (2006) *Gairaigo to Gendai Shakai (Loanwords and Contemporary Society)*. Tokyo: Kokuritsu Insatsukyoku. These reports are also available on WWW at http://www.kokken.go.jp/public/gairaigo/index.html. Accessed 29 September 2006.

Kokuritsu Kokugo Kenkyūjo (eds) (1988) *Jidō Seito no Jōyō Kanji no Shūtoku (The Acquisition of the Jōyō Kanji by School Children)*. Tokyo: Shoseki.

Komori, Y. (2002) Japanese language booms and nationalism. *Japanese Book News* 40, 1–2.

Kondo, M. and Wakabayashi, J. (1998) Japanese Tradition. In M. Baker and K. Malmkjaer (eds) *Routledge Encyclopedia of Translation Studies* (pp. 485–493). London: Routledge.

Lee, S., Graham, T. and Stevenson, H.W. (1996) Teachers and teaching: Elementary schools in Japan and the United States. In T. Rohlen and G. LeTendre (eds) *Teaching and Learning in Japan* (pp. 157–189). Cambridge: Cambridge University Press.

Lo Bianco, J. (2004) *Brief Outline of the Australian Language Policy Experience*. On WWW at http://www.nlconference.org/docs/LoBianco_paper.doc. Accessed 8 November 2006.

McConnell, D. (2000) *Importing Diversity: Inside Japan's JET Program*. Berkeley, CA: University of California Press.

McVeigh, B. (2004) Foreign language instruction in Japanese higher education: The humanistic vision or nationalist utilitarianism? *Arts and Humanities in Higher Education* 3 (2), 211–227.

Maher, J. (2002) Language policy for multicultural Japan: Establishing the new paradigm. In S. Baker (ed.) *Language Policy: Lessons from Global Models* (pp. 164–180). Monterey, CA: Monterey Institute of International Relations.

Maher, J. (1995) The *Kakyo*: Chinese in Japan. In J. Maher and K. Yashiro (eds) *Multilingual Japan* (pp. 125–138). Clevedon: Multilingual Matters.

Maher, J. and Kawanishi, Y. (1995) On being there: Korean in Japan. In J. Maher and K. Yashiro (eds) *Multilingual Japan* (pp. 87–101). Clevedon: Multilingual Matters.

Mason, J., Anderson, R., Omura, A., Uchida, N. and Imai, M. (1989) Learning to read in Japan. *Journal of Curriculum Studies* 21 (5), 389–407.

Matsumori, A. (1995) Ryūkyūan: Past, present and future. In J. Maher and K. Yashiro (eds) *Multilingual Japan* (pp. 19–44). Clevedon: Multilingual Matters.

MEXT (2007) *Zenkoku Gakuryoku, Gakushū Jōkyō Chōsa (National Survey of Knowledge and Learning)*. On WWW at http://www.mext.go.jp/a_menu/shotou/gakuryoku-chousa/07012901/002.pdf. Accessed 7 February 2007.

MEXT (2006a) *Japan's Education at a Glance 2005*. On WWW at http://www.mext.go.jp/english/statist/05101901.htm. Accessed 10 November 2006.

MEXT (2006b) *Nihongo Shidō ga hitsuyō na Gaikokujin Jidō Seito no Ukeire Jōkyō (Foreign Students needing Instruction in Japanese Language)*. On WWW at http://www.mext.go.jp/b_menu/houdou/18/04/06042520/001/001.htm. Accessed 15 September 2006.

MEXT (2006c) *"Shōgakkō Eigo Katsudō Jisshi Jōkyo Chōsa (Heisei 17 Nendo)" no omona Kekka Gaisetsu (Outline of the major results of the 2005 survey on the current state of implementation of English activities in elementary schools)*. On WWW at http://www.mext.go.jp/b_menu/houdou/18/03/06031408/001.htm. Accessed 4 October 2006.

MEXT (2006d) *Wagakuni no Ryūgakusei Seido no Gaiyō (Outline of Japan's International Student System)*. On WWW at http://www.mext.go.jp/a_menu/koutou/ryugaku/06082503/001.pdf. Accessed 15 December 2006.

MEXT (2005a) *Monbu Kagaku Hakusho (White Paper on Education, Culture, Sports, Science and Technology)*. On WWW at http://www.mext.go.jp/b_menu/hakusho/html/hpba200501/index.htm. Accessed 29 November 2006.

MEXT (2005b) *Redesigning Compulsory Education: Summary of the Report of the Central Council for Education*. On WWW at www.mext.go.jp/b_menu/shingi/chukyo/chukyo0/toushin/06051511.pdf. Accessed 4 October 2006. The full report is available in Japanese at http://www.mext.go.jp/b_menu/shingi/chukyo/chukyo0/toushin/05102601.htm. The full report lists the teaching of English at elementary school level as a response to globalization.

MEXT (2004) *Gaikokugo Senmon Bukai ni okeru Shingi Jōkyō ni tsuite (The Activities of the Specialist Committee on Foreign Languages)*. On WWW at http://www.mext.go.jp/b_menu/shingi/chukyo/chukyo3/gijiroku/015/05032201/006.htm. Accessed 9 November 2006.

MEXT (2003a) *Action Plan to Cultivate "Japanese with English Abilities"*. On WWW at http://www.mext.go.jp/b_menu/houdou/15/03/03033101/001.pdf. Accessed 26 September 2006.

MEXT (2003b) *Heisei 14 Nendo Kōtō Gakkō nado ni okeru Kokusai Kōryū nado no Jōkyō (Gaisetsu) (Outline of the Situation of International Exchange in High Schools and Other Schools in 2002)*. On WWW at http://www.mext.go.jp/b_menu/houdou/16/05/04051101.htm#06. Accessed 14 September 2006.

MEXT (2003c) *Regarding the Establishment of an Action Plan to Cultivate "Japanese with English Abilities*. On WWW at http://www.mext.go.jp/english/topics/03072801.htm. Accessed 26 September 2006.

MEXT (2003d) *The Course of Study for Foreign Languages*. On WWW at http://www.mext.go.jp/english/shotou/030301.htm. Accessed 27 September 2006.

MEXT (2002) *Developing a strategic plan to cultivate "Japanese with English abilities."* On WWW at http://www.mext.go.jp/english/news/2002/07/020901.htm. Accessed 26 September 2006.

MEXT (2001) *'JET Puroguramu Hyōka Chōsa' Ankeeto Kekka Gaiyō (Summary of Results of a Survey evaluating the JET Program)*. On WWW at http://www.mext.go.jp/b_menu/houdou/13/11/011121/02.htm. Accessed 26 September 2006.

Miller, R. A. (1982) *Japan's Modern Myth: The Language and Beyond*. New York: Weatherhill.

Ministry of Education (1998) *Gakushū Shidō Yōryō: Kokugo (Course of Study Guidelines: Japanese Language)*. On WWW at http://www.mext.go.jp/b_menu/shuppan/sonota/990301b/990301d.htm. Accessed 22 September 2006.

Ministry of Education (1997) *Monbusho's budget for the Fiscal Year 1997*. On WWW at http://www.mext.go.jp/english/yosan/970401.htm. Accessed 28 November 2006.

Ministry of Education (1991) *'Wagakuni no Bunkyō Shisaku' Heisei 3nendo: Dai2 Bunkyō Shisaku no Dōkō to Tenkai: Dai1shō Kyōiku Kaikaku (Japan's Cultural Policies 1991: No. 2 Trends and Development in Cultural Policy: Chapter One, Education Reform)*. Tokyo: Okurasho Insatsukyoku.

Ministry of Justice Japan (2006) *Kako Jūnenkan no Kika Kyoka Shinseisha-sū, Kika Kyokasha-sū nado no Imin (Migrants by numbers of applicants for naturalisation approval in the past ten years, numbers approved and others)*. On WWW at http://www.moj.go.jp/TOUKEI/t_minj03.html. Accessed 11 September 2006.

Ministry of Justice Japan (2004) *Number of foreign nationals registered (Dec. 2004)*. On WWW at http://www.moj.go.jp/ENGLISH/IB/ib-01.html. Accessed 8 September 2006.

Ministry of Public Management, Home Affairs, Posts and Telecommunications (2006) *Heisei 18 Nenban: Jōhō Tsūshin Hakusho (2006 Information and Communications in Japan)*. On WWW at http://www.johotsusintokei.soumu.go.jp/whitepaper/ja/h18/index.html. Accessed 6 November 2006.

Mizui, Y. (2006) SELHi in action: Schools' water study helps English flow. *Daily Yomiuri Online* 7 March 2006. Archived on WWW on the Linguist List at http://listserv.linguistlist.org/cgi-bin/wa?A2=ind0603a&L=edling&P=3652. Accessed 29 September 2006.

Monbu Kagakushō Kōtō Kyōiku-kyoku Daigaku Shinkō-ka (2006) *Daigaku ni okeru Kyōiku Naiyō nado no Kaikaku Jōkyō ni tsuite: 1. Karikyuramu Kaikaku no Jisshi Jōkyō (Regarding the Reform of Educational Content in Universities: 1. The Implementation of Curriculum Reform)*. On WWW at http://www.mext.go.jp/b_menu/houdou/18/06/06060504/001.htm. Accessed 14 September 2006.

Monbu Kagakushō Shotō Chūtō Kyōiku-kyoku Kokusai Kyōiku-ka (2005) *Heisei 16 Nendo Kōtō Gakkō nado ni okeru Kokusai Kōryū nado no Jōkyō ni tsuite (International Exchange in High Schools and Other Schools in 2004)*. On WWW at http://www.mext.go.jp/b_menu/houdou/17/10/05102501/001.pdf. Accessed 14 September 2006.

Murakami H. (2003) A slow boat to China (Alfred Birnbaum, trans.). *The Elephant Vanishes* (pp. 218–239). London: Vintage.

Neustupný, J. (1987) *Communicating with the Japanese*. Tokyo: The Japan Times.

Nikkei (2005) *Comparison of Japanese & Overseas Media*. On WWW at http://www.nikkei-ad.com/media_data/en/japan_market/j_market_compare.html. Accessed 2 November 2006.

Nikkei Shakai (2002) *Giron hyakushutsu no dekasegi seminaa – imaya 'Burajiru imin' – keizai ni sayū sarenai kōzō (Controversial seminar on soujourners – now we are Brazilian migrants – a structure not controlled by the economy)*. On WWW at http://www.brazil.ne.jp/nikkey/news/126.html. Accessed 3 November 2006.

Nippaku 21 Seiki Kyōgikai (2006) *Aratana Nippaku Kankei o mesashite (Towards a new Japan-Brazil Relationship)*. On WWW at http://www.mofa.go.jp/mofaj/area/brazil/pdfs/21_kyogikai_t.pdf. Accessed 3 November 2007.

Nishimura, Y. (2004) Establishing a community of practice on the Internet: Linguistic behaviour in online Japanese communication. In Berkeley Linguistics Society (eds) *Proceedings of the 29th Annual Meeting of the Berkeley Linguistics Society* (pp. 337–348). Berkeley, CA: University of California Press.

PACE (2005) *A Practical Guide to Publishing in Japan*. On WWW at www.pace.or.jp/English/practical%20guide/p-14-16.pdf. Accessed 6 November 2006.

Pang, C. (2000) *Negotiating Identity in Contemporary Japan: The Case of Kikokushijo*. London: Kegan Paul International.

Prime Minister's Commission on Japan's Goals in the Twenty-First Century (2000) *The Frontier Within: Individual Empowerment and Better Governance in the New Millennium*. On WWW at http://www.kantei.go.jp/jp/21century/report/overview.html. Accessed 18 October 2006.

Ricento, T. (2000) *Ideology, Politics, and Language Policies: Focus on English*. Amsterdam: John Benjamins.

Round-table Committee for the Improvement of English Teaching Methods (2000) *Eigo Shidō Hōhō nado Kaizen no Suishin ni kansuru Kondankai: Shingi Keika Hōkoku (Progress report on investigations into the improvement of English teaching methods)*. On WWW at www.mext.go.jp/b_menu/houdou/12/06/000609.htm. Accessed 17 October 2006.

Ryang, S. (1997) *North Koreans in Japan: Language, Ideology and Identity*. Boulder, CO: Westview Press.

Sakamoto, T. (1981) Beginning reading in Japan. In L. Ollila (ed.) *Beginning Reading Instruction in Different Countries* (pp. 16–25). Newark, NJ: International Reading Association.

Seeley, C. (1991) *A History of Writing in Japan*. Leiden: Brill.

Shibatani, M. (1990) *The Languages of Japan*. Cambridge: Cambridge University Press.

Shiramizu, S. (2004a) Japan's Ethnic Media: Brazilian Newspapers Evolve with Community. *Japan Media Review*. On WWW at http://www.japanmediareview.com/japan/research/1099706235.php. Accessed 7 September 2006.

Shiramizu, S. (2004b) Japan's Ethnic Media: Little Fish in Big Pond Reach Out to Expats. *Japan Media Review*. On WWW at http://www.japanmediareview.com/japan/research/1099706235.php. Accessed 7 September 2006.

Siddle, R. (2002) An epoch-making event? The 1997 Ainu Cultural Promotion Act and its impact. *Japan Forum* 14 (3), 405–423.

SMJ (Solidarity Network with Migrants Japan) (2004) *Who and what migrant workers are*. On WWW at http://www.jca.apc.org/migrant-net/English/migrantworker/migrants_is_e.html. Accessed 9 November 2006.

Spolsky, B. (2004) *Language Policy*. Cambridge and New York: Cambridge University Press.

Statistical Research and Training Institute, Ministry of Internal Affairs and Communication, Japan (2006) "Registered foreigners in Japan." *Japan in Figures 2006*. On WWW at http://www.stat.go.jp/english/data/figures/index.htm. Accessed 11 September 2006.

Statistics Bureau, Ministry of Internal Affairs and Communication, Japan (no date) *Foreigners by Nationality (44 Groups), Age (Five-year Groups) and Sex*. On WWW at http://www.stat.go.jp/English/data/kokusei/2000/gaikoku/00/hyodai.htm. Accessed 11 September 2006.

Student Services Division, Higher Education Bureau, MEXT (2005) *Outline of the Student Exchange System in Japan*. On WWW at www.mext.go.jp/a_menu/koutou/ryugaku/06021615/002.pdf. Accessed 17 October 2006.

Taira, K. (1997) Troubled national identity: The Ryukyuans/Okinawans. In M. Weiner (ed.) *Japan's Minorities: The Illusion of Homogeneity* (pp. 140–177). London: Routledge.

Tamaoka, K. (1996) *A Japanese Perspective on Literacy and Biliteracy: A National Paper on Japan*. ERIC ED408563.

Tanabe, Y. (2004) *Tanabe Memo: Daigaku no Eigo Kyōiku no Arikata o kangaeru (Tanabe Memorandum: How English Education in Universities should be)*. On WWW at http://www.jacet.org/2004/040620tanabe_memo.pdf. Accessed 16 October 2004.

Taylor, I. and Taylor, M. (1995) *Writing and Literacy in Chinese, Korean and Japanese*. Amsterdam: John Benjamins.

The Japan Forum (1998) *Kankoku Chōsengo to Chūgokugo Kyōiku no Torikumikō (Schools involved in Korean and Chinese language Education)*. On WWW at http://www.tjf.or.jp/korean/pdf/jk_j2.pdf. Accessed 18 October 2006.

The Japan Times (27 April 2006) *Record 20,962 foreign kids lack Japanese fluency*. On WWW at http://search.japantimes.co.jp/print/nn20060427b1.html. Accessed 11 September 2006.

The Japan Times (18 April 2006) *Portuguese-language texts aid Brazilian kids*. On WWW at http://search.japantimes.co.jp/cgi-bin/nn20060418f1.html. Accessed 8 September 2006.

The Japan Times (18 October 2005) *Aso says Japan is nation of 'one race'*. On WWW at http://search.japantimes.co.jp/cgi-bin/nn20051018a7.html. Accessed 22 February 2006.

Torikai, K. (2005) The challenge of language and communication in twenty-first century Japan. *Japanese Studies* 25 (3), 249–256.

Trends in Japan (1996) *Multicultural Publications: Foreigners in Japan Find an Oasis of Information*. On WWW at http://web-japan.org/trends96/honbun/tj960904.html. Accessed 8 September 2006.

Twine, N. (1991) *Language and the Modern State: The Modernization of Written Japanese*. London: Routledge.

United Nations Development Programme (2003) *Human Development Indicators 2003*. On WWW at http://hdr.undp.org/reports/global/2003/pdf/hdr03_HDI.pdf. Accessed 6 December 2006.

United Nations Population Division (2001) *Replacement Migration: Japan*. On WWW at http://www.un.org/esa/population/publications/migration/japan.pdf. Accessed 8 November 2006.

Vasishth, A. (1997) The model minority: The Chinese community in Japan. In M. Weiner (ed.) *Japan's Minorities: The Illusion of Homogeneity* (pp. 108–139). London: Routledge.

Wetzel, P. (2004) *Keigo in Modern Japan: Polite Language from Meiji to the Present*. Honolulu: University of Hawaii Press.

World Association of Newspapers (2005) *World's 100 Largest Newspapers*. On WWW at http://www.wan-press.org/print.php3?id_article=2825. Accessed 1 November 2006.

Yohan Inc. (2006) On WWW at http://www.yohan.co.jp/english/index.html. Accessed 7 November 2006.

Yomiuri Online (28 March 2006a) *Shō5 kara no Eigo no Hisshūka, 2010 Nendo nimo Dōnyū e (Towards mandatory English from elementary Year 5, beginning in 2010)*. On WWW at http://www.yomiuri.co.jp/kyoiku/news/20060328ur11.htm. Accessed 4 October 2006.

Yomiuri Online (28 March 2006b) *Chūō Kyōiku Shingikai, Shō5 kara no Eigo no Hisshūka o Teigen" (Central Council for Education proposes English become mandatory from elementary Year 5).* On WWW at http://www.yomiuri.co.jp/kyoiku/news/20060328ur02.htm. Accessed 4 October 2006.

Yoshida, A. (2002) The curriculum reform of the 1990s: What has changed? *Higher Education* 43, 43–63.

Yoshida K. (2005) A comparison of the English proficiencies of Japanese (SELHi vs. non-SELHi), Korean, and Chinese high school students. *ASTE Newsletter* 53, 1–10. On WWW at http://pweb.sophia.ac.jp/%7Eyosida-k/%91%E6%82T%82R%8D%86.pdf. Accessed 16 October 2006.

Yoshida, K. (2002) From the fish bowl to the open seas: Taking a step toward the real world of communication. *TESOL Matters* 12 (1). On WWW at http://www.tesol.org/s_tesol/sec_document.asp?CID = 193&DID = 913. Accessed 9 November 2006.

The Language Situation in Nepal

Sonia Eagle
English Department, Kanda University of International Studies, 1-4-1 Wakaba, Mihama-ku, Chiba-shi, Chiba-ken, 261-0014, Japan

This monograph describes the language situation in Nepal in its historical and social perspective as well as language planning and policy implemented by the national government over the last fifty years. Discussion is included on the local languages, multilingualism and lingua franca. Consideration is given to languages in specific domains such as national and private education, the military and the Gurkha regiments, literature, the media, tourism, trade, international affairs and daily life. The relationship between caste, class, ethnic groups and language is also outlined. Case studies are incorporated to illustrate certain language issues. Ecological variables affecting language use and register, language death and language revival are considered. Finally, recommendations are suggested in regard to the future of language planning in Nepal.

Introduction

Nepal is an isolated and diverse nation, which presents a number of complex factors related to language planning and policy.[1] To understand the intricacies of the language problems and the multilingual and multicultural make-up of the nation, several background factors need to be considered. Geography and ecological variables, economic alternatives and limitations, migrations of people, religion, social stratification and the political history of the region are all factors that directly impinge upon language issues in Nepal, both historically and at present. In addition, recent changes related to the emergence of a modern democratic nation are having a significant impact on current language policies.

For over one hundred years the borders of Nepal were effectively closed to all foreign residents and travellers. After the opening of the country in 1950, the government made efforts to modernise the political system, develop the economy and make education available to a larger number of the people. An important part of this modernisation involved what Kaplan (1989) has referred to as 'top-down' language planning. Since 1950, official government language planning and policy has emphasised the need to adopt one language, Nepali, as the national language.

While top-down language planning, in the modern sense, began only after 1950, recorded information on languages dates back more than 2000 years. Most language matters in Nepal have not been planned; they have evolved in response to historical circumstances. However, official government involvement in language policy is not new and dates back several hundred years.

Background on Nepal

Nepal extends along the Himalayan mountain range in the north and the Ganges plains in the south. It is bordered on the south, east and west by India and on the north by the Tibetan region of The People's Republic of China. Thus it lies between two major civilisations which are culturally, linguistically and racially distinct. The impact of these two large cultural areas on Nepal is closely tied to the diverse linguistic and ethnic make-up of the country. The following summary of the background on Nepal has been greatly simplified to cover only those aspects of Nepalese culture that are particularly relevant to language issues.

The environment

The country covers an area of 147,181 square kilometres, extending about 880 kilometres in an east–west direction and less than 200 kilometres in a north–south direction (Sill & Kirkby, 1991: 35). Although Nepal is completely landlocked, it is remarkably diverse ecologically. There are three distinct geographic zones extending the length of the country in east–west directions.

The Terai

The southern part of Nepal, called the Terai, extends from the Indian border to the bottom of the foothills. The original inhabitants of the region spoke a variety of Indo-Aryan languages. The inner Terai was a swampy, tropical forest area until the mid 1950s when DDT was used to eradicate the malarial mosquitoes. The area was then opened up to extensive agricultural development and the subsequent migration of primarily Nepali speaking people from the hill and mountain regions. Due to the flat topography and an adequate supply of water, the Terai today includes the richest agricultural land in Nepal. For similar reasons, along with the relative ease of transportation to outside sources and markets, the area is also the primary industrial area of Nepal.

The hills and fertile valleys

Lying south of the high Himalayas, a number of fertile valleys and high hills make up the central region of Nepal. The altitude ranges between 900 and 2100 metres (3000 and 7000 feet) and the climate is temperate. The valleys below 1200 metres (4000 feet) were originally tree-covered, but intensive agriculture and deforestation have depleted much of the forested areas. The hills have been terraced intensively and both rainfall and irrigation farming are practised. These midlands have been the most populous regions of Nepal, although recent expansion into the Terai has altered the demographic pattern. The capital city, Kathmandu and Kathmandu Valley lie in the centre of the midlands. This region has been, and to some extent remains, the political, cultural and religious heart of the nation.

The Himalayan ranges and high plateaux

The Himalayas extend across the north of Nepal and include Mount Everest (Sagarmatha) and seven other peaks of over 8000 metres (26,000 feet). The mountain zone makes up about 25% of the landmass of Nepal and about 10% of the population, mostly Tibeto-Burman speakers, live in the area. Villages and footpaths wind up the mountains higher than 4600 metres (15,000 feet). There are no roads in the mountains. The high ranges are dissected by several north–south river systems, with villages strung along the river gorges. Animal trains, as well as human porters, traverse the stony footpaths travelling north–south throughout Nepal. These paths connect the Tibetan plateau with the Indian subcontinent and are the major trade routes running through Nepal. These trade routes are very old, dating back possibly as far as 2000 years, and they have made multilingualism a necessary and inherent part of life in Nepal from earliest times. Small airports are scattered in a few mountain valleys allowing light aircraft (up to 16 seats) to take off and land; however, they are used primarily by tourists and a few wealthy Nepalis. Few goods are brought into the mountains by air, so that even today goods are transported over the mountains by pack animals or humans. Mountaineering and trekking contribute significantly to tourism in Nepal.

The people of Nepal

By 1995, the estimated population of Nepal was 21.3 million. Population density is high and the per capita income in 1995 was estimated at US $180. The infant mortality rate is high and life expectancy is low, averaging only 54 (Anonymous, 1995a: 47–48). Nepal ranks as one of the poorest, least developed and least industrialised nations in the world. This poverty and lack of development is a critical aspect of language planning and policy in Nepal.

Despite the economic poverty of the nation, Nepal is a culturally complex and diverse country. Estimates of the number of different ethnic groups in Nepal vary greatly. Bista (1987) describes about 35 distinct ethnic groups. If language is a defining factor in determining ethnic identity, Malla (1989: 449) claims that there are about 70 mutually unintelligible languages spoken inside Nepal. Since Nepal sits at the crossroads between India, Tibet and Indochina, ethnic, racial and linguistic diversity is not surprising.

The prehistoric period

Both Buddhist and Hindu manuscripts, written in Sanskrit, date from well over 2000 years ago. They mention and include tales about the people of Nepal. Gautama Buddha was born in Lumbini in the Nepalese Terai in 563 BC and, according to legend, he or his earliest disciples were already spreading Buddhism in Nepal during the Buddha's lifetime. These early religious writings indicate that Nepal was settled more than 2000 years ago.

The Kirats and the Khas

Over the last 2000 years, several groups of people moved into Nepal at different times and from various directions. It is not always clear whether ethnic differences are the result of independent immigrations or whether the linguistically related groups evolved *in situ* into distinct cultures, as a result of isolation and ecological adaptation. In some cases, people with very different languages and traditions have lived side-by-side or in close proximity for centuries while maintaining their separate identities.

There is some evidence that Aryan cow herders ranged through the region as early as 2500 BC, but little else is known about the earliest settlers in Nepal. Over 2000 years ago, two major cultural groups, the Kirat and the Khas, migrated into the area. The Kirat (Kiratas in some sources) entered the area from the north and east. They were Mongoloid people speaking Tibeto-Burman languages. It is likely that all of the Tibeto-Burman language groups who settled in the hills and valleys (e.g. Newar, Magar and Gurung) are descended from the Kirats. Originally, these people practised Buddhism and shamanism.

An Indo-Aryan people, the Khas, entered Nepal from the west. They spoke an Indo-Aryan language and had ties with west central Asia. In time, these Aryan Khas spread from the western hills across the valleys of Nepal. They practised a form of non-caste Shiva religion and Shamanism.

In the 12th and 13th centuries, a second wave of Hindu migration spread into Nepal. High-caste Hindus, escaping the Muslim invasions, fled into the Terai and the hills. This new wave of immigrants consisted of traditional caste Hindus who spoke Indo-Aryan languages. Although their largest concentration was in the western part of Nepal, they spread throughout the country replacing, dominating, converting, or intermarrying with many of the other groups.

About 500 years ago people with close racial and cultural ties to Tibet, such as the Sherpas, migrated into the high mountain regions. They herded sheep and cultivated high mountain crops. Like Tibetans, they spoke Tibeto-Burman languages and practised Buddhism and in some cases Bonpo, a type of pre-Buddhist Tibetan animism.

In Nepal today, about 3% of the population are Muslim. They first arrived in Kathmandu around 1500. They came primarily from Kashmir and were traders in woollen goods and glass bangles. The largest group of Muslims migrated into Nepal after the Sepoy mutiny (1857–1859) in British India. In the western Terai, they are farmers and usually speak Urdu. Those who live in the towns and cities of Nepal, as traders and shop keepers, usually speak Nepali as their mother tongue. The language of religion is of course Arabic.

As this discussion suggests, Nepal has been a multicultural and multilingual country for most of its history. Although the various Tibeto-Burman speaking groups have strong and viable local cultures and identities, for most of Nepal's history the Indo-Aryan speaking people have dominated the broader political domains.

Early kingdoms and city-states

The early history of Nepal is strewn with an array of changing kings and kingdoms. Several states both in the midlands and the Terai arose, flourished and faded. Two of the most important were the Licchavi and Malla dynasties. The Licchavi period, often described as the golden age of Nepal, lasted from about AD 200 to 879. The Licchavis were apparently high-caste Hindus forced from their kingdom in northern India. After moving into Nepal, they united much of the area and established the Licchavi Kingdom. Literature flourished during the Licchavi period; most of the writings were in Sanskrit using Gupta script. Most of the Hindu Licchavi kings were tolerant of Buddhism and maintained the major Buddhist sites.

The Mallas were another Indian Kshatriya (Chhetri in Nepali) warrior caste with a kingdom in India dating back before the time of the Buddha. They dominated Nepal from AD 1200 to 1768. This period is marked by a florescence of art, literature, construction and architecture. During this period books were written in Sanskrit and Newari, and according to Tharpa (1990: 45) some still exist in the government library. Sanskrit was used for religious texts and court poetry. Although the Mallas claimed Indo-Aryan ancestry, Yadav (1990: 175) states that the language of the Malla courts was Newari, the Tibeto-Burman language of the local residents of Kathmandu Valley.

Perhaps the most significant contribution of the Mallas was the codification of new religious and social laws that restructured Nepalese society along a strict, orthodox Hindu configuration. At this time, even many of the Buddhist groups adopted at least an incipient caste system. Towards the end of the Malla period, feuds and instability fragmented the country again. Nepal was divided into a large number of feudal city-states and there was little unity in the region.

One problem, which relates even to the present historical period, is determining the origins of the various ruling kings of Nepal. One theory, which has just been discussed, asserts that they were high-caste kings and warriors from India who conquered and ruled the local population. Another theory (Bista, 1994: 19) suggests that these early kings were indigenous Nepalese who justified their right to rule by adopting Hindu caste privilege. Bista refers to their 'borrowed pedigrees' and their 'alleged' Indian background. Both theories appear in the literature. This issue is relevant to the Licchavi and Malla dynasties as well as to the Shah/Rana rulers of modern Nepal.

Traditional Languages of Nepal

Statistics on the number of languages spoken in Nepal are inconsistent. Official government census data are also variable. The 1952/54 census recorded 36 separate languages, whereas the 1981 census listed only 18. These languages are divided into 11 or 12 major languages spoken by over 1% of the population and a large number of minority languages spoken by less than 1% of the people. The principal languages of Nepal (Nepali, Maithili, Bhojpuri, Tamang, Abadhi, Tharu, Newari and other) by ecological zone for the 1952 and 1981 census data are listed in Figure 1. Other scholars claim that there are about 70 mutually unintelligible languages in Nepal. Table 1 lists what Malla (1989: 449) refers to as some of the better-known languages, together with government census data for those languages that were recorded in the 1952/54, 1961, 1971 and 1981 censuses.[2]

Language families and race

On the basis of Table 1, a number of generalisations may be made. Four language families can be found in Nepal:

(1) Dravidian;
(2) Austroasiatic;
(3) Sino-Tibetan (Tibeto-Burman branch);
(4) Indo Aryan.

Both of the first two language groups are small in number and, according to Bista (1987: 146/138 respectively), these groups migrated into the Terai region of Nepal from India in fairly recent times.

With regard to the two predominant language families in Nepal, the number of Tibeto-Burman languages (36) is considerably larger than the number of Indo-European languages (14). In the 1981 census, however, there were slightly less than two million Tibeto-Burman speakers and over twelve million

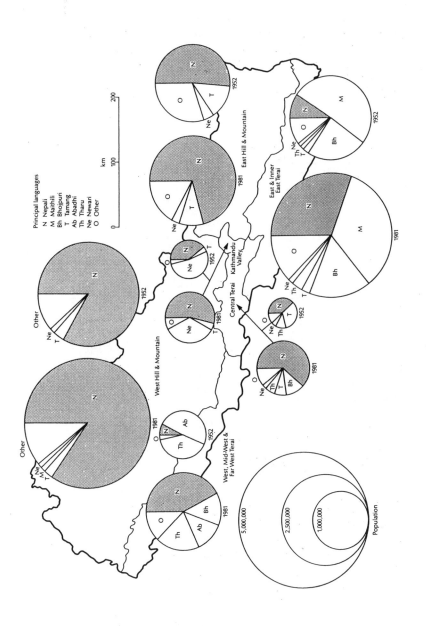

Figure 1 Map of principal languages of Nepali (1952 and 1981 census) by ecological zone (adapted from Sill & Kirkby, 1991: 97)

Table 1 Languages of Nepal and available census data

Languages	1952/54	1961	1971	1981
Dravidian Languages				
None Listed	–	–	–	–
Austroasiatic Languages				
Santhal/Satar	–	10,645	3,193	5,804,
Sino-Tibetan Languages				
1. Bhujel	–	–	–	–
2. Bramu/Bhramu	–	–	–	–
3. Byansi	1,786	–	–	–
4. Chantel	–	–	–	–
5. Chepang	14,216	9,247	–	–
6. Dhimal	5,671	8,186	–	–
7. Dolpali	–	–	–	–
8. Dura	–	–	–	–
9. Gurung*	162,192	157,778	171,609	174,464
10. Jangali	–	–	–	–
11. Jirel	–	–	–	–
12. Kagate	–	–	–	–
13. Kaike	–	–	–	–
14. Kham	–	–	–	–
15. Khambu	–	–	–	–
16. Kusunda	–	–	–	–
17. Lepcha/Rong	–	1,272	–	–
18. Lhomi	–	–	–	–
19. Limbu*	145,511	138,705	170,787	129,234
20. Magar*	273,780	254,675	288,383	212,628
21. Managba	–	–	–	–
22. Meche	523	938	–	–
23. Newari*	383,184	377,727	454,979	448,746
24. Nishangba	–	–	–	–
25. Pahari	864	3,002	–	–
26. Rai-Kirat*	236,049	239,749	232,264	221,333
27. Raji	1,514	801	–	–
28. Routya	–	–	–	–
29. Sherpa	70,132	84,229	–	73,589
30. Sunuwar	17,299	13,362	20,380	10,650
31. Surel	–	–	–	–
32. Tamang*	494,745	518,882	555,056	522,416
33. Thakali	3,307	4,134	–	–
34. Thami	10,240	9,046	–	–
35. Tibetan	–	–	–	–
36. Vayu/Hayu	233	–	–	–

Table 1 (*cont.*)

Languages	1952/54	1961	1971	1981
Indo-European Languages				
1. Avadhi*	–	447,960	316,950	234,343
2. Bhojpuri*	16,355	557,357	806,480	1,142,805
3. Bote	649	–	–	–
4. Chauraute	–	–	–	–
5. Danuwar	9,138	11,624	–	–
6. Darai	3,084	1,645	–	–
7. Hindi	80,181	2,867	–	–
8. Maithili*	300,768	1,130,401	1,327,242	1,668,308
9. Majhi	5,729	5,854	–	–
10. Marvari	4,244	6,716	–	–
11. Nepali*	4,013,567	4,796,528	6,060,758	8,767,361
12. Rajvamsi	35,543	55,803	55,124	59,383
13. Tharu*	359,594	406,907	495,881	545,685
14. Urdu	32,545	2,650	–	–
Totals	6,686,364	9,263,408	10,969,045	14,230,271

*These languages are classified as the major languages of Nepal.
– indicates that the number of speakers of these languages was unrecorded.

Indo-European speakers, making the Indo-Aryan language group the largest in Nepal.

Table 1 also shows a dramatic increase in the number speakers of some Indo-European language groups. Bhojpuri and Maithili speakers significantly increased in number, and the number of Nepali speakers more than doubled from about four million in the 1952/54 census to nearly nine million in the 1981 census. Nepali has spread throughout Nepal, but the other two languages are spoken primarily in the Terai region. Another Indo-European language group from the Terai, Tharu, shows a modest increase in number, while Avadhi speakers show a sharp decline. Speakers of Newari, the original Tibeto-Burman language of the Kathmandu Valley, increased in number by 15%. With regard to the other mountain dwelling people who speak Tibeto-Burman languages, Gurung, Rai-Kirat, Tamang and Sherpa remained relatively the same across the census periods, Limbu has an erratic pattern and Magar and Sunuwar speakers have both declined in number.

Several language groups that were recorded in the original first or second census went unrecorded in the later census. In most cases (e.g. the Buansi, Dhimal, Lepcha/Rong, Meche, Pahari, Raji, Thakali, Vayu/Hayu, Bote, Majhi and Marvari), their numbers in the first census were low, amounting to less than 10,000. For other large language groups such as Hindi and Urdu, which were not recorded in the last two censuses, one can only speculate that since these are languages are closely related to Nepali, they were included in the Nepali count.

Although originally there may have been a relationship between race and language families, this distinction is no longer clear cut. The original Gorkha rulers, who were Indo-Aryan Nepali speakers, today appear to be Mongoloid or mixed race people. Similarly, although the Newari speakers were originally Mongoloid, today they include both Indo-Aryan and mixed race people. In the Terai, although they speak an Indo-Aryan language and their culture is Hindu-based, the Tharu are classified as Mongoloid.

Census data reliability

The census data in Table 1 suggest that there have been several rather surprising changes in language demography over the last 50 years. No doubt there are valid reasons for some of these variations. The population of the country has been increasing at a rapid rate. The number of people tabulated went from 6,686,364 in 1952–54 to 14,230,271 in 1981, an increase of 47%. People have migrated into the Terai, both from the hills and from India, altering the demographic picture and the attendant language statistics. With a new emphasis on Nepali as the national language, language loss may have occurred in some areas. However, Malla (1989: 448) questions the scientific accuracy of the censuses and recommends that they be used with scepticism and caution, and Yadav (1990: 41) suggests that there may have been some politically-motivated manipulation of the language data. For example, the very large jump in recorded Nepali speakers seems too great to be accounted for only by population growth or language shift. At the same time, the large number of Hindi and Urdu speakers recorded in 1952–54 and 1961 went unrecorded in 1971 and 1981. Such an omission seems unlikely unless the criteria for determining language classifications were altered in the later census questionnaires.

Early Religions and Related Language in Nepal

Religion is an integral part of the daily lives of most Nepalis. Two world religions, Hinduism (Shiva sect) and Buddhism, have existed in Nepal for well over 2000 years with each claiming precedence. The 1962 constitution defined Nepal as an 'independent, indivisible and sovereign monarchical Hindu state' (Burghart, 1994: 5), and for many Nepalese people, the Nepalese king is still believed to be an incarnation of Lord Vishnu (Sharma, 1989: 333). The 1981 census claims that 89% of the people are Hindu, 5% are Buddhist and 3% are Muslim. Jains, Sikhs and Christians make up the remaining 3%. The census, as previously noted with regard to languages, may also involve politically-motivated manipulation of the religious data, and it is likely that the Buddhist percentage has been somewhat under-recorded. Over the centuries, the two religions have mingled and a synthesised form has been practised by many Nepalese people.

The earliest form of Hinduism in Nepal is associated with Shiva (Pashupath in Nepal). The early Licchavi kings built the Temple of Pashupatinath next to Kathmandu. This golden-roofed temple complex is, even today, a major pilgrimage site. Early Hindu scriptures, inscriptions, and various forms of writing were in Sanskrit in Gupta script. Sanskrit, as the language of the Hindu scriptures, was not a spoken language and its impact on the local population was limited to priestly rituals. Malla (1989: 446) writes:

> With the arrival of the Licchavis around the early centuries AD, Sanskrit was encouraged and patronised as the language of epigraphy. As against

the local vernaculars it was probably the symbol of the ruling and cultural elite. The very remoteness of this language from the speech of the common man presented itself as the voice of authority requiring the services of the initiated mediator (*dutaka*) for interpreting the edicts. Steadily, literacy became the preserved function of the priesthood and Sanskrit was the language of both religions in Nepal. This is evident from the fact that all the extant ancient sacred texts of both Hinduism and Mahayana Buddhism found in Nepal are in Sanskrit. Ancient Nepalese manuscripts belonging to the 9th and 10th centuries are … [in] Sanskrit. As the priesthood built a stronghold in society in the first millennium AD, they sanctified Sanskrit in all rituals and localised literacy as a priestly occupation.

While the general populace was influenced by rituals in Sanskrit, they were never literate. This limited the impact of the religious language on the common people.

Buddhism spread to Nepal during or shortly after the lifetime of Gautama Buddha about 2500 years ago. Buddhist structures and monuments are found throughout Nepal. The language of early Buddhism was Sanskrit, but by the time of the Malla kings, Buddhist manuscripts and inscriptions were also written in Newari. The high mountain Tibeto-Burman people, such as the Sherpas, who have close cultural and linguistic ties to Tibet, use Tibetan script in Buddhist writings.

In addition to these two major religions, various forms of Shamanism were and are practised throughout Nepal by all but the highest caste Hindus. Most of the Tibeto-Burman speakers practise a kind of ecstatic Shamanism, while Shamanism associated with Hinduism is more allied with divination and fortune telling. Both forms involve faith healing and curing, and native Shaman curers are often the only alternative for many rural Nepalese who may have no access to Western-trained medical doctors. Shamanistic religious rituals are conducted in the local vernacular and the practitioners are usually non-literate. The Shaman-istic practices exist side-by-side with both Buddhism and Hinduism. Each reli-gion operates in a separate domain and there is little or no conflict between them. Religious tolerance and diversity has a long history in Nepal.

Despite this religious tolerance, the general belief that Hinduism is the most prestigious and important religion of the area is widespread, particularly in regard to regulations of caste, status, and privilege. Masagara's (1991) study of the impact of French Christianity on Rwanda society concludes that religion 'not only changed the language structure, but it also changed the nature of familial relationships, the social hierarchy, and the economic structure' (cited in Kaplan & Baldauf, 1997: 228). Over a period of several hundred years, the Hinduisation of much of Nepal has had comparable ramifications, affecting the economic system, the family structure, marriage patterns, and inheritance rights, as well as the social organisation tied to caste and privilege. The language of this change was not the language of religion, Sanskrit, but Nepali (Gorkhali), the Indo-European vernacular language of the Gorkha king and his armies. Through military conquest and legislation, the Gorkhas effectively enforced on the local populations the Hindu belief in the divine origin of the caste system, including the vertical and fatalistic social structure that it perpetuates. A review of the caste system and social hierarchy in Nepal illustrates how this was brought about.

Caste, Social Hierarchy and Language in Early Nepal

Caste distinctions were not a marked part of the early cultures of Nepal. Animistic and Shamanistic religions and societies were egalitarian. Buddhism, when it followed the original teachings, rejected the concept of fixed castes. The Shiva-worshipping and animistic Aryan Khas were also non-caste Hindus. Although the early kings, such as the Licchavis, may have recognised and practised the Hindu caste system, this hierarchical classification was accepted only by the elite in the ruling courts. It had few ramifications for the common people or the tribal groups in Nepal. After the Muslim invasions of India, a large number of high-caste Hindus fled from India into Nepal. To establish their distinct identity and to defend their cultural traditions, these new immigrants emphasised caste rankings and actively spread their belief system throughout Nepal. This Hinduisation or Sanskritisation of Nepal remains a major political controversy in this newly emerging democracy today.

Tibeto-Burman speakers, even now, tend to live in geographically circumscribed rural areas and constitute distinct, tribal-like cultures. The Indo-Aryan Hindu people first settled in western Nepal, but gradually spread across the hill and valley regions, occupying whatever land was available or could be claimed. Their identity was determined by their relatively uniform caste system, religion, and language, rather than by a specific geographic location or a tribal identity. The majority of them owned and cultivated land. In Nepal the occupation castes, while not exactly untouchables, were at the bottom of the caste system. Ethnic or tribal people (most of them Mongoloid, Tibeto-Burman speakers) were ranked in the middle castes. The spread of this fixed system of caste relegated the Tibeto-Burman speakers to an inferior caste and effectively eliminated them from high-ranking positions.

Traditional Education in Early Nepal

During the early years in Nepal, two systems of education existed associated with the two major religions. Instruction in both traditions was generally classical and formal rather than practical. The Sanskrit system of education was based mainly on Hindu classical scriptures, requiring a high proficiency in Sanskrit. According to Vir (1988: 29), the Sanskrit schools were single-teacher schools and only the highest caste Hindus were educated. The Buddhist *gompas* or monasteries, originally only for the monks, were later opened to all people. According to Vir, these two distinct systems of education continued in Nepal until the end of the 12th century. By the 13th century, the Hindu influence on education became increasingly important.

In 1745, during the late Malla period, the first Christian Capuchin missionaries entered Nepal. After being driven out of Peking and Lhasa, they settled in Patan in the Kathmandu Valley (Kansakar, 1989: 46). Their impact on Nepal in terms of religion, education, and language appears to be minimal. Vir states that while some missionaries translated Hindu manuscripts into English, other missionaries from Italy destroyed thousands of Hindu manuscripts, offending the Hindu kings (Vir 1988: 31). Kansakar (1989: 46) states that 'before they could make any great progress in conversion, the Gurkhas entered into the Kathmandu Valley and expelled them from Nepal with their converts, mostly Newars'.

The great diversity of people, cultures, languages, and religions in Nepal has been a critical factor influencing the nationalisation and modernisation of this developing nation. The modern era in Nepal began in 1768 when the invading Gorkha army conquered the Malla kings in Kathmandu Valley.

The Gorkha Era (1869–1951)

The end of the medieval period in Nepal

By the 18th century, the Malla kingdom of Kathmandu Valley had fragmented into several kingdom states. At the same time, in the western part of Nepal, other kingdoms and empires had existed concurrently with the Mallas. In the early 18th century, the Shah-king of the Khas state of Gorkha, Prithvi Narayan, united the disparate western kingdoms and created a powerful army that included Khas, Magar, and Gurung soldiers. The army marched east and, in 1769, defeated the remaining states of the Malla kingdom (Stiller, 1989: 101). The two countries, Gorkha and Nepal, were thus united creating the present-day nation of Nepal. The capital was established in Kathmandu from which the Gorkha kings ruled the nation.

One factor credited to the Gorkhas was that they were able to create a united and secure Nepal in the face of the continuing encroachment of the British into the area. The Roman Catholic missionaries, who had entered and established missions in Nepal under the Malla kings, were suspected of covertly supporting the British. They were expelled from Nepal by the Gorkhas and the nation was closed to all foreigners from that time until 1951. The Gorkha armies proceeded eastward, by 1789 annexing land as far as Sikkim, and Nepal maintained unity over this expansive nation until the Anglo-Nepal War in 1814. The language of the Gorkha kings was the Indo-Aryan language, Gorkhali, now called Nepali.

The impact of British India on Nepal

Although Nepal always remained an independent nation, it was nonetheless strongly influenced by the British Raj in the 18th and 19th centuries. In 1814, the British declared war on Nepal and the Nepalese army was defeated. The British claimed the Terai and parts of eastern Nepal, but they were never able to subdue the whole of Nepal.

Although Nepal lost the battle, the British soldiers were impressed by the extraordinary bravery of the Nepalese soldiers. They made an agreement with the government to recruit Nepalese soldiers to help maintain and extend British rule in India. Thus the famous Gurkha regiments in the British and Indian army were begun with the first recruitment organised in 1815. Most of the Gurkha regiments, from the earliest times until the present, came from the hill and mountain regions of Nepal and were Mongoloid or mixed-race people. Generally, they were not from the high-caste ruling elite. Most of them spoke a Tibeto-Burman language, not Nepali, as a first language, but Nepali became the lingua franca of the whole Nepalese army, including the British-Gurkha regiments. Even the

British officers in the Gurkha regiments were required to learn Nepali (Farwell, 1985: 118).

In 1857, the Gurkha regiments helped the British suppress the Sepoy mutiny in India. As a reward, the Terai was returned to Nepal and the current borders of the nation were established.

The Rana oligarchy

In 1847, a series of palace plots, intrigues, and a massacre resulted in a successful *coup d'état* in which the royal family was overthrown. Jung Bahadur Rana took over the government as the Prime Minister of Nepal. Although Nepal did not have a colonial background, it

> ... was kept under the worst form of isolation, backwardness and economic exploitation, and the country remained a feudal state controlled by the Ranas. Their only interest was the collection of revenue and the maintenance of law and order. (Bista, 1994: 28)

Realising the inevitable fact that he must in some way deal with the British, as well as maintain his position as ruler of Nepal, Prime Minister Rana took an unprecedented trip to England in 1850. On his return he set up two specific goals:

- remodel the Nepalese army along British lines, and
- teach English and provide a Western-style education to his children and close family members.

Thus, during the Rana era, English and a Western-style education were not only a privilege of the elite, but a factor in reinforcing their despotic rule.

Education for the elite

Before the Rana regime, education was primarily the domain of the religious leaders. Few people other than the priests and royalty were literate. After visiting England, Jung Bahadur Rana set up a school in the palace for the children of close family members. Teachers were brought from England or India and classes were taught in English. From this time, a Western-style education was, by definition, an education in English. In 1885, the school was moved to present-day Durbar High School in Kathmandu, but education was still the prerogative of the affluent and the ruling elite. Higher education was pursued in India, usually at the English-medium convent schools. In 1918, an English-medium, Western curriculum college, Trichandra College, was set up in Kathmandu, primarily for graduates of Durbar High School. Later, schools teaching in Hindi existed in the Terai and a school in Nepali was established to train high-ranking males in clerical skills to meet the needs of the Rana government.

Muslims, being classified as low-caste or untouchable, were not allowed to attend any Nepali schools, although some traditional Urdu schools existed (Bista, 1987: 152). Bista adds that towards the end of the Rana period, the government opened a Muslim primary school, and by the 1940s Muslims were allowed to attend secondary schools and later college.

In 1950, at the end of the Rana regime, the literacy rate in Nepal was 2%. Skinner and Holland (1996: 276) state that at this time there were 8,500 students enrolled in primary schools (less than 1% of the population) and there were 332 primary and secondary schools in the country. The students in the Rana era schools were almost exclusively high-caste males and education for the masses was discouraged or even forbidden by the Ranas as being potentially subversive.

The Gurkha soldiers and education

The Gurkha regiments were educated, after enlistment, by the British in both Nepali and English. In this century this has included eight weeks of English language education. Fluency in English was a requirement for any Gurkha officer. Children of the soldiers were often educated abroad in places such as England, India, or Hong Kong. Most of the schools they attended were English-medium schools and colleges. The Gurkhas and their children were thus the first commoners to speak English in Nepal. This, along with a degree of relative affluence based on their retirement pensions, has elevated the social rank of returning soldiers and their families. Their modest pensions make possible the purchase of land and housing. Many of them became headmen or opened schools for the local children in their native villages. Some choose to live abroad or to set up residences and businesses in the Kathmandu Valley. Their unique position has been a factor in affecting the status of English in Nepal.[3]

Writing and publishing during the Gorkha period

Prior to the Gorkha period most writing was in Sanskrit. With the spread of Nepali as the lingua franca, in the 18th century, poets and writers began to write in the Nepali language. The earliest poems and writings extolled the virtues of the king, the expansion of the Gorkha kingdom, and the heroism of the soldiers. The Sanskrit epics were also popularised in Nepali and a travelogue of Jung Bahadur Rana's trip to England was written anonymously. Also, some poets wrote poems describing individuals, the cities, and the lives of the common people.

The earliest publications in Nepali were printed by Nepali students studying in Banares (Subedi, 1989: 429). By 1896, a press was set up in Kathmandu and the first Nepali magazine and newspaper were published. Other journals were published in Nepali in Banares and Darjeeling. In 1913, the Gorkha Language Publication Committee was established in Nepal and made responsible for the publication of books in Nepali.

In 1905, Nepali was made the official language of law and government, and the Prime Minister declared that documents written in languages other than Nepali were not legal in the courts. Prior to this time, Nepali had been the language of trade and the military.

Because British officers in the Gurkha regiments had to learn Nepali, the first dictionaries in Nepali and the earliest linguistic studies of Nepali were written by British scholars. Malla (1989: 458) lists several publications on the Nepali language. In 1920, A.J. Ayton published the first grammar of Nepali, and in 1931 *A Comparative and Etymological Dictionary of the Nepalese Language* was published by Ralph Turner. Dictionaries written by Nepali scholars were published in 1912, 1920 and 1949. An English-Nepali version of the Concise Oxford Dictionary was printed in 1936 and the first monolingual Nepali dictionary was published as late as 1951. Thus some standardisation of Nepali, by both British and Nepalese scholars, had begun before the end of the Rana era.

By the early 1900s, European influences on Nepali writing increased. Subedi (1989: 430) states that young people being educated abroad, as well as soldiers returning from Europe after the First World War, wrote in Nepali about change, innovations, civil rights, and even revolution.

The end of the Rana regime

Repression continued to be the hallmark of the Rana regime. Rivals of the Ranas within the family were banished to the provinces with land grants and governorships, and the landed aristocracy, who supported the Rana rulers in the kingdom, became increasingly more powerful. With the help of government officials, they increased their holdings by forcing farmers off the land, leaving many people landless. Many of the dispossessed fled to Assam, Bhutan, Burma, and Darjeeling. In the British hill areas of Darjeeling, they played an important role in establishing and working on the newly developing tea plantations. As they migrated out of Nepal, their language, Nepali also spread beyond the national boundaries. However, the increasing power of the landowners increased the poverty and exploitation inside Nepal.

After World War II, there was a significant movement towards decolonisation and independence throughout the Third World, and Nepal was affected by these world events. In 1947, India gained its independence, and by 1949, China had become a communist country. Educated Nepalese living in India organised anti-Rana political parties and B. P. Koirala, leader of the Nepali Congress Party, led an armed revolution in Nepal in 1950. In 1951, a compromise government was established creating a coalition between the Rana family, the Shah-king, and the leaders of the Nepali Congress Party. In this way, a major revolution was averted, the political power of the Ranas was reduced, the figurehead king regained power, and the people were allowed some measure of political participation. Thus Nepal began its first steps towards democracy, representative government, and the adoption of new policies in education and language planning.

The Modern Period: Politics, Education and Language Planning

Following the reforms of 1950, Nepal entered a period of political instability and unrest. After King Tribhuvan died in 1954, his son King Mahendra agreed to hold parliamentary elections. Within five years, five different cabinets were formed and political instability continued. After the elections were finally held in 1959, the Nepali Congress won a majority. However, reactionary forces opposed the reforms of the elected government, and the ensuing panic led to the take-over of the government by the king. Borre *et al.* (1994: 8) attribute illiteracy and lack of political awareness of the masses to the increasing consolidation of power in the royal family.

After assuming absolute power, the King 'dissolved parliament, imposed a ban on political parties, arrested the Prime Minister and his cabinet colleagues, locked up thousands of party workers in jails and suspended the fundamental rights of the people' (Borre *et al.*, 1994: 10). King Mahendra stated that the parliamentary system was not suitable for Nepal and was not effective in bringing about the necessary modernisation and nationalisation of the country. The King then implemented the concept of a partyless Panchayet democracy, which was continued after King Mahendra's death in 1971 by his son King Birendra, the present King of Nepal. While the government from 1950 to 1990 was marked by corruption and abuse of civil rights, it also implemented a number of changes relevant to education and language planning.

Emerging nationalism in Nepal

Although Nepal was effectively united under the Gorkha kings, the concept of Nepal as a nation was not universal. Many people living outside the central valley defined Nepal as Kathmandu and the Kathmandu Valley (formerly called the Nepal Valley). They did not consider themselves to be a part of that political entity. Given the precarious and strategically important position of Nepal, situated between India and China, developing a sense of nationhood and national unity became a priority for the central government. This policy was supported by India, since India regarded Nepal as a buffer zone between India and China. Other countries, such as the United States, were concerned about the possibility of a Chinese communist takeover of Nepal. Nepal also feared India, especially after its annexation of the country of Sikkim, and chose to maintain and strengthen an identity separate from India. As a result, a nationalisation policy was stressed by the central government of Nepal with the support of a number of countries. As a part of this policy, education and literacy were given a high priority. Also, the designation of Nepali as the only official national language, essential for uniting the country and educating the masses, was enforced. Malla (1989: 456) states that the 1959 and the 1962 Constitutions of Nepal granted the status of national language to Nepali. The slogan of this policy was 'one nation, one language'. The 'one-nation/one-language' idea originated in Europe, primarily in the 18th century, as the nations gradually emerged (Fishman, 1972). The idea or myth that a national language was essential to national unity has pervaded language planning activities everywhere during much of the post-World War II period, for example, in France, the United States, and the Philippines. The Nepalese single-language policy, associated with efforts to consolidate national unity, is consistent with this belief.

With respect to designating one language as a national language, Kaplan and Baldauf state that the language selected is sometimes assumed to be the one spoken by a majority of people in the nation, but in reality 'it is more likely to be a language associated with a power group – e.g. the people living in and around the capital city, the tribal groups which traditionally make up the army, the group with the highest level of education, or the group which controls the greatest part of the wealth' (1997: 16). In the Nepalese case, all of these criteria are relevant.

Educational policies and changes, 1950–1990

Educational reforms introduced after 1954 included the creation of a Ministry of Education and the appointment of a Secretary of Education and a Chief Inspector of Schools. At the same time, the United States offered technical advice to the government of Nepal, particularly in educational development. The American advisors, along with the Ministry of Education, organised a National Education Planning Commission (NEPC) to report on the educational needs of the country. The first college of education was founded, and teacher training and Normal Schools were begun. In 1956, the United States advisers helped organise the first university in Nepal, Tribhuvan University. Entrance to the university required high school graduation and passing grades on the School Leaving Examination (SLE). The United States advisers also stressed the need for the establishment of technical training institutions in Nepal (Bista, 1994: 123). At this time, English was the sole medium of instruction beyond high school. During the 1950s and 1960s, the school system was expanded to some extent, to include local schools in towns and villages. In 1969, the government began to institute its language planning policy, making Nepali the language of education in the elementary and high schools.

In 1969, the National Education System Plan was set up by the government with the goal of further expanding education in Nepal for the masses. The National Educational System was implemented from 1971 to 1976. Education was standardised and a national curriculum as well as textbooks in Nepali were designed. Schools were nationalised and Nepali was designated as the sole preferred medium of instruction in all of the national schools. The policy was prescribed and enforced, to a large extent, in the remaining private English-medium schools. English was designated as an International Language and was added to the curriculum in the fourth grade. While Nepali was the preferred language of instruction at the university level, courses in mathematics, science, technology, and the social sciences continued to be taught in English.

By 1985, the number of schools had increased to 11,869 primary schools, 3578 lower secondary schools, and 1321 secondary schools (Jha, 1989: 78). By 1989, there were over a million students enrolled in grades one through five (Skinner & Holland, 1996: 276). Entrance examinations and the semester calendar were incorporated into the school system and the educational budget was increased. Polytechnical schools were set up, including a women's technical school. By the late 1980s, there were 150 university campuses in Nepal with 80,000 students being admitted to the universities, while 18,000 entered the science colleges and technical schools. By 1990, the national literacy rate in Nepali was estimated variously at between 29 and 36%. In major urban centres, such as Kathmandu, it is considerably higher.

Sill and Kirkby (1991: 147) discuss the serious issue of the attrition rate of students in the Nepalese school system. They state that of the children enrolled in grade 1 between 1973 and 1979, only 30% completed grade 5. At least half of those who left school did so in the first grade. In 1981, at the secondary level, only 6.8% of the enrolled students successfully completed the secondary school leaving certificate. Sill and Kirkby add that although the number of graduates who have completed college has increased significantly from about 10,000 in 1971 to 37,330 in 1981, they still represent only a small fraction of the total school population of 2.3 million. Several Nepalese scholars have tied this high attrition rate to the government language policy that requires the use of Nepali throughout most of the school system.

The choice of Nepali as the sole national language of Nepal and the sole language to be used in the school system was, and continues to be, highly controversial. The central government rationale for this decision, strongly supported by the King and the ruling elite, was based on the fact that Nepali had been the lingua franca of the country for at least 150 years. Nepali was already established as the language of the government, the law courts, trade, the military, and the police. It was the local language that was most spoken, written and used by the people. For about 50% of the population, it is the first language,[4] and another 20 to 30% of the people are said to be bilingual in Nepali. Since it is closely related to several other Indo-Aryan languages of Nepal (e.g. Hindi and Maithili) the government claimed that it was easy for people to learn. The government policy stressed the importance of adopting a native Nepalese language (as opposed to Indian Hindi or English) to unify the nation and to establish a strong national identity. In short, it appeared to be the most logical, practical, and financially feasible language to be used as a link language and as the language of wider communication within multilingual Nepal. Some case studies, particularly of traditional Tibeto-Burman speaking culture groups, do seem to suggest that at least some level of fluency in Nepali is widespread.

Case studies related to the use of Nepali

(1) In his study of the Chantyal people of Nepal who traditionally spoke a Tibeto-Burman language, Noonan (1996: 121) states that at present all Chantyals speak Nepali, with only a quarter continuing to speak their ethnic language. The Chantyal people are a small ethnic group living in a relatively inaccessible mountain area of central Nepal. Chantyal language speakers use their ethnic language within their family and the village context. However, the Chantyal come in daily contact with Nepali speakers such as the blacksmith caste, Magar farmers, peddlers, goldsmiths, traders, police, health workers, and teachers. These people are always addressed in Nepali. Since only a quarter of this ethnic group speak Chantyal, Noonan states that '[o]ne's identity as a Chantyal is not, then, in any way related to one's ability to speak the language' (1996: 127). The decision to speak Nepali is tied to economics and status, not ethnic identity. Ethnic languages in Nepal, he adds, are in general spoken by the poor and are signs of backwardness and poverty. Economic success in the national context requires Nepali and English. He states that despite the remoteness of their location, all of these Chantyals, even children, speak Nepali and are bilingual. Changes in the Chantyal language, as it is spoken today, have involved a considerable amount of lexical borrowing and his analyses show that 74% of the words are of Nepali origin, 4% of English origin, and only 20% are Tibeto-Burman. Also, the more formal the speech, the more Nepalised it becomes. Since all schooling, by law, is in Nepali, education is likely to increase this trend, particularly since there is no Chantyal writing system. All writing in the community is necessarily in Nepali. In conclusion, Noonan states that '… it is hard to see how the language can survive' (1996: 135). Since this situation is likely to continue, he predicts the death of the language in the near future.

(2) James Fisher's (1987) study of the Magars of Tarangur, who live in the mountain region of north-west Nepal, illustrates both the multilingual abilities of the people of Nepal, as well as the increasing hegemony of Nepali and the implicit threat to indigenous languages. The Tarangur, who speak an unwritten Tibeto-Burman language, Kaike, live in three remote mountain

villages situated between the northern Tibetan-speaking, Buddhist Bhotia and the Nepali-speaking Hindus to the south. The Tarangur are farmers and middlemen traders between these two distinct groups, transporting market goods, commodities, and grain from south to north and salt from north to south. As middlemen, in addition to Kaike, all adults speak two other languages – Nepali and Tibetan (Fisher, 1987: 21). Fisher adds that the Tarangpurians not only speak these two languages but, in what he calls 'impression management', they are able to adjust their behaviour, religion, and even names to operate successfully in these two cultural traditions. In his study, Fisher has described in detail 'the present cultural heterogeneity of Tarangpur – a society which is nominally Buddhist, strongly Hinduised and still partly tribal' (1987: 189). He concludes that the motivating factors of Tarangpur life are power, status, and wealth and that the key to these pursuits lies in the hands of the Nepali Hindus and the central government. He states that there is no comparable pull from the north or from the Bhotia culture. Thus, he predicts the further Nepalisation of Tarangpur.

(3)   In a study of the Gurungs, a large community of Tibeto-Burman speaking mountain people scattered through much of the central hill region of Nepal, Regmi (1990: 61) states that all native Gurung are bilinguals; they speak Gurung as well as Nepali. But all eastern Gurungs of Ramjatar are monolinguals, speaking only Nepali. Regmi adds that the contemporary Gurung language has no script and no literature.

(4)   Another study of the Gurung by Ragsdale (1989) presents a somewhat different picture. He studied the impact of the educational reforms of the central government, along with the national exams, on Gurung students. All the children in Lamasa village, where he did his research, failed the new third grade examination administered in 1974. Many Gurung men were recruited into the Gurkha regiments in India and Britain. For example, of the Gurkha veterans who collect their pensions in the town of Pokara, 11,620 or 70% are Gurung. To be accepted in the regiments, literacy and a pass in the primary level exams was essential. According to Collett (1994: 100), most of the Gurkha recruits now are educated to Grade 9 and 10. Thus, student failure had particular ramifications for the military Gurung. Ragsdale (1989) attributed the failure to Nepal's elitist system of education, which showed little regard for its suitability to the country's needs. The third grade test, centrally prepared by high-caste Hindus and Newars, often required an abstract understanding of Nepali. The culture content of the test, while it may have been comprehensible to students in the Kathmandu Valley, was sometimes outside the experience and vocabulary of the Gurung students. Ragsdale stressed that language was a significant factor in student failure. He writes:

> Gurungs have proved highly adaptable in learning to speak Nepali and through the auspices of the army have achieved a relatively high rate of literacy in the national language. ... Gurung remains the language of kinship and home life. Outside the classroom it dominates the play-ground. ... Further, the Nepali brought home from the army has been notorious for its simplicity and lacks sophistication. Nepali spoken

in Gurung villages lacks the infusion of Sanskrit terms or complex constructions that mark educated speech. ... The Gurung students in 1974 did not completely understand the instructions of the proctors or of the test itself. (Ragsdale, 1989: 149)

He goes on to say that the proctor who explained the examination procedures spoke in a highly Sanskritised fashion which the Gurung children had trouble understanding.

This example, while it refers to the Nepali understood and spoken by the Gurung, is no doubt representative of other Tibeto-Burman speakers, many of whom are illiterate and use only spoken Nepali. It illustrates how the nationally prescribed curriculum and examination system favours native Nepali speakers and the urban elite and does not take into account the cultures, experience, and needs of the ethnic minorities. Ragsdale suggests that, given the high degree of competition for civil servant and academic jobs in Nepal, it is possible that the tests were designed to benefit urban Newar and Indo-Nepalese students, even if this was done unconsciously. Gurung parents were angry about the test results and this may account, in part, for the recent increase in attendance at English-medium boarding schools.

(5) Webster (1994) conducted a study/survey on Nepali proficiency in rural Nepal using the Nepali Sentence Repetition Test. His study included participants from different ethnic groups including Gurung, Thakali, Magar, and Ghale/Bhotia. He pointed out that while there is some level of Nepali proficiency in every village in Nepal, different speakers have varying abilities to speak and understand Nepali depending on factors such as education, amount of travel, village location, and gender. In conclusion, he wrote, 'those who are uneducated and illiterate are nowhere near as proficient in Nepali as those who are educated and literate' (1994: 45). Only 12% of the population surveyed, those who were in the most educated category, were proficient enough in Nepali to handle complex language material. The results of his survey call into question the popularly held belief in Nepal that everyone speaks Nepali.

Summary of Nepali bilingualism

Malla (1989) points out that there are no sound and reliable studies on the incidence of bilingualism in Nepal. The level of fluency is highly variable and may often best be defined as partial bilingualism. Nepali is used in specific domains and for specific purposes. Since many bilingual people are not literate, their children are not able to compete with native Nepali speakers in educated Nepali. Malla (1989: 452) writes that:

According to the 1952/54 Census Report, Nepali is used as a second language by 13.3% of the total population of Nepal. Some 19% of the population in the Hills and the Inner Terai used Nepali as a second language, whereas only 2.9% did so in the Eastern and Western Terai. The later census reports do not give any figures relating to bilingualism.

The lowland Terai had been the Maithili, Bhojpuri, Awadhi and Tharu-speaking areas in the past. But the resettlement and land distribution policies of His Majesty's government have both encouraged hill settlers in these areas. Consequently, there has been a greater incidence of bilingualism and weakening of linguistic homogeneity of these regions.

This last point is significant since in the past the medium of education in the Terai was Hindi. After the eradication of the malarial mosquito, the Terai has become the most important agricultural area of Nepal as well as the major industrial region of the country. The ties between India and the people of the Terai are close, and the central government, situated comparatively far away in Kathmandu, has a weaker hold on the people there. For these reasons, the strengthening of Nepalese nationalism, national identity, and the national language were seen as particularly critical in this part of the country.

With regard to the Tibeto-Burman speakers, Malla points out that while many of them have no writing or literacy tradition, others such as the Sherpa and the Limbus have a rich oral and literate tradition. However, he concludes that:

> ... their links with their traditions and past have become weaker day by day. Although once in a while a few cultural patriots among these speech communities have published sundry items on their cultures and language, the usual tendency among them is to adopt Nepali and become bilinguals. This tendency is most pronounced in the western hills among the Gurungs, the Magars and the Thakalis. (1989: 453)

Malla also suggests that any attempt at language loyalty or revival was often interpreted as communalism or tribalism. As such it was defined as subversive to the goals of nationalism and the national government, so it was discouraged. Consequently, a number of minority languages in Nepal, particularly those spoken by less than 1% of the population, may be said to be dying.

Opposition to Nepali

Those who oppose Nepali as the sole medium of instruction and the only national language stress that it is the language of a long-time repressive government. Since it is the language of the ruling castes, it re-enforces a stifling, oppressive, and fatalistic caste system. Some people fear that the national language policy is not so much a means to promote national unity as a tool of cultural dominance for the ruling elite. Requiring Nepali throughout the system of education accounts in part for the high attrition rate of children whose first language is not Nepali. Also, Nepali was imposed on minority people, who had no say in the decision. Students are forced to learn in a language that is inadequate to meet the needs of a modernising, industrialising, internationally-oriented nation. In terms of science and technology, Nepali has not been adequately standardised or modernised. Even literature, academic texts, and resource materials in Nepali are severely limited.

The problems of standardisation and elaboration of languages has been considered in detail by Haugen (1983: 275). Standardisation for purposes of science and technology involves a classic language planning dilemma. As Kaplan and Baldauf (1997: 31–33) point out, standardisation is an expensive, time-consuming, and resource-intensive process. When a government is unwilling or unable to undertake such a process, it compels one indigenous language to serve the purpose of national unity at the expense of modernisation and development. In Nepal, English, by necessity, has had to fill this gap, especially at the tertiary level, imposing an additional language burden on the students.

By the 1980s and 1990s, Nepali and central government language planning policies became highly political and controversial issues. The demand for first language education was a part of the people's demands during the riots and protests of the late 1980s, which led to the end of the Panchayat government and to the beginning of a multi-party, democratic, parliamentary government in 1990.

Movements for First Language Education and Revitalisation

The political turmoil of the 1980s in Nepal included a demand for the language rights of non-Nepali speakers. In particular, the leftist writers, intellectuals, politicians, and journalists argued for equal language rights. Several organisations and journals were founded to express this opinion and to state the resentment of these people towards the national government's language policy. Malla (1989: 462) says that three main ideas have emerged from this movement:

(1)   All languages are equal.
(2)   No language should be given the privileged status of national language at the cost of other languages.
(3)   A contact language will emerge on its own, and the State should not interfere in order to promote any single language.

The new left-wing political parties emphasised that equality, not unity, was the most important value to be considered. Other scholars have suggested that while Nepali may be designated as a contact language, it should not be elevated to the position of sole national language.

Organised groups in support of first language policies include the Mother Tongue Council, the All Nationalities Forum for Equal Rights, the Nepal Langbali Family, the Tamang Service Trust, the Maithili Sahitya Parisad, and the Nepalabhasa Manka Khala. A conference held by the last group approved:

> a ten point resolution demanding equal 'constitutional status', right to educate in mother tongue, representation of all languages in the media, information and publicity, non-discrimination of non-Nepali language, MAs for public service, and the protection of all scripts, cultures, literature and languages through the Royal Nepal Academy and other government sponsored corporations. (Malla, 1989: 463)

In reference to early language movements in the Terai region, Yadav (1990) states that in the 1950s, a language movement was begun in the Terai that opposed the government language planning policy. 'Save Hindi' committees were formed in several towns proposing a more liberal policy towards languages. Protests and strikes against making Nepali the compulsory medium of instruction were held. However, the national government issued a ban on all forms of protest and the movement died out. Yadav concludes that the people of the Terai feel discriminated against and have been deprived of a role in the mainstream of national life. This marginalisation has been a motivating factor behind the push for L1 education.

The new language policy, 1990

The constitution of Nepal in 1990 guaranteed the fundamental right of the individual to receive primary education in his/her first language. It also guaranteed the fundamental right to preserve and foster the growth of language, script, and culture of a speech community in Nepal.[5] Following this constitutional change, the National Education Commission Report in 1992 recognised the need for clear-cut policy and planning to influence primary education through the medium of the first language.

Although these new policies may have resulted in a new awareness and appreciation of local languages and cultures, according to Toba (1992) nothing has been done to implement these policies. Instead, there has been an increase in pressure, from a small elitist group, to make Sanskrit a compulsory subject in the school curriculum. Shrestha and van den Hoek (1994: 46) state that in 1994 only two L1 medium schools existed in Nepal, one Magar school in Pokhara and one Newari school in Kathmandu. They add:

> Only one Newari school for the whole valley, which is flourishing with so-called English Boarding Schools? Yes, and that one Newari school is on the outskirts of the city and has apart from nursery classes, only two primary school classes. It has 123 pupils in total, 36 of them subsidised by N.B. Japanese foster parents! (Shrestha & van den Hoek, 1994: 46)

They add that the Newari school has an impressive executive committee, fully dedicated to the ideal of education in the first language. However, a noted Newar linguist told me in an interview that he was doubtful that this Newari experiment would succeed. In fact, most Newars who can afford it send their children to English-medium schools.

As an example of the need for first language education, Yadav describes the case of the Tharus, a large group of Indo-Aryan speakers in the Terai, who are defined as educationally disadvantaged. He quotes a report by the Research Centre for Educational Innovation and Development (CERID) which concludes that:

> ... the greatest problem faced by [Tharu] children in their school is the problem of communication. Nepali as the medium of instruction obstructs learning. They hardly understand anything taught in Nepali. They cannot express themselves adequately in it. The compulsion of learning through Nepali retards their educational growth. (1992: 180)

Following distinctions made by Robins and Uhlenbeck (1991), Yadav goes on to distinguish between 'elaborate' and 'restricted' codes. He states that this has grave implications for non-Nepali speaking children in Nepal who are able to communicate and understand only the restricted code, while the school curriculum, textbooks, and instruction make extensive use of the elaborate code. This opinion agrees with the findings of Ragsdale (1989) in reference to the Gurung.

Another study by CERID (Yadav, 1992: 179) deals with the wastage in primary education in Nepal. In the first grade, 50% of the students drop out, while only 35% complete the five years of primary school. The study concluded that the use of Nepali as the medium of instruction for non-Nepali speakers is one of the major contributing factors to the high drop-out rate. The language disadvantages of non-Nepali speakers limit their educational potential and assure that they will be kept at the bottom of the socio-economic scale.

The question of how many known languages there are in Nepal remains unresolved. The list in Table 1 by Malla (1989: 449), with accompanying census statistics, included 36 of the better-known languages. However Malla (1989: 448) points out that:

> Nepal's language demography is not inspired by a spirit of scientific accuracy; it is dictated by the expediences of census operations. Neither the instruments of data collection, nor the collectors of data are irreproachable. … No wonder that nearly 18 mutually unintelligible East Himalayish languages are lumped together as 'Rai-Kirat' in the language census of Nepal! … The 1981 Census provided tabulations on 18 languages 'leaving a residue of 764,802 persons in the category of "other/unstated". This group accounted for 5.09% of the population'. (Census Bureau Statistics, 1987: 67)

In an effort to account for all the languages spoken in Nepal, Toba (1992) lists 70 languages (see Table 2).[6] He uses the following abbreviations to indicate the language family to which each language belongs:

AA – Austro-Asiatic
IA – Indo-Aryan
D – Dravidian
ST – Sino-Tibetan (generally referred to as Tibeto-Burman in this study).

Table 2 Languages of Nepal (Toba, 1992: 6)

1	Athpariya	ST
2	Awadhi	IA
3	Bahing	ST
4	Bantawa	ST
5	Belhariya	ST
6	Bhojpuri	IA
7	Bhujeli	ST
8	Bote	IA
9	Byangsi	ST
10	Chamling	ST
11	Chantel	ST
12	Chepang	ST
13	Danuwar	IA
14	Darai	IA
15	Darmiya	ST
16	Dhangar	D
17	Dhimal	ST
18	Dolpo	ST
19	Dumi	ST

20	Dungmali	ST
21	Dura	ST
22	Ghale	ST
23	Gurung	ST
24	Helambu Sherpa	ST
25	Hayu	ST
26	Humla Bhotia	ST
27	Jerung	ST
28	Jirel	ST
29	Kag	ST
30	Kagate	ST
31	Kaike	ST
32	Khaling	ST
33	Kham	ST
34	Koi	ST
35	Kuling	ST
36	Kusunda	extinct, unclassified
37	Lepcha	ST
38	Lhomi	ST
39	Limbu	ST
40	Lohorong	ST
41	Lopa	ST
42	Ma gar	ST
43	Maithili	IA
44	Meche	ST
45	Mewahang	ST
46	Nachering	ST
47	Nepali	IA
48	Newari	ST
49	Ny i-shang	ST
50	Puma	ST
51	Rajbangi	IA
52	Raji	ST
53	Rangkas	ST
54	Raute	ST
55	Sangpang	ST
56	Satar	AA
57	Sherpa	ST
58	Sunwar	ST
59	Tamang	ST
60	Thakali	ST
61	Thami	ST
62	Tharu	IA
63	Thulung	ST
64	Tibetan	ST
65	Tichurong	ST
66	Tilung	ST
67	Umbule	ST
68	Yakha	ST
69	Yanphu	ST
70	Other languages such as Hindi, Sanskrit, and Urdu	IA

Toba states at the end that the list is tentative since no comprehensive survey of languages has been carried out in Nepal. This would indicate that such a survey is badly needed (see also Subba, 1976). Many of these languages are as yet unrecorded and many have no script or literature. Of these 70 languages, one is extinct, one is Dravidian, one is Austro-Asiatic, nine are Indo-Aryan and the remaining 58 are Sino-Tibetan. It is the Sino-Tibetan languages that are most neglected in the official census count. Malla (1989: 449) suggests that the difficulties of mountain terrain, comprising 83% of Nepal's land mass, in part accounts for some of the discrepancies.

Given the large number of first languages spoken in Nepal, the expense and magnitude of implementing first language education programmes in all of these languages would be prohibitive. Taking into consideration Haugen's (1983: 275) language planning model, which includes the need for language selection, codification, implementation, and elaboration, the skilled manpower needed to carry out such a process would not be available in Nepal, even if some funds were forthcoming.

In an attempt to respond to the problems of first language education, Yadav (1992) points out that 12 languages are spoken by more than 1% of the population in Nepal. These languages are:

(1) Nepali 53.21 %
(2) Maithili 11.83 %
(3) Bhojpuri 6.60 %
(4) Tharu 4.85 %
(5) Tamang 4.66 %
(6) Newari 3.44 %
(7) Magar 2.24 %
(8) Rai-Kirati[7] 1.94 %
(9) Abadhi (Awabhi)1.72 %
(10) Limbu 1.30 %
(11) Gurung 1.14 %
(12) Urdu 1.03 %

He then determines criteria by which languages might be selected for first language programmes:

- the linguistic demography or the number and percentages of speakers of the language;
- the literary status of the language in terms of a writing system and the availability of printed texts, grammars, dictionaries, folk and other literatures.

This is a simplistic solution to a very complex problem, and other criteria might have been considered. However, on this basis, Yadav suggests that Nepali, Maithili, Limbu, and Newari might prove to be good candidates for initial first language programmes. All four are spoken by more than 1% of the population and have an established written tradition. Nevertheless, they would all require considerable standardisation and elaboration, particularly in terms of scientific and technical terminology. Other widely spoken languages, he suggests, might be added at a later time.

Newari language and revitalisation

Perhaps the most effective case for language rights and revitalisation has been made for Newari. The Newars are the original inhabitants of Kathmandu Valley, where they made up 55% of the population in 1954 and constitute about 33% today. Also, Newars are to be found scattered throughout Nepal in urban areas, district headquarters, and trade centres. In 1981, 20% of Nepal's urban population spoke Newari, a Tibeto-Burman language that has had a writing tradition for hundreds of years. In 1909, the old Newari script was abandoned and the Devanagari script, also used for Nepali, was adopted. While this has standardised the scripts of written languages in Nepal, particularly for the purposes of printing and publication, it has led to the loss of the traditional Newari script which very few people can now read.

Malla states that since the 1920s, the Newari literary elite have been struggling to revive their language. However, during the period from the 1920s through the 1940s, Newari poets and writers opposed the Rana regime, and 'several of them were fined, tortured and jailed and had their property confiscated for writing or publishing in Newari' (1989: 462). Since 1946, publishing in Newari has been permitted, and about 2000 book titles have been printed, mostly financed and sponsored by writers and organisations within the speech community. In addition, 25 journals and magazines have been published – mostly by campus-based literary groups. At present, one daily and two weekly newspapers are available in Newari. According to Malla, there are approximately 110 Newari literary-cultural groups in Nepal, and literary conferences, poetry recitals, and staged plays in Newari have been held by these groups. Music and films in Newari have also been sponsored by Newari speakers. According to Shrestha and van den Hoek (1994: 46), Newari was taught in every school in the valley until 1972. After 1972, Nepali was enforced as the language of instruction, leading to the suppression of Newari in education and literature.

Newar culture, both Hindu and Buddhist, is caste structured, and high-caste Newars are a part of the wealthy, ruling, urban, and academic elite. Traditionally centred in and around the capital city, they wield considerably more power than most other ethnic minorities. If Newari cannot be revived and maintained successfully, revitalisation of other Tibeto-Burman languages is likely to be difficult. Many of these lesser-used languages have no written tradition, the people are dispersed throughout the often inaccessible mountain areas, and they are poorly represented in the national power structure.

Critics of first language education

Until the present time, the government of Nepal has not provided adequate funds for the study and preservation of the minority languages in Nepal, and it has made no effort, at the national level, to implement first language education. Yadav (1990: 165) refers to the government policy towards minority languages as 'benign neglect'. Given the poverty of Nepal and the need to enact land reforms, enforce forest conservation, build roads and irrigation systems, provide safe drinking water, and develop health care services, first language education is seen as an added financial burden. Yadav (1992: 182) points out that those who object to the first language as a medium of instruction argue that 'the nation is "just not ready" for it – in view of the lack of textbooks and reading materials written in the medium of the bewildering mass of languages spoken in Nepal'. First language education, while a valid ideal, is not seen as a financial or pragmatic necessity. Critics of first language education suggest that it is an academic and political issue rather than a felt need by most of the rural farmers and villagers of Nepal. Yadav (1992: 181) adds that a major objection to the use of the first language is that it is perceived as a threat to national unity and is unsuited to promote the national interests.

Dead and dying languages

Mühlhäusler (1995: 4), referring to the seriousness of the loss of languages says:

> There is now a considerable body of evidence suggesting that the diversity of human languages is decreasing at a rate many times faster than at most if not all previous periods in the history of human languages.

As majority languages (such as Nepali) capture larger numbers of registers, minority languages are under an increasing threat of extinction (Kaplan & Baldauf, 1997: 227). Consequently, the Nepalisation and/or death of languages in Nepal, as illustrated by Noonan's (1996) Chantyal example, seems inevitable without the intervention of some type of planning and research. Dahal (1976: 155) states that many Nepalese languages are in the process of extinction. He specifically mentions Majhi, Kumbale, Bayu, and Kusunda. Since these four languages were not included in Toba's 1992 list of seventy languages in Nepal, it is possible that they are already extinct. Toba (1992), in reference to the Kusunda language, states that while one man admitted to still speaking the language, efforts to tape and record his speech were unsuccessful, and it was impossible to classify the language family to which Kusunda belonged. It is now regarded as unclassified and extinct. There is an urgent need to conduct linguistic studies of the dying languages in Nepal before they are irretrievably lost.

Languages taught in Nepal

For over two decades, Nepali has been used as the medium of instruction in all national schools in Nepal. However, the primary level textbooks assume a spoken knowledge of Nepali and nowhere is it taught as a foreign language to non-Nepali speakers. English is added to the national school curriculum in the fourth year of primary school, as an international language, and is continued as a compulsory subject from that point on throughout the school curriculum. Both Maithili and Newari are said to be offered as subjects in some high schools.

According to the *Course of Study* (1992) in the Faculty of Humanities and Social Sciences at Tribhuvan University, Compulsory Nepali, Alternative English, and Compulsory English are required courses for the Bachelor of Arts degree. In addition, the journal, *Nepalese Linguistics*, (1994: inside front cover) states that the Faculty of Humanities and Social Sciences offers Hindi, Urdu, Maithili, Newari, and Sanskrit as optional subjects applicable to a BA. Thus, the study of some minority languages is possible at advanced levels of education. The Campus of International Languages at Tribhuvan University offers language courses in Chinese, English, French, German, Japanese, Russian, and Spanish. Nepali,

Sanskrit and Tibetan are also offered for international students.[8] According to an unofficial count by the Japanese Embassy, 22 language institutions in Nepal offer instruction in Japanese, making it the most studied foreign language in Nepal after English.[9] Language studies appear to be an important part of tertiary education in Nepal.

Immigrants and refugees in Nepal

There are a number of Sikhs residing in Nepal, although they were not mentioned in the available literature. According to Devendra Jung Rana in an interview, many of the Sikhs fled Burma/Myanmar during the military take-over. They dominate the trucking and transport industry between the Terai and the hill regions, as well as between the Terai and India. The Sikhs I met informally in shops and restaurants spoke fluent English.

A particularly pressing problem in Nepal is the presence of over 85,000 refugees from Bhutan, who have been settled in refugee camps in the south-eastern area (Kumar, 1993). Since the 1700s, Nepalese people migrated to Assam, Darjeeling, Sikkum and Bhutan in search of better economic opportunities. In Bhutan, the Nepalese settled in the south where they constitute a majority. The Bhutanese government has accused the Nepali-speaking Hindus of trying to usurp the power of the Bhutanese King, the elite, and the Buddhist religion. As a result, the government has imposed on the Nepalese majority the compulsory use of the Bhutanese language and traditional Bhutanese dress, which are characteristic of only 16% of the population (Baral, 1993: 197). In a further move towards 'ethnic cleansing', Bhutan also passed citizenship laws which discriminated against long-time Nepali speaking residents. As a result, many Nepali speakers fled Bhutan and entered Nepal as refugees. This population flow has led to increased land pressure and deforestation, exacerbated ecological problems, and intensified the political instability of the south-eastern districts of the country. Little has been written on the literacy, education, or language of the refugees other than to state that they are Nepali speakers. English is apparently the medium of instruction in Bhutan, and Nepali has been banned in the country since 1985. Guragain (1993: 42) states that 'while the refugee educators are trying their best to follow the Bhutanese system, the fact that they teach Nepali using the textbooks from Nepal's curriculum means that the children are becoming "Nepalised".'

Since 1959, over 10,000 people have fled Tibet and settled in a number of locations in Nepal. The Tibetans speak a Tibeto-Burman language which includes a group of languages within the Sino-Tibetan language family (Kansakar, 1993). According to Kansakar (1993: 165), 'the Tibetan and Newari scripts are variations of the Brahmi (Devanagari) alphabet of northern India, which has its origins in the *Kutila* writing system invented in the 7th century AD'. Tibetans did not use Chinese script for Tibetan writing prior to 1959, marking the Chinese take-over of Tibet. Wilkinson (1994: 17) states that:

> Relations between the Chinese and those Tibetans seeking 'independence' have been severely strained. To the Chinese, Tibet is a strategically vital region that must also be led from feudalism to socialism. ... To the Tibetans,

their country was invaded and despoiled by the Chinese, who must leave before there can be peace.

In an effort to escape Chinese persecution, many people fled from Tibet and settled in the mountain regions of India and in parts of Nepal. The Tibetan refugees endured considerable hardship during their early re-settlement.

Several organisations including the Indian Red Cross, the International Committee for Assistance to Tibetan Refugees in Nepal (founded by Father Moran, SJ), US AID, Oxfam, and particularly Swiss Overseas Aid have all helped in the feeding, care, resettlement, and training of these Tibetan refugees. Also, the government and people of Nepal have played an important role in accepting and resettling the refugees. The carpet industry and a number of other handicrafts have helped the Tibetans to become self-supporting, and even relatively prosperous.

Based on a survey by Jha (1992: 57), the literacy rate of Tibetan refugees is comparatively high for Nepal, with 57.95% of the people classified as literate. Nowhere did the study specify in which language the Tibetans were literate. Furthermore, Jha (1992) states that, of the educated Tibetans, 52% have a primary education, 1.77% have a middle-level education, 4.43% have their School Leaving Certificate, 12.39% have an intermediate education, 10.62% have a BA education and 0.88% an MA education. Another 17.70% have a monastic education. It is likely that the secularly educated would be literate in Nepali and/or English, while those educated in the monasteries have been primarily educated in Tibetan.

One of the major Tibetan refugee centres is in Jawalakhel, located near Kathmandu and adjoining the city of Patan. Initially, the children of this settlement were educated at a nearby national Nepalese school, in Nepali, but in 1984, the Atisha Primary School was opened in the settlement. The school follows the Nepalese syllabus, but the medium of instruction is English with Tibetan and Nepali as compulsory subjects.

The Tibetans have stimulated the revitalisation of two important Buddhist centres near Kathmandu – Swayambath Stupa and Bodnath Stupa. Both areas have become Tibetan settlements as well as handicraft and tourist centres. As of 1988, there were four English-medium Tibetan schools in the Kathmandu Valley, including Namgyal High School (Jha, 1992). Schools for Tibetans have also been established in several other refugee areas outside the Valley. Jha indicates that Tibetan refugees near Pokhara felt that studying in Nepali was not particularly useful for Tibetans, so they asked the national government for permission to set up an English-medium primary school. Permission was granted in 1986. Jha also adds that some well-off refugees send their children to English-medium boarding schools in Pokhara, Kathmandu, and India. Chetri (1990: 268) states that among the refugees in Nepal, there is a strong emphasis on the need to learn three languages (Tibetan, Nepali, and English). He also notes that the monks in Tibetan monasteries in Nepal have expanded their curriculum to include English. This is consistent with the general spread of English-medium schools in Nepal, although it was not clear why the Tibetans elected to educate their children in English. Jha (1992: 82) says that despite the current relative affluence of the Tibetans in Nepal, 'as high as 98.46% of these people are still determined to return to their homeland provided the political condition in Tibet improves and the Dalai Lama returns there'.

Education and local self-government

The implementation of first language education in Nepal would require the participation of local people in the education system, the curriculum, and language planning. In this regard, Martinussen (1995) states that the government of Nepal has implemented a plan for decentralisation throughout the country, establishing both village and district level governments and representation. In 1993, a new education act provided for the formation of district education development committees. However, he indicates that there is no assurance of the presence of local authorities on the committees. Educational policy continues to be handed down from the national level, and the district government's 'influence upon the decisions regarding education policies and priorities within their own areas will remain limited' (1995: 101). Since the central government has not implemented first language education programmes, despite its change in written policy, it would seem that given Martinussen's conclusions, the prospect for first language education in most parts of Nepal is rather cloudy. On the other hand, as in the Tibetan case, English-medium education is clearly on the increase, even in the rural areas.

The problems associated with language, education, and language planning are not simple. Perhaps the most common position taken is one of resignation. In his 1994 presidential address at the conference of the Linguistic Society of Nepal, the society president, C.P. Sharma, pointed out that he was first educated in the Terai in Hindi; Nepali was his third language. He added:

> Today at least we have one of the native languages of Nepal as the language of the nation. I know that this language has become 'the language' because it was spoken by the ruling class. But it has reached that place not in a day or two. It has taken decades to make it acceptable to the whole nation. ... Nepali as a language is widely in use and people of Nepal have started to identify with it. Yes, I agree that we should also help improve other mother tongue languages of Nepal without any discrimination but we should not make a mistake of putting the languages of the nation in the same weighing pan as 'the national language'. My reasons are pragmatic not prejudiced. (Sharma, 1994: 2)

If Sharma's opinion is widely shared by other non-Nepali speakers, the present government language policy is likely to continue.

English in Nepal

English is the second most widespread language in Nepal in terms of popularity, education, and use. It is spoken at all socio-economic levels, by both literate and non-literate people. No statistics are available for the number of people who speak or read English. The general impression is that a large percentage of the population speak at least some English, with varying levels of accuracy and fluency. Jha (1989: 111) quotes Professor H. D. Purcell, who wrote as early as 1971, that:

I am bound to start by saying that, in world terms, the standard of English here strikes me as comparatively high. ... better English is spoken at Tribhuvan University than at any University in the Middle East ... and that goes for the whole of South America, most of Africa, and all of the Far East, with the exception of Malaysia, Singapore, Hong Kong and the Philippines.

Today, this fluency extends beyond the university, making English the primary language of communication in education, trade, commerce, tourism, mass media, international aid projects, and international communication. Jha (1989: v) states that, in practice, the English language functions as a second language in Nepal because it is used in more domains than any other language in Nepal, including the national language, Nepali.

English and education

For over 100 years in Nepal, a Western education meant an education in English, albeit reserved primarily for the elite. Before 1950, several English-medium schools existed in Nepal, including Durbar High School and Trichandra College. In addition, wealthy Nepalese sought advanced education abroad in England or India where they were educated in English. Between 1950 and 1970 other private English-medium schools were opened including the Jesuit St. Xavier School for boys, founded by Father Moran, SJ, and St. Mary's School for girls, operated by the Loretta Sisters. Protestant mission schools also existed in parts of the country, for example in the Gorkha area.[10] The mission schools were given over to the government after 1970, as part of the process of nationalisation. St. Xavier changed to meet government requirements in 1977,[11] when English, mathematics, and science continued to be taught in English, and other classes were converted to Nepali. Although both Catholic and Protestant schools have existed in Nepal since the 1950s, the nationalisation of the schools in the 1970s effectively limited their influence on Nepal and the Nepalese people. The impact of Christianity on Nepal has remained minimal. Although there are some schools run by missionaries,[12] most of the English-medium schools today do not have any religious affiliation, and are operated by educated Nepalese.

After the 1970s, the official policy defined English as the international language and the language of science and technology. English was no longer the medium of instruction in the first three grades, but it was introduced into the national curriculum in the fourth year and remained a compulsory school subject through to the BA. An English School Leaving Exam, prepared at the national level, was introduced, and a pass on the exam was required for entrance into university, colleges, and technical schools. In addition to compulsory and optional English language classes, courses in mathematics, science, medicine, and technical subjects are taught in English at the advanced levels. Other courses are increasingly being taught in Nepali at the post-high school levels, although English textbooks may be required or recommended. English is regarded as essential to the modernisation, development, and internationalisation of Nepal, and continues to play an important role in higher education.

In addition to these institutions of higher education, there are over 20 English language institutes in Kathmandu alone, and others throughout the country.

These include the American Language Center (USIS) and the British Council School, as well as Nepalese operated institutes.

With regard to libraries, the Tribhuvan University Central Library has the largest collection of English books in the country. Jha (1989: 110) states that of the 145,000 books in the library in 1989, more than 80% were in English. Other libraries, where 60 to 100% of the books are in English, include the British Council Library, the USIS Library, the Kesar Library, the Indo-Nepal Library, the Russian Cultural Library, and the Integrated Women's Development Library. Jha adds that almost 95% of the journals, magazines, and newspapers in these libraries are written in English. The English language plays a central role in education and research in Nepal.

Recent developments in English-medium education in Nepal

English-medium schools, often referred to as boarding schools even when no boarding facilities are available, have mushroomed throughout Nepal in the last two decades. Jha (1989: 114) states that in the whole of Nepal, the number increased from 35 in 1977 to 785 in 1988. No statistics were found after this date, but the number has increased significantly since the new democratic government was inaugurated in 1990. One professor[13] at Tribhuvan University told me:

> Anyone who can possibly afford it will send their children abroad to study in England or India. If that is not possible, then they will send them to the best possible English-medium school they can afford in Nepal. If that is too expensive they will send them to an inferior English-medium school. As a result, only the very poor, who have no choice, send their children to the national schools to be educated in Nepali.

Attitudes towards the use of English as a medium of instruction

Those who support education in English stress that it was never the native language of an oppressive government, colonial or domestic; it is therefore a comparatively neutral language in the national political debate. It has a long history as the language of Western education and it remains important for the development of science, technology, and modernisation in Nepal. English is closely tied to the identity of a modern, educated, international citizen. According to Jha (1989: vi), it is not confined to specific domains; it is used even in socio-cultural gatherings, family weddings, birthday celebrations, and in the interpersonal communication of ideas and views. English is an essential tool in both upward mobility and the job market. M. Agrawal states that:

> Without a knowledge in the English language it has become almost impossible these days to get a job. In my opinion proficiency in the English language is essential to get any one of 90% of the available jobs. (cited in Jha, 1989: v)

The opposing view points out that, as English is not a native language, it contributes nothing to a national identity or to national pride. The failure rate in English on the School Leaving Examination (SLE) is very high, and only 40% of the candidates or fewer pass each year. Requiring English favours the wealthy who can afford to attend good English-medium schools. Making English a requirement for higher education limits the number of people eligible for advanced level training. Since 93% of the people in Nepal are farmers, they have no need to learn a foreign or international language, so English should not be included in the curriculum as early as the fourth grade. Furthermore, as Nepali is the language of the national government, the civil service, the legal system, the national military, and the police, English is not necessary for many positions in these fields.

Yadav, who is personally in favour of reducing the role of English in higher education, points out that many intellectuals in Nepal would prefer to enhance the status of English. He quotes a recommendation by the Second National Convention of Tribhuvan University Teachers of English, stating:

> English cannot be considered a foreign language like say French or Arabic. In the context of Nepal it is the only language of education and communication for a majority of people and the number of such people is increasing at a fast rate. It needs, therefore, to be given the recognition of this reality in our national language policy document, and funds should be accordingly allocated to the effective teaching/learning of English in Nepal (1990: 280).

One interpretation of the popularity of English-medium schools in Nepal today is that it is a passing trend or fad, termed 'English-mania' by some. In interviews, possibly for political reasons, people were very adroit at side-stepping the issue, even when I asked directly why they chose to educate their children in English. One Newar businessman, whose children, aged five and seven, both attended English-medium schools and spoke fluent English, avoided the language issue and said that he sent them to the English school because the system of education was superior, the teachers were better trained, and the facilities were much better. This is generally the opinion expressed by many, and there is some evidence to indicate that it may be true.

Several reports (Davies *et al.*, 1984; Giri, 1981; Karki, 1989) have discussed the problems of lack of teacher training, overcrowded classrooms, and poor facilities in the national schools. Skinner and Holland (1996: 279) write:

> From our perspective, Naudadan schools appeared sparsely furnished and austere. They were long buildings made of stone walls, concrete floors, and slate or tin roofs. Since there was no electricity, light came only from a few small windows. Some of the lower grades had no chairs or desks. Children in these classrooms sat on mats on the floor ...

While they are describing a national school, the description is also fairly accurate for some of the English-medium schools that I saw or visited outside of Kathmandu. While superior facilities and teaching may be a fact in the better English-medium schools, especially in the urban areas, it does not explain why people choose to educate their children in English-medium private schools rather than establish and operate good private Nepali-medium or first language medium schools.

The MA in English Language Teaching at Tribhuvan University, set up along British lines, appears to be a model curriculum. Courses are taught, for example, in language teaching, language acquisition, and linguistics. The programme involves two months of practice teaching and the writing of 36 lesson plans, complete with materials designed by the student. Both are evaluated and graded. Several MA theses in English which I read were well written and of professional quality. They indicate familiarity with the latest scholars and methods in the field from Britain, the United States, and India. However, because of the class size and lack of facilities in national schools, it is difficult to implement modern methods in the classrooms. For those not hired by the institutions of higher learning, teaching at a good English-medium school allows for greater freedom and better working conditions. The availability of trained English teachers may make the opening and operating of English-medium schools particularly attractive. However, no real studies of the English-medium schools, teachers, or curriculum were available.

In my opinion, choosing to educate children in English is not merely a fad. For non-Nepali speakers, particularly those who speak a Tibeto-Burman language, education in the first language is neither possible nor practical. Thus education for them, whether in Nepali or in English, is education in a foreign language. Education in two foreign languages is an additional burden. For those who strongly object to the national policy of Nepali as the sole medium of instruction in the national schools, opting to send children to an English-medium school may be viewed as a form of protest. Also, English is possibly more advantageous in the job market, particularly for those jobs available to people classified as middle or lower caste.

English education, class and caste

While an English education was once the prerogative of the elite, this is no longer entirely true. Jha (1989: 114) writes:

> Thus English in the education system in Nepal appears to have a very important place, and its ever spreading popularity among the common Nepalese can be gauged from the fact that even low-paid jobbers, such as peons and watchmen send their children to English-medium boarding schools. ... Several of the low-paid jobbers I interviewed said that they send their children to 'boarding school' with the hope of bringing them at least a rung higher than they themselves are on the socio-economic ladder of their society.

My own interviews confirm this position, as the following examples indicate:

- One trekking guide, Ang Kami Sherpa, who spoke good English, was sending his son to a Buddhist lamasery in the Sherpa region. His two younger daughters, however, attended English-medium schools in Kathmandu.
- My house cleaner, a high-caste Newar, worked to help send her children to boarding school.
- While in Marpha, a small Thakali mountain town (at 9000 feet) on the Kali-Gandaki trade route from Tibet to Pokhara, I stayed at a modest guest house. Marpha is accessible only on foot or by pack-animal trains. It is about a two-hour trek from Jomosum and the nearest airport where very small planes land. Trekking down from Jomosum to Pokara in the valley, takes five to seven days. The Thakali owner of the guest house, who had a

two-year-old son, was teaching him to speak Nepali and English (not Thakali). She explained that he needed Nepali because it was the national language, and he needed English because as soon as he was old enough she would send him to an English school in Jomosum. Despite the remoteness of the town, on trekking back to Jomosum I photographed two small stone English-medium schools. I was told there was a third.

While preference for education in English among non-Nepali speakers is understandable, it is also popular among Nepali speakers, including the elite. Jha (1989: 386) states, 'It is, however, intriguing to note that the same vocal supporters of Nepali language and culture-based nationalism send their children to the best possible English-medium schools'. He also remarks that, '… the use of the English language is becoming indulged in by those who do not want others below them socially, educationally and economically to join them and their class' (1989: 358).

Under the educational reforms of the National Education System Plan in 1972, the School Leaving Examinations were introduced for admission into colleges, the university, and technical schools. In reference to this, Bista (1994: 127) states:

> … the requirements of examination threatened the system of privileges by emphasising competence. Some of those in higher positions became concerned that their own children might not be able to achieve the same status, if they were to fail entrance examination. Previously, their positions were guaranteed by social status and *afno manchhe*[14] connections.

Since the examinations most often failed were English or in the medium of English, even high-caste Nepali speakers choose to send their children to English-medium schools. For them, it is one means of maintaining their privileged social position.

Elsewhere, Bista (1994) points out that the vast majority of teachers, university professors, intellectuals, and journalists are high-caste Hindus. He adds that they are strongly represented in the government, the administrative bureaucracies, the civil service, and politics; positions which they obtain through *afno manchhe* connections. With the exception of some teachers, Nepali is the language used in most of these occupations, as well as in the national military and the police. High-caste Nepali speakers may not need English to have access to many good positions. For most of the middle and lower classes and castes, however, these jobs are not available because they lack the necessary connections or social position. Tibeto-Burman speakers, as well as other tribal groups, are classified as middle caste, and all artisans and labourers are low caste or untouchable. Concerning business and trade. Bista (1994: 160) writes:

> Mercantile activity has been successfully practised by the ethnic people of Nepal since the earliest days … but under fatalistic caste principles imported from India, mercantile activity was disparaged as a polluting activity. Not only is it a form of labour, but it is crassly materialistic. Merchants were thus considered low caste.

I do not believe that this attitude is so widely held by most high-caste Nepalese today, and many of them are engaged in trade and commerce. Education and wealth have largely replaced caste as the primary definers of status in Nepal, although until recently these factors have been contiguous. However, this attitude does point out that, while government jobs are not easily available, business and service activities, including tourism, are traditionally the occupations of many middle and lower class/caste people. Although English may be a privilege for the high-caste Nepali speakers, it is a necessity for many other people; this appears to be a contributing factor in the felt need for English among these people.

Language acquisition outside the school system

Up to this point, considerable attention has been given to education and multilingualism. In fact, most language acquisition in Nepal occurs informally and outside the classroom. Given the low literacy rate in Nepal, this includes both Nepali and English. In Nepal, one encounters street peddlers, bicycle rickshaw drivers, taxi drivers, trekking guides, porters, and street children who speak surprisingly fluent English. Most of them are unschooled. Jha states that 'in fact fluency in the spoken English, not always grammatically correct, of these people [in tourism] is developing mainly because they interact a lot with foreign tourists' (1989: 195). In his opinion '... most of the graduates of Tribhuvan University do not speak as fluently as children speaking with the tourists ... even among those [children] who have never been to school' (1989: 191).

Gulmez and Shrestha (1993) conducted a study of formal and informal language exposure on EFL development. The formal group was university students educated outside of Kathmandu who had little or no exposure to native English speaking people; the informal group was made up primarily of Sherpa mountaineering and trekking guides, who learned English on the streets or on the hills and mountains of Nepal. Most of them had no formal schooling. Gulmez and Shrestha concluded that the students who learned English in the classroom scored higher on accuracy, in terms of grammar and structure, but their speech was marked by '... pauses, hesitations, repetitions, false starts and fragments ...' (1993: 80). In contrast, the Sherpas were more concerned with communication and meaning. As a result, they were rated higher on fluency. While this study deals specifically with English acquisition, most multilingual people in Nepal acquire other languages informally, rather than through study in the classroom.

Multilingualism and Language Domains

Multilingualism in Nepal is frequently tied to specific domains. People code switch depending on the environment and the audience. I rarely met anyone who spoke less than three languages. Many spoke several. For example, one Newar businessman, U. Shrestha (1995, interview) spoke Newari, Nepali, and Hindi. He majored in English at the university and spoke native-like English as well as passable French. After six years of study in Japan he spoke and wrote fluent Japanese. He said that although he could read and correspond in Japanese, he preferred to write papers and proposals in English. An unschooled Sherpa mountain climber of my acquaintance spoke Sherpa, Nepali, English, and Japanese, the latter two learned on mountain climbing expeditions. Multilingualism, with varying degrees of fluency, is the norm throughout Nepal.

Literature in Nepal

Although multilingualism is virtually universal in Nepal, most literature and creative writing forms are in Nepali. According to Hutt (1988), the most popular genre of Nepali literature is poetry. Prose was not developed until the 20th century, following efforts to standardise the language.

Early poetry was derived from Sanskrit verse, with traditional themes, including heroic and devotional poetry. By the mid-1900s, romanticism and innovations in metre and verse influenced and modernised Nepali poetry. Contemporary issues and events, as well as political dissent and disillusionment, became important themes in later poems. Hutt (1988: 225) states that Nepali poetry by the 1960s and 1970s was no longer only the privilege of high-caste males. Now young men and women, who were graduating from the universities, wrote about the aimlessness of life, often with political overtones. In the late 1970s there was a 'Street Poetry Revolution', in which young intellectuals criticised the Panchayat government in popular poems. The poets recited their works in the streets of Kathmandu during the summer of 1979. The short story is the second most popular literary genre of the 20th century in Nepal. Writers, influenced by foreign literature and ideas, were concerned with social realism and psychological themes. Nepali short stories were published in journals in Nepal and Darjeeling.

By the 20th century, novels had also appeared in Nepali. At first they were translations from Hindi and other foreign works. Later, original novels were written and published by Nepali writers. The lives of exiled Nepalese were a popular early theme. By the 1950s novelists began writing about middle-class experiences and the lives of common people. For the first time, novels were often set in the rural areas of Nepal. With the continuing standardisation of Nepali, Hutt predicts that innovation and experimentation are likely to continue, giving rise to an 'increasingly rich literature of the national language of Nepal' (1988: 228).

Languages in commerce and trade

As indicated in the case studies, Nepali has been the lingua franca of trade throughout Nepal at least since the 1700s. Tibetan and Hindi are also used as trade languages at the extremes of the Nepalese trade routes from Tibet to India. Most trade transactions in these remoter areas rely on the spoken language rather than on writing.

With the opening of Nepal to the outside world in 1950, international trade beyond Nepal's border regions became increasingly important. According to Jha (1994), the primary language of international trade is English. Letters, contracts, and other business-related papers are written in English. In fact, Jha states that even in domestic trade, English is the second most important language after Nepali, with letters, advertisements, and slogans frequently using English (1989: 186). Trade has been a primary incentive for the acquisition of languages, particularly Nepali, throughout Nepal.

Tourism and language

Since 1950, the tourist industry has grown rapidly in Nepal, accounting for 30% of the total foreign exchange entering the country (Jha, 1994: 5). The primary language of tourism, at all levels, is English, from the street merchants and the mountain guides to the employees in the five-star hotels. English is used even with tourists who come from non-English speaking countries. People with proficiency in English are found not only in the urban and religious centres, but also all along the mountain trekking trails in shops, small rest houses, tea houses, and restaurants. Competence in English is a requirement for all jobs available in the tourist industry. Although at the service and street level, English is usually learned through interactions with the tourists, the many tour agencies, hotels, and tourist shops require written as well as spoken fluency, and often demand computer literacy in English as well. Tourism has been a major factor in the use and spread of English in Nepal.

Diplomacy and international agencies

The language of diplomacy and international affairs in Nepal is English. Correspondence and communication with countries outside Nepal is conducted in English. Jha (1994: 4) states that scores of domestic and international seminars, symposia, conferences, and meetings are held in Kathmandu every year. The language used on these occasions is English.

Nepal receives aid in various forms from several countries in Europe, and from the United States, Canada, Japan, India, and China, as well as from international organisations such as the World Bank and the United Nations. Aid projects include agricultural development, water projects, reforestation, hydroelectric power dams, the building of roads, bridges, irrigation projects, government buildings, medical centres, and a variety of other projects funded by aid-donor countries.[15] The language of all aid projects, no matter the country of origin, is English. Also, in general, English proficiency is a requirement for Nepalese who are hired to work on foreign aid projects. However, owing to the recent move towards the decentralisation of the government, including the activities of foreign donor programmes, the emphasis on English may change. According to Martinussen (1995: 103), at least some of the donor-funded projects and programmes have been making efforts to work more closely with the local village and district governments, rather than solely through the national, central government.

Language and mass media in Nepal

One area where Nepal is making inroads towards modernisation is in the development and availability of mass media. Nepali and English are the two most important languages in the media, with Hindi occupying the third place, particularly in popular music and film. Prior to 1990, publications in the other native languages of Nepal were discouraged or even suppressed. (Data on publications in Newari can be found on p. 298).

By 1989, the number of Nepali books totalled about 22,000 titles. Literary works as well as textbooks and readers have been published in Nepali. The Education Material Production Centre, established in 1962, has produced 150 standardised Nepali textbooks. The Curriculum Development Centre of Tribhuvan University has published about 120 textbooks in Nepali for use at university level. The Royal Nepal Academy, founded in 1957, has put out about 367 Nepali works (Malla, 1989: 459). As a result of these publications, an increasing number of courses at the university can be offered in Nepali. Nevertheless, Malla (1989) comments on the acute dearth of textbooks and reference materials available in the national language. If, as some scholars suggest, Nepali is to become the primary language of higher education, many more books, particularly in science and technology, will need to be written or translated into Nepali. Given the poverty of Nepal, financial considerations to some extent limit these possibilities.

English remains important in higher education, especially in the areas of science and technology. As stated previously, 80% of the books in the Tribhuvan University library are in English, and English textbooks are used throughout the universities and colleges. Bookstores abound in Nepal, and most of the books for sale are in English. While most of the literature and poetry in Nepal is written in Nepali, many creative writers do write in English. In addition, Jha (1994) states that a number of Nepalese scholars have published books and papers in English on history, politics, economics, culture, religion, and philosophy. Nepalese writings in English are 'a part of the national literature of Nepal and it reflects almost the same human emotions and feelings with all human conflicts and challenges as literature produced in the Nepali languages' (Jha, 1994: 6).

With regard to newspapers, in 1986–87 there were 455 registered newspapers in Nepal; 417 were in Nepali, 32 in English, three in Newari and one each in Hindi, Maithili, and Bhojpuri (Malla, 1989: 460). Many magazines are also published in Nepali and English. In 1994, the popular English magazines included the *Mountain Tribune*, the *Weekly Mirror*, *Current Affairs*, *Spark*, the *Everest*, the *Himalayan Times*, *Himal*, and the *Sunday Dispatch*.

Radio programming began in Nepal in 1947. In 1989, the one radio station in Kathmandu broadcast predominantly in Nepali, with 11.23% of the programmes in English, usually the news (Jha, 1989: 152). In August 1994, Radio Nepal began broadcasting in eight national languages. Five-minute news bulletins were aired in Rai-Bantawa (Bantawa), Limbu, Tharu, Bhojpuri, Tamang, Magar, Gurung, and Abadhi (Shrestha, 1994: 32). Some music programmes also include broadcasts in languages other than Nepali.

Television broadcasts on the national station began in 1985. By 1994, about 30% of telecast time was devoted to English language programmes and the rest was in Nepali (Jha, 1994: 6). In 1994/95 Nepal had five other channels available with a satellite dish – Star Plus (mostly American TV programmes in English), Prime Sports (in English), Star Shangri-La Channel (movies in English), the BBC (mostly news and business in English), and Channel V (the programmes were listed in English but they were not familiar; one came from Manila; most of them seemed to be music/variety shows). Music programmes that I saw included MTV and Indian variety/musical shows in English. The huge satellite dishes that pull in these stations can be found on many houses in the Kathmandu/Patan area. Traditionally, people in the area live in large extended family compounds. While many single families may not be able to afford a satellite dish or a VCR, the extended family, as well as the Gorkha veterans, apparently can. Television sets were also common in many bars and restaurants in the urban areas.

In 1988 there were 33 'cinema halls' in Nepal, most of the films being in Hindi or English. During the same period, according to the Department of Information, there were 150 video 'parlours' in Kathmandu, with 35% of the films in English and most of the remainder in Hindi (Jha, 1989: 161). The video shop owner, whom I interviewed in 1995, said that the mix in his shop was about 50% in English and 50% in Hindi. Movies in both Hindi and English are neither dubbed nor subtitled in Nepali.

In February 1994, the first film festival, *Film Himalaya*, was held in Kathmandu. It extended over a period of three days, showing documentaries and films on the Himalayan region and its people. The films included a wide variety of subjects, produced by a number of countries outside Nepal, the majority of them in English. The festival, which was put together with a budget of only US$8000, was screened in two small theatres at the Russian Cultural Centre. While many of the films were panned, the festival itself was acclaimed a success. Plans were in place for a second festival in March 1996. A film archive, with an initial holding of 71 films on the Himalayan region, was set up by *Himal* magazine. This archive would be made available, for a minimal fee, to film-makers, researchers, students, and film connoisseurs (Prasad, 1994: 8). Verma states that while Nepal has almost no documentary film-making tradition, it was hoped that the festival would 'inspire and provoke the latent filmmaking talents of Nepali documentarists' (1994: 13).

The most popular and widely known music in Nepal remains Hindi film songs, which are sung in Hindi. The popularity of both Hindi films and film songs, in part, accounts for why so many people claim to speak Hindi. British and American pop music is popular with the young. Bars and restaurants often played New Age music by international artists such as Kitaro, although this practice may have been intended to cater to the tourists. Probably the most popular Western album heard in 1994/95 was *Unplugged* by Eric Clapton.

During the nine months I lived in Nepal, computers seemed to spring up everywhere. In 1995, the Computer Association of Nepal (CAN) organised a four-day fair, the first of its kind in Nepal. The aim was to display the new methods and tools in information technology and to consider their impact on Nepalese society. The fair included 46 stalls, as well as seminars and technology talks, with 10,000 people in attendance. According to one article, the Information Technology Industries in Nepal have a growth rate of over 40% annually (Anonymous, 1995b: 28). Although software was advertised in Devanagari script, every computer that I saw used English.

It should be noted that English usage in the written media in Nepal is not only fluent but makes extensive use of various forms of humour, puns, double-entendre, plays on words, tongue-in-cheek comments, and sarcasm. Debate and controversy are highly developed, and Nepalese English speakers are remarkably adept and adroit in their use of English.

Nepal does not seem to lag far behind the rest of the world in catching up with the information age, and for much of the media, the language used is English. It is probable that fluency in English has, in part, made the media explosion possible, while in turn, the common use of English in the media is likely to further improve English fluency.

The status of linguistics and language studies

Linguistics was first introduced into Nepal in 1969 by Professor Alan Davies, when he taught three courses on linguistics and applied linguistics for college teachers of English. In 1972, the Institute of Nepal and Asian studies (INAS), in conjunction with the Summer Institute of Linguistics (SIL), began an MA in Linguistics in the English Department at Tribhuvan University. Also, in 1973, professors at Tribhuvan University made initial efforts to establish a Department of Linguistics. The first Seminar in Linguistics was held in 1974, and a journal, including the papers presented, was published by INAS (Tuladhar, 1994: 51). In 1979, the Linguistic Society of Nepal was founded; the society has held a Linguistics Conference every year since. Also, a journal, *Nepalese Linguistics*, is published by the society. The Linguistics Conference held in 1993 had four sessions: General Linguistics (four papers), Applied Linguistics and Language Teaching (four papers), Sociolinguistics and Language Planning (five papers) and Syntax and Semantics (six papers). Of the 19 papers presented, 12 were by Nepalese linguists and seven were given by non-Nepalese. The list of Linguistic Society Members includes five honorary members, all non-Nepalese, and 116 life members. Of the life members, 27 have non-Nepalese names and 89 appear to be Nepalese. The interest and participation in linguistic matters on the part of Nepalese scholars seems clear.

In 1977, the Centre for Nepal and Asian Studies (CNAS) was established and INAS was dissolved. As a non-teaching institution, CNAS is primarily concerned with research matters and publications. Each CNAS journal, *Contributions to Nepalese and Asian Studies*, published biannually, usually includes at least one article on linguistics or language matters.

At present, the linguists at Tribhuvan University are scattered in four different departments. Once again, in 1992, meetings were held to prepare a list of courses and teachers that could be used to begin a Department of Linguistics. However, by 1995, the department had not yet been established. Despite the need for linguistic research and field studies in Nepal, linguists continue to struggle for funds and recognition.

In 1993, the Nepali English Language Teaching Association (NELTA) held its first annual conference. At the Second Annual NELTA Conference, in 1994, there were three keynote speakers, 30 presentations, a panel/plenary, as well as book and poster exhibitions. The only language used for talks and presentations at both the Linguistic Society Conference and the NELTA Conference was English. All articles that I saw in the Linguistics Society Journals were in English, and all the articles, except one, in the CNAS journal were in English, although CNAS states in its editorial policy that papers are welcome in both Nepali and English. This outcome underlines the importance of English in academia in Nepal.

The Summer Institute of Linguistics has produced a number of descriptions of different languages in Nepal, particularly those in the Tibeto-Burman family. This work continues today, as illustrated by Toba's presentation at the Linguistic Conference in 1994 on 'Implosive Stops in Umbule', a Rai language. However, many native languages in Nepal remain unrecorded and further linguistic field studies are needed.

The Future of Language Planning in Nepal

The new democratic government in Nepal, with a multiparty system, began in 1990. Since that time, several elections have been held, and the parties in power have changed back and forth between the Nepali Congress Party and a Communist Coalition group. The period has continued to be characterised by a degree of instability. Under the new government, Nepali remains the primary language in the national schools. Little progress has been made so far in the use of first languages in the school system, although it is now a constitutionally approved alternative. To date, the more liberal attitude towards language choice seems to have led to an increase in the number of English-medium boarding schools. While it is too soon to tell what the final direction of education and language planning will take, given the alternatives, a number of recommendations might be considered. Most of them have been suggested, in some form, by a variety of scholars in Nepal.

The first priority for future language planning is the need to produce a comprehensive survey of the native languages existing in Nepal, with an accurate count of the number of speakers of each language. Data on first languages, bilingualism, and multilingualism also need to be collected. It is possible that more explicit language information could be incorporated into subsequent Nepalese census questionnaires, although Clyne (1982) has discussed the many difficulties of collecting and interpreting language data through the national census. Scholars and linguists in Nepal, who question the validity of earlier language statistics, have expressed the need for a more accurate method of data collection. A more reliable alternative would be to implement a sociolinguistic survey independent of the national census (see Kaplan & Baldauf, 1997: 102). Such a survey would require a considerable amount of pre-planning, the training of a survey team, and the appropriate interpretation of the collected data; the cost of a comprehensive survey is substantial.

Language planning and Nepali

The importance of Nepali as a link language, as well as the most important language in education, is certain to continue. It is the first language for at least 50% of the population and if current trends towards Nepalisation continue that number will increase. Thus, Nepali will continue to be the main language of instruction for much of the country. Despite the recent increase in the number of books and texts in Nepali, if it is to become the language of higher education many more will need to be written and translated. A considerable amount of work remains to be done by linguists, language specialists, and writers with regard to Nepali.

Nepali is still in the process of being standardised and modernised. No reference grammar of the language, written on modern linguistic principles, is yet available (Yadav, 1992: 186). Nepali has several dialects, and there has been little standardisation of spelling or orthography. One area of particular dispute involves the degree of Sanskritisation of Nepali vocabulary. Nepali has to rely on

Sanskrit roots for learned, abstract and technical vocabulary. According to Malla (1989: 458) 80% of its vocabulary is cognate with Hindi, and at a certain level it becomes indistinguishable from Hindi. Nepali language purists have tried to preserve the language by creating new terms from indigenous roots, but it is becoming increasingly difficult for these terms to be accepted since the Sanskrit alternatives are widely in use, and Sanskrit oriented writers continue to borrow most words from Sanskritised Hindi. If Nepali is to survive as a separate academic language, greater efforts will be needed to preserve its distinct identity.

At the primary school level, current textbooks in Nepali are written for students who already speak Nepali. No school texts are available which teach Nepali as a second language. Whether Nepali is begun in the first year or added later in a bilingual programme for non-Nepali speakers, textbooks for teaching Nepali as a second language will need to be designed. Also, new reading textbooks, which more adequately take into account the multicultural realities of the country, will be needed, particularly for students outside the urban areas. The matter of restricted and unrestricted code will have to be considered in developing school material for students who are only familiar with spoken Nepali and the restricted code. For this work, there would probably be a sufficiently well-trained manpower base among Nepalese-speaking scholars, writers, and linguists to undertake the further modernisation of Nepali, provided the funds are made available to implement such studies.

The United Mission to Nepal (UMN), a non-denominational missionary organisation, has begun developing a series of readers in Nepali for school children and new adult literates. It has been designed to provide meaningful literature for use in adult literacy classes all over Nepal. As of 1994, eleven books were available in the series. They are graded into four levels, from easy to very difficult, covering topics such as soldiers' lives, women's stories, and earning a living. The texts are authored by people in the villages whose stories are taken down and minimally edited (Anonymous, 1994: 43). While this is a very modest beginning, it indicates the potential for providing interesting Nepali readings and oral histories for beginning readers, both children and adults. I found no studies of adult literacy programmes in Nepali, but this review would suggest that such programmes are to be found throughout the country. There is probably a need to study and expand the existing literacy programmes.

The future of other Nepalese languages: Preservation and education

The current government and the Ministry of Education are committed, on paper at least, to the implementation of first language education and to the development and preservation of minority languages. If genuine progress is to be made in this direction, considerable work will be needed. Reasons for implementing first language education are well documented in studies around the world. However, given the realities of the large number of community languages, as well as the lack of funds and trained manpower for such a project, the possibilities of any full-scale implementation of such a plan may seem overwhelming. Nepal is one of the poorest and least industrialised countries in the world, and funding for any programme in language studies and education has a relatively low priority. Some scholars have suggested that funding might be found from countries already providing aid projects in Nepal. Apparently,

UNECEF has helped fund bilingual programmes in other countries and may extend financial help to Nepal. The Japanese foster parent programme is already giving money to help support children in the Newari school. Financial aid will be a priority if first language education is to be developed.

If the people of Nepal are determined to enact such a plan, considerable work will need to be undertaken. Both Morton (1976) and Yadav (1992) have laid out recommendations for the implementation of programmes for bilingual education and the use of first languages in the primary grades. The following outline is a synthesis of some of their proposals along with an outline of the language planning model suggested by Haugen (1983) and Kaplan and Baldauf (1997).

A bilingual programme would involve the use of the minority language in all beginning classes taught by native speakers of the language. After literacy has been established in the early grades, there would be a gradual shift towards the national language, involving first oral Nepali classes and then reading classes. Important decisions involving status planning would have to be made to decide which of the minority languages would be developed for use in education. Textbooks and teaching material would have to be written for those languages that already have an existing writing system. Native-speaking teachers would have to be trained, and a plan for implementing the programme into the education system would need to be designed.

For languages that do not have an existing writing system, a more extensive language planning programme would be required. Corpus planning and codification of the language would be essential, and decisions would need to be made regarding the selection of a suitable code. Hornberger (1992) has pointed out some of the problems involved in code selection. Haugen (1983) has stated that three aspects are involved in codification: graphisation, grammatication and lexication. According to Kaplan and Baldauf (1997), the results of codification work are a prescriptive orthography, grammar, and dictionary.

In Nepal, the issue of selecting, creating, or modifying a writing system for first language education has usually favoured the adoption of Devanagari script, currently used for Nepali. This would standardise writing systems in the country and facilitate the transition to Nepali. The use of Devanagari, described as a syllabic writing system (Bandhu, 1976), particularly for Tibeto-Burman languages, may present a number of problems. For example, phonemes in these languages include vowels, differing vowel lengths, and glottal stops not present in Nepali. Some work has been done in this direction by SIL and linguists at Tribhuvan University. Adjustments will need to be made to adapt this script to the minority languages.

The languages selected would need to be standardised by developing dictionaries, reference grammars and textbooks, as well as the standardisation of spellings and punctuation. In the final process of elaboration, the vocabulary necessary to meet the educational needs of the language would have to be compiled and modernised while technical terms may have to be devised. Primers, supplementary reading texts, and pedagogical material will have to be written in the minority languages – material which reflects the different cultures and the multicultural nature of the communities. Material will also need to be developed to facilitate the transition into Nepali, particularly in textbooks to be used in beginning oral language classes.[16]

Implementing L1 classes at local level is complicated by the fact that most local communities in the country are not monolingual; local languages and Nepali exist side-by-side. This problem is due, in part, to the very early diaspora of Hindu, Indo-Aryan speakers, who spread across the country mixing with the local tribal groups, as well as to the more recent migration of Nepali speaking Hill people into the Terai.

Finding trained linguists, minority language writers, and L1 teachers will be essential and problematic. Higher education training for such positions would be needed. Yadav (1992) strongly recommends establishing a Central Institute of Languages in Nepal, similar to the Central Institute for Indian Languages (CIIL) in Mysore India, to promote linguistic research in the languages of Nepal (see Pattanayak, 1986). While these may seem to be daunting tasks, Yadav points out that forty years ago no studies or textbooks existed for Nepali either. If the minority languages of Nepal are to be preserved, and if education for the masses is to be extended effectively, consideration of these proposals will be essential. There is a need for more linguistic studies, both theoretical and applied, to be implemented and funded.

Language planning and education in English

No mention was made in the literature regarding the possibility of bilingual education in Nepali/English or L1/English, although in the light of current trends this does seem to be a possible alternative. The present widespread growth of English-medium boarding schools needs to be reviewed and studied. If, in fact, it is a passing fad, the present government policy of ignoring the trend may be valid. If, however, it becomes a continuing alternative for education in Nepal, serious consideration should be given to the quality and standardisation of private English education. Many writers are critical of some of these English schools. Khanal (1995: page unknown) writes:

> ... the people have started opening boarding schools in remote villages where most students have to walk more than ten to fifteen miles a day to reach schools. Even more boarding schools are being opened in the Kathmandu Valley today. ... Most of the principals of such schools are either under-qualified or former primary teachers expelled from their schools on charges of corruption or leakage of question papers. ... The most surprising thing is that the people themselves are not complaining against these malpractices!

In an even more dramatic vein, an English teacher, Upadhyay (1995: page unknown), writes in a news article:

> Language teachers teaching Nepali in schools are already bemoaning that the students' skills in the Nepali language are deteriorating because of an overemphasis in English. ... Many schools in Kathmandu have been able to dupe parents into believing that their children are indeed learning English. ... I find it amazing that parents have bought lock, stock and barrel what these schools claim to be teaching. ... Sooner or later we are bound to discover that our English-mania has managed to produce a whole breed of new Nepali intellectuals who can converse in dog-English with stilted

American accents at hip joints while gyrating to whatever trash is in fashion, but who can neither write a single sentence worth reading in English or Nepali, nor display analytical thinking that is the hallmark of an educated person.

These comments seem more emotional than factual, and it is not always clear if such critics are complaining about education in English rather than Nepali, or if they are questioning the quality of English being taught. Articles and writers often lament the fact that English grammar, accuracy, and literature are being neglected in the English-medium schools and language institutes. What does seem clear is that English-medium schools are rapidly increasing in number throughout Nepal, and there seems to be no means of regulating the quality of most of these schools, in part because they are not officially recognised by the present government language policy.

If English should continue as an alternative medium of instruction in Nepal, some degree of standardisation of the curriculum may be necessary and a system of accreditation for the schools and the teachers would be advisable if the standards of education are to be regulated. Also, it may be necessary to establish a system to evaluate materials, teaching methods, and textbooks to prevent the rather haphazard approach to English education currently in place. English teaching textbooks and materials, relevant to Nepalese cultures and experiences, would need to be written and included in the curriculum. Given the demand for English fluency in higher education and on the job market, as well as in the felt needs of at least some of the people, it seems unlikely that the current trend towards English-medium schools will die out in the near future. Consequently, it may be necessary for the national government to recognise and incorporate the English school stream into the national language policy.

The relevance of material in English literature in the national school curriculum was discussed at the NELTA conference. Too often the English texts and readings used in Nepal are too difficult or are without context; for example, students in Nepal, who have never seen a circus or a seal have difficulty relating to readings on such subjects. Also the vocabulary, style, and content of many selected readings are too often outdated and impractical. This suggests that the English curriculum in the national schools needs to be re-evaluated and updated to include relevant texts, to which the students can relate.

Despite all of the above mentioned problems, at least for the first time in the history of the country, the people have the possibility of making a choice as to how their children will be educated. With a democratic government and the beginning of decentralisation, they may even have a say in the decisions which will be made in the future.

Class, caste, ethnic identity and education

How the government of Nepal deals with ending caste prejudices, promoting equality, and incorporating the middle and lower castes into the mainstream of the Nepalese political system will be an important test of the new administration. Bista (1994: 163) states:

> ... the very simplicity of most of the ethnic cultures allows a greater flexibility than does the cumbersome and ossified structure of urbane upper

class-caste society in the Kathmandu valley. Nepal's future hopes lie with them. … Confidence in themselves and pride in the nation, currently crippled by fatalism, will have to be carefully cultivated.

Language choice and educational opportunities for the ethnic minorities and the non-elite castes would play a critical part in the future of the people of Nepal. Already education has begun to replace caste as a status marker in Nepal and, even in the national schools, education has had an important impact on the social structure of the country. Skinner and Holland (1996: 273) write, 'in Nepal, school participants – teachers and students – were often struggling to turn the schools from a site of state control to a site of opposition not only to the state, but also to systems of caste and gender privilege hegemonic in the society'. Similarly, Vir (1988: 159) concludes that '[t]he process of modernisation is able to cut across the barriers of caste, class and religion: [F]or, the students tend to share common modern attitudes and values. Education thus becomes a leveller in a society'. Education, even in Nepali or English, has been a factor in changing Nepalese society and forging a new identity for individuals as educated persons. With a renewed interest in the possibilities of preserving the languages and cultures of Nepal, essential to the ethnic identity of the local people, the status of these people should improve and be assured.

Multilingualism and nationalism

Nepal, like many multilingual countries in the world, is faced with the dilemma of trying to establish itself as a modern, industrial nation, while at the same time preserving the languages, cultures and ethnic identities of the people. The policy of the central government, until recently, has stressed the importance of a single national language along with the development of a modern industrial state. Yet Nepal would still be classified as an agrarian culture. Sill and Kirkby (1991: 14) state that 93% of the population is engaged in agricultural activities. Gellner (1983) believes that modern nations and nationalism emerge only with the advent of industrialisation. Sill and Kirkby (1991) point out that Nepal is one of the least industrial countries in the world. Only about 1% of the workforce was employed in manufacturing in the mid 1980s. The modern industrial sector along with cottage handicrafts contributed only 5% of the GDP. Sill and Kirkby attribute the weak development of manufacturing to a limited infrastructure, a small domestic market, lack of seaports and competition from India – factors that have hindered economic development and kept the standard of living low. During the revolution of the late 1980s, Nepalese people also blamed the slow economic development of the country on the government and the Royal Family, who were accused of graft, corruption and the misuse of aid funding. By 1995, goods from China, regarded as superior to the Indian equivalents, could be found in Nepal. Competition from China, as well as India, has become a significant factor in limiting Nepalese industrial potential. Without an industrial base and a manufacturing work force, the arguments for a single national identity are weakened. Gellner (1983: 13) writes:

> In traditional milieu an ideal of a single overriding cultural identity makes little sense. Nepalese hill peasants often have links with a variety of religious rituals, and think in terms of caste, clan or village (but not of nation)

according to circumstances. It hardly matters whether homogeneity is preached or not. It can find little resonance.

These realities do not encourage optimistic predictions for the future development of a modern industrial nation in Nepal. While some advances have been made in education, writers are already complaining that there are not enough jobs to employ the present number of college graduates. Given the horrors that extreme nationalism and patriotism have bequeathed to the world in the 20th century, perhaps Nepal should not be in too great a hurry to create a nation on the old European model.

As mentioned previously, Nepal already seems to be entering the post-industrial information age. For example, Nepalese handicrafts and Buddhist thankas (religious paintings) already can be ordered from Kathmandu over the Internet. By 1999, internet cafes had become popular in Nepal, and were found in Kathmandu, Patan, and Pokara. They are frequented by both tourist and locals. If it is possible for a nation to leap-frog over the industrial–national stage and jump with both feet into the post-industrial, global era, Nepal may be on its way.

Conclusions: Language planning and language ecology

Referring to language planning in context, Kaplan and Baldauf (1997: 13) state that:

> It appears to be the case that languages which serve important societal functions for their speakers survive, regardless of the ministration of government. But it is also the case that, if languages come to serve fewer functions outside the home, as the speakers of those languages are drawn away from their home communities by the siren call of urbanisation, by the need for increased economic mobility, and by other powerful societal forces, as majority languages or languages of wider communication replace smaller languages in important registers, smaller languages die, larger languages struggle and no amount of educational interventions is likely to save them.

Elsewhere they add that:

> In sum, language death occurs when at least the three following conditions pertain:
>
> (1) Parents are reluctant or unable to pass on a language to their children.
> (2) The language ceases to serve key communication functions (registers) in the community.
> (3) The community of speakers is not stable and/or expanding, but rather is unstable and/or contracting. (1997: 273)

The language situation in Nepal reflects a number of these ecological factors:

- Nepali is the language of the people in power and as such it occupies a number of significant domains and registers throughout the country, for example in national trade, the political system, the legal courts, the military, the police, and the national education system.

- English is the language which occupies the second largest number of significant domains throughout the country, including the tourist industry, international trade and business, international affairs, aid projects, the media, private education, and science and technology.
- As Nepal becomes more urbanised, the prestige languages, Nepali and English, are replacing the local languages in the cities.
- Given the poverty of Nepal and the limited number of job opportunities, fluency in Nepali and/or English is essential to compete in the job market, even to some extent in the rural areas.
- Education and literacy are spreading the use of both Nepali and English, to the detriment of the local languages.
- Language death of the smaller languages in Nepal is occurring (see Noonan, 1996; Toba, 1992 and Dahal, 1976). The smaller the number of speakers of a language, the greater the likelihood of language death, and many of the languages of Nepal have a small number of speakers (Malla, 1989: 453). Also, the fewer the number of speakers of a language, the harder it is to justify the expense of teacher training, materials production etc., so that it may not be economically feasible to extend L1 education to all the languages in Nepal.
- At least some parents of minority languages are choosing to teach their children Nepali and/or English rather than the local language (see case study on page 306 about the Thakali in Marpha). The parents state that these two languages are essential for education and job opportunities.
- Efforts have been made to revitalise languages such as Newari (see page 298) but most Newars are bilingual in Newari and Nepali, or trilingual in Newari, Nepali and English. Languages which are spoken and read outside the borders of Nepal, such as Maithili, Hindi, and Urdu have a broader support base than most Nepalese languages, so they may be able to maintain their vitality. Languages and ethnicities are not bound by political borders. Several languages spoken in Nepal, including Nepali, are also spoken in neighbouring areas on all sides of the country.
- Since little or no government or financial support has been given to develop or preserve the minority languages in Nepal, it is likely that in future more of the smaller languages will die out and the larger minority languages will occupy a reduced number of communicative functions, registers, and domains – being limited to the family, the local community, and ceremonial activities.

Given the above facts, in the future Nepali, and possibly English, are likely to occupy an increasing number of domains and registers in Nepal. Kaplan and Baldauf (1997: 13) write:

> ... it is not merely a matter of declaring politically that it is for some reason desirable to preserve or promote or obstruct some language: it is not merely a question of charging the education sector to teach or not to teach some language. ... it is a question of trying to manage the language to support it within the vast cultural, educational, historical, demographic, political, social structure in which language policy formation occurs every day.

The government of Nepal has tended to relegate the implementation of national language planning to the educators and the Ministry of Education. While the leftist politicians include the need to educate children in their first language as a part of their platform, their stated policy seems to have had little impact, as yet, on the national system of education. In the national schools, education in Nepali continues. A language policy that effectively promotes one national language inevitably affects the whole network of languages within the system, limiting the number of domains and registers of all the other languages in the country. Such a policy also has social and political ramifications, since it favours native speakers of the chosen language in terms of prestige, education, and the job market.

Colin (1984) states that language is the repository of a group's ethnic identity and linguistic concerns are often central to ethnic political activity. On the basis of his three case studies he adds that:

> ... Language promotion was not mere cultural attachment, but often a rational and instrumental attempt to reduce socio-economic inequality, to wrest more power from the state and opposition groups, and to determine an increasing amount of the ethnic group's role in the wider political structure. (1984: 215)

Similarly, in Nepal, language issues may be seen as representative of the broader issues of powerlessness, prejudice, and inequality felt by minority groups throughout the country. Efforts need to be made to incorporate the ethnic populations into the economic and political mainstream of the country, in addition to revitalising and preserving their ethnic identities and languages. These broader issues transcend the simplistic solution of including first language instruction in the system of education. If minority languages and cultures are to be maintained in Nepal, and if the position of the ethnic groups is to be improved, it will require the determination of the local people, as well as the foresight of the national government.

Although nationalism and monolingualism have been instrumental political values in the past, today, this may be changing. With a United Europe, and other trade alliances and mergers forming around the world, in the future multilingualism may become an incentive, as well as a necessity. Multiculturalism, with renewed and redefined ethnic identities, is becoming an integral part of most nations. The 18th century myth 'one nation/one language' does not work in Europe, where it was born, and it does not function in polyglot polities such as Nepal (see Fishman, 1972). How the new government of Nepal deals with the many ethnic groups and languages in Nepal, within the national context, will be a challenge.

Acknowledgements

I would like to express my appreciation to Sano Foundation of Japan for the one-year research/sabbatical grant, 1994–95, which supported my study and research in Nepal, and to president Kazuko Inoue of Kanda University of International Studies for her support and encouragement.

I am deeply indebted to Robert B. Kaplan for his sound advice and guidance while I was in Nepal and during the writing process. His wisdom and patience made this work possible. I would also like to thank both R. B. Kaplan and R. B. Baldauf Jr. for their expertise in editing the manuscript.

Because I am not Nepalese, I have had to rely heavily on the works of many Nepalese scholars. My indebtedness to professors K. P. Malla, B. Jha, B. D. Bista, R. Yadav, S. K. Yadav and many others is apparent throughout the study. In particular, I would like to thank Nirmal Tuladhar of CNAS at Tribhuvan University for his help and advice and for his introductions to others during my research in Nepal. Any errors of interpretation are, of course, my own, but I hope, as an outsider, that I have managed to remain objective and relatively untouched by the political and emotional debates on language issues in Nepal.

Thanks go to many people I talked to or interviewed, especially to Udaya Shrestha, Father Maniyar SJ, and Devandra Jung Rana for their time and their valuable input on language and education in Nepal. I would also like to thank D. J. Rana and his family, Bhupendra Raj Raut, Pierte Jirel and Goma Shrestha for welcoming me and making my stay in Nepal a pleasure.

Special thanks go to my husband Daijiro Suzuki for his support and care both in Nepal and during the time spent writing in Japan. This work is dedicated to my children, Antonia Diaz-Lindsey and Andres Diaz for their love, sacrifice and understanding throughout my career.

Correspondence

Any correspondence should be directed to Professor Sonia Eagle, English Department, Kanda University of International Studies, 1-4-1 Wakaba, Mihama-ku, Chiba-shi, Chiba-ken, 261-0014, Japan.

Notes

1. Data on the language situation in Nepal were gathered during a research/sabbatical leave that included residence in Nepal from September 1994 to May 1995. Funding for the study was provided by a grant from the Sano Foundation of Japan and Kanda University of International Studies (Kanda Gaigo Daigaku), Makuhari, Japan. The research in Nepal was undertaken with the approval of Tribhuvan University, Kirtipur, in association with the Centre for Nepalese and Asian Studies (CNAS). Field-work, conducted primarily in the Kathmandu Valley, included interviews with teachers, administrators and parents, as well as classroom observations and filming. I participated in the 1994 Conference on Linguistics at Tribhuvan University and the 1994 Nepali English Language Teaching Association Conference (NELTA). Both conferences were an important source of information on the language situation in Nepal. Nepalese books, journals, graduate theses and articles in newspapers and magazines were purchased or copied. Many of these sources are difficult or impossible to obtain outside Nepal. These writings provided important data for this work.
2. English spellings of Nepalese languages are highly variable from source to source. These spellings are taken from Malla (1989: 499). Later references from different sources may use alternate spellings.
3. Today, the future of the Gurkha regiments in the British army is in question. The Gurkhas were the major military presence in Hong Kong prior to the turnover of the territory to China. Their participation in the Falkland war and in the peace-keeping activities in Kosovo suggest that they will continue to remain a part of the British military, but it is likely that their numbers will be reduced. There has been talk of forming a United Nations military force in which the Gurkha soldiers would play an important role, but this has not materialised.
4. Throughout the Nepalese literature the term *mother tongue* is used. Kaplan and Baldauf (1997: 19) state that 'The notion *mother-tongue* is extremely difficult to define;

in its simplest meaning it can be understood literally – "The language of one's mother" or the language one speaks with one's mother. In reality, one may in fact be a native speaker of a language even though one's mother was not. … It is not a useful term, but it is, nonetheless, one that is widely used'. For this reason, I have chosen to use the term first language or L1, recognising that this term too has problems of definition.

5.   Translated in Yadav (1992: 178).
6.   Since transcriptions from Nepali into English are highly variable, spellings in this list do not always conform to Malla's spellings. The same is true of Yadav's list that follows. This problem also arises with names and places. For example, some words are spelled with the native pronunciation and others with the Nepali form. In addition, some writers mark the retroflex sound with an 'h' and some do not.
7.   According to Malla (1989: 448) the Rai-Kirati (Kirat) designation lumps together 18 mutually unintelligible languages. Toba has listed them separately. Yadav (1992) has grouped them together following the national census criteria. If Malla is correct this would complicate the matter of first language education in Rai Kirati.
8.   The international students are a heterogeneous group but I have no information as to which countries they are from.
9.   Japan is one of the major aid donor countries to Nepal. The Japanese built an important hydro-electric dam and a cement factory in Nepal and in 1995 they were constructing the new Bagmati bridge between Kathmandu and Patan, as well as a large government building in the area. They also fund other projects in the rural areas, such as the building of schools and medical centers. Many of these projects are sources of employment for the local people. With the beginning of the first direct flight to Nepal, operating out of the new airport in Osaka, tourism from Japan was expected to increase. One Nepalese art shop owner, when asked why he learned to speak Japanese so well, replied, 'The Japanese people don't seem to be able to speak English, so we have no choice but to learn Japanese'. There are also a large number of Nepalese currently working in Japan, particularly in Indian or Nepalese restaurants. Some are in the country on student visas to study at Japanese universities. According to Sharma (1995: 12) 1700 Nepalis have been trained in Japan and 1400 Japanese experts and Japanese Overseas Cooperation Volunteers have been sent to Nepal.
10. Interview 1995 with Mr Rana, private Nepali tutor, educated in the Gorkha mission schools.
11. Interview with Father Maniyar, SJ, principal of St. Xavier school 1994–95.
12. Father Maniyar in an interview in 1995, said that a Japanese Jesuit priest, Ooki, Akijiro, ran a school for mentally retarded children in Pokara. Also, four Japanese Sisters of Notre Dame operate a school in Bandipur, 150 kilometres from Kathmandu. They teach in English following the same curriculum as St. Xavier. A member of the Four Square Church told me, in conversation, that the church operates a school for homeless children and orphans. The children are being educated and trained to be church missionaries in Nepal. It would appear on the basis of a short article in the *Himal* (Anonymous, 1994) that the United Mission to Nepal is active in teaching adult literacy classes in Nepal.
13. Since some people were hesitant about expressing opinions which were in opposition to government policy, I have chosen not to specify the names of interviewees whenever the issue has political overtones.
14. *Afno manchhe* is defined by Bista (1994: 98) as one's circle of association; not what you know but whom you know.
15. A number of studies on matters associated with foreign aid, language development, and manpower training are relevant to these issues (see Albin, 1991; Crooks & Crewes, 1995; Kaplan, 1997, 1998; and Kenny & Savage, 1997).
16. The kinds of language planning issues and problems described in relation to Nepal have been explored in other polities in the recent past; e.g. the Philippines (Gonzalez, 1999), Malaysia (Omar, 1995), and Indonesia (Alisjahbana, 1976).

References

Ablin, D. (1991) *Foreign Language Policy in Cambodian Government: Questions of Sovereignty, Manpower Training and Development Assistance*. Paris: UNICEF.

Alisjahbana, S.T. (1976) *Language Planning for Modernization: The Case of Indonesia*. The Hague: Mouton.

Anonymous (1994) Stories from the heart of Nepal. *Himal*, May/June, 43. [Lalipur, Nepal: Himal Association].

Anonymous (1995a) Business section, The bottom line and vital signs. *Asiaweek*, Feb. 3, 47–48.

Anonymous (1995b) Computer: World Perfect. *Spotlight*, March 10–16, 101–120. [Kathmandu: Prompt Communication Services].

Ayton, A.J. (1920) *A Grammar of the Nepalese Language*. Calcutta.

Bandhu, C. (1976) Transcription and orthography. *Seminar Papers in Linguistics* (pp. 103–116). Tribhuvan University: Institute of Nepal and Asian Studies.

Baral, L.R. (1993) Bilateralism under the shadow: The problems of refugees in Nepal–Bhutan relations. *Contributions to Nepalese Studies* 20 (2), 197–212. [Nepal: CNAS].

Bista, D.B. (1987) *People of Nepal*. Kathmandu: Ratna Pustak Bhandar.

Bista, D.B. (1994) *Fatalism and Development: Nepal's Struggle for Modernization*. Calcutta: Orient Longman.

Borre, O., Pandey, S.R. and Tiwari, C.K. (1994) *Nepalese Political Behaviour*. New Delhi: Sterling.

Burghart, R. (1994) The political culture of the Panchayat democracy. In M. Hutt (ed.) *Nepal in the Nineties* (pp. 1–13). Delhi: Oxford University Press.

Chetri, R.B. (1990). Adaptations of Tibetan refugees in Pokara: A study of persistence and change. PhD Dissertation, University of Hawaii.

Clyne, M. (1982) *Multilingual Australia* (1st edn). Melbourne: River Seine.

Colin, H.W. (1984) More than tongue can tell: Ethnic separatism. In J. Edwards (ed.) *Linguistic Minorities, Policies and Pluralism* (pp. 108–118). London: Academic Press.

Collett, N. (1994) The British Gurkha connection in the 1990s. In M. Hutt (ed.) *Nepal in the Nineties* (pp. 98–105). Delhi: Oxford University Press.

Course of Study: Bachelor (1992) Faculty of Humanities & Social Sciences, Curriculum Development Centre, Tribhuvan University, Kathmandu.

Crooks, T. and Crewes, G. (eds) (1995) *Language and Development*. Jakarta: Indonesian and Australian Language Foundation.

Dahal, B.M. (1976) Linguistic perspectives and priorities in Nepal. *Seminar Papers in Linguistics* (pp. 153–160). Nepal: INAS, Tribhuvan University.

Davies, A., MeLean, A., Glendinning, E., Awasthi, J.R., Pradhan, A. and Bajaracharya, N.K. (1984) The English Language Survey of Nepal, 1983–84. Unpublished report prepared by a British Council/ODA survey team.

Farwell, B. (1985) *The Gurkhas*. England: Penguin Books.

Fisher, J.F. (1987) *Trans-Himalayan Traders: Economy, Society and Culture in N.W. Nepal*. Delhi: Motilal Banarsidass.

Fishman, J.A. (1972) *Language and Nationalism*. Rowley, MA: Newbury House.

Gellner, E. (1983) *Nations and Nationalism*. Ithaca: Cornell University Press.

Giri, R.A. (1981) A comparative study of English language proficiency of the students studying Grade Ten in the secondary schools of Doti and Kathmandu. MA Thesis, Tribhuvan University, Nepal.

Gonzalez, A., FSC. (1999) The language situation in the Philippines. In R.B. Kaplan and R.B. Baldauf, Jr (eds) *Language Planning in Malawi, Mozambique and the Philippines* (pp. 133–171). Clevedon: Multilingual Matters.

Gulmez, Y. and Shrestha, T.B. (1993) The relative effectiveness of formal and informal exposure in ESL development. *Contributions to Nepalese Studies* 20 (1), 77–90. [CNAS, Tribhuvan University].

Guragain, G. (1993) Living out a refugee welcome. *Himal*, Jul/Aug., 40–42. [Lalitpur, Nepal: Himal Association].

Haugen, E. (1983) The implementation of corpus planning: Theory and practice. In J. Cobarrubias and J.A. Fishman (eds) *Progress in Language Planning* (pp. 269–289).Berlin: Mouton.

Hornberger, N.H. (1992) Bilingual education success, but policy failure. *Language in Society* 16, 14–29.

Hutt, M. (1988) *Nepali: A National Language and its Literature*. New Delhi: Sterling Publishers.

Jha, B. (1989) A sociolinguistic study of the use of English in Nepal. PhD Dissertation, University of Patna.

Jha, B. (1994) English in Nepal in sociolinguistic perspective. Unpublished paper presented at the Linguistic Conference 1994, Tribhuvan University, Nepal.

Jha, H.B. (1992) *Tibetans in Nepal*. Delhi: Book Faith.

Kansakar, T.R. (1993) The Tibeto-Burman languages of Nepal: A general survey. *Contributions to Nepalese Studies* 20 (2), 165–173. [CNAS, Tribhuvan University].

Kansakar, V.B.S. (1989) Population of Nepal. In K.P. Malla (ed.) *Nepal: Perspectives on Continuity and Change* (pp. 28–51).Kirtipur, Nepal: Centre for Nepal and Asian Studies.

Kaplan, R.B. (1989) Language planning vs. planning language. In C.H. Candlin and T.F. McNamara (eds) *Language, Learning and Community* (pp. 193–203).Sydney: NCELTR.

Kaplan, R.B. (1997) Review of 'Language Development: Teachers in a Changing World' by B. Kenny and W. Savage (eds) *Asian Journal of English Language Teaching* 7, 121–126.

Kaplan, R.B. (1998) Review of 'Language and Development' by T. Crooks and G. Crewes (eds) *English for Special Purposes* 17, 317–320.

Kaplan, R.B. and Baldauf, R.B., Jr (1997) *Language Planning: From Practice to Theory*. Clevedon: Multilingual Matters.

Karki, M. (1989) Attitudes of campus students towards English language: Field study. MA Thesis, Tribhuvan University, Nepal.

Kenny, B. and Savage, W. (eds) (1997) *Language Development: Teachers in a Changing World*. London: Longman.

Khanal, S. (1995) Time to evaluate the private schools. *The Rising Nepal*, February 1.

Kumar, D. (1993) Thinking through Nepal's Bhutan problem. *Contributions To Nepalese Studies* 20 (2), 213–219.

Malla, K.P. (ed.) (1989) *Nepal: Perspectives on Continuity and Change*. Nepal: Centre for Nepal and Asian Studies.

Martinussen, J. (1995) *Democracy, Competition and Choice: Emerging Local Self-Government in Nepal*. New Delhi: Sage.

Masagara, N. (1991) Oath-taking in Kirundi: the impact of religion on language. PhD Dissertation, University of Southern California, Los Angeles.

Morton, B. (1976) Applied linguistics: Toward bilingual education programs for Nepal. *Seminar Papers in Linguistics* (pp. 117–135). Nepal: INAS, Tribhuvan University.

Mühlhäusler, P. (1995) The ecology of small languages. In R.B. Baldauf, Jr (ed.) *Backing Australian Languages: Review of the Aboriginal and Torres Strait Islander Languages Initiatives Program* (pp. 1–14).Canberra: National Languages and Literacy Institute of Australia.

Nepalese Linguistics (1994) Volume 11, November. Kathmandu: International Offset Press.

Noonan, M. (1996) The fall and rise and fall of the Chantyal language. *Southwest Journal of Linguistics* 15 (1-2), 121–135.

Omar, A.H. (1995) Language policy and management in Malaysia. *Journal of Asian Pacific Communication* 6, 157–165.

Pattanayak, D.P. (1986) Language and the new education policy of India. *New Language Planning Newsletter* 1 (1), 1–2.

Prasad, A. (1994) Notes from the festival. *Himal* 7 (2), 8–12. [Lalipur, Nepal: Himal Association].

Ragsdale, T.A. (1989) *Once a Hermit Kingdom: Ethnicity, Education and National Integration in Nepal*. New Delhi: Monohar.

Regmi, M.P. (1990) *The Gurungs: Thunder of Himal, a Cross-cultural Study of a Nepalese Ethnic Group*. Jaipur: Nirala.

Robins R.H. and Uhlenbeck, E.M. (eds) (1991) *Endangered Languages*. Oxford/New York: Berg.

Sharma, C.P. (1994) Presidential Address, Fifteenth Annual Conference, Linguistic Society of Nepal. Tribhuvan University, Nepal, 26 November.

Sharma, R.S. (1989) Monarchy and the democratic development in contemporary Nepal. In K.P. Malla (ed.) *Nepal: Perspectives on Continuity and Change* (pp. 333–366). Kirtipur, Nepal: Centre for Nepal and Asian Studies.

Sharma, S. (1995) Japanese aid: Yen for more. *Spotlight*, March 10, 12. [Kathmandu: Prompt Comumunications Services].

Shrestha, B. and van den Hoek, B. (1994) Education in the mother tongue: The case of Newari. *Nepalese Linguistics* 11, 46–47. [Nepal: Linguistic Society of Nepal].

Shrestha, M. (1994) Broadcasting tongue twisters. *Himal* 7 (5), 32. [Lalipur, Nepal: The Himal Association].

Sill, M. and Kirkby, J. (1991) *The Atlas of Nepal in the Modern World*. London: Earthscan.

Skinner, D. and Holland, D. (1996) Schools and the cultural production of the educated person in a Nepalese hill community. In B.A. Levison *et al.* (eds) *The Cultural Production of the Educated Person: Critical Ethnographies of Schooling and Local Practice* (pp. 273–299). Albany: State University of New York Press.

Stiller, L., S.J. (1989) Modern Nepal. In K.P. Malla (ed.) *Nepal: Perspectives on Continuity and Change* (pp. 101–120). Kirtipur, Nepal: Centre for Nepal and Asian Studies.

Subba, S. (1976) *The Languages of Nepal*. Seminar Papers in Linguistics (pp. 139–159). Nepal: INAS, Tribhuvan University.

Subedi, A. (1989) Nepali literature: A critical survey. In K.P. Malla (ed.) *Nepal: Perspectives on Continuity and Change* (pp. 423–444). Kirtiput, Nepal: Centre for Nepal and Asian Studies.

Tharpa, P. (1990) *Nepal: Socio-economic Change and Rural Migration*. New Delhi: Vikas.

Toba, S. (1992) *Language Issues in Nepal*. Kathmandu: Samdan Books.

Toba, S. (1994) Implosive stops in Umbula. Unpublished paper presented at the Linguistic Conference 1994, Tribhuvan University, Nepal.

Tuladhar, N.M. (1994) Linguistic Society of Nepal: A brief history. *Nepalese Linguistics* 11, 30–31. [Nepal: Linguistic Society of Nepal, Tribhuvan University].

Turner, R.L. (1931) *A Comparative and Etymological Dictionary of the Nepalese Language*. London: Kegan, Paul & Trench, Trubner and Co.

Upadhyay, S. (1995) English, oh English. *The Sunday Post*, February 26.

Verma, S. (1994) Because they are there. *Himal* 7 (2), 13–14. [Lalipur, Nepal: Himal Association].

Vir, D. (1988) *Education and Polity in Nepal*. New Delhi: Northern Book Centre.

Webster, J. (1994) Nepali proficiency in rural Nepal. *Nepalese Linguistics* 11, 43–45. [Tribhuvan University, Linguistic Society of Nepal].

Wilkinson, J. (1994) *Tibet*. Hong Kong: The Guidebook Company.

Yadav, R. (1992) The use of the mother tongue in primary education: The Nepalese context. *Contributions to Nepalese Studies* 19 (2), 177–190. [Nepal: Tribhuvan University]

Yadav, S. K. (1990) Language planning in Nepal: An assessment and proposal for reform. PhD Dissertation, University of Rajasthan, Jaipur.

The Language Situation in Nepal: A 2007 Update

Sonia Eagle
Port Moody, BC, Canada

Introduction

The last ten years in Nepal have been marked by continual instability, protests, riots, civil war, bombings, strikes, school closures and general unrest. A brief summary of these recent difficult times is essential to explain how issues of language planning and education have been obstructed or undermined by this social and political upheaval. Since 1990 the elected government of Nepal and the parliament have essentially been unable to function. Parliament was frequently dissolved, and several turnovers of parties and policies occurred. By the mid 1990s the Maoist 'people's war' was initiated, and the build-up of the People's Liberation Army (PLA), as well as a larger people's militia, continued to undermine the elected government. At one point, the Maoists claimed to control two-thirds of the nation. The number of deaths attributed to both sides of the insurgency exceeds 13,000. Schools were taxed or closed and often converted to military training grounds and barracks. The unrest and civil war, which began in the west, soon spread throughout the country.

On June 1, 2001, the palace massacre occurred, eliminating the reigning royal family and everyone in the immediate line of succession to the throne. This was devastating in a Hindu country where the King and his family were considered to be descended from the gods. Crown Prince Dependra (who also died) was blamed for the massacre by the official investigating commission, but conspiracy theories abounded (see Gregson, 2002; Raj, 2001; Willessee & Whittaker, 2004). Both the new King, Gyanendra (younger brother of the massacred King, Birenda) and his son Paras, the new Crown Prince, were extremely unpopular and were even suspected of complicity in the murders in some of the conspiracy theories.

As the Maoist insurgency continued, the elected government was blamed for not being able to control the uprising. In February 2005, King Gyanendra dissolved parliament and took control of the government of Nepal. Politicians, journalists, and others were imprisoned, and the media were brought under royal control. Civil and political rights were suppressed. Conflict between the Maoist soldiers and the national army and police increased in frequency and in deadliness. Many people, who were not Maoist sympathizers, were opposed to the actions of King Gyanendra and helped the unrest to spread.

In a spontaneous 19-day people's movement in April 2006, hundreds of thousands of people demonstrated against King Gyanendra in the cities and villages throughout Nepal. On April 23, 2006, the leaders of the seven-party alliance re-instated the parliament to form an interim government, headed by Prime Minster Koirala of the Nepali Congress Party. The seven-party alliance had been established before King Gyanendra dissolved parliament; it is composed of the seven major political parties, including the two largest parties, the Nepali Congress Party (NC) and the United Marxist-Leninist Party (UML). On May 18, 2006, the House of Representatives stripped the King of his power, declared Nepal to be a secular state, and removed the King as commander of the army. The name of the army was changed from the Royal Nepalese Army to the Nepal Army, and the Prime Minister was declared head of the Nepal Army. An interim constitution, drawn up by the interim government, deprived Gyandendra of any administrative rights, and all royal possessions of the massacred family members were taken from him. As a secular state, Nepal plans to change all symbols associated with the Hindu religion and the royal family, including the national anthem, the national bird and the national flower. An image of *Sagarmatha* (Mount Everest) will replace the image of the King on Nepalese currency.

In November 2006, a Comprehensive Peace Agreement was signed between the Maoist Party and the seven-party alliance under the supervision of the United Nations. The Maoist party members, after they had agreed to disarm, were included as ministers in the interim government, thereby creating an eight-party alliance.

By January 2007, the United Nations organization was expanded and named the United Nations Mission to Nepal (UNMIN), headed by Ian Martin. In September 2007, the UNMIN had established five regional offices in Nepal and recruited 772 staff, 65 of whom were international members with the remainder hired in Nepal. Martin said that the Mission would need more than 1,000 workers, 133 international posts and 947 Nepalese to complete their mission (*Nepalie Special*, Jumbo mission 2007: 1). Controversy exists because of the differential in pay and allowances for the two groups, as well as the high profile of UNMIN offices, vehicles, aircraft and helicopters.

The Deputy Special Representative of the Secretary General for Nepal and Deputy Head of UNMIN, Tamsat Samuelo of Eritrea, in an interview with the *Nepali Times*, stated the goals of the UNMIN:

> UNMIN is a special political mission established by the Security Council to support Nepal in its political transition toward an elected constituent assembly. The specific elements of the mandate are monitoring of arms and armed personnel, electoral assistance and support to the monitoring (by a national mechanism) of the cease-fire/peace agreements. (*Nepali Times*, Nov. 2, 2007: 2)

Both India and China have expressed concern about the role and presence of the UNMIN in Nepal (Khadka, 2007: 1). India is particularly distrustful of the activities of the UNMIN in the Terai region bordering India (Jha, 2007: 1). In Nepal there is also considerable dissatisfaction and disillusionment with the work of the UNMIN (Subedi, 2007: 1). The international community and the UN are hoping that the peace agreement and the deadlock will be settled as soon as possible so that the UNMIN can withdraw from Nepal.

The UN mission has made some progress. Under the direction of the United Nations arms monitors, 31,000 Maoist soldiers have disbanded and been placed in camps throughout Nepal. Their weapons have been confiscated and sequestered until after the national election. The soldiers have been granted amnesty and the government may give consideration to allowing some of them to be integrated into the Nepal Army. In June 2007, the Nepalese government agreed to give a monthly stipend of 3,000 rupees (US $46) to the Maoist soldiers confined in the camps.

In November 2006, the Nepalese Government granted a Maoist spokesperson, Krishna Bahadur Nahara, 70 million rupees to manage the camps or cantonments of the PLA as a part of the weapons management deal. Twenty-one camps were set up in seven districts of Nepal. Reports on life in the camps, however, indicate that the situation is difficult. The secretary of the cantonment of Maoist fighters in the Chitwan (jungle) area, Comrade Abiral, states that he faces many problems including insufficient food and drinking water. The Nepali government promised him 30 rupees a day per inmate, but Abiral says that he has not received any of this money and now the camp owes 60 million rupees to local traders. This, in turn, puts considerable pressure on the local traders and villagers. Scorpion and snakebites are common in some camps, and medical treatment and/or medicine are not available. Mutinies have been planned and thwarted, and thousands have deserted or fled the camps. While the UNMIN has succeeded in initial containment and disarmament of the Maoist soldiers, many problems remain.

The national elections were originally planned for November 29, 2007. Due to dissention among the eight parties, these elections were cancelled. One contention was that the Maoist Party demanded that Nepal be declared a republic before the election was held. The Nepali Congress Party (NC) and others insisted that the newly elected government should vote on this decision. Lack of concession or compromise on other matters by the eight parties stalled and cancelled the November 27 election, although Jimmy Carter had arrived on November 26 to monitor the pending proceedings. UNMIN, which had hoped to ensure the success of the election process, could not prevent the eight party deadlock. International opinion is pushing to set a new election date before the fragile peace agreement falls apart. UNMIN has now been granted an extension of six months stay in Nepal (Khadka, 2007: 1) with the hopes that the election can be held by April 2008.

Structure of the Future Government of Nepal

Many issues related to the structure and nature of the future government of Nepal must be decided, either by the current interim government, or by the newly elected government after April 2008. One major issue, an important factor in the cancellation of the November 2007 election, is the question of whether Nepal should become a republic or if the Hindu King should somehow have a role in the future of Nepal. Some traditional Hindus, as well as those generally tied to the right wing of the NC party, have proposed the possibility that King Gyanendra and Crown Prince Paras immediately abdicate in favour of the next generation. Prince Navayuvaj Jridayendra is about four years old and would, under this plan, function only as a ceremonial figurehead. All political power would remain with the elected government. Although this token monarchy might appease some of the Hindu population of Nepal, the Maoists and others are very strongly opposed to this suggestion and are demanding that Nepal become a republic.

Another important issue is whether Nepal should remain a centrist or unitary nation with the government and decision-making continuing to be centred in Kathmandu. Several groups, including the Maoist, the hill tribal groups (Janajatis), and the people of the Terai (Madhises), are demanding that a federal government be instituted. These groups state that they have been poorly represented and generally neglected by the government in Kathmandu, and they hope that a decentralized provincial or state government would allow them more control over local matters.

In regard to a federal nation, several proposals have been presented by the various political groups and parties as to how Nepal might be divided into states or provinces. Some of these proposals, generally favoured by the hill tribes, are based on, or take into consideration, issues of language and ethnicity. However, with the exception of a few remote groups, the identifiable ethnic and linguistic tribes do not occupy a distinct or clearly bounded geographic area. While they may, in general, be identified with a geographic region, they are intermixed in these areas with Indo-European cast Hindus, Newari traders and other ethnic people. For this reason, provinces based on language and ethnicity alone could cause a number of complex problems, including the dislocation of large numbers of people. In contrast, the people of the Terai favour divisions based on population size, and since they make up over 30 per cent of the population of Nepal, they would, on this basis, be allocated several provinces and have a larger representation in the government. Federation issues are far from resolved and will require extensive consideration in the new government and constitution.

Were Nepal to become a federation, some matters presently controlled by the central government would be delegated to the state or provincial governments. If the US and Canada were used as models, language and education would constitute issues transferred to the jurisdiction of state or provincial governments. Previous language planning and policy decisions made by the central government could become obsolete, and new state or provincial policies would need to be decided and acted upon at that level. For this reason, until the final constitution and government have been decided, issues in language planning and policy will remain in a state of uncertainty.

Major Disadvantaged or Marginalized Groups

Dalits

Dalits were previously defined as untouchables. A fault of the original study defining the various population groups was that it did not include information on this group; that study relied on research and material related to language issues. Since the valley and hill dalits are Hindu and speak Nepali as their first language, they were overlooked. The 1990 Constitution declared that untouchability was abolished, but despite this law, discrimination, exclusion and suppression of dalits continue to be commonly practised by Hindus, Newars and non-caste groups. According to the 2001 census, about 15 per cent of the total population were classed as untouchable, but the actual number is likely to be higher – one estimate states that one-fifth of the population or 4.5 million people are dalit (Bhattarai, 2004: 6). The dalit have the lowest social and economic status of any group in the country. Despite the fact that they speak Nepali as a first language, their literacy rate is estimated at 22.8 per cent, compared to the national average of 39.6 per cent. Dalits in the Terai are further disadvantaged, since Nepali is not their first language; thus, the results are supported by the literacy rate for this population – 11 per cent, compared to the national average and the rate for Nepali-speaking dalits (Bhattarai, 2004: 6). However, even literate, Nepali-speaking dalits are excluded from political, administrative and academic fields.

Janajatis

Janajatis are the hill and mountain ethnic or tribal groups who usually speak a Tibeto-Burman language. They make up about 22 per cent of the population. (Bhattarai, 2004: 2) In the traditional Hindu legal code, they were ranked as a middle level caste called *matwali* or 'alcohol drinking groups'. The term *nationalities* is now preferred over the term *janajatis,* and the people so called also prefer to be considered 'non-caste people'.

The *janjatis* claim that they have always been discriminated against and dominated by the Hindu power elites, and since 1990 ethnic awareness and activism has increased. The Nepal Federation of Nationalities (NEFEN) was formed in 1990 to represent 42 ethnic groups or associations. They are demanding more recognition of their distinct languages, cultures, histories and religions, as well as an expanded role in the government along with a fairer share in the national economy. They would also like their identification with a specific geographic territory to be taken into consideration in the plans for federation.

Madhesi

Madhesi are the people of the Terai, both the original inhabitants and the large number of people who migrated there after the eradication of the malarial mosquito. In regard to Madhesi identity, a *Nepali Times* article states:

> Close to a year after a powerful assertion of *madhesi* identity, the PM simply refused to recognize or accept that the *madhesi* exist. It is true that there is heterogeneity within (the) Tarai, and groups that reside there claim a distinct identity for themselves. And 'madhes' is now a distinctly political term preferred by *madhesi* activists for mobilization. (November, 2007: 1)

The *madhesi* or people living in the Terai region make up about 33 per cent of the total population of Nepal – 18% of the caste Hindus, about 10% of the ethnic groups and about 4% of the Muslim population (Bhattarai, 2004: 2).

In the spring of 2007, *madhesi* uprisings and riots spread throughout the Terai. To some extent *madhesi* riots, as well as their newly defined identity, developed as a response to Maoist policies and activities in the region, which did not address some of the specific regional concerns of the local people. In addition, the *madhesi* avow that they have always been ignored by the central government in Kathmandu Valley, and currently they are not adequately represented in the government, including the eight-party interim government. *Madhesi* are demanding the creation of a federal government, a voice in designing the plans for a new Nepal, and more elected representatives from the Terai in the parliament. Although their demands at present are regional and political, they have a long record of objecting to Nepali as the sole language in the schools and government.

Kamaiya or Bonded Labourers

In many respects, Nepal remains a feudal society. The dominant groups have frequently appropriated land from the disadvantaged and disenfranchised. Absentee landlords, as well as a system of *kamaiya* or bonded labour, continue to be problematic in some areas of Nepal, particularly in the western districts. For example:

> A 1995 government study estimated the *kamaiya* population in these (western) districts to be 25,700 from 16,400 families. Three-quarters of them were bound to their landlords by perpetual debt. Under this system the burden of debt repayment shifts automatically to the eldest son after the death of the head of the family. Non-government organizations, however, estimate the number is closer to 200,000. (Rai, 2000: 1)

On July 17, 2000, the government of Nepal abolished the *kamaiya* system, which has been described by Rai (2000: 1) as a system of virtual slavery, and the freed *kamaiyas* were released from all debt obligations binding them to their masters. Plans and funds made by the government to retrain and/or relocate the free *kamaiya* were seriously inadequate. The landlords evicted them from their lands, leaving the *kamaiyas* with no homes and no place to live or work. Those who were freed are now in a worse situation than they had been before, and nothing is being done to solve the problem. While the Tharu tribal people of the Terai, as described by Guneratne (2002), were particularly oppressed by this economic system, other groups such as the nomadic forest people and the dalits are also affected by these remnants of feudalism and oppression (Bhattarai, 2004: 7).

The new government and the interim constitution must deal fairly and responsibly with these disadvantaged groups and with these social issues and inequalities. All of these groups claim that they are lacking representation in the government and in the political parties, both of which are controlled by the powerful, elite castes. This view is supported by an article in the *Nepali Times*, which states:

> . . . you'd expect the Maoists (CPN-M) to at least show tokenism, but they are even worse than the NC (Nepali Congress Party) and the UML (United Marxist Leninist Party). Of the 35 member CPN-M central committee, 25 are bahun-chhetri. Even in the western region where the Maoists declared (an) autonomous Guring and Magar zone, nine of the 13 districts have bahun or chetri chiefs. Of the 37 central committee members of the NC, there is only one dalit. Of the 15 permanent members of the UML, 13 are bahuns. (*Issue* 349, 2007: 2)

Clearly, the two highest castes dominate all levels of politics in Nepal, including the communist parties. Complaints by the marginalized groups seem valid and will need to be addressed in any future government of Nepal.

Women, the Largest Disadvantaged Group

Women certainly are the largest disadvantaged group in Nepal, having a much lower literacy rate than males and holding very few decision-making positions. In light of this situation, the Maoist Party has demanded that patriarchal exploitation and discrimination against women be stopped; to set an example, many armed soldiers in the PLA and the militia were women. They were trained in combat and the use of arms. In an effort to rectify the discrimination, the interim government has recommended inclusionist policies that would give women a voice. In May, 2007, parliament passed a resolution directing the government to reserve at least 33 per cent of the seats in state bodies for women (*Issue* 361, 2007: 1). Also, to ensure a fairer voting process, the seven-party alliance agreed that 33 per cent of the voting list should be made up of women (Magar, 2007: 1). Women have expressed doubt that such resolutions will be implemented, and they asked 'Why not 50 per cent'? (*Issue* 361, 2007: 1).

Update on Other Groups in Nepal

The Gurkha soldiers

Many soldiers in the Gurkha regiment were stationed in Hong Kong prior to the handing over of the territory to China. There was concern in Nepal that the Gurkhas would no longer be recruited by Britain. However, currently, 3,400 Gurkhas are serving in the British Army. Competition for these positions is very high, with sixty applicants for every opening, because the pay is 30 times higher than even a good job in Nepal. Another 40,000 Gurkhas serve in the Indian Army, although the pay there is considerably lower. In June, 2007, possibly in response to the large number of women soldiers in the PLA, Britain began to recruit female Gurkhas for the first time in history. The women will serve in combat support units, and fifty women will be recruited as a test group in 2007 (*Strategy Page*, 2007: 1).

The Bhutanese refugee problem in 2997

More than 100,000 Nepali refugees from Bhutan (Raj, 2007) continue to live in refugee camps in Nepal. Before the Bhutanese government expelled the Nepali speakers from Bhutan, it was estimated that 45 per cent of the population of Bhutan was originally from Nepal.

Language and Education

Language policy continues to be an important political issue in Nepal. The significant increase in private English medium school since 1990, said to offer a superior education, has been a matter of concern to the Nepalese central government and particularly to the Maoist Party. An obvious solution to the increase in the number of private schools would have been to improve the quality of education in the government schools and to address some of the needs and demands of the people. In this regard, following some of the UNESCO recommendations (2003), plans were made to expand free education beyond the primary grades, to introduce early education in the first language, and to begin the teaching of English in the first grade rather than in the fourth grade. Unfortunately, the people's war and the unrest throughout Nepal have drastically limited or entirely arrested these plans; for example, first language education was initiated for some Indo-European languages in the Terai and for Newari in the Kathmandu Valley, but a lack of textbooks, an insufficient supply of trained teachers and inadequate management have seriously impeded the establishment of both first language education as well as first grade primary English education.

In September 2007, the Ministry of Education and Sports issued a draft proposal for consultation and dissemination: *School Sector Reform, Core Document: Policies and Strategies*. The report – taking note of the cultural and linguistic diversity of Nepal – emphasizes the need for a holistic and integrated approach to education from grade one to grade twelve. Goals include decentralization and the need to improve technical and vocational training at the local high school level. The report also points out that loss of life and the psychological damage to students, teachers, and parents that occurred during the ten years of conflict disrupted education services and damaged the educational infrastructure (p. 9). The authors of the report believe that peace has now created an atmosphere more conducive to education and development. The report states: 'Each community will have the right to receive basic education in mother languages as provided by law (p. 9).' The report adds that a child's first language (i.e. 'mother tongue') shall be used as the medium of instruction up to the third grade (p. 38). With respect to language schools, the report avows that existing Sanskrit schools and other traditional schools may continue to operate; however, they must follow the National Curriculum Framework (p. 26); indeed, all private schools shall follow the National Curriculum Framework (NCF), and textbooks shall be selected based on the NFC guidelines. With respect to institutional (private) schools (presumably the English medium schools), a regulatory framework (yet to be specified) shall define 'the governance, management, quality, and finance functions' of such schools (p. 27). In private schools with up to 200 students, the schools shall provide free education to 15 per cent of students from disadvantaged groups. In private schools having more than 200 students, 20 per cent of the students shall be provided free education. These provisions are in keeping with the Maoist policies of taxing or closing the private schools in Maoist occupied areas. The report asserts that the medium of instruction in high schools may be either Nepali or English as determined by the School Management Committee (SMC) and the local government (p. 38). This policy follows the three-language formula endorsed by UNESCO and the Council of Europe; however, the policy is not clear with respect to practice in private and government schools. With respect to teacher selection, the report insists that priority shall be given to the recruiting and training of females, dalits, and other disadvantaged groups (pp. 40, 49). Scholarships and training programs shall be developed to improve the skills of disadvantaged teachers, especially those who will be teaching first language classes.

With respect to funding, the report specifies that a minimum of 20 per cent of the national budget will be reserved for education. The Ministry of Education states that while financing this educational policy will be a challenge, it is essential to meet local needs as well as the economic needs of the new Nepal. Obviously, this brief update can only touch on a few highlights of the interim proposal (*School Sector Reform, Core Document: Policies and Strategies*) specifically related to language issues. The Ministry of Education and Sports does seem to be dedicated to improving and upgrading government-funded education and to reducing the need to rely on private schools. However, it should be kept in mind that the *School Sector Reform* was written by the interim Ministry of Education and Sports. Following the elections in 2008, the Constitutional Assembly will draft a new Constitution that may restructure the state. Depending on the extent to which the state is reconceived, some of the contents of this reform draft may need to be revised.

All of the actors in this political drama are not in full agreement with the interim government's proposed language policy. Several scholars have considered the interim proposal to be too complex and consequently unworkable, while others suggest that, like similar plans in the past, it will never be effectively implemented. Prem Phyak, a professor in the Department of English at Tribuvan University, in an article entitled 'Nepal: Linguistic Black Day', is critical of what he perceives to be the limitations of the proposal. He points out that, although the indigenous nationalities (tribal groups) have been making demands about their linguistic rights since 1990:

> [T]here is no[t] any commendable effort from the part of the government to address linguistic issues; . . . in practice there is no linguistic pluralism. Eight parties have made political decision(s), but they have never consulted with other stakeholders of language planning like linguists, economists, educationalists and native speakers. The provision in [the] interim constitution is not functional at all (2007: 1).

This was a concern frequently expressed by scholars in 1994/95, and apparently the situation has not changed.

Nepal English Language Teachers Association (NELTA)

NELTA is affiliated with such other ELT associations as IATEFL and TESOL, and works closely with the British Council, the American Center and the Ministry of Education and Sports in Nepal. NELTA held its twelfth annual conference in February 2007. The topic of the conference was 'English and Social Mobility: Empowerment or Marginalization'. In the last ten years, NELTA has opened eleven branches and seven resource centres, designed to improve the quality of teaching, research and teacher training; consequently it offers seminars, short-term teacher training programs, and one-day workshops in various parts of the country. These activities are especially important in upgrading the English language teaching skills of primary school teachers, who now have to begin English classes in grade one. Clearly, NELTA is playing a critical role through its efforts to improve English language teaching in government public schools.

Recent Technology

Despite the war and the civil unrest, Nepal has made some advances in technology in the last ten years. For example:

(1)   The market in mobile phones is expected to grow very rapidly in the near future. Nokia is now entering the Nepalese market with plans for providing easy to use entry-level phones in a market where most cell phones are brought in illegally (Chand, 2007: 1).

(2)   Cable net is now available in Nepal, offering high-speed connections along with many more television channels (Khadka, 2004: 1).

(3)   Despite the fact that outsourcing jobs have also been impeded by the unrest, companies are beginning to set up operations successfully in Nepal. The company Geospace, established by investment from Japan, combines aerial pictures and topographic data to make three-dimensional maps. The company has 80 fulltime staff and can employ up to 250 people. Another company, HiTechValley.iNet, employs 200 staff (Upadhaya, 2006: 1). Stability in Nepal should increase outsourcing opportunities.

(4)   The annual computer show – greatly expanded from prior years, with 100 companies exhibiting and 100,000 visitors expected – was held in Katmandu in March 2006 (Upadhaya, 2006: 2).

(5)   Blogging became particularly important and active in Nepal when the King took control of the government. During this period, members of the press and the media were jailed, and the media were suppressed, and censored. Blogging was used to bypass censorship, to protest against the King and the government, and to provide a vehicle for free speech (Aryal, 2006: 1).

However, Aryal (2006: 2) points out that blogging is a limited resource in Nepal since less than one per cent of the population (only 0.7%) has access to the Internet. Argal concluded that the future of Nepal looks brighter thanks to bloggers.

Conclusion

Change in the economic and social system is essential at many levels if Nepal is to survive as an independent nation. The Maoist movement and the public protests have attracted considerable sympathy in Nepal, even though the tactics of violence are regarded as unacceptable. Both of Nepal's closest, largest and most important neighbours, India and China, are going through a period of rapid growth and economic change. It is hoped that, with peace and a new constitution, the future of Nepal will indeed become much brighter.

References

Aryal, M. (2006) Citizen scribes. *Nepali Times e Special*. www.nepalitimes.com, Issue 353.

Bhattarai, H. P. (2004) Cultural diversity and pluralism in Nepal: Emerging issues and the search for a new paradigm. *The Free Library*. www.freelibrary.com, July 1 (pages in this article are not numbered; I hand-numbered the pages and my numbers [19 pages total] are used in this text).

Chand, P. P. (2007) A mobile telecom revolution. *Nepali Times e Special*. www.nepalitimes.com. Issue 353, June 15.

Gregson, J. (2002) *Massacre at the Palace: The Doomed Royal Dynasty of Nepal*. New York: Hyperion Press.

Guneratne, A. (2002) *Many Tongues, One People: the Making of Tharu Identity in Nepal*. Ithaca: Cornell University Press.

Jha. P. (2007) Delhi view. www.nepalitimes.com, Issue 372, November 2, 2007.

Khadka, N. S. (2007) Mission impossible. www.nepalitimes.com, Issue 376, November 30.

Khadkaj, N. S. (2006) Cable net. *Nepali Times e Special*. www.nepalitimes.com. Issue 206, July 23.

Magar, J.P. (2007) Moving ahead. *Nepali Times e Special.* www.nepalitimes.com. Issue 353, June 15.

Ministry of Education and Sports (2007) *School Sector Reform. Core Document: Policies and Strategies.* (Draft: For Consultation and Dissemination) Nepal. September 2007. Kathmandu: Government Printer.

Nepali National Commission for UNESCO (2003) *Education for All: National Plan of Action.* Ministry of Education and Sports, Kathmandu: Government Printer.

Nepali Times e Special. (2007) Longer the deadlock, greater the danger for the peace process. www.Nepalitimes.com, Issue 372, November 2, 2007.

Nepali Times (2007) Jumbo mission. www.nepalitimes.com, Issue 367, November 21.

Parajuli, J. N. Going nowhere. *Nepali Times e Special.* www.nepalitimes.com, Issue 356, July 06.

Phyak, P. Nepal: Linguistic black day. www.Telegraphnepal.com, neolinx,Vol. 24, No. 18, June 23.

Raj, P.A. (2001) *Kay Gardelo: The Massacre in Nepal.* New Delhi: Rupa & Co.

Raj, P.A. (2007) Nepal: How did the Bhutan refugee problem start? www.Telegraphnepal.com, Vol. 24, No. 18, June 23.

Strategy Page ((2007) Gurkha women being recruited. www.strategypage.com/htmw/articles/20070622.aspx.

Subedi, S. (2007) Futile neutrality. www.nepalitimes.com, Issue 371, October 19, 2007.

Upadhaya, G.R. Not doing too badly in IT outsourcing. *Nepali Times e Special.* www.nepalitimes.com, Issue 291, March 24.

Willesee, A. and Whittaker, M. (2004) *Love and Death in Kathmandu.* New York: St. Martin's Press.

The Language Planning Situation in Taiwan

Feng-fu Tsao

Institute of Linguistics, National Tsing-Hua University, Hsinchu, Taiwan, China

This monograph presents a detailed study of the language planning situation in Taiwan. After a general account of the socio-historical context in which the planning activities have taken place, a brief review of what happened in terms of language planning in Mainland China under the Nationalist government between 1911 and 1945 is presented. The following section provides a critical examination of the language planning activities in both language policy and language cultivation that have happened in Taiwan since the island was returned to Chinese jurisdiction in 1945. A turning point in the short history of language planning in Taiwan was reached in 1987, when martial law that had been in existence for forty years was lifted. Many changes have taken place since then and many more are in the making. The final section is therefore a careful examination of some important recent developments in language planning. In that section an optimistic outlook for the future is provided and an explanation for that optimism is given.

Introduction

What is language planning?

Following Fishman (1974: 79), language planning in the present monograph will be broadly defined as 'the organised pursuit of solutions to language problems'. As implied by the definition, the scope of activities covered by language planning is rather wide, and within language planning scholarship, an important distinction is usually maintained between what is called policy or language determination issues, and cultivation or language development issues (Neustupný, 1970; Jernudd, 1973; Figueroa, 1988). Paulston (1984: 55) makes this distinction most clear when she states, 'I find it useful to distinguish between *language cultivation* and *language policy*, where language cultivation deals with matters of language and language policy deals with matters of society and nation' (Emphasis in original).

In reviewing the language planning efforts in Taiwan, I too find it useful to maintain such a distinction, as will be made clear in the following discussion.[1] Furthermore, for ease and convenience of presentation, language-in-education issues will be examined separately from language planning issues, even though it is very clear that language education policy and implementation is a very important part of language planning.

The design of the monograph

Before I take up the issues in language planning and language education, it will be useful to give a general account of the socio-historical context under which the planning activities have taken place (see following section). There follows a brief examination of what happened in terms of language planning in Mainland China under the Nationalist government 1911–1945. The next section provides a critical examination of the language planning activities that have happened in Taiwan since the island was returned to Chinese jurisdiction in 1945. The final section is a careful review of some important recent developments in language planning in Taiwan. In that section I take a look at possible future developments, explaining at the same time why I am rather optimistic in my outlook.

Socio-historical Context

Taiwan, which is separated from the south-eastern coast of the Mainland China by 150 kilometres of the Taiwan Strait, is an island with an area of 35,981 square kilometres and a population of about 21 million. This population consists mainly of four ethnic groups: the Taiwanese or Minnanren (Southern Min people), the Mainlanders, the Hakka and the Austro-Polynesian aborigines. According to Huang's (1991: 21) estimate, the percentage of population of each group is as follows:

- Minnanren 73.7%,
- Mainlanders 13%,
- Hakka 12% and
- Austro-Polynesians 1.7%.[2]

Taiwan's complex and bitter historical past has left the country with this diverse ethno-linguistic heritage. The Austro-Polynesians are the aborigines of the island, who, according to the most up-to-date research in linguistics (Li, 1979, 1992, 1995), anthropology and archaeology (Chang, 1995) arrived on the island from the south-eastern coast of the Asian continent about 6000 to 8000 years ago.[3] Those early settlers, who are now generally believed to be the oldest known ancestors of the Austronesian people, were in time divided into two groups according to the places where they resided. Those who live in the coastal plains are called *Pingpu Zu* (the plain tribes) and those who live in the mountain areas are called *Gaoshan Zu* (the mountain tribes). Unfortunately, very little is known about the movements of these people either within or outside of the island. Chinese historical records on the contact between the Mainland and the island are few and scattered. The earliest record of Chinese contact dates as far back to AD 230, when, during the period of the Three Kingdoms, Emperor Sun Quan tried without success to send troops to conquer the island. A thousand years later, Emperor Kubla Khan (1260–1295) of the Yuan (Mongol) dynasty made two similar futile attempts. Unsuccessful as they were, it was these early efforts that paved the way for the gradual increase in contacts between the Mainland and Taiwan in later years (Chen, 1996).

But before the massive presence of Chinese on the island took place, the Dutch invaded the south of the island in 1624 and established colonial rule there (1624–1661). A year later, the Spanish, not to be outdone by the Dutch, invaded the north of the island and ruled the area until they were driven out in 1648 by the colonial government in the south. Even though the Dutch treated the indigenous aborigines like slaves, their language policies were not particularly oppressive and discriminatory. The missionaries that came with the colonial government even created a writing system for Siraya, an aboriginal language serving as a lingua franca in the south. The writing system, invented at first for missionary purposes, was later used to keep records and to write contracts. It was in use for more than a hundred years before Chinese characters eventually replaced it.

During the Dutch colonial rule, the island was still largely inhabited by the Austro-Polynesian aborigines. According to Tsuchida's (1983) and Li's (1990, 1992) research, the *Gaoshan Zu* (the mountain tribes) and *Pingpu Zu* (the plain tribes) can each be further divided into nine tribes. The former consists of Atayal, Saisiyat, Bunun, Tsou, Rukai, Paiwan, inhabiting from north to south the central mountain areas, and Amis, Puyuma and Yami in the east. In addition to Siraya just mentioned in connection with the Dutch colonial rule, the latter group comprises, from north to south, Ketagalan, Kavalan, Taokas, Pazch, Papura, Babuza, Hoanya, and Thao. The exact geographical distribution of these groups of speakers is shown on the map (adapted from Li, 1992) in Figure 1.

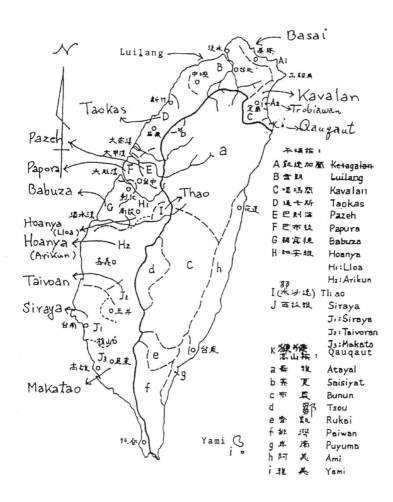

Figure 1 The distribution of Aboriginal languages in Taiwan in the 19th century (adopted from Li, 1992)

Having successfully driven out the Dutch in 1662, Zheng Cheng-kong (better known in the west as Koxinga), his Ming royalists and his family ruled the island for 21 years (1662–1683). As Zheng himself was from Southern Fujian, and his followers were mostly from the same region, they spoke the Southern Min dialect. Zheng's rule was replaced by the Manchus of the Qing dynasty and about two hundred years of Qing rule ensued (1683–1895). In the late Ming period and the early years of Qing rule, the coastal provinces of Fujian and Guandong were suffering from economic hardship and political turmoil; many inhabitants in the area were forced to leave their home towns in search of a better life in south-east Asia or Taiwan. Those who went to Taiwan were mostly from the Quanzhou and Zhangzhou districts of Fujian province, speaking the Zhangzhou or Quanzhou variety of the Southern Min.

The Hakka mostly from Kuangdong province, speaking either the Hai-lu or Si-hsien variety of Hakka according to their place of origin, soon joined this new wave of immigration. When these different groups of immigrants came to Taiwan, they tended to occupy areas on the island similar to their home regions in the Mainland; Quanzhou people, being shop and factory owners or workers, settled mostly along the coastal areas and ports. Zhangzhou people settled mostly in the inland plains and were devoted to agriculture. The Hakka, who were skilled in farming in hilly areas, settled in table lands and foothill regions (Shi, 1987: 1–6).

The coming of all these different groups of people led to a number of fierce struggles. The Han settlers with their larger numbers, better farming and irrigation skills and often with the implicit support of the Qing government soon outmanoeuvred the Plain tribes of aborigines, who, as a result, lost their land and were fast assimilated. The Mountain tribes, being separated by high mountains and deep valleys, were kept out of harm's way, at least for the time being.

In 1895, a year after Taiwan was ceded to Japan by the Qing government as a result of losing the first Sino-Japanese war, the Han inhabitants on the island already outnumbered the aboriginal people by a clear majority, and among the Han, Southern Min speakers account for 82%, Hakka speakers for 16% and the rest for only 2% (Lamley, 1981: 291–293). By 1905, the year when the first census was taken, ethnic Chinese had emerged as the majority group by a sizable margin (2,970,000 Chinese vs. 113,000 aborigines) and they have remained so ever since.

The Japanese rulers made it clear at the very beginning of their occupation that they intended to integrate Taiwan fully into the Japanese Empire. To this end, policies of complete Japanisation were designed. The Japanese rulers, however, were pragmatic enough to realise that such an end could not be achieved in a short time. They therefore implemented these policies in three stages of educational planning which were increasingly assimilatory in nature. During the first stage (1895–1919), which is generally referred to as the stage of pacification, private Chinese schools called *Shu-fang* (book house), where ethnic Chinese sent their children to study Classical Chinese with Southern Min or Hakka pronunciation, were tolerated, while at the same time the Japanese government urged people in Taiwan to send their children to the public elementary school, where Chinese was taught as a required subject.

During the second stage – the stage of assimilation (1919–1937) – all private Chinese schools were banned and Chinese as a subject was made elective. During the final stage – the stage of complete Japanisation (1937–1945)– not only was Chinese banned in all public domains, but even the few Chinese pages of the basically Japanese newspaper *Xinminbao*, the largest in Taiwan at that time, and all other publications in Chinese were banned. The ethnic Chinese living in Taiwan were thus completely cut off from their Chinese cultural print tradition. Earlier, in 1938, a year which saw the beginning of the second Sino-Japanese war, the Japanese government in Taiwan, in order to further obliterate Chinese influence, launched a fierce 'only-Japanese-speaking-families' campaign whose purpose was to drive the indigenous languages out of the family domain, usually believed to be the best stronghold for language maintenance (Chen, 1996; Tsao, 1997a). With all these repressive and discriminatory measures in force, ethnic Chinese and native Austro-Polynesians were in fact second-class citizens and their languages could not but be seriously damaged.

When Taiwan was returned to China at the conclusion of the Second World War, the people in Taiwan were overjoyed, firmly believing that their social and political status would be greatly improved. However, as the irony of life would have it, their high expectations have never been realised, as we shall see in some detail in the following discussion.

In 1949, four years after Taiwan was returned to China, the Nationalist government lost Mainland China to the Chinese Communists and was forced to retreat to Taiwan. Those immigrants and their children, now known as 'the Mainlanders', constitute the second largest ethnic group in Taiwan, even though at the time of their arrival they did not form a homogeneous group as they originated from different parts of Mainland China, speaking a variety of Han dialects or minority languages. Most of the Mainlanders were at least receptive bilinguals when they arrived in Taiwan. They had acquired Mandarin either through educational channels or during army service. The better educated among them could certainly write Mandarin and probably also classical Chinese. Upon their arrival Mandarin was a natural lingua franca for inter-dialectal communication for the group. Most of their children also acquired it either as a first or a second language. Today, the majority of the Mainlanders are located in large cities, especially in Taipei, the capital city.

On the economic front, things turned out much better. In the early fifties, about ten years after the Nationalist government took over Taiwan, a very successful land reform programme was launched. This reform programme not only directly paved the way for agricultural development but also indirectly paved the way for later industrial development (Huang, 1998). This dynamic transformation started in the 1960s. The industrialisation of Taiwanese society took place between 1961 and 1980. In the total workforce, the proportion of agricultural workers decreased dramatically from 56% in 1953 to 19% in 1983, while the proportion of the industrial workers increased significantly from 18% in 1953 to 41% in 1983 (Wen, 1985). In the meantime, the per capita gross national product of the country rose from US$203 in 1950 to US$2344 in 1980 and to US$12,439 in 1995.[4]

With the radical economic growth, education was no longer a luxury for the people of Taiwan. In 1950, there were 139.64 students for every 1000 people; in

1982, there were 255.18 students. In 1950, only 31.99% of primary school children continued their middle school education; in 1982, the percentage that continued education increased to 98.6%. As literacy became widespread and opportunities to receive higher education increased (Tsao, 1998a), the indigenous residents (the Southern Min, the Hakka and the Austro-Polynesian people) were more likely to obtain better occupations and higher incomes, which in turn upgraded their social status. Today, with greater socio-economic and political resources, these less powerful groups are better equipped to compete with the Mainlanders.

The economic prosperity, however, has not entirely been a blessing. In the course of development, the aboriginal people, who used to be protected by high mountains and deep valleys, have become more and more exposed to Han people. Furthermore, well-paved roads now lead right into their territory and television networks bombard them with Han language and culture. The inevitable result has been a rapid decrease in speakers of the aboriginal languages. In fact, of all eleven tribes among whom we can find speakers, seven have fewer than 10,000 speakers and are in serious danger of extinction.

In summary, Taiwan, as it stands today can be characterised as:

- a multi-ethnic and multilingual society with four major ethnic groups; the Mainlanders, the Southern Min people, the Hakka and the Austro-Polynesians;
- an immigrant society, the latest group being the Mainlanders;
- a Chinese society, and above all,
- a modern industrialised society.

A Brief Account of the Language Planning Efforts in China from 1911 to 1945

As mentioned earlier, at the conclusion of the Second World War in 1945, Taiwan was returned to China. By that time a number of language policies had already been formed and implemented in Mainland China and so when the Nationalist government took over Taiwan, the laws and regulations pertaining to language and language education were simply taken over from China with very slight adaptations. Therefore, in order to fully understand the language planning situation in Taiwan after 1945, it is necessary to begin on the Mainland.

A brief history of the national language movement

When the Republic of China was established in 1911, it faced two pressing problems: unification and modernisation. Ethnolinguistically, the country was composed of more than 50 ethnic groups, each speaking one or more languages, representing the Sino-Tibetan, Austronesian, Altaic, and Indo-European linguistic stocks. Even though the Han group was by far the largest, accounting for more than 90% of the population, it actually consists of seven major dialects, dozens of mutually unintelligible forms of speech and hundreds of sub-dialects. Yuan (1960: 22) lists the major dialects and population percentages as: Mandarin 70%, Wu 8.4%, Xiang 5%, Cantonese 5%, Min 4.2%, Hakka 4% and Gan 2.4%.

It is obvious that in a country with so much ethnolinguistic diversity and complexity linguistic unity has been a serious problem. Actually towards the end of the Qing dynasty as the Western powers encroached ever more upon China's territory, leaders of the country realised that for China to become a strong country, it must have a unified national language and mass literacy.

The lack of a single language for use among all Chinese had long been taken to be a serious impediment to national unification and political, economic and social development. At the national level, it is reported that in the early days of the Qing dynasty the emperor had a hard time communicating with officials from the southern provinces, especially Fujian and Guandong. The problem actually became so serious that the government had to set up a special school to teach them Mandarin.

Another serious problem was mass illiteracy. Statistics on illiteracy in China in the early years of the Republic have never been more than rough approximations, but even as late as the middle and late 1950s estimates from a number of sources suggest that from one half to two thirds of the adult population were functional illiterates. The figure could only have been higher twenty or thirty years earlier.

But to tackle these two serious and urgent problems, two questions involving language planning needed to be answered: (1) which dialect should be chosen as the national language? and (2) how should it be written so that the mass could learn it in the shortest possible amount of time?

Realising the urgency of the problems, the new republican government worked on them immediately. On 10 July, 1912 a meeting on national education was held at the Ministry of Education (henceforth MOE) in Peking. An important resolution passed at the meeting was to organise the Committee for the Unification of Pronunciation (henceforth CUP) whose functions were:

- to examine and authorise the pronunciation of all the words in the national language (NL);
- to analyse the phonemes of the NL and decide on the number of phonemes;
- to adopt phonetic alphabets: one alphabetic symbol for each phoneme (Fang, 1965: 131).

Established officially on 15 February, 1913 as a subordinate committee of the MOE, the CUP had 45 members, representing different provinces and special districts of the country. At its first meeting, the important question of which dialect should be chosen as the national language was discussed. There were two serious contenders, Mandarin and Cantonese.

Considering everything, Mandarin should have been chosen as the national language as it has the following advantages over all other dialects:

(1) Mandarin, as previously mentioned, is by far the largest dialect group, its speakers accounting for 70% of the total population, and furthermore, its four major sub-dialects, namely, Northern, Northwestern, Southwestern, and Lower Yangzi, are said to be mutually intelligible (Chao, 1943: 61).
(2) Geographically, Mandarin speakers occupy a very broad territorial belt running all the way from the northernmost reaches of Manchuria to the borders of Yunnan and Sichuan in the south-west.
(3) Peking has been the national culture centre for about a thousand years and much of the vernacular literature written in this long period was in Northern Mandarin.

(4)   The final advantage is that Peking has been the capital of China from Liao
times through the Jin, Yuan, Ming and Qing dynasties up to today with only
brief interruptions. Since Peking was the seat of government, officials from
all parts of China had always had to learn a form of Mandarin (called
guanhua, 'official speech') in order to be able to conduct government business. This *guanhua*, or lanqing *guanhua* 'blue-green Mandarin', as it was
sometimes called because of traces of all kinds of different dialect backgrounds in the speech of its speakers, was regarded by many Chinese as the
lingua franca of all China.

However, despite all of these advantages, in the meeting where all provinces
and special districts were equally represented a compromise solution was more
likely to be adopted. The national language finally chosen was actually an artificial form of Mandarin containing the maximum distinctions found in the major
dialects: i.e. the entering tone, the jian-tuan distinctions (dental and velar initials
occurring before a high front vowel respectively, FT), two mid-vowel phonemes
/o/ and /e/ (where most northern dialects have only one). The choice seemed to
be a happy one as it pleased most of the parties concerned, and that partially
accounts for the fact that in the process of selection (even though there were
heated debates interspersed with skirmishes involving flying teacups and
saucers), when the NL was thus decided, there were no serious riots of the order
of those in India and Sri Lanka, when Hindi and Sinhalese were selected as their
national language. Another contributing factor to the relative smoothness of
selection is that, as mentioned earlier, there was a common concern among the
elites at that time about the necessity of establishing a national language to facilitate inter-lingual and inter-dialectal communication.

This compromise solution, while it seemed to be able to satisfy most of the
representatives, actually contained an insurmountable difficulty for propagation. Since it was an artificial language, there was not a single teacher who could
claim to speak it natively. Teachers who had to teach it were soon divided into
two camps according to the strategy they adopted. Those who spoke a Northern
dialect close to the Peking dialect used the Peking dialect as their basis, with an
approximation of the entering tone used in reading pronunciation when they
read Classical Chinese. Those who spoke a Southern dialect used the entering
tone they had in their native dialects, which in actual pronunciation varies from
dialect to dialect, and they had to approximate the other four tones found in
Peking phonology. The two camps fought about what standard pronunciation
was for more than a decade and this controversy has come to be known as 'Jing
Gou zhi zhen' (controversy over Peking pronunciation and national language
pronunciation) (Chao, 1976b; Tsao, 1987).

This serious drawback of trying to use an artificial national language, coupled
with the fact that a majority of the Chinese people already spoke some type of
Mandarin, finally tipped the scale in favour of Peking Mandarin as the NL of
China.[5] In 1932, without publicly announcing any radical changes, the
Pronouncing Dictionary of the National Language, which was authorised by the
MOE in 1919 on the basis of the recommendation of CUP, was quietly revised in
the form of the *National Pronunciation of Common Vocabulary* and was authorised
by the MOE as the dictionary of standard pronunciation. It included 9920 words

and 2299 synonyms and was based exclusively on the educated speech of Peking (Chao, 1976b).

The selection of the writing system

Let us now return to the question of what writing system should be selected for the national language. As early as the late Qing dynasty there were heated debates as to whether the Chinese characters, as they were at that time, were a suitable writing system for Chinese. The most serious drawback of the system is that it is too complex to be learned by a great number of people within a short time. Part of the reason for this difficulty is that a great many Chinese characters, chiefly due to historical sound changes, are at this stage of development devoid of any association with their pronunciation. This lack of association between sound and meaning certainly makes the learning task much more difficult as learners often have to resort to rote memory. To put it differently, the writing system is perceived as a great impediment to the promotion of mass literacy, which was regarded as imperative for the modernisation of China. On the other hand, it has been the medium with which Chinese culture and Chinese literature have been recorded and any drastic change in the writing system entails the danger of disconnecting the present from the cultural past. Various proposals were made which include keeping the character writing system intact but supplementing it with an auxiliary transcribing system to indicate the pronunciation, replacing it with simplified characters, and finally, using a romanised spelling system.

At the meeting on national education held at the MOE in 1912 (mentioned previously), an important decision was taken that Chinese characters were to be kept intact but an auxiliary system of phonetic alphabets was to be adopted in education. It was the CUP's duty to devise such a system.

In the year immediately after the CUP was convened, it was decided that the traditional transcribing alphabet rather than a Latin alphabet should be adopted as the official phonetic (transcribing) device supplementing the characters. This was essentially a spelling system that fell between the Latin alphabet and the Japanese syllablary in function, but was like simplified Chinese characters in shape.

After the close of the first meeting, the work of the committee was suspended because of political turmoil. However, in the private sector, the work continued. In the few years that followed, some 'transcribing alphabet classes' were established in Peking and in 1916 a periodical named the 'Transcribed Mandarin Paper' was published in which articles were printed in characters with the transcribing alphabets beside them (henceforth to be called 'transcribed characters' for short).

On 23 November, 1916 the transcribing alphabets were authorised by the MOE. The system consisted of symbols for 24 consonants, 3 glides, 12 vowels and 4 tones. From a purely linguistic point of view, these symbols, with the exception of the tone symbols, are not completely phonemic symbols. Some of them represent sounds (allophones) rather than phonemes. The tone symbols, however, represent phonemic tones, and morphophonemic sandhi rules are stated separately.

Immediately after the Committee for the Preparation of a Unified National Language (CPUNL) was founded in April 1919, its members set to work to improve the transcribing alphabets. The revised system formed the basis of the National Phonetic Symbols (henceforth NPS), which were officially promulgated by the MOE in 1930. These symbols were to play a very instrumental role in the propagation of the national language in Taiwan.

In 1928, the MOE on the recommendation of the CPUNL authorised a romanisation system for transcription, chiefly developed by Chao, Y.R. and Lin, Yu-tang, and promulgated the regulations for the romanisation of the national language. From then on until its revision in Taiwan in 1984, this romanised phonetic transcribing system, whose chief feature was the representation of the tones in spelling rather than by diacritic marks, was known as the second form of NPS (NPS2, for short).

The change from 'Chinese Literature' to 'Chinese Language' as a subject in the elementary school

Another major contribution of CPUNL was the change from 'Chinese Literature' to 'Chinese Language' as a subject in the elementary school. This change may appear to people unfamiliar with the traditional way of teaching Chinese as a trivial change of name, but in reality it involved a change of great consequence. Traditional Chinese literature had always been written in a special literary style closer to Classical Chinese than to the everyday spoken language. The transcribing alphabets, devised as an aid to the rapid spread of literacy and common education, were actually based on the spoken language. So in order for the transcribing alphabets to have the greatest effect and for the textbooks, which before the change were uniformly written in the literary style, to be readily readable for elementary school students, the content of the language course had to be changed and the textbooks re-written. Therefore, at the first meeting of the CPUNL, it was recommended that the textbooks on Chinese for elementary schools be revised so that all the lessons were written in the colloquial spoken style. In 1920, the required subject 'Chinese Literature' for the first two grades in the elementary school was changed to 'Chinese Language' by the MOE, and in time this change was extended to all six grades in the elementary school. In this way, the teaching of the literary style in elementary education went into history.[6]

Language planning activities in connection with language development

While it seems that much was going on in the area of language policy and policy implementation during this period, despite many interruptions due to political turmoil and the Sino-Japanese War, nothing much seemed to be happening in the area of language development. One noticeable exception was the work of the Institute for Compilation and Translation in the compilation of lists of vocabulary equivalents in scientific and technical fields. The Institute was founded as a branch office of MOE in 1932, and between its inception and the Nationalist government's retreat to Taiwan in 1949, it compiled and published 25 volumes of word lists covering a variety of modern scientific disciplines such as mathematics, physics, chemistry, various specialties in medicine, several branches of engineering as well as five areas in social science (including economics, psychology and education). However, in spite of such a respectable showing in the standardisation in scientific terminology, language development was undeniably a peripheral concern at best during this period.

Summary: Special features of the language planning activities in the period

A careful examination of the language planning activities in this period reveals the following important features.

Firstly, the process of the selection of the national language was in general quite smooth. To be sure, there were heated exchanges of words and blows in the meetings, but once the national language was decided upon, there were no serious riots. Two important reasons account for this relative smoothness. First, there was a general consensus among the opinion leaders in the late Qing dynasty and the early years of the Republic that, in order for China to become a modernised, strong country, a unified national language was an essential. Second, a compromise selection was made in the sense that even though it was based on the Northern Mandarin, the national language also included some other features such as the entering tone found in other major dialects and this artificial version of Mandarin was able to satisfy all the parties concerned.

Secondly, even though the selection process was, comparatively speaking, rather smooth, the national language selected was not completely satisfactory. Being an artificial language based on the Northern Mandarin, the norm in some cases existed only on paper, there being no native speakers to exemplify the exact pronunciation. This lack of 'live norm' in the national language, so to speak, actually presented a serious challenge to its later propagation. The situation was not corrected until 1932, almost two decades after the norm was first conceived. This aspect offers a good lesson for those planners who wish to adopt a compromise-made language as a national language.

Another feature of the planning process is its almost exclusive concern with the pronunciation of the national language. The first official committee set up for planning purposes was called the Committee for the Unification of Pronunciation and it set the tone for the later processes. This exclusive concern with pronunciation was probably due to a misconception among the general public that the differences between different dialects lay mostly in the area of phonology. This misconception, in turn, was probably induced by the fact that in the Qing dynasty literate people in China were able to communicate through writing in Chinese characters even though they read the characters differently in their own dialect. Whatever the reason, this concentration on phonology in the early stages of the planning was probably justified, but the persistent emphasis on only the phonological aspect of the national language could justifiably be seen as being too restrictive in scope.

The fourth feature is that, as far as language planning activities are concerned, much attention was paid to language policy matters and very little to language development issues. This bias was probably due in part to the fact that there was no standing committee whose function was to guide all activities pertaining to language planning. Every committee was *ad hoc* in nature and once the assigned mission was deemed accomplished, it was dissolved.

Finally, no systematic evaluative measures are to be found in any part of the planning and propagation process in the period. The lack of an evaluation component is a feature common to many language-planning projects throughout the world as Rubin (1971) has pointed out. Since this feature also has persisted in language planning endeavours undertaken subsequently in Taiwan, I will examine its consequence more closely in a later section of the monograph.

Language Planning Activities in Taiwan since 1945

For more than five decades that the Nationalist government has ruled the island of Taiwan, the most important language policy has been the propagation of Mandarin, the national language. I will therefore begin our discussion in this section with an account of the so-called National Language Movement (NLM) to be followed by a brief evaluation of the movement. However, as made clear in the previous section, since Taiwan is a multi-ethnic and multilingual society, the propagation of the national language has inevitably affected other languages spoken on the same island. At the same time, as much of the country's resources have been pumped into the propagation of the national language in the educational system, it has also had serious effects on the other languages, chiefly English, which are being taught in the school system. I will therefore go into the policy matters related to these languages in the second part of this section. Part 3 of this section focuses on language development issues, which have been gaining in importance as Taiwan has become modernised. The final part of this section sums up the previous discussion by pointing out the special features of the language planning activities in this period.

National language movement in Taiwan

National language movement: A historical account

At the close of World War II in 1945, the Japanese government surrendered unconditionally to the Republic of China (ROC) and Taiwan was returned to the rule of the Chinese government. In the same year the Taiwan Provisional Provincial Government was set up with Chen Yi as its Administrative Head. Although the Nationalist government was not unprepared for the recovery of Taiwan (as preparatory work had started in 1944), when the end to the war began to seem inevitable (Kubler, 1985), the appointment of Chen as the administrative head was a hasty, ill-considered decision. Chen, a Nationalist general, who once ruled Fujian Province, turned out to be rather ill-prepared for the work lying before him to rule an island inhabited by millions of Southern Min, Hakka, and Austro-Polynesian speakers, most of whom had received some Japanese education and some of whom spoke fluent Japanese as a high language. His lack of preparation is clearly revealed in an interview with a Da-Gong Newspaper journalist before he took up his new post. He boasted in the interview that with his experience in the propagation of the national language in Fujian Province, he should be able to make great headway in four years. He also strongly advocated that strict measures should be taken in promoting the national language.

Very little is known about what Chen was able to achieve in Fujian Province, but judging from its present-day much poorer showing in the propagation of Mandarin (called Putonghua (PTH) in Mainland China) when compared with that of Taiwan (Zhou, 1992; Tsao, 1997a), Chen's statement cannot be taken very seriously. It was also foolhardy of him to advocate strict promotional measures because the sociolinguistic situation of the island at that time can be roughly characterised as a diglossia without societal bilingualism (Fishman, 1967; Tsao, 1998b). In other words, in the Taiwanese society, there existed a ruling class of Mainlanders, most of whom could speak some form of Mandarin and a lower class of people comprising Southern Min, Hakka and Austro-Polynesian speakers, and there was no way for these groups to communicate with each other except through translation. The situation was extremely delicate and needed to be handled with care. In this connection, one is reminded of the well-thought-out and very cautious language policy of appeasement used by the Japanese when they first arrived on the island (see above). In sharp contrast to the Japanese, Chen advocated strict measures. Indeed in 1946, less than a year after he took up his post, he banned the use of Japanese completely in order to eradicate the Japanese influence in Taiwan. While the grounds for doing so might have been justifiable, the timing was unfortunate and the consequences were hardly what he had expected. As previously indicated, Japanese was the high language that many elites used in the public domain. This being the case, banning the Japanese language was like shutting their mouths, or taking away their voices. Little wonder that thousands of intellectuals strongly protested at this arbitrary act of the government (Hsu, 1991). Ill-considered acts like this coupled with the reports that a number of people from the indigenous groups were either deposed or demoted because of their poor proficiency in Mandarin soon turned the indigenous groups of people against the government and the Mandarin-speaking Mainlanders. This anti-government sentiment, enhanced by many reports of government inefficiency and corruption, reached its peak when the tragic February 28 incident broke out in which thousands of Taiwanese and Mainlanders were killed and the relationship between the indigenous groups and the Mainlanders was greatly traumatised.[7] Soon after the tragic incident, Chen was deposed and was eventually executed on the grounds of conspiring with the Communist Chinese against the government.

On the national language promotion side, things were far more fortunate. The National Committee and Fujian Chapter of the Committee for the Promotion and Propagation of the National Language took active parts in the deliberation on the reconstruction of Taiwan as early as 1944 (Kubler, 1985). In November 1945, soon after the Japanese surrendered on 9 September of that year, several dozen members of the Mainland Committee of CPPNL, led by Wei Jiangong, a philologist, and He Rong, a grammarian, arrived in Taiwan to set up the machinery for the promotion of the national language there. Because there were still not sufficient teachers and promoters to staff the various Mandarin centres, some thirty primary school teachers with high proficiency in Mandarin from Fujian Province were brought in in the spring of 1946. Later, several dozens advanced university students in Mandarin training classes at various Mainland universities were also recruited for the same reason (Fang, 1965).

The Taiwan Provincial CPPNL was established in April 1946 subordinate to the Educational Department of the Provisional Provincial Government. It included among its charter members, Wei Jian-gong, He Rong, Fang Shiduo, Li Jiannan, Wang Yuchuan, Lin Shaoxian, Zhu Zhaoxiang, and Wu Shouli, several of whom were to play important roles in the promotion of the national language in Taiwan for years to come. However, in addition to the main office of the Committee located in Taipei, other branch offices called Mandarin Promotion Centers were opened in Taichung, Taitung, Hsinchu, Kaohsiung, Changhua, Chiayi, and Pingtung. They were staffed by the recruits from Mainland China and they operated in close cooperation with the local school systems and city governments (Fang, 1965: 133). The Committee set to work at once; the first few urgent tasks that called for immediate attention were:

- to set up the standards (chiefly in pronunciation) for the national language,
- to devise the working outline of the NLM in Taiwan, and
- to compile the Standard Pronunciation Dictionary of the national language.

In the early days after Taiwan's restoration to China, enthusiasm for learning the national language was extremely high, but this high enthusiasm, instead of being fully utilised, was soon dampened by the bad administration of the Provisional Provincial Government headed by Chen Yi on the one hand and by the lack of qualified teachers, on the other. As can be imagined, teachers were from very different backgrounds, ranging from those who were native speakers of the national language to those who had had very little exposure to the national language and could only speak it with a very heavy accent. Standard textbooks were also unavailable. The members of the Taiwan CPPNL thus began a series of efforts to explain to the public through the mass media (mainly radio and newspaper) the meaning and the purpose of NLM, and the definition of the national language (Fang, 1965).

Another achievement of the Committee was to designate an outline for NLM in Taiwan. The following six principles were decided on:

(1) to recover the Taiwanese dialect so as to enable the public to learn the national language by comparison between the dialect and the national language;
(2) to emphasise the standard pronunciation;
(3) to eradicate the influence of Japanese as reflected in the daily speech of the people;
(4) to promote the contrastive study of morphology so as to enrich the national language;
(5) to adapt the NPS so as to promote communication among people of different races and origins; and
(6) to encourage the intention of learning the national language so as to facilitate the teaching of it (Fang, 1965: 131).

Of the six principles, 2, 3 and 6 all look practical and practicable. In fact, I have already mentioned some of the work done in accordance with the sixth principle. Principle 5 was a very wise decision, and NPS were to play a vital part in the propagation of the national language. I have more to say about this in connection with the Mandarin Daily News in a later section. Unfortunately, as Taiwanese society is becoming internationalised, this system is now facing a stiff challenge from competing romanised systems, especially the one propagated by the People's Republic of China. It is still too early to say what the outcome of this competition will be.

Principles 1 and 4 were either controversial or impractical. When Principle 1 was announced, it immediately spawned a heated debate. There were people who argued that dialects should be done away with once and for all, but there were other people who argued that the national language can be best learned through people's mother tongue, namely the dialect. It was not clear whether there was a consensus among the committee members and if so what that consensus was. Judging from the fact that there was only one series of textbooks called the 'Bridge Series' (which utilised the comparison method to teach the Southern Min speakers the national language), and, from the fact that no members of the Committee were known to take part in the debate, it seems fair to say that the Committee was not really too enthusiastic about this principle. As for Principle 4, it looks more like a utopian blueprint, as there were no experts on Taiwan at that time who were able to conduct a contrastive study of Mandarin and Southern Min, not to mention Hakka and the aboriginal Austro-Polynesian languages.

Yet another major effort of the Committee was the compilation of the Dictionary of the Standard Pronunciation of the national language. The first Taiwan edition was published in 1952. In the ensuing years, it became so popular that almost every teacher had a copy of it. It certainly played a very important role in the standardisation of the national language in Taiwan.

The Taiwan Provincial CPPNL was established in April 1946 and abolished in 1959. A lower-level committee in the Provincial Department of Education was founded to replace it. Three reasons were given for the abolition of the Committee:

(1) the policy objective of NLM (i.e. standardisation and propagation) was deemed to have been achieved;
(2) the cultivation of the NL, a long-term enterprise, could be continued through the joint efforts of the school, the media, and the whole nation; and
(3) a lower-level committee was thought to be sufficient to guide the development of the national language.

As all three of the reasons given were highly questionable, the true reasons for its abolition remain a mystery. Kubler (1985) has argued that budget considerations must have played an important part as it was not too long after the battle of Quemoy with the Chinese Communists, and the Nationalist government could have been contemplating an expensive, large-scale military offensive. (I am of this opinion.) In any case, the feeling that much in terms of language planning remained to be done and that a lower-level committee was insufficient for guiding the operation soon became widespread. In 1980 the government was pressured into re-establishing under the MOE a body equivalent to the CPPNL, which had existed on the Chinese Mainland before the Nationalist government's retreat.

Scholars' evaluation of the Taiwan Provincial CPPNL seems to be in general favourable (Tse, 1986; Kubler, 1985). Three tasks in particular are held up as exemplars: first, there was a step-by-step promotion programme. Training of Mandarin promotion personnel was the first step. Training of primary and secondary school teachers was the second. Finally, training of students still in school as well as those already working in society was the third. This step-by-step promotion method was deemed to be effective. Second, the effective Pronunciation Demonstrating Broadcasting Program was regarded by many as an excellent example as to how the mass media could be used as an aid in language planning efforts. Finally, the Taiwan Provincial CPPNL should be credited for its effort in the formulation of policy and strategy to teach only the spoken language through the NPS for the first 12 weeks in the first semester of the first grade in elementary schools. The policy was made on the basis of the experimental results conducted by the Committee on the improvement of teaching methods and teaching materials in the national language (Tse, 1986: 69).

In the 1960s and 1970s, with the disbanding of the Taiwan Provincial CPPNL, large-scale, organised efforts to promote Mandarin were largely stopped. Language planning activities in this period, however, took a new turn. Attention was now paid to areas that hitherto had been pretty much neglected – such as the teaching of reading and composition at the elementary school level. There were even plans to construct a Mandarin proficiency test including a taped interview for the oral section for all sixth-grade children in Taiwan (Zhang, 1974: 224).

There was also a movement, spearheaded by President Yen Jia-gan, to reform the language of official government documents. At that time most of the documents were composed using semi-Classical Chinese. The aim of the movement was to make the language more in line with the vernacular *Baihua* style.

In the late 1970s, the work of promoting Mandarin in Taiwan by the lower-level committee under the Provincial Department of Education and other educational organisations included activities such as school spelling bees, pronunciation competitions, Mandarin speech contests, as well as Mandarin adults' education classes and literacy programmes for employees of various government and private institutions. Research activities during the period included scientific character counts of different genres of current publications for use in reading research or textbook compiling, Chinese speed reading, Mandarin shorthand, Chinese typewriter development, and Chinese character computer technology, some of which will be reviewed more extensively in the section on language development (Kubler, 1985).

Special mention must be made in this connection of a movement that was very active in the late 1960s and 70s – the Chinese Cultural Restoration Movement. When the Taiwan Provincial CPPNL was disbanded in 1959, some of the language planning activities were picked up by the committee in charge of the Movement. As many of the committee members showed great concern over what they perceived to be a much slower rate of progress in the promotion of the NL since the disbanding of the Taiwan Provincial CPPNL, they passed a six-point resolution which they presented to the MOE. The MOE accepted and announced them on 26 November, 1970. These resolutions were (Chen, 1996; Kubler, 1985):

(1) Immediately revive the Committee for the propagation and promotion of Mandarin in the Ministry of Education to make unified plans and positively oversee the promotion work of the Mandarin committees at every level.

(2) Increase funding for personnel in the Committee for the Promotion of Mandarin in the provincial capital and the chief sites of each county.

(3) To achieve the goals of the Mandarin movement, we should start simultaneously from the following four aspects:

   (a) Strengthen Mandarin education in the schools and cultivate Mandarin-teaching personnel.
   (b) Strengthen Mandarin education in society and start supplementary education programmes in the villages, in mines, factories, among adults in the aboriginal tribes, and for all those who lack formal schooling.
   (c) Improve radio and television programmes. The amount of foreign language (i.e. English – FFT) and dialect (i.e. Southern Min – FFT) programming should be decreased and Mandarin programmes increased.
   (d) Strengthen Mandarin education among overseas Chinese, making use of textbooks, records, and films, etc. to promote the Mandarin language abroad.

(4) Ask the people's representatives to use Mandarin when speaking at conferences so as to increase its influence.
(5) Require organisations, schools, offices, and all public areas to use Mandarin. Civil servants and, above all, teachers in the public schools should set an example for others.
(6) To increase interest in speaking Mandarin, various kinds of contests and activities should be employed that increase awareness among the people of the importance of speaking Mandarin.

During the 1970s, some of these measures were put into effect. But as previously mentioned, the revival of the Committee for the Promotion and Propagation of Mandarin in the MOE had to wait until 1980.

After the Committee was established, language planning activities again became active on the national scene. The following are some of the most important things that the Committee has done since its establishment.

In 1984, the MOE announced a revised system of romanisation of the Chinese characters. The older system, originally developed by Y.R. Chao, Lin Yu-tang and their colleagues more than half a century ago, had been felt to be exceptionally complicated in that the four tones were represented by letters instead of by diacritic marks, and the rules of spelling tried to reflect not only the phonemic system, but also narrow phonetic information. The revised system employs diacritics for the four tones: – for high level, / for rising, 'v' for dipping and \ for high falling. These marks, which are quite iconic in their representation of the actual tone values, are also ones that are used in NPS, and in the Pinyin system used in Mainland China. In addition, the spelling rules are made to reflect only the phonemic system, thus greatly simplifying the system. This new revised system is mainly designed for the use of teaching Chinese to foreigners and overseas Chinese (i.e. those who cannot read Chinese characters) and for local people to use in transcribing their names in romanised forms (in letters). These last statements of purpose are felt to be necessary because the government wants to reiterate its stance of not abolishing Chinese characters.

Many critics, this writer included, have serious doubts about whether the revised system, created after the Pinyin system in use in Mainland China since the 1950s and which has gained world-wide recognition, would be extensively employed in the teaching of Mandarin abroad. As for its local application in the area of the transcription of personal names and place names, it has scarcely been used since most people, including scholars and linguists, are not familiar with it. In a word, many scholars feel that its creation was more to satisfy the need of the policy than to meet any actual demand at that time.

In early 1999 the issue of whether NPS or some romanised spelling system should be used in the teaching of Mandarin was raised again and has been heatedly debated. In the discussion, the appropriateness of the new revised system has again been questioned. This issue will be taken up again in that larger context in the last section of the monograph.

In addition, in line with the Nationalists' claim to authenticity and its policy of not using simplified characters, the Committee has invested a great deal of its resources to standardise the Chinese orthography (the characters). Before the establishment of the Committee, an *ad hoc* committee spent six years (from 1973 to 1979) in the compilation of a list of standard orthography and another three years in its trial use (*Central Daily News*, 9 May, 1983). In April 1981, this list of standard orthography of commonly used characters was authorised and published by the MOE at the recommendation of CPPNL (*Central Daily News*, 27 April, 1981).

Any account of NLM in Taiwan would be incomplete without mentioning the role played by the army and the *National Language Daily*. In the 1940s and 1950s, all young men planning to enter the army were encouraged to enrol in a Mandarin course first since Mandarin was (and still is) the language of the Taiwan military forces. Later on, the army, in cooperation with the Taiwan Provincial CPPNL, published special manuals for teaching Mandarin as part of its basic training. Since two to three years' military service is required of every young man, many who had not had a chance to learn Mandarin picked up the language during their compulsory military service. This has not only helped propagate the national language, but it has helped promote literacy in the country as well (Tsao, 1998a).

Another important factor that has contributed to the success of NLM is the *National Language Daily*, a newspaper using transcribed characters, which has been popular for the past fifty years especially among lower-grade students. Since its founding in 1948, it has made a great contribution to the standardisation and propagation of the national language. Its significance in the promotion of the national language was never more keenly felt than after the abolition of the Taiwan Provincial CPPNL. The National Language Daily Press Service Committee for national language education was organised in 1960 to provide service to education in the national language. Totally supported by the *National Language Daily*, it provides the following services:

- to compile and publish textbooks and teaching materials in the national language;
- to assist in the training of teachers and promoters of the national language;
- to answer, research, and experiment with problems related to the national language;
- to provide other services related to the education in the national language.

An evaluation

Like many other language planning programmes, evaluation, no doubt, is the weakest aspect of language planning endeavours in Taiwan. In fact, little is known about whether there has been any provision made for continuing evaluation of the NLM at the national or local level. To date, to the best of my knowledge, no official assessment has ever been attempted. Those essays that appeared in the anthology of papers collected by The Executive Yuan in 1982 were all impressionistic and, generally speaking, devoid of useful information. This lack of information makes this present attempt at evaluation a difficult, but a worthwhile task. Fortunately for our present endeavour, many evaluative reports about what has been going on in language planning in Mainland China since 1949 are readily available. In the evaluation which follows, these reports are cited for comparison whenever feasible.

Taiwan's successful propagation of Mandarin Chinese as the national language has been well documented (Tse, 1987; Zhou, 1992; Tsao, 1997a). While it is certain that Tse (1987) was over-optimistic in his estimate of the percentage of people unable to speak the national language (5%), as Huang (1993) and Tsao (1997a) have pointed out, he was not too far off the mark. A more realistic figure has been given by Ke (1990), who based his estimate on the school enrolment and people's educational attainment figures provided by the Executive Yuan, as displayed in Table 1.

Table 1 Percentages of educational attainment for people above six in Taiwan in 1987

Elementary School	37.54%
Junior High	19.12%
Senior High	7.40%
Vocational School	16.17%
Junior College	5.15%
College	4.37%
Graduate School	0.22%
Self-study	1.65%
Illiterate	7.79%
Total	100.00%

His calculation is as follows. The total percentage of people with a middle school education or higher is 52.43%. If we then add 37.54%, the percentage of people who had only elementary education or who were at that time enrolled in an elementary school, then the total comes up to 89.97, roughly 90% of the population aged 7 or above. In other words, it is safe to estimate for those over six years old in Taiwan in 1987, roughly 10% of them were not able to speak Mandarin. This figure, though not as high as Tse's estimate, is actually quite remarkable. Zhou You-Guang, who is a very senior scholar and researcher in the propagation and development of Mandarin in Mainland China, is of the same opinion. In his recent book (1992), he compared the speed with which Mandarin Chinese has been propagated in Taiwan and Singapore with a dragon flying and that in Mainland China as a turtle's crawling.[8]

Two points should be made in connection with this phenomenal success of Mandarin promotion in Taiwan. First, being able to speak Mandarin Chinese means that speakers with this ability are able to make themselves understood in the language when called upon to do so. It does not include the ability to carry on a sustained conversation in the language, nor does it imply that they are able to speak like a Peking resident, as the norm suggests people should be able to do. Quite the contrary, after fifty years of strenuous propagation, a number of discrepancies in all aspects of the grammar, but especially noticeable in phonology (pronunciation), have been found (Cheng, 1985; Li, 1983; Kubler, 1985; Tsao, 1987). Many of the features have been fossilised to the extent that this variety has come to be known as 'Taiwan Mandarin'. Such discrepancies between the norm and the actual speech are not unexpected. It is this expected discrepancy between the norm and the actual performance in the speech community that has prompted both Rubin (1971) and Karam (1974) to stress the need for evaluation in language planning and of using the evaluation results to adjust the norm after the language has been propagated for a certain extended period of time. However, in the case of the propagation of the national language in Taiwan, either the authorities concerned are not aware of the need for doing an evaluation or they are reluctant to do so because they think that the issue is still politically sensitive. No evaluation of this kind has been done since the norm was set up some seventy years ago, and the failure to adjust the norm has caused language teachers a lot of problems. To begin with, they are torn between what they are expected to teach and what they feel they should teach. If they teach according to an unrealistic norm, they will be teaching their students a language that not many people use in Taiwan, but if they teach what they think they should teach, they are not doing the thing that they have been taught to do. To complicate the matter even more, they actually cannot teach what they are expected to teach in any real sense, since many of them are 'Taiwan Mandarin' speakers, and therefore they cannot serve as models for their students.

Secondly, the phenomenal success has been achieved at the expense of the indigenous languages, i.e. Southern Min, Hakka and the aboriginal Austro-Polynesian languages. In other words, while Mandarin has been gaining in popularity, the indigenous languages have been fast eroding. Many scholars (Huang, 1993; Li, 1994; Tsao, 1994, 1996a, 1996b, 1997a, 1997b among others) have seen this as a natural consequence of the government's policy of promoting Mandarin, the national language, while neglecting and at times suppressing the indigenous languages, a subject which is examined in the next section.

Language policy effects on other indigenous languages

The policy and its implementation

Romaine (1995: 242), after an extensive study of the language policies of many countries has come to the following conclusion:

> The traditional policy, either implicitly assumed or explicitly stated, which most nations have pursued with regard to various minority groups, who speak a different language, has been eradication of the native language/culture and assimilation into the majority one.

Taiwan's past experience shows clearly that it is no exception. Although this policy in an overt written form is nowhere to be found, all the indications are it has been the covert policy all along. Evidence for this is that when some open-minded scholars such as Hong Yen-chiu spoke up for the minority peoples' language rights and argued against a hard-line approach, he was immediately attacked by many hard-liners who criticised his views as not leading to national unity (Hong, 1978).

In fact, this hard-line, high-handed propagation of Mandarin was very prevalent up to ten years ago. Romaine (1995: 242) reported that in Australia, the United States, Britain and Scandinavia, minority children were until recently still subject to physical punishment in school for speaking their home language. In Turkey, where Kurdish is a minority language whose existence is not recognised, the situation was even worse. Thus one Kurdish woman who attended a special boarding school provided for Kurdish children described her heartbreaking experience vividly (Clason & Baksi, 1979: 79, 867, translated by Skutnabb-Kangas, 1984: 311–12):

> I was seven when I started the first grade in 1962. My sister, who was a year older, started school at the same time. We didn't know a word of Turkish when we started, so we felt totally mute during the first few years. We were not allowed to speak Kurdish during the breaks, either, but had to play silent games with stones and things like that. Anyone who spoke Kurdish was punished. The teachers hit us on the fingertips or on our heads with a ruler. It hurt terribly. That's why we were always frightened at school and didn't want to go.

Many short articles, appearing in Lin's (1983) collection of essays, described similar experiences that many indigenous language speakers had in their early years of schooling. My own experience in learning the national language in a suburban primary school in Taipei also bore this out. Even though punishment was not as severe as the one the Kurdish sisters underwent, there were several ways of punishing a student when he or she was caught speaking Taiwanese Southern Min in school. However, as we were all indoctrinated with the idea of the imminent threat of communism as well as the importance of national unity, and therefore the necessity to speak the national language, these unnecessarily severe punishments were not thought to be very drastic at the time. Furthermore, many indigenous language speakers were informed by their teachers that their languages were base and vulgar and that they should feel ashamed for being speakers of such languages.

Control of newspapers and electronic media was equally oppressive. Newspapers were exclusively in Mandarin, with one or two English papers being the exceptions. In the fifties, soon after the Nationalist government moved to Taiwan, it was stipulated that, in view of the fact that most people did not know Mandarin, Taiwanese programmes in electronic media would be allowed on condition that they be gradually replaced by Mandarin programmes. In the seventies, it was further stipulated that programmes in the 'dialects', meaning Taiwanese and Hakka, would be aired for only one hour a day. The ban was in effect for about ten years before it was finally lifted together with the lifting of martial law (Huang, 1993; Tsao, 1997a).

Under the double oppression of school education and the mass media, it would indeed be odd if indigenous languages did not begin to die out.

The effect of the policy and its implementation

Huang and Chang (1995), in a recent paper on the sociolinguistic history of the Gavaland Pingpu tribe, report that in I-lan area around 1650 there were nearly ten thousand Gavaland speakers, but by the time Professor Ruan did his field work in 1969, only about 800 speakers remained there. If we include the number of people who migrated to Hua-lian, the total would not exceed two thousand. But less than thirty years later even those 800 speakers have disappeared, leaving the I-lan area with no Gavaland speakers.

The Gaoshan group, though luckier than the Pingpu tribe as it is protected by the mountains, is actually not doing too well. According to statistics released by the government in 1989, the population of the nine Goashan tribes was:

- Amis 129,220
- Atayal 78,957
- Paiwan 60,434
- Bunun 38,627
- Puyuma 8,132
- Rukai 8,007
- Tsou 5,797
- Saisiyat 4,194
- Yami 4,335.

According to Huang's (1991, 1993) calculations, based on a questionnaire survey of Aboriginal College Students, the attrition rate was estimated to be 15.8% between two generations and 31% between three generations. If Huang's estimate was correct, almost half of the existing aboriginal languages are going to disappear from Taiwan in another two generations.

Similar results also were obtained in Lin's (1995) survey report. After surveying one thousand junior high school students studying in 25 schools, Lin found that, for the aborigine students, only 37% claimed that the aboriginal language was the one most frequently used at home. Only 68% claimed that they could speak their parents' language and among the latter group only 16% claimed to be fluent.

The Hakka students' performance was only slightly better than that of the aborigines; 40% of the students surveyed said that Hakka was the most frequently used language at home. Elsewhere, according to Huang's (1993) survey of 327 Hakka students in the Taipei area and 404 Hakka Taipei citizens, only 70% of those people whose parents were both Hakka speakers claimed that they could speak Hakka.

As for Taiwanese, both Huang's and Lin's survey results indicate that it too shows signs of erosion, although the rate is relatively slow. Furthermore, Chan's study (1994) shows that the domains traditionally attributed to Taiwanese, such as the home and the marketplace, are shrinking, indicating that the dominant language, Mandarin, has made inroads upon it as well.

Based on an island-wide telephone survey of 934 subjects conducted by the Formosa Cultural and Educational Foundation, the relationship between the

Table 2 Relationship of ethnic group identity and mother tongue identity in three age groups for Hakka

	I *Ethnic group identity(%)*	II *Mother tongue identity (%)*	III *II/I (%)*
L (18-30)	7.4	5.7	77
M (31-40)	13.5	12.2	90
H (41-50)	11.9	10.6	89

N.B. Figures in Columns I and II of the table refer to the percentages of subjects in that age group who claimed that identity out of total survey population, and those in Column III are the percentages obtained by dividing the figure in Column II by that in Column I.

Table 3 Relationship between ethnic group identity and mother tongue identity in three age groups for Taiwanese

	I *Ethnic group identity(%)*	II *Mother tongue identity (%)*	III *II/I (%)*
L (18-30)	80.2	70.8	88
M (31-40)	76.9	74.2	96
H (41-50)	76.9	79.1	99.4

proportion of subjects claiming to be of Hakka ethnic descent, and that of subjects claiming to have Hakka as their mother tongue, for three age groups, is shown in Table 2. Table 2 clearly indicates that the erosion of the Hakka language has intensified among younger people (those aged below 30), with the erosion rate reaching a dramatic 13% decline between younger and middle-aged Hakka.

For comparison, consider the corresponding figures from the Taiwanese group shown in Table 3. From Table 3 it is quite clear that the Taiwanese group shows signs of erosion as well, although the rate is slower, being 8% between the mid- and low-age groups, as compared to 13% for the Hakka group.

My own large-scale survey (Tsao, 1997a) also yields basically the same result, i.e. while Mandarin was gaining popularity, all the indigenous languages were rapidly fading. These two tendencies are clearly demonstrated in Figures 2 (Mandarin proficiency) and 3 (mother tongue proficiency) respectively. From the above statistics it is clear that the indigenous languages in Taiwan are disappearing with the aboriginal languages declining the fastest, Hakka close behind and Taiwanese less markedly. This shows unmistakably the effect of the government's policy on the indigenous languages other than Mandarin, the national language.

Teaching English and other foreign languages in Taiwan

Like many developing countries in the world, Taiwan's past language-in-education policy has been to a large extent determined by two main factors: (1) nationalism and national unification and (2) modernisation and economic growth. These two factors are not in agreement at all times. The language-in-education system can be seen as a resultant state of the interaction

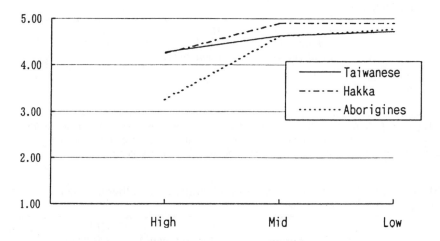

Figure 2 Comparison of Mandarin proficiency in the three ethnic groups

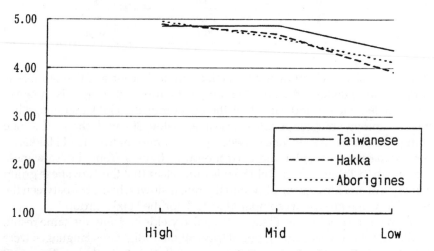

Figure 3 Comparison of mother tongue proficiency in the three ethnic groups

between these two factors, but to see this clearly, we need to take a look at the system first.

In describing a language-in-education system, Bamgbose's (1991: 62) characterisation is very useful. He suggests characterising a language-in-education system by seeking answers to the following three questions: (1) What language? (2) For what purpose? and (3) at what level? For our present purpose, the languages involved can be classified into three types: the mother tongue, the national language, and other languages used for wider communication. As has been shown in the previous sections, in Taiwan the mother tongue may be Southern Min, Hakka, Mandarin or one of the aboriginal Austro-Polynesian languages. The major language of wider communication (LWC) taught in Taiwan is English, but French, German, Spanish and Japanese are also taught.

Table 4 Language type and function in education in Taiwan

	Literacy	*Subject*	*Medium*
Mother tongue	O	O	O
National language	X	X	X
LWC	O	X	O

If we now concentrate on the first two major questions, namely, 'what language?' and 'for what purpose?' we may arrive at nine possibilities, each represented by a cell in the matrix shown in Table 4. By filling in the possibilities that are actually realised with 'X', and those unrealised as 'O', we get the table as shown.

Educational practice as represented by Table 4 has existed almost unchallenged for fifty years.[9] As is apparent in the table, Mandarin, the national language, has played a very important role in the system. It is taught to everybody, regardless of their mother tongue or home language, as a language for literacy. It is also a subject taking up at least five hours of instruction every week from the first grade up to college freshman level, and is by far the most important subject in all elementary and secondary courses. Finally, it is the sole medium of instruction in the school system. Competency in it plays a decisive role in a student's scholastic achievement.

In distinct contrast is the role of English in the system. It is required of every student in the secondary school and the first year of college. It used to take up five hours of instruction per week in all years of secondary education. However, when compulsory education was extended from six years to nine in 1970, the hours of instruction were cut to two or three in the first two years of junior high school.

Despite its widely recognised importance in literacy, the mother tongue, except where it is also Mandarin, played absolutely no role in the system officially until the 1997 school year, when mother tongue education began to be allotted one hour per week in the elementary school programme. I will have more to say about this change in the final section of this monograph when some recent developments are examined.

The mother tongue was excluded from the system on the grounds that it has been seen as an impediment to national unification. However English, as a representative of the so-called languages of wider communication, has been included for the purpose of providing information access to the world of technology and science which Taiwan needs for social modernisation and economic growth. This role for English, however, has never been emphasised because it is, at the same time, perceived as a potential threat to nationalism. The equilibrium was achieved by assigning English the role as set out in Table 4.

This being the case, it came as no surprise when a national survey of English teaching in Taiwan was conducted in 1974–1976 and a number of problems were found, these problems did not receive much attention from the media or the authorities concerned. The survey was part of a cooperative project between the Department of Linguistics, University of Southern California (USC) and the English Research Institute, National Taiwan Normal University (NTNU). It was jointly conceived, planned and implemented by Prof. Robert B Kaplan of USC and Prof. C. M. Yang of the NTNU. Dr Philip Sedlak, who spent about two years in Taiwan implementing the plan, conducted the actual survey. The survey was able to gather a wealth of data about English teaching in the secondary school in Taiwan, but for some reason, the first report, which was published in June 1976, was so hastily composed that it left much to be desired. As pointed out by Tsao (1982) and Tse (1987), there are specifically three important shortcomings:

- much of the data collected in the survey was left unanalysed;
- the statistical analysis was not very revealing; and
- some of the recommendations proposed were highly impractical.

Fortunately, these shortcomings were corrected by Tse, who reanalysed much of the raw data gathered in the survey. The results were reported in Tse's PhD dissertation written at USC in 1979 and later published in a slightly revised form in Taiwan (Tse, 1987).

The reanalysed survey presented a large number of significant findings, which tell us much about English teaching in the secondary schools in Taiwan at that time. The important findings include the following:

(1) Most English teachers were inadequately trained, both in English and educational methodology.
(2) Learning and writing had been emphasised in their training.
(3) Despite being highly desirable, the availability of in-service training was low.
(4) The weekly hours of English instruction were inadequate.
(5) Grammar and translation were given disproportionate emphasis.
(6) Most tests focused on reading and writing.
(7) Audiovisual aids were woefully inadequate and underutilised.
(8) English contact outside school was very limited.

This amended survey gave a true picture of English teaching at secondary level, and yielded a number of important shortcomings that called for immediate attention. However, for some reason, it did not have as much impact on the English teaching profession as had originally been planned. As a result, English teaching remained pretty much the same for some twenty years after the survey was conducted with only two possible exceptions. First, in-service training is now much more available to teachers, although what effect such a change has brought to actual teaching remains to be examined. Second, English teachers' educational training does seem to have improved over the years. This is clearly revealed in Table 5, where the English teachers' educational training in 1976, the time when the survey was conducted, is compared with that in 1996.[10] However, this upgrading of teachers' educational training has been due in large part to the general expansion of universities and graduate schools in Taiwan. The effect of this upgrading of teachers' qualifications remains to be determined.

These shortcomings notwithstanding, in all fairness it might be said that judging from the economic success of Taiwan in the past 30 years, some credit has to be given to the successful implementation of this particular area of educational policy.

Table 5 Secondary school English teacher's educational training in 1976 and 1996

	Total	*Master and Doctorate*	*Normal university graduates*	*Graduates of other universities or colleges*	*Graduates of junior college and others*
1976	100%	0.4%	28.30%	61.30%	10.0%
1996	100%	9.8%	44.64%	35.66%	9.9%

Prior to the reanalysis of the survey data, Tse conducted a small-scale survey of language use in Taiwan. Among its many interesting findings, the following are particularly notable (Tse, 1987: Chapter 4):

(1) English is the foreign language most often used at work. After English, Japanese is most often used. German and French are rarely used.
(2) Even English is not frequently used at work.
(3) When English is used at work, reading and writing skills are most often required.
(4) Cram schools and English programmes sponsored by employers generally are not considered helpful.
(5) Although significantly more respondents' attitudes towards English were positive, over one-third of them have an unfavourable attitude for nationalistic reasons.

Points 1 and 5 deserve some further comment. The respondents' attitudes as revealed in the survey were basically in line with the government's language policy, but even as early as twenty years ago, there were signs that nationalism was slowly giving way to pragmatic considerations. This comment applies to English as well as to Japanese. Recall that in the mid-1940s, when Taiwan had just been restored to the Republic of China, the language policy was to wipe out the Japanese influence in the indigenous languages and culture. However, by the late 1970s, because of Taiwan's heavy trade with Japan, Japanese had already replaced French and German as the second most frequently used foreign language in Taiwan. This change was to be reflected in the educational language policy in the 1980s and 90s when enrolment in Japanese classes offered by various universities showed a rapid increase and several Japanese departments were established in national as well as private universities. At the same time the enrolment figures in German and French classes offered at universities dropped considerably.

As far as English is concerned, the pragmatic attitude of the people has actually made English become increasingly popular. This general popularity coupled with the general affluence of the populace and traditional Chinese people's emphasis on children's education has induced many parents to send their young children to English language classes, which have mushroomed in the past decade. As this trend has grown rapidly, it has recently pushed the government into changing its earlier policy of beginning English education in secondary school, a matter that I will take up in some detail in the next section.

Language planning activities connected with language modernisation and development

Similar to what happened in Mainland China under the Nationalist administration, language planning activities in Taiwan have been centred on the problem of language unification, especially pronunciation. Comparatively little has been done in the area of language development and modernisation. However, as the national language has been increasingly used in various domains and in the educational system in the Republic, a number of problems occurred that called for solutions.

One of these problems has to do with whether in printing Chinese horisontally, the direction should be from left to right or from right to left. Traditionally, Chinese texts are printed vertically and are read from right to left. This was fine until Chinese was used for materials in science and technology, which often consist of quantitative data and sometimes include special terminology in Roman letters which are read from left to right. This kind of printed material, therefore, often contains matters printed in different directions, causing great confusion in reading.

A related debate broke out in the seventies about the direction of printing Chinese horizontally between the traditional purists and the modernists, and the MOE was called upon to provide a set of guidelines governing the printing of Chinese. Finally, after much deliberation and discussion, a compromised solution was reached. When printing vertically, the direction should be from right to left, but in order to accommodate scientific exposition, when printing horizontally the direction from left to right is allowed. Such a compromise, which might seem to have pleased the contenders of both camps at the time, actually ended up not solving all the problems it was intended to solve. In fact, it has created a number of others. Let us take a concrete example. In Taiwan there are two major newspapers, the *China Times* and the *Liberty Times*. While both follow the guidelines propagated by the MOE in printing vertically, i.e. from right to left, they do it differently when printing horizontally. The *China Times* prints from right to left, thus creating confusion when numerals and roman letters appear, whereas the *Liberty Times* prints from left to right, thus requiring readers to adopt different strategies when reading vertically and horizontally.

Standardisation of orthography of personal names and place names has been promoted to facilitate the use of the Chinese language with computer technology. Specifically, the issue is that some characters used in personal names, both surnames and given names, and place names, are very rarely used items or in some extreme cases, are the idiosyncratic inventions of the individuals concerned. As such, they can complicate computer processing and have to be standardised (*Central Daily News*, 29 March, 1983).

A major contribution of the CPPNL after its re-establishment in 1980 has been the re-compiling and updating of the *Dictionary of the National Language* (henceforth the Dictionary), which was first published in 1936 in Mainland China and enlarged and brought up to date in 1981. The recompilation work began in June 1988 and was completed in January 1994. The Dictionary with its 160,000 entries boasts the largest list of Chinese characters in existence. It has been posted on the computer network since 1993 by the MOE and recently a CD version of the

Dictionary has been made available to the general public for only the cost of mailing. A concise version is being compiled and is expected to be completed soon (*The Sixth Educational Yearbook of ROC 1996*: 1853).

Developing efficient computer input systems for Chinese characters has been a common concern of the CPPNL and the Institute for Information Industry. The latter is a non-profit organisation founded in 1979 with the following main functions (The Institute for Information Industry, 1998):

(1) to assist the government in information industry planning and in promoting national information construction;
(2) to introduce information and communication techniques and concepts and to promote information industry development;
(3) to propagate information science and to train information science professionals;
(4) to create a milieu and a condition favourable to the development of the information industry and to assist its development; and
(5) to assist the government in setting up information and communication standards.

Since its establishment the Institute has taken a very active part in these functions. However, in the area of developing new ways of processing Chinese characters, it is fair to say that private companies have done the lion's share of the work with the Institute playing the role of the coordinator. The Institute and the CPPNL have cooperated over the years to complete successfully registration with the International Standardisation Office (ISO) for the standardised coding of all the standardised Chinese characters (*The Sixth Educational Yearbook of ROC*, 1996: 1850).

Finally, there is the perennial problem of the unification of technical terminology. In Taiwan, as in Mainland China under the rule of the Nationalist government, the agency responsible for this has been the Institute of Compilation and Translation whose roles, since its inception in 1932, have been stipulated as:

(1) the reviewing and compiling of all books on Chinese culture, the humanities, social sciences, and natural sciences and of all textbooks for all levels;
(2) the translating and reviewing of all the translated works on world literature, humanities, social sciences and natural sciences;
(3) the translating and compiling of technical terminologies for different sciences; and
(4) the compilation of textbooks for all levels (*The Fifth Educational Yearbook of ROC*, 1974: 895–913, Taipei: MOE).

In recent years, however, the Institute has been chiefly concerned with the compilation of textbooks at all levels and the compilation of books on Chinese culture. Even though there is still a section on Natural Sciences, it has been understaffed and very few advances have been made in the area of the unification of technical terminology. From 1932 to 1974, 66 specific scientific and technical terminologies had been authorised by the MOE through the Institute of Compilation and Translation. However, since 1974 only two more have been added and, to date, no effort has been made to evaluate how well these terms have been accepted and put to use (The National Institute for Compilation and

Translation, 1997: 13). There is every indication that they have been neglected. There are probably two reasons for this. First, according to Liu (1970), a former Director of the Institute, in a number of cases in the wordlists prepared by the Institute and authorised by the MOE, more than one translation equivalent occurs. While this practice may actually reflect the current situation, it is definitely against the principle of standardisation and is a reflection on the inefficiency of the Institute. Second, and more importantly, authors and teachers who are familiar with the foreign language in which the loan terms originate, tend to use the original form rather than the loan (Barnes, 1974: 473).

Recent Developments in Language Planning

The language planning scene in Taiwan as depicted in the previous section may seem rather unremarkable to some people, and I can readily agree with that observation if our focus is on what had been done before 1987, the year in which martial law was lifted. However, since its lifting, a number of exciting things have been happening. As most of them lie in the area of language-in-education planning, it is in this area that I will begin my discussion.

Recent changes in language-in-education policies

Shifting of emphasis to Baihuawen in Chinese courses in secondary education

As discussed in the previous section, in China for more than a thousand years before the founding of the Republic, the extreme linguistic diversity meant that Classical Chinese had always served as a written lingua franca, much like the role that Latin played in medieval Europe. Thus, Classical Chinese was the school language as well as the language used in the government and in the civil service examinations. As a consequence, a huge volume of fine literature was produced in the language. Therefore, in the earlier years of ROC, when the school language was changed from Classical Chinese to Mandarin, it took effect quietly and only in the elementary school. This difference in content was reflected in the names used to identify the programmes. In elementary school it was called *Guoyu* 'National Language' and in the secondary school *Guowen* 'National Literature'. When the Nationalist government came to rule Taiwan, this distinction was preserved. Even though the *Baihua* (vernacular) literature flourished in the 1930s and 40s in Mainland China, especially for fiction, much of it was tinged with pro-communist ideology and was consequently banned in Taiwan. In practice, this strongly biased the contents of the Chinese courses in the secondary school and the curriculum of the Chinese departments in the universities, including the normal university, towards Classical Chinese literature and against the modern language and the vernacular literature. Let us take for example the Chinese Department of the National Taiwan Normal University, the leading department where thousands of Chinese teachers were trained. In the Chinese Department at the university, there are about 70 faculty members, about 20 of whom are listed under the linguistics section. However, in actuality, half of those twenty were teachers of Mandarin pronunciation, a course which up to five years ago used to be required of every normal university student. Nine out of the remaining ten professors specialise in philology rather than modern linguistics.

Another indication that modern linguistics and the methodology of language teaching have been flagrantly neglected can be clearly shown by examination topics for the masters' theses and doctoral dissertations that have been written at the department. From 1961 to 1995, a total of 158 doctoral dissertations were written falling under the following categories:[11]

Chinese classics	64
Chinese philology	24
Chinese history	2
Chinese literature:	61 (classical, 57; modern, 4
others	7

The 531 masters' theses produced from 1958 to 1995 fall into the following categories:

Chinese classics	180
Chinese philology	74
modern Chinese studies	7
Chinese history	21
Chinese literature	231 (classical, 224; modern, 7)
Chinese arts	7
others	11

Looking at these dissertations and theses from another perspective reveals that there is not a single thesis or dissertation on anything remotely related to language teaching. Another point that cannot be missed is the extremely skewed distribution towards classical as opposed to modern Chinese; in the case of dissertations 153 relate to classical topics, 5 to modern, and in the case of theses 517 are classical, 14 are modern.

It does not take much imagination to see how effective a Mandarin teaching programme can be, when it is taught by teachers trained in a programme with such a strong bias towards Classical Chinese literature. In fact, Taiwan's college-bound students are found to be quite low in their written Chinese proficiency. As a language professor at a leading Taiwan university, I frequently have been surprised by the number of complaints I have received from my colleagues in science and technology about the poor command of Chinese that their graduate advisees have as reflected in their reports, papers, and theses.

The students' low proficiency in Chinese must have been the reason that prompted the MOE to re-examine its earlier policy of placing so much emphasis on the teaching of Classical Chinese in the secondary school curriculum. In the end, a sensible decision was made in the curriculum standard; as of the 1997 school year, the ratio of modern Chinese to Classical Chinese in the first year of the junior high (equivalent to the 7th grade in the United States) was to be 8 to 2, but the Classical Chinese proportion will be gradually increased as the students progress through their secondary education.

This is in fact a long overdue change in the right direction. However, like so many other changes that will be discussed, there is a serious hiatus in the decision making. The change was made without taking the teachers' prior training into consideration and hence no provision has been made to retrain or re-educate them.[12] Consequently, its expected effect on promoting students' Chinese proficiency remains to be seen.

Issues concerning the national phonetic symbols

A heated debate has been raging in Taiwan for the past three years having to do with the National Phonetic Symbols (NPS). Recall that there are actually two sets of NPS. NPS1, which employs components of traditional Chinese characters as symbols, was promulgated by the MOE on 23 November 1918 and has played a very important role in promoting Mandarin, the national language, in Taiwan. NPS2, which employs romanised letters as symbols, was first devised by the famous linguist, Y.R. Chao and his colleagues, and was promulgated in 1926. NPS2 was later revised in Taiwan on the ground of its extreme complexity and promulgated by the MOE in 1986. The revision of NPS2 was evidently prompted at least in part by the fact that the set of phonetic symbols promoted by Mainland China since 1956, officially known as *Hanyu Pinyin Fangan* 'Chinese Phonetic Scheme' (henceforth CPS), has become so widely accepted that the very existence of the original NPS2, and even NPS1, was threatened.

In Taiwan this has led to a debate, on-going now for some time, that has to do with two closely related issues:

(1) In teaching Mandarin Chinese to Chinese people and to speakers of other languages, is NPS1 a better scheme than one employing romanised symbols?
(2) If the answer to (1) is no, then which of the three currently available schemes, i.e. NPS2, CPS or Tong-Yong Phonetic Scheme (Yu & Xu, 1998) (henceforth, TYPS for short), a newly devised phonetic scheme designed by an anthropologist working at Academia Sinica, is the most suitable one? These questions are addressed in the following two sections.

NPS1 vs. a romanised phonetic scheme

Opinions with regard to the first issue have been divided. On the one hand, we have the traditionalists who argue that NPS1 should continue to be used, pointing for their support to the following two observations. First, since Taiwan's policy is to continue to teach Chinese characters, the NPS1, being made up of symbols derived from components of traditional characters, inevitably is more compatible with writing and printing of Chinese characters. The fact that its symbols are derived from Chinese characters will also enable it to provide a better transition from learning the phonetic symbols to learning Chinese characters. Second, and perhaps more importantly, NPS1, as has been repeatedly pointed out, has played a very important role in the promotion of Mandarin Chinese in Taiwan.

The modernists, on the other hand, have argued that a romanised phonetic scheme should be employed in the teaching of Mandarin, at home and abroad. They have two arguments in support of their view. First, the continued use of NPS1 is an impediment to the modernisation of the Chinese language since it fails to provide either a universally available way of indexing or an easy input system to the computer, as the system is only known in Taiwan and some restricted areas of the world. Second, NPS1's presumed advantage of being a better instrument than a romanised phonetic scheme is called into doubt since a romanised phonetic scheme has never been tried in Taiwan and since a romanised system has been in use in Mainland China for more than forty years with no reported undesirable effects.

Currently (in 1999), the issue is still unresolved, and it is difficult to see what the outcome of this policy deliberation will be. However, I am of the opinion that since Taiwan has internationalisation as a major objective, easy access to information exchange and communication through the computer will be a factor that will only gain in importance with time. This consideration, coupled with the fact that many children actually recognise letters in the English alphabet even before they enter elementary school, will eventually tip the scale in favour of using the romanised phonetic scheme instead of NPS1.

Which of the three romanised phonetic schemes is the most suitable?

There are three romanised phonetic schemes currently in use in Taiwan (namely, the NPS2, the TYPS, and the CPS), but which one is the best? To answer this question, let us first set up some criteria for comparison. In devising a phonetic scheme or more commonly a writing system for a language, there are three important considerations: economy, consistency and convenience (Fishman, 1968). Economy usually means that a phonetic scheme is primarily based on the phonemic system of the language, i.e. there is a symbol for each phoneme and where there is no phonemic contrast no additional symbols need be provided. Consistency means that one symbol stands for one sound and there are no other symbols that stand for the same sound. Conversely, one sound is represented by only one symbol and there are no other sounds represented by the same symbol. There are a number of notions subsumed under the general rubric *convenience*. First, a set of phonetic symbols is regarded as convenient if it can be easily learned. For example, the symbols are so devised that the letters can be easily associated with the sounds they represent. Secondly, a set of phonetic symbols is also convenient if it is easily processed in writing and in printing, which in our present day technology means easily processed by using a computer. Finally, a set of symbols is taken to be convenient if it can be generally used, allowing for slight modifications, in a number of closely associated languages.

Since the CPS promoted in Mainland China is the oldest system, I will begin my discussion with the CPS and then compare it with the other two schemes. The CPS, which was approved by the Congress of the PRC in February 1958, can be briefly summarised in Table 6.

In examining the scheme, the following points may be noted (De Francis, 1967):

(1)   The symbol *u* represents a high back rounded vowel except after *y* and the palatal initials *j, q, x*, when it represents a high front rounded vowel. This is a fairly ingenious solution to the problem of the symbol ?, the use of which can now be confined to combinations with *l* and *n*.

(2)   The symbols have been so chosen that there are but rare occasions to use the juncture symbol.

Table 6

Initials					
	Unaspirate d stops	*Aspirated stops*	*Nasals*	*Fricatives*	*Voiced continuants*
Labials	b	p	m	f	
Alveolars	d	t	n		l
Alveolar sibi-lants	z	c		s	
Retroflexes	zh	ch		sh	r
Palatals	j	q		x	
Gutterals	g	k		h	

Finals (Rimes)	
1.	simplex rimes: a, e, i, u, *u*
2.	duplex rimes : ai, ei , ao, ou, an, en, ang, eng
3.	semivowels (as initials): y, w
Tones	
1. ma-; 2. ma/; 3. mav3; 4. ma\; 5.ma (neutral tone)	
Juncture	
	pi'ao

(3) The symbol *i* represents a high front unrounded vowel except after retroflexes and alveolar sibilants when it represents the two distinctive vocalisations of these two sets of initials.

(4) The schema is in general quite economical in that it is based on the phonemic system of Mandarin. Take *i* mentioned in point 3 for instance. Even though phonetically at least three different pronunciations can be found depending on the kind of consonant that precedes it, only one symbol *i* is used since these different pronunciations are non-contrastive.

(5) It is also in general quite consistent. The only point at which the question of consistency may be raised is in the fact that the symbol *h* is used both for the glottal fricative and for retroflexion as in the case of *zh*, but since in the latter case it is the second part of a digraph and in the former it occurs independently, the possibility of causing ambiguity is very small.

With respect to convenience, it has the following merits. (1) Digraphs are rarely used, there being only three in the initials. (2) All the 26 letters in the English alphabet are put to use in representing one sound or another, thus making certain that the English keyboard is fully utilised. (3) Diacritic marks have been reduced to the minimum, there being four for the five tones and the umlauting mark for *ü*, which we just observed has been reduced to two cases, i.e. after *l* and *n* where minimal pairs between *ü* and *u* can be found. On the other hand, some symbols used have been found to be not so easily associated with the

Table 7 Differences between CPS and NPS2

	Initials						Finals (Rimes)		
	Dental sibilants		*Palatals*	*Retro- flexes*	*Semivowels (as initials)*		*Simplex vowels*		*Complex vowels*
CPS	z	c	q	x	zh	y	w	i	ü	ao
NPS2	tz	ts	ch	sh	j	i	u	Ø (after r,z)	iu	au

sounds they represent, namely, *c*, an alveolar sibilant, *q*, an aspirated palatal, and *x*, a palatal fricative. In this way, they complicate the acquisition of these symbols.

With this brief description and evaluation of the CPS as backdrop, we can now proceed to compare CPS with NPS2 and TYPS. Table 7 summarises the differences between CPS and NPS2. From Table 7, it is clear that, as far as initials are concerned, the major differences lie in how the alveolar sibilant series and the palatal series are treated. While NPS2 stresses the virtue of sound–symbol association, thus choosing digraphs to represent affricates, CPS attempts to find some letters in the English alphabet as yet unoccupied by other Chinese sounds with a view to fully utilising the English keyboard.

In the area of vowels, the differences are few and of minor importance. Take the case of high front rounded vowel for example. CPS chooses *ü*, a letter found in French and German, but not in English, thus requiring a diacritic mark if English keyboard is adopted. NPS2, on the other hand, selects a digraph *iu* to represent the sound, obliterating the need for a diacritic mark but at the same time running up the cost in typing as two keys have to be pushed instead of one.

Overall, however, it seems to many that the two schemes are actually quite similar. But since NPS2 was devised about thirty years later than CPS, it has to be better in some way to justify its existence and this consideration is fully reflected in the final choices made.

This general attitude is also reflected in TYPS, the most recent invention, as can be clearly seen in Table 8, which shows that TYPS is even more similar to CPS than NPS2. Actually, the inventor, Mr Yu, has made a virtue of the fact that the scheme can be easily converted to either NPS or CPS and can also be easily modified to represent other Han dialects such as Southern Min and Hakka, as well as the aboriginal Austro-Polynesian languages spoken in Taiwan. This is the reason

Table 8 Differences between CPS and TYPS

	Initials			Finals (Rimes)			
	Dental sibilants			*Simple*		*Complex*	
CPS	j	q	x	I	ü	en	eng
TYPS	z	c	s	ii*	yu	un**	ong***

* only after dental sibilants and retroflexes
** only after w
*** only after w & f

why the inventor calls his scheme *Tong-Yong Pinyin* 'literally, general-use spelling' and has actually written a few pamphlets demonstrating how this can be done.

Returning to our comparison between TYPS and CPS, we find that our previous remarks on the differences between CPS and NPS2 can be applied here, i.e. the two systems are basically the same with some adjustments made by TYPS as 'improvements' over the CPS. These 'improvements' are necessary, as in the previous case of NPS2, to justify its existence. However, there is another more important factor that should be taken into consideration in the final decision regarding these modifications, and this factor has to do with how Taiwan perceives itself in relation to the Mainland China, a topic that I will discuss in the next section. Here, in order to facilitate discussion, I will assume that Taiwan tends to perceive itself as a separate entity, independent of Mainland China, even though at the same time it admits that culturally it is closely related to the latter and there is a very strong need for communication. This self-perception and general attitude towards Mainland China are fully reflected in the designs of NPS2 and TYPS, i.e. against the general backdrop of similarity, there are some differences to keep them distinct. Since NSP2 is official while TYPS is not, the former tends to be more conservative than the latter.

It is still too early to say for sure how this issue will be decided, but the whole issue has aroused the attention of the Executive Yuan and the MOE. As this writer was working on this monograph, the Minister of Education, Dr Lin Qing-Jiang announced on 11 February, 1999 that a meeting will be held in March to deliberate on the issue. He has proposed that the scheme to be used be determined according to the following three principles:

(1) The scheme should be instrumental in helping the nation to promote internationalisation.
(2) It should be easily learnable given the present language-education situation in Taiwan.
(3) The selection should take into consideration the fact that the MOE decided in 1996 that, as of that year, the street names and road signs should use NPS2; some counties and cities have already allotted some money for the change (*China Times*, 11 February, 1999: 9).

An arising new supra-ethnic identity

As indicated in our discussion of the socio-historical context, Taiwan is, among other things, an immigrant society and like many immigrant societies, it is beset with problems of ethnicity, language loyalty and group (i.e. supra-ethnic) identity. In fact, there is perhaps no other place in the modern world where people are as divided in their opinions with respect to their group identity as in Taiwan. Fortunately, as a result of some recent socio-political developments, a new group identity seems to be emerging, indicating that ethnic harmony could be achieved if the trend continues. There have been clear indications that more and more Taiwan residents have come to identify themselves with the place in which they live and call themselves 'Taiwanese'. In order not to be confused with 'Taiwanese' in its old sense of referring to the indigenous people of Taiwan in contradistinction with 'Mainlanders', a new term has been coined – 'New Taiwanese' – to refer to this rising new supra-ethnic identity. In this section, in addition to identifying what this new identity is, I explain why it has taken so long for this new group identity to emerge and what role language plays in the process.

Socio-political context: A brief recapitulation

Recall that earlier we said that during the Qing dynasty as more and more Chinese immigrants from Kuangtong and Fujian came to settle on the island, four ethnic groups were gradually formed: the Zhangzhou people, the Quanzhou people, the Hakka and the aboriginal Austro-Polynesian, the first two groups being Southern Min speakers with different accents. Small-scale ethnic conflicts were almost daily occurrences during that period, and large-scale bloodshed and feuds were not uncommon (Lamley, 1981). However, when it was announced at the conclusion of the First Sino-Japanese War that Taiwan was to be ceded to Japan, people in Taiwan felt frustrated and humiliated because they had been deserted by their motherland, and because they felt an urgent need to do something to protect themselves. It was this sense of humiliation and the fear of being ruled by a foreign people that stirred them into action. The First Taiwan Republic was hastily founded on 16 May, 1895. Unfortunately, the Republic, lasting only 148 days, was soon defeated and overthrown by the Japanese army. This incident, together with other signs, was interpreted by Huang (1993) as the beginning of the process of transforming Taiwan society from a purely immigrant one into one of more-or-less native ethnicity (different from their ethnic Chinese origins).

When the Japanese came to rule the island, they of course did everything they could to prevent this group identity from coming into being, as this trend was diametrically opposed to their interest in Japanising Taiwan. This being the case, no progress in the formation of group identity was made during those fifty years of Japanese administration. However, being put under a repressive foreign rule evidently created a feeling of being 'related' or being 'in the same boat'. In addition, during that half century the Chinese immigrants were largely cut off from their ancestral home in Mainland China and ethnic Chinese on the island gradually came to identify with the places in which they resided (e.g. *Zhanghua* or *Tainan*) rather than their places of origin on the Mainland. Partly because of this changing concept of their place of origin and partly because of the Japanese government's policy forbidding fighting between ethnic groups, ethnic conflicts gradually died down.

When Taiwan was returned to China in 1945, people in Taiwan, having been placed under oppressive, discriminatory foreign rule for half a century, warmly welcomed the opportunity to become citizens of the Republic of China, expecting to be treated as equals under the new government. This high expectation, as I indicated earlier, never materialised. Misunderstandings abounded during those few years when the rulers and their followers from the Mainland came into contact with the local people because they lacked a common language and they did not share a collective memory, having been completely cut off from each other for fifty years. However as it turned out, the misunderstandings, instead of being removed through patient and careful explanation, were actually increased by the inefficient administration of the Provisional Government headed by Chen Yi.

On 28 February, 1947, the tragic 228 incident broke out, killing thousands of people, Mainlanders as well as the indigenous inhabitants; the relations between the indigenous groups of the people and the Mainlanders were severely strained. Even though this accident was soon put down by troops from Mainland China and even though Chen Yi, the administrative head, was sentenced to death, the relationship between the indigenous people and the Mainland newcomers was not truly restored until very recently. For many people the tragic event was the seed of separation that later developed into the Taiwan Independence Movement.

Two years later, the Nationalists, having lost their war with the Communists, retreated to Taiwan, bringing about a million followers with them. Even though this group was composed of people from virtually every province of Mainland China, speaking all the major Han dialects and a number of minority languages, they and their children born locally after 1949 were perceived as *Waishenren*, 'Mainlanders' by the indigenous people, who referred to themselves as *Benshenren*, 'Taiwanese', or to use the more colourful metaphor of the local people, the distinction is between *yam* 'Taiwanese' and *taro* 'Mainlanders'.[13]

The Mainlanders (partly because many of them were associated with the Nationalist government in one way or another, partly because they were, on average, better educated than the local people at that time, and partly because most of them could manage to communicate in Mandarin, having learned Mandarin in school or picked it up in the military) occupied most of the important positions in the government (see Huang, 1993, and the references cited therein). These discriminatory official hiring practices continued for about thirty years, even though the educational level of the local people soon caught up with that of the Mainlanders. That hiring practice began to change in 1972 when Chiang Ching-Kuo, the former ROC president who was then serving as the Premier, began to introduce young local talent into his cabinet.

On the language front, things were no better. The language policy of the Nationalist government can be briefly described as uni-directional bilingualism (Chan, 1994), i.e. while all speakers of a local language have to learn to speak Mandarin, the national language, the Mainlanders, most of whom could speak some form of Mandarin were not required to study a local language. This policy was implemented more effectively in schools where those who spoke their mother tongue were punished. Students were taught that it was unethical and unpatriotic to speak their mother tongue if it was a language other than Mandarin. In the mass media, the use of indigenous languages was, for a long time, severely restricted. With all these repressive measures in effect for more than thirty years, it is little wonder that the use of the indigenous languages has declined significantly and that some of them face extinction in a generation or two.

The adoption of these relatively discriminatory policies in language and in the appointment of public officers, especially at higher levels, was conducive to conflicts between ethnic groups. These ethnic conflicts, in their turn, worked against a genuine group identity. As a consequence, people were split in their views on identity, with most Mainlanders considering themselves Chinese and most local people considering themselves Taiwanese.

In addition, the government's policy towards Mainland China had been ultra-conservative. For about forty years, the Nationalist government considered Taiwan a temporary residence, their final goal being to recover Mainland China. While most Mainlanders understandably honoured and cherished this policy, most local people had long ago realised how unrealistic and wishful such a policy was. This split of opinions also contributed to widening the ethnic divide and was again not conducive to the emergence of a supra-ethnic identity.

Signs of ethnic reconciliation and the emergence of the new identity

The first sign of ethnic reconciliation appeared when indigenisation of the island's politicians occurred in 1972, under the process begun by Chiang Ching-kuo. Soon after that, in order to make his intention clear, Chiang, who was born and raised in Mainland China, proclaimed, 'I'm a Taiwanese, too' (Chung, 1999). Later, he chose Lee Teng-hui to be his successor, and when Chiang died in 1988 the latter went on to become the first Taiwan-born Hakka to govern Taiwan.[14]

Democratisation in politics began in 1986 when the first opposition party, the Democratic Progressive Party (henceforth DPP) (whose members were chiefly Taiwanese natives advocating separatism) was founded and was tolerated even while the repressive martial law was still in effect. The DPP gained strength when martial law was revoked in July 1987. In 1992, the party made an impressive showing in the first major democratic legislative election based on universal suffrage, winning about one-third of the seats in the Legislature, which had been occupied by Mainlanders since the Nationalist government retreated to Taiwan in 1949. Meanwhile, the ruling party also underwent democratisation as more and more Taiwan-born Kuomingtang legislators appeared. As the voice of the local majority began to be heard, relations between different ethnic groups improved.

In 1993, a second opposition party, the New Party (which was mainly composed of Mainlanders who advocated unification with China) was founded and Taiwan was on its way to experiencing preliminary multi-party democracy. In March 1996, the people of Taiwan elected Lee Teng-hui as their president through direct general election for the first time in the history of the island. As political resources have become increasingly proportionally distributed among the ethnic groups, ethnic disharmony began to thaw, giving the new supra-ethnic group identity a chance to emerge.

Not everything, of course, has gone well. On the diplomatic front, setbacks have come one after another since 1970 when Taiwan (known as the Republic of China) left the United Nations in anticipation of the passage of a resolution admitting the People's Republic of China, and expelling Taiwan from the world organisation. This traumatic event started a three-decade-long process of diplomatic setbacks with the United States taking the lead in severing diplomatic relations with the Republic of China (ROC).

But fortunately, as Taiwan experienced the setbacks which greatly reduced its international diplomatic space, a new sense of group identity began to emerge – more and more people in Taiwan came to identify with the island instead of

Mainland China, where they or their ancestors originated. The changes were accelerated in 1996 when, during the height of the presidential election, the Mainland Chinese conducted a series of military exercises and missile tests with the obvious intention of intimidating Taiwan people into voting against separatism. However, this sabre rattling backfired and helped many people in Taiwan decide to identify themselves with the place in which they lived. This change can be clearly seen by the following comparison of survey results. In a 1992 survey, 26.9% of the respondents identified themselves as Taiwanese (Wang, 1993). When the same categories were calculated in a 1996 survey taken immediately after the missile threat (Sun and Ma, 1996), the figure was 46%, indicating a strong shift towards the Taiwanese and away from the Chinese end of the identity spectrum within the short time span of four years.

Meanwhile, government policies also showed changes in the same direction. As previously mentioned, since 1997 Taiwanese Southern Min as well as Hakka and the aboriginal languages have been promoted on the island to the extent that they are now taught in elementary schools. When compared to the national language, Mandarin, all the indigenous languages, especially Southern Min, are getting more and more attention and now are spoken in public by many government officials in the hope of relating better to the general public.

At the same time, some of the villages for military dependants around the island have been reconstructed into new communities where Taiwanese residents mingle with the original residents of Mainland origin.

Another major measure that reflects the government's desire to blur the line between ethnic groups was taken when the Ministry of Internal Affairs decided to change the format of ROC identification cards. For cards issued before 1992 there was a small box printed on the back of the card that provided a space for the identification of the cardholder's 'native place', which meant the place from which his or her father originated on the China mainland (if the father immigrated to Taiwan around 1949), or the place in Taiwan which was considered the cardholder's home town (if his or her father had arrived prior to 1945 or was a Taiwan native). This box was removed from cards issued after 1992. Such a change signalled a de-emphasis on one's connection with Mainland China and an emphasis on personal identity with Taiwan.

In line with this governmental attitudinal change was a view expressed by Chen Shui-bian, Taipei's former mayor and a presidential hopeful likely to represent DPP in the upcoming presidential campaign in 2000. Chen dismisses the metaphor of 'yam' and 'taro', preferring the image 'peanut'. 'In fact, we are all peanuts', he said at a public gathering in late 1998, adding that, just like peanuts, people in Taiwan should take root easily and be able to identify with the land on which they dwell and which they think of as their permanent home (Chung, 1999: 8). Such a message coming from a high-profile figure in the DPP strongly indicates that the DPP is taking a pragmatic approach and will likely embrace ethnic reconciliation in its platform in the forthcoming presidential election.

The role language has played in the process

Mandarin chauvinism, as I reported earlier, used to be quite common in Taiwan. But with the concept of 'New Taiwanese' becoming prominent, will Southern Min, a language spoken by about 70% of the people in Taiwan, take the place of Mandarin? While some observers express apprehension about this (see Chung, 1999), others have reported that the role played by language in characterising this new supra-ethnic identity does not seem particularly salient. According to Sun and Ma's (1996) survey, only 22% of the young people considered a Taiwanese to be a person who could speak Southern Min, and only 9% defined a Mainlander as a person who could not speak Southern Min. These results indicate that the ability to speak Southern Min is not an important criterion in distinguishing a Taiwanese from a Mainlander. The more salient factors, according to the same survey, are being born in Taiwan (55%); living in Taiwan (49%); regarding oneself to be Taiwanese (39%); and having Taiwan listed as 'native place' (38%) (items allowed for multiple choices).

From these findings, it does seem that language plays a salient role in characterising the emergent concept of 'New Taiwanese'. However, if we examine the role that language has played while the new identity concept has been developing, we will find another story. The strenuous promotion of the national language in the first thirty years after Taiwan's Retrocession in 1945 resulted in the functional allocation of the four major languages in Taiwan. Mandarin served as the high language and Southern Min, Hakka and the indigenous aboriginal languages served as the low languages, forming a diglossic society with societal bilingualism where Mandarin also served as the effective lingua franca. If the promotion of Mandarin had been kept at this level, the resultant state would have been a lot more acceptable to all ethnic groups concerned. However, as we have repeatedly pointed out, the repressive policies were kept for too long, and as a result all languages except Mandarin are either quickly diminishing in use or are on the verge of extinction. The sad state that many indigenous languages were in caused great resentment among the people. Once martial law was revoked, the resentment that had been suppressed for so long broke out in strong protests in some cases, or manifested itself in the increasing use of the local mother tongue as a symbol of defiance against the government authority or simply as an expression of ethnic identity.

For a while it seemed that language would serve as a dividing force rather than as a unifying one in Taiwan. But as the concept of 'New Taiwanese' began to take shape, a change of attitude with regard to the use of language took place – the use of language began to be 'less emotionally loaded and more pragmatically oriented' (Tse, 2000). This trend towards pragmatism can be detected in the use of language in the televised campaign speeches given by the four sets of presidential and vice-presidential candidates in 1996 (Tse, 2000) as well as in the more recent Taipei and Kaohsiung mayoral elections and the legislative election (Chung, 1999; Kuo, 1998). To be more specific, a common characteristic in all these campaign speeches was the use of language to win votes rather than to rally for ethnic identification and division. In other areas involving the use of language, the same attitude is also found. A radio station run by the New Party, which is largely composed of Mainlanders and sympathisers for reunification with China, has certain call-in programmes conducted in Southern Min.

As the attitude of treating language more as a means of communication and less as a marker of ethnicity gains ground, Mandarin, which has developed into a lingua franca in Taiwan, is likely to be used more by people who used to employ Southern Min or Hakka as a gesture of defiance. Indeed, it has been observed that some politicians of the DPP show less apologetic attitudes when they use Mandarin in public domains, especially in the mass media (Tse, 2000; Kuo, 1998). Today, the only group of people who insist on using Taiwanese as a symbol of group solidarity are the members of the Taiwan Independence Party (TIP), a newly established breakaway group from the DPP, dissatisfied with the less radical and more practical stance on the separatist issue. This view on the use of language is not even shared by DPP Legislator Ye Ju-lan, who otherwise is a great sympathiser with the TIP. Instead, Ye advocates the idea that the term 'Taiwanese language' should be used to refer to all languages used on the island rather than for Southern Min alone (*Global Views Monthly* 121, June 15, 1996. pp. 79–80).

Summary

To summarise, in Taiwan in the past few years we can clearly see a new sense of group identity emerging. This emerging sense of new identity, which has been termed 'New Taiwanese', has more to do with the shared feelings among people of different ethnic groups, towards the land in which they live, Taiwan, towards modernity and democracy, and towards the uncertainty of their future relations with Mainland China. In short, it is an identity built on a shared way of life and the common fate of living on the same island under the military threat of the People's Republic of China. While this newly arising group identity is not tied to any language at this moment, language has been observed to play an important role in its development.

A Look at the Future

In this monograph, after a brief account of the socio-historical context, I have ventured to examine critically the language planning situation in both Mainland China before the Nationalist government moved to Taiwan and in Taiwan after its Retrocession, paying special attention to some recent developments occurring after martial law was lifted in 1987. While this examination seems to have found more inadequacies than strengths, I am, nonetheless, quite optimistic when thinking about how future language policy and planning might develop. This optimism stems from the following observations.

(1) To begin with, language policy-making before martial law was lifted in 1987 had always been a one-way affair, i.e. it had always been top-down, allowing very little input from the general public and from experts. Now there are clear indications that, as Taiwan moves towards democracy, public opinion and expert advice are playing an increasingly important role in the process of language policy making. This is something that people in Taiwan could hardly have imagined even ten years ago. As far as policy implementation is concerned, we find that the legislative body of the government is paying more attention to it so that its practice may be sound.

(2) In the closely related area of language education, the old system (as represented in Table 4), that existed for about forty years unchallenged and unchanged, has been closely examined since the lifting of martial law. Some changes, such as adding one hour of mother-tongue instruction to the elementary school curriculum, have been implemented. Other changes, like

beginning English education in the fifth grade and starting the instruction of other LWCs in secondary school, will be implemented in 2001.

(3) Plans are now being made to reduce the class sizes in primary and secondary schools from the present 45 to 50 per class to about 30 per class. When implemented, these plans will certainly greatly facilitate language teaching and learning.

(4) An important improvement in teacher training has been implemented beginning in 1997. Previous to that, the three normal universities and nine teachers' colleges were the principal sources of primary and secondary school teachers. It is easy to imagine that problems might have emerged out of such a closed system over the years. Realising the ills, the Ministry of Education decreed two years ago that universities and colleges other than those normal universities and teachers' colleges will be allowed to train primary and secondary school teachers. It is hoped that this new addition to the teacher supply can provide the additional teachers needed as a result of the planned class-size reductions. At the same time, by making the job market for teachers more competitive, the development should induce changes in the old teacher training institutions, which had become stagnant due to lack of competition.

(5) Finally, and most importantly, as the use of language is becoming less emotionally charged and more pragmatically oriented, inter-ethnic relations in Taiwan between the four major ethnic groups have shown signs of improvement. There is hope that Taiwan will be able to emerge healthy from its bitter past, which was full of ethnic conflicts and tensions. While ethnic harmony may not be easily achieved, ethnic reconciliation may well be in sight. Rather than 'yams' or 'taros', people may choose to be 'peanuts'.

Correspondence

Any correspondence should be directed to Professor Feng-fu Tsao, Institute of Linguistics, National Tsing-Hua University, Hsinchu, Taiwan, China (fftsao@mx.nthu.edu.tw).

Notes

1. Bamgbose (1991) in his chapter on language planning also maintains this distinction although he does mention some overlapping cases. In this monograph, whenever such a case occurs, an arbitrary decision will be made as to which category it belongs to.
2. No census data are available because questions concerning people's ethnolinguistic background were considered too sensitive to be included in the previous census questionnaires.
3. See Li (1992) and the references cited there for a summary of arguments in support of this view.
4. *Taiwan Statistical Data Book,* various issues, Council for Economic Planning and Development as cited in Shieh (1998).
5. For a general discussion of the drawbacks in selecting an artificial or made-up composite language as the national language see Bamgbose (1991).
6. In retrospect, it is certainly a great pity that the extension was stopped at the elementary school level, for language education in a living language in all four skills cannot be completed in six years. The effects of this oversight have been keenly felt in Taiwan today. Please refer to the section on 'Recent changes in language-in-education policies' for more discussion.

7. The February 28 incident, commonly known in Taiwan as the 228 incident, occurred on 28 February, 1947. Although there have been a number of theories as to why it occurred, no consensus has been reached. It is doubtless, however, the most serious ethnic conflict in Taiwan during this century. Among its many far-reaching effects is the spawning of the Taiwanese Independence Movement (TIM) that has been in existence for more than forty years. Official studies of the incident were forbidden under martial law and reconciliatory measures such as making 28 February a public holiday were taken only after martial law was lifted in 1987. For further discussion relating to the incident see the section on the 'Socio-political context' of this monograph.

8. Knowledgeable as Zhou was, he was not able to give an estimate of how many people in Mainland China in about 1990 were able to speak Mandarin. A survey conducted by *Kuang Ming Daily* in 1998 indicated that only 22% of the respondents claimed to be native speakers of Mandarin. The report, however, did not mention how many are able to speak it as a second language (*China Times*, 14 December, 1998, p. 14).

9. The only minor change in the system in its fifty years of existence is the addition of four hours of mother-tongue instruction in the third to the sixth grade in elementary schools, starting in the 1997 school year.

10. Data for the year 1996 were adapted from Table 3-5 of the *Statistical Abstract of Education in the Republic of China, 1997*, published by the MOE. The figures in the original table refer to secondary school teachers as a whole but since we have no reason to expect that English teachers as a group will be different from secondary school teachers, we have used the figures for comparison.

11. The data are adapted from the appendix to *Papers by the Faculty and Graduate Students at the Graduate Institute of Chinese, National Taiwan Normal University, Vol. 39*.

12. The lack of training in teaching modern Chinese also explains why, soon after the MOE made the announcement of the change in 1994, many Chinese teachers went into a panic and protested.

13. The local people call themselves 'yam' because on the map, Taiwan looks like a yam.

14. Lee Teng-hui is ethnically a Hakka, but his first language is Southern Min.

References

Bamgbose, A. (1991) *Language and the Nation: The Language Question in Sub-Saharan Africa*. Edinburgh: Edinburgh University Press.

Barnes, D. (1974) Language planning in mainland China: Standardization. In J.A. Fishman (ed.) *Advances in Language Planning* (pp. 457–80). The Hague: Mouton.

Chan, H.C. (1994) Language shift in Taiwan: Social and political determinants. Unpublished PhD dissertation. Georgetown University.

Chang, K.Z. (1995) An examination of some approaches to the study of indigenous Taiwan from the standpoint of archeology. In Y. H. Shi *et al.* (eds) *Papers from the First Conference in the Indigenous Culture of Taiwan* (pp. 1–8). Taipei: College of Humanities, Taiwan Normal University.

Chao, Y.R. (1943) Language and dialects in China. *The Geographical Journal* 102, 63–66.

Chao, Y.R. (1976b) What is correct Chinese? In A.S. Dil (ed.) *Aspects of Chinese Sociolinguistics* (pp. 72–83). Stanford, CA: Stanford University Press.

Chen, M.R. (1996) A study of language educational policies in Taiwan after its retrocession. Unpublished MA thesis, National Taiwan University [in Chinese].

Cheng, R.L. (1985) A comparison of Taiwanese, Taiwan Mandarin, and Peking Mandarin. *Language* 61 (2), 352–377.

Chung, O. (1999) Neither yam nor taro. *Free China Review* (February), 6–13

De Francis, J. (1967) Language and script reform. In J.A. Fishman (ed.) *Advances in the Sociology of Language II* (pp. 450–75). The Hague: Mouton.

Fang, S.D. (1965) *Fifty Years of the Chinese National Language Movement*. Taipei: Mandarin Daily Press. [in Chinese]

Figueroa, E. (1988) Evaluating language policy in Taiwan – some questions. In R.L. Cheng and S.F. Huang (eds) *The Structure of Taiwanese: A Modern Synthesis* (pp. 285–299). Taipei: Crane.

Fishman, J.A. (ed.) (1967) Bilingualism with and without diglossia: Diglossia with and without bilingualism. *Journal of Social Issues* 32: 29–38.

Fishman, J.A. (1974) Language planning and language planning research: The state of the art. In J.A. Fishman (ed.) *Advances in Language Planning*. The Hague: Mouton.

Formosa Cultural and Educational Foundation (1997) A survey on people's language ability and their attitude toward language policy. In F.F. Tsao (ed.) *Ethnolinguistic Policy: A Comparison of the Two Sides of the Taiwan Straits. Appendix 7* (pp. 181–188) Taipei: Crane [in Chinese].

Hong, Y. C. (1978) *Miscellaneous Talks on Language*. Taipei: Mandarin Daily Press.

Hsu, S. J. (1991) The language problems in the early years of Taiwan retrocession. *Si-Yu Yuan* (Thought and Language) 29, 4–23.

Huang, C.C. (1998) Historical reflections on the postwar Taiwan experience from an agrarian perspective. In C.C. Huang and F.F. Tsao (eds) *Postwar Taiwan in Historical Perspective* (pp. 17–35). Bethesda, MD: University of Maryland Press.

Huang, S.F. (1991) Some sociolinguistic observations on Taiwan. *The World of Chinese Language & Literature* 7 (6), 16–22. [in Chinese]

Huang, S.F. (1993) *Language, Society, and Ethnicity: A Study of the Sociology of Language in Taiwan*. Taipei: Crane [in Chinese].

Huang, S.F. and Chang, Z.C. (1995) A sociolinguistics investigation of Kavaland: An Aboriginal language. In P.R. Li and Y. Lin (eds) *Collection of Papers on the Austronesian Languages in Taiwan* (pp. 241–256). Taipei: Council on Educational Research, Ministry of Education.

Jernudd, B.H. (1973) Language planning as a type of language treatment. In J. Rubin and R. Shuy (eds) *Language Planning: Current Issues and Research* (pp. 11–23). Washington, DC: Georgetown University Press.

Karam, F.X. (1974) Towards a definition of language planning. In J.A. Fishman (ed.) *Advances in Language Planning* (pp. 103–24). The Hague: Mouton.

Ke, J.-X. (1990) The national language education in the Taiwan Province: Past, present, and future. Paper presented at the Annual Conference of the Chinese Language Teachers Association, Nashville, Tennessee, USA.

Kubler, C.C. (1985) *The Development of Mandarin in Taiwan: A Case Study of Language Context*. Taipei: Student Book.

Kuo, S.H. (1998) Language has a dividing as well as a unifying function. In the opinion forum section, *United Daily* (Dec. 15), Taipei [in Chinese].

Lamley, H.J. (1981) Subethnic rivalry in the Ching Period. In E.M. Ahern and W. Gates (eds) *The Anthropology of Taiwanese Society*. Stanford, CA: Stanford University Press.

Li, David C.C. (1983) The sociolinguistic context in Taiwan: Trends and developments. In C. Chu, S. Coblin and F.F. Taso (eds) *Papers from the Fourteenth Conference on Sino-Tibetan Linguistics and Languages* (pp. 257–78). Taipei: Student Book.

Li, Paul J.-K. (1979) The origin of the Taiwan Aboriginal peoples: Linguistic evidence. *Dalu Journal* 59 (1), 1–14 [in Chinese].

Li, Paul J.-K. (1990) Classification of Formosan languages: Lexical evidence. *Bulletin of the Institute of History and Philosophy* 64 (4), 813–848.

Li, Paul J.-K. (1992) *The International and External Relationships of the Formosan Languages*. National Museum of Prehistory Planning Bureau [in Chinese].

Li, Paul J.-K. (1995) The distribution of the Austronesian languages in Taiwan and the migration of their speakers. In F.F. Tsao and M. Tsai (eds) *Papers from the First International Symposium on Languages in Taiwan* (pp. 1–16). Taipei: Crane [in Chinese].

Li, P. O. (1994) An evaluation of the current language policy on Mandarin and the indigenous dialects and languages. In P.R. Huang (ed.) *Papers on Current Language Problems Taiwan* (pp. 147–164). Taipei: Chinese Department, National Taiwan University.

Lin, J. (ed.) (1983) *Collected Papers on Language Problems in Taiwan*. Taipei: Taiwan Wenyi Zazhishe [in Chinese].

Lin, J.P. (1995) Mother tongue and cultural transmission. In R.K. Li and Y. Lin (eds) *Collection of Papers on the Austronesian Languages in Taiwan* (pp. 203–222). Council on Educational Research, Ministry of Education.

Liu, T. (1970) An interview by Dayle Barnes, as cited in Barnes (1974).

Ministry of Education (1974) *The Fifth Educational Yearbook of the ROC*. Taipei: MOE [in Chinese].

Ministry of Education (1996) *The Sixth Educational Yearbook of the ROC*. Taipei: MOE [in Chinese].

Ministry of Education (1997) *Statistical Abstract of Education in the Republic of China 1997*. Taipei: MOE [in Chinese].

Neustupný J.V. (1970) Basic types of treatment of language problems. *Linguistic Communications* 1, 77–99. Reprinted in J.A. Fishman (ed.) (1974) *Advances in Language Planning* (pp. 37–48). The Hague: Mouton.

Paulston, C.B. (1984) Language planning in education. In C. Kennedy (ed.) *Language Planning and Language Education*. London: George Allen and Unwin.

Romaine, S. (1995) *Bilingualism* (2nd edn). Cambridge, MA: Blackwell.

Rubin, J. (1971) Evaluation and language planning. In J. Rubin and B.H. Jernudd (eds) *Can Language be Planned? Sociolinguistic Theory and Practice for Developing Nations* (pp. 218–52) Honolulu, HI : University of Hawaii Press.

Shi, T.F. (1987) *The Geographical Distribution of the Han Ethnic Groups During the Qing Dynasty and Their Ways of Living in the Place of Origin*. Taipei: Department of Geography, National Taiwan Normal University [in Chinese].

Shieh, S.C. (1998) Unique features of Taiwan's economic development (1955–1995). In C.C. Huang and F.F. Tsao (eds) *Postwar Taiwan in Historical Perspective* (pp. 36–54). Bethesda, MD: University of Maryland Press.

Skutnabb-Kangas, T. (1984) *Bilingualism or Not: The Education of Minorities*. Clevedon: Multilingual Matters.

Sun, S.H. and Ma, S.R. (1996) Who are the new Taiwanese? *Global Views Monthly* 121, June 15, 1996: 46–50.

The Executive Yuan (1982) *Review and Criticism of the NL: Policies and Implementation*. Taipei: The Executive Yuan, ROC [in Chinese].

The Institute for Information Industry (1998) *Profile of the Institute for Information Industry*. Taipei.

The National Institute for Compilation and Translation (NICT) (1997) *Profile of the NICT*. Taipei: NICT [in English and Chinese].

Tsao, F.F. (1982) The National Taiwan Normal University–University of Southern California Survey of English Teaching in the Republic of China: An evaluation report. *English Literature and Linguistics* 8, 128–134 [English Department, National Taiwan Normal University].

Tsao, F.F. (1987) Re-identifying the norm for Guoyu. In A. Brankamp *et al.* (eds) *Chinese–Western Encounter: Studies in Linguistics and Literature: Festechrift for Franz Giet, SVD on the Occasion of his 85th Birthday* (pp. 385–409). Taipei : Chinese Materials Center Publications.

Tsao, F.F. (1994) Social changes and linguistic adaptations. In P.-R. Huang (ed.) *Papers on Current Language Problems* (pp. 27–52). Taipei: Chinese Department National Taiwan University [in Chinese].

Tsao, F.F. (1996a) Language education in Taiwan: A review in sociolinguistic perspective. In P. Storey *et al.* (eds) *Issues in Language in Education* (pp. 153–166). Hong Kong: The Hong Kong Institute of Education.

Tsao, F.F. (1996b) The teaching of the national language and the mother-tongue in Taiwan. In S.Y. You *et al.* (eds) *Papers from the Conference on the Future of the Chinese Language in Hong Kong after 1997* (pp. 15–31). Hong Kong: The Chinese Language Society of Hong Kong [in Chinese].

Tsao, F.F. (1997a) *Ethnic Language Policy: A Comparison of the Two Sides of the Taiwan Straits*. Taipei: Crane [in Chinese].

Tsao, F.F. (1997b) Preserving Taiwan's indigenous languages and cultures: A discussion in sociolinguistic perspective. In N. Inoue (ed.) *Globalization and Indigenous Culture* (pp. 97–112). Tokyo: Institute for Japanese Culture and Classics, Kokugakuin University.

Tsao, F.F. (1998a) Postwar literacy programs in Taiwan: A critical review in sociolinguistic perspective. In C.C. Huang and F.F. Tsao (eds) *Postwar Taiwan in Historical Perspective* (pp. 158–180). Bethesda, MD: University of Maryland Press.

Tsao, F.F. (1998b) Diglossia, bilingualism and Taiwan's language education. In C.S. Tung (ed.) *The Proceedings of the International Symposium on Languages in Taiwan and their Teaching*. Taipei: The Association of Languages in Taiwan.

Tse, K.-P (1986) Standardization in Chinese in Taiwan. *International Journal of Sociology of Language* 59, 25–32.

Tse, K.-P (1987) *Language Planning and English as a Foreign Language in Middle School Education in the Republic of China*. Taipei: Crane.

Tse, K.-P (2000) Language and a rising new identity in Taiwan. *International Journal of the Sociology of Language* 143, 151–164.

Tsuchida, S. (1983) Austronesian languages in Taiwan (Formosa). In S.A. Wurm and S. Hattori (eds) *Language Atlas of the Pacific Area*. Canberra: The Australian National University.

Wang, F.C. (1993) The nature of ethnic assimilation. In M.K.Chang (ed.) *Ethnicity and National Identity* (pp. 53–100). Taipei: Ye-Chiang Publishing Co. [in Chinese].

Wen, C.Y. (1985) The industrialization and the social changes in Taiwan. The China Forum editorial committee (ed.) *Social Change and Culture Development in Taiwan* (pp. 1–40). Taipei: Lianging Publishing [in Chinese].

Yu, B.-Q. and Xu, Z.-Q. (1998) *Tong-Yong Mandarin Phonetic Scheme*. Taipei: Lan-tian Book Co. [in Chinese].

Yuan, J-H. *et al.* (1960) *A Survey of Han Dialects*. Peking: Wenzi Gaige Chubanshe [in Chinese].

Zhang, B.-Y. (1974) *Historical Data of the National Language Movement in Taiwan*. Taipei: Commercial Press [in Chinese].

Zhou, Y.-G. (1992) *A Synchronic and Diachronic Account of the Languages in China and Their Writing Systems*. Peking: Renmin Jiaoyu Chubanshe.

Further Reading

Chang, K.Z. (1987) The archaeological study of the southern coast of China and the origin of the Austronesian People. *The Archeology of Southern People* 1, 1–14.

Chao, Y.R. (1976a) Some contrastive aspects of the Chinese national language movement. In A.S. Dil (ed.) *Aspects of Chinese Sociolinguistics* (pp. 97–105). Stanford, CA: Stanford University Press.

Chen, E.S.H. (1988) Functional perspective on the modernization of the Chinese language. *Journal of Chinese Linguistics* 16 (1), 145–50.

Chen, S.H. (1979) *Population Changes and Social Changes in Taiwan*. Taipei: Lianjing.

Cheng, C.C. (1975) Directions of Chinese character simplification. *Journal of Chinese Linguistics* 3 (2/3), 213–220.

Cheng, C.C. (1976) Chauvinism, egaliterianism, and multilingualism: China's linguistic experience. *Studies in Language Learning* 1 (2), 45–58.

Cheng, C.C. (1979) Language reform in China in the seventies. *Word* 30 (1/2), 45–58.

Fang, S.D., Zhang, F.P. and Zhang, X.Y. (1972) A brief history of the national language movement in the past sixty years. In F.R. Chang (ed.) *The Chinese Studies in the Past Sixty Years* (pp. 461–554). Taipei: Zhengzhong.

Hsiau, A.-C. (1998) Language ideology in Taiwan: The KMT's language policy, the Tai-yu language movement and ethnic politics. *Journal of Multilingual and Multicultural Development* 18, 302–315.

Li, X. (1998) A critique of Tong-Yong romanized symbols. *The Word of Chinese Language* 90, 27–35 [in Chinese].

Lu, L-j. (1988) A survey of language attitudes, language use and ethnic identity in Taiwan. Unpublished MA Thesis, Fu Jen Catholic University.

Sedlak, P.A.S. (1976) *Report of the National Taiwan Normal University–University of Southern California Survey of English Teaching in the Republic of China*. Taipei: Wan Pang Press.

Sung, Wen-hsiun (1980) The prehistory of Taiwan: An archeological perspective. In Chen, C.L. (ed.) *Taiwan: A Part of China*. Taipei : Zhongyang Wenwu Gongyigshe [in Chinese].

Tse, K.-P. (1982) Language policy in the Republic of China. In R.B. Kaplan (ed.) *Annual Review of Applied Linguistics* (pp. 33–47). Rowley. MA: Newbury House.

Tse, K.-P (1995) Bilingual education and language planning. *The World Chinese Language* 75, 32–36 [in Chinese].

van den Berg, M.E. (1986) *Language Planning and Language Use in Taiwan*. Taipei: Crane.

van den Berg, M.E. (1988) Taiwan's sociolinguistic setting. In R.L. Cheng and S.F. Huang (eds) *The Structure of Taiwanese: A Modern Synthesis* (pp. 243–261). Taipei: Crane.

Yang, B.C. (1987) *A Conies History of Taiwan*. Kaohsiung: The First Publishing [in Chinese].

Yang, R. (1989) *Language Maintenance and Language Shift among the Chinese on Taiwan*. Taipei: Crane.

The Language Planning Situation in Taiwan: An Update

Feng-fu Tsao
Institute of Linguistics, National Tsing-Hua University, Hsinchu, Taiwan

Introduction

In the monograph, we took a historical journey to see how things in language planning evolved up to 1999. In this update, we will continue our exploration. The turn of the century seems to be a perfect dividing line because it was in the year 2000 that the Kuomintang (KMT), which had ruled the island for 55 years, lost the presidential election and had to turn over administration to the Democratic Progressive Party (DPP), which, as we mentioned in the monograph, emerged as a serious political player in the 1980s and contended aggressively for domination in the 1990s.

The new ruling party moved quickly into action and, with their 'pent-up' energy, they have brought about quite a few changes in language planning; we will take up these changes in detail, exploring the DPP's process of policy formation and examining their implementation.

Indigenization-driven Language Planning

Policy Change: From *Mandarin Only* to *Mandarin Plus*

We mentioned earlier that the default language policy that the KMT practiced can be characterized as a nationalism-driven monolingualism in which a non-indigenous minority language, Mandarin, was the national language; it was the only language allowed in the education system and in public domains. After 50 years of very successful promotion, an estimated 90 per cent of the population is able to communicate in that language. But because of the high-handed and oppressive promotion measures, all the minority languages – Southern Min, Hakka and the aboriginal languages – soon became marginalized and diluted as we reported in the monograph. As Taiwan became democratised, people's ethno-consciousness was awakened; KMT's nationalism-driven and China-centred language policies came under serious attack in the 1980s and 1990s. As the criticism mounted, the KMT elite was forced to reflect about the way in which Taiwan should maintain external relations with China and at the same time deal internally with its interethnic relations. Thus, Kuo Wei-fan, a former minister of the Ministry of Education (MOE), in 1994 came up with the idea of *tongxinyuan* (concentric circles) in one's identity development. The idea posits that Taiwanese youth should go through three stages in preparing themselves for outside reality; i.e. they should 'stand on Taiwan, have consideration for China, and open their eyes to the world' (Corcuff, 2002: 87). In a similar vein, former president Lee Teng-hui, in campaigning for Ma Ying-jeou in the 1998 Taipei mayoral race, proposed redefining the 'new Taiwanese' to include anyone who identifies with Taiwan, regardless of personal ethnicity, language or nationality (Tse, 2000). At the same time, while the KMT was contemplating putting bilingualism or multilingualism on its political agenda, some oppressive measures were removed, and tolerance was practised in the implementation of its national language policy. Thus,

- punishment for speaking the minority languages at school was officially prohibited in 1987 (Huang, 1995: 57–58),
- the Broadcast Bill was revised in 1993 allowing the use of native languages in domestic broadcasts (*Gazette of the Legislative Yuan*, 1993), and
- the local language-in-education policy was formulated, allowing the teaching of Taiwanese local languages, cultures and histories in primary school beginning in 1993 (*Gazette of Ministry of Education*, 1997).

So the road was paved for a full-scaled multilingual education policy to come on line when the DPP became the ruling party.

The DPP, in fact, lost no time in setting up its new language policy and putting it into practice. To make known the new government's intention, President Chen Shui-bian proclaimed, soon after he became President, the fourteen languages spoken in Taiwan to be 'national languages'; following the proclamation, the official English name of 'the National Language Promotion Committee' was changed to 'the National Languages Committee' in 2003, though the Chinese name remained unchanged because it was specified clearly in the Organization Law of the Committee and can not be changed without first changing the law.[1] In order to increase representation and to protect the language rights of minority groups, in addition to the Council of Indigenous Peoples (CIP), a ministerial-level agency that had been established in 1996 by the former government, the Council for Hakka Affairs (CHA) was set up in 2003. A major function of both councils is to preserve the first languages and to revitalize the traditional cultures of the minority groups. Colleges for the study of both the Hakka people and the Austronesian peoples have consequently been set up at four universities, and two television stations were established, one for the Hakka people and the other for the Austronesian peoples. To show its extraordinary concern for the language equality issue, three versions of language equality laws were drafted by the MOE, the Council of Hakka Affairs, and the Council of Indigenous Peoples respectively. After much discussion and negotiation, the final version of the law, which was renamed 'The Law for the Development of National Languages' was recently passed by the Executive Yuan and was sent to the Legislative Yuan for final ratification on February 1, 2008. A new course, 'Taiwanese Native Languages', in the Grades 1–9 curriculum got under way in 2001. Southern Min, Hakka and the aboriginal languages were included in the curriculum, and elementary school students were required to take one hour of one of these subjects per week.

As we mentioned earlier, the Mandarin only policy was closely associated with a China-centred ideology; when the policy was being re-evaluated, a heated debate arose concerning the official status of Mandarin in a democratizing Taiwan. With indigenous languages and English added to the elementary school language subject area (Kaplan & Baldauf, 2003), the teaching of Mandarin was naturally affected. The hours of instruction for the languages area were reduced from ten to six in the new curriculum. In addition, the area was deprived of its unique national-language status since the government had redefined its concept of 'national language' by making the term plural instead of singular. By presidential decree, Taiwan now has 14 national languages including Mandarin, Southern Min, Hakka, and the 10 aboriginal Austronesian languages.

Despite these various impediments, Mandarin remains the most important language in both the elementary school and the high school curricula. This decision was made on the basis of the following three pragmatic considerations:

(1)   Taiwan, being a multilingual country, will naturally require a lingua franca for efficient government and for interethnic communication. Even though many independence-minded radicals would have strongly preferred other languages such as Southern Min or English to take the place of Mandarin (Cheng, 1993), they realize that such a proposal is impractical at the present time. As a result, Mandarin still retains its official status by default.

(2)   Second, Mandarin is still in demand as the symbolic language of business and politics throughout the Chinese Diaspora. This is so because economic growth and political stability are high on the political agenda of many governments, Taiwan included.

(3)   Third, after fifty years of high-handed promotion, Mandarin has become the first language of a large group of Taiwanese who have grown up speaking the language in public domains as well as in the family. To these people, the use of such other Chinese varieties as Southern Min or Hakka is non-pragmatic and has no value other than fostering ethnic solidarity.

Implementation

A major challenge facing the New Policy that the new DPP government put in place at that time was the implementation of the new policy of teaching Southern Min, Hakka and aboriginal languages in grades 1 to 9. It is useful to explore some of the problems faced and the measures taken to solve them and to offer an evaluation. The following discussion will be given in terms of the target population, syllabus, teacher supply, resources and evaluation, adapted from Kaplan and Baldauf (1997: 113–117). The identification of the target population refers to the decision about who will have access to learning the language and who must learn the language. In the nine-year integrated curriculum, every elementary school student is required to learn one of the local languages offered by their school. The actual offering of the local languages at each school is determined on the basis of the ethnic origin of the majority of students and the availability of teachers.

Since so much of the final decision depends on the principal's evaluation of the conditions involved, a large number of other factors may go into the decision. A recent survey undertaken by Chen (2004) found that elementary schools predominantly offered courses in Southern Min. Thus, in Chiayi city, all 20 schools offered Southern Min and one of them in addition offered Hakka. In Changhwa county, 173 out of 174 schools offered Southern Min. When the school teachers and administrators in Chiayi city and Changhwa county were asked why they made that decision, they replied that they took that implementation decision because there were no appropriate teachers available or because there was a lack of appropriate student numbers to make it possible to offer courses in other languages (i.e. the policy requires at least five students). Such a predominance of Southern Min instruction distorts the purpose of the language policy. Even though Southern Min speakers constitute by far the largest ethnic group, comprising 73.3 per cent of the total population, such a practice, if unchecked, may actually result in undesirable consequences, as claimed by Hsiao (1997: 313), to the effect that 'a movement intended to save a minority language may turn out to be a new form of oppression that threatens other minority languages.'

In 2002, according to a MOE estimate, Southern Min alone, if taught from Grade 1 through Grade 4, would require 3,000 teachers. But very few qualified teachers were available at the time. This came as no surprise, since none of the local languages were ever offered as a subject at any level of formal schooling, not to mention as a medium of instruction; in response to this urgent need, the MOE went to work immediately, recruiting and training teachers. Two specific measures were taken:

(1)   encouraging colleges to set up local-language teaching departments or short-term training programs;
(2)   setting up a teacher certification system.

In fact, the first certification test was given by the MOE in 2002. About 7,400 candidates took the test, which consisted of a written and a spoken part, and only 1,287 candidates (17%) passed. Those who passed the test would need to undergo a teacher-training program to be qualified as a local language teacher at a primary school. As it turned out, very few of those who passed the test actually ended up being full-time primary school teachers (*Taipei Times*, August 14, 2002: 2)

Consequently, in 2004, according to Chen's (2004) study, local languages were taught by teachers with basically three different levels of training:

(1)   full-time teachers who are well-qualified and certified in the teaching of a local language;
(2)   substitute or *zhiyuan jiaoshi* (supplementary teachers, most of them certified), who may not have professional knowledge or adequate teacher training;
(3)   regular homeroom teachers having a certain level of knowledge of a local language who are assigned, voluntarily or involuntarily, to teach a local language along with other subjects.

Among the three types of teachers, the second and the third type constituted the largest group. Only a few certified and well-trained local-language teachers currently fill full-time positions. In short, the education-authorities still have to face a grueling up-hill struggle in the implementation of local language policy.

The syllabus for the local language policy stipulates the starting year of instruction, the number of teaching hours allotted, the content to be taught and finally the teaching methods to be used. The following discussion will therefore be organized in terms of the starting year, the teaching hours, the teaching content and the methodology.

As mentioned previously, from the school year 2001 on, all students in elementary school have been required to study at least one local language. The objectives for teaching local languages are stated as follows:

(1)   to increase students' understanding of their native culture, and to help develop concepts about preserving, transmitting and creating native languages and culture;
(2)   to develop students local language proficiency so as to enable them to use the language effectively in the four areas of listening, speaking, reading and writing;
(3)   to promote native language education and foster respect for multilingualism.

Despite the MOE's stipulation that local language courses were compulsory, as of 2002, only 53 out of 1,345 elementary schools nationwide (i.e., only four per cent) had yet to offer local-language instruction (*Taipei Times*, August 14, 2002: 2). According to Chen's study (2004), some schools simply offered local language courses perfunctorily because they were far more interested in offering English classes. Most of the schools chose to teach a local language for only one hour per week to meet the minimal requirement set by the MOE.

The teaching methods for local languages were not clearly stated in the curriculum standards for the teaching of local languages. The specification of teaching methods was probably left open on purpose due to the lack of institutional programs responsible for training local language teachers, but lack of specificity actually led to great confusion as to the proper teaching methods to be employed. It has been observed that some teachers choose to teach listening and speaking without introducing the phonetic system and Chinese characters, while others chose to teach the local language the way that they had taught Mandarin; i.e. teaching the phonetic symbols in the very beginning before moving on to teach scripts. Some teachers introduce words to students in Romanized spelling enabling them to read even during the initial stages, while others synchronize their teaching of the local languages with the teaching of Mandarin, making use of large numbers of words, phrases and Chinese characters shared by both. Chen (2004), after observing a variety of local language classrooms, concluded that the methodological decision depends on individual teachers and school administrators. Such inconsistency in teaching methods and procedures would, of course, seriously limit the effectiveness of local language teaching.

The standard of textbook editing for local languages is far below that for English or Mandarin. This lowering of the standard was to be expected, and there were several reasons for it. To begin with, as Mr. Liao, an officer of the National Institute for Compilation and Translation, explained in an interview, most publishers are not willing to invest heavily in local-language textbooks for two reasons:

(1)   the local language textbooks have very restricted distribution, and
(2)   neither the phonetic transcription system nor the scripts have been standardized, and so, in many cases, parallel systems have to be simultaneously displayed, running up cost and causing confusion.

In addition, the production of such textbooks does not need authorization from the National Institute for Compilation and Translation.

But third, and perhaps most important, the use of textbooks in classes is not required. Teachers are allowed to write or adapt material for their own use. In fact, many teachers prefer to use material that they have developed or adapted for their own classes; i.e. they teach proverbs, old sayings, nursery rhymes and folk songs. They take this approach for three reasons:

(1)   they think their materials are more interesting than the cut and dried materials presented in the published textbooks;
(2)   they are not familiar with the phonetic symbols and Chinese characters used in the textbooks, and finally,
(3)   some local language teachers believe that the purpose of teaching the local languages is to enable the students to communicate with the elder members of the family only, not to develop literacy among the students.

There are very few agreed-upon criteria for assessing student's performance in local languages. In Chen's (2004) survey, it was found that most teachers used formative rather than formal assessment. Most teachers also conduct assessment with a view to stimulating students' interest in local languages rather than to measuring their achievement. In my view, this is not a bad assessment method, as in the current state of local languages teaching it seems far more important to maintain students' interest in the language rather than to gauge their level of attainment.

Summary and Evaluation

The preceding two sections have been devoted to a discussion of recent language planning in the areas of acquisition and status planning, following Hornberger's (1990, 1994) classification scheme. In status planning, in order to promote language equality and to protect minority groups' language rights, a national languages development law was recently drafted by the Executive Yuan and on February 1, 2008, was sent to the Legislative Yuan to await ratification.

In the area of acquisition planning, local language education policy was established and put into practice in 2001. The purpose of setting up such a policy is clear: the government intends to revitalize these rapidly disappearing languages through formal school instruction, as has been done in many other places of the world. But has it attained its goal? Perhaps it is still too early to tell, but according to a use survey conducted in 2004 (Yeh *et al.*, 2004), only Southern Min is showing an increasingly reversed shift. Hakka continues its long-term shift toward Mandarin, and the Austronesian languages are experiencing an even greater shift toward Mandarin. From our examination of the implementation process, such a result is hardly surprising.

Another unexpected but welcomed result of this indigenization movement is that a new national identity is gradually emerging. There used to be a line of demarcation between mainlanders – those who migrated to Taiwan after the KMT lost in the civil war – and the local inhabitants, but throughout these years of the democratizing process of open discussion, a new national identity with the land of Taiwan has been developing across ethnic linguistic boundaries.

Another issue that has been debated is whether Local Language Education (LLE) policy should include the development of standardized writing systems for Southern Min and Hakka. At present, both languages lack vocabulary for the more formal registers, and it has been cogently argued that this lack reinforces their low status and forces the speakers to code-switch when they are speaking in the academic and official domains, thus impeding the promotion and propagation of these languages (Chiung, 2001). As Chen (1999: 205) has pointed out, a written code is essential for the standardization and elaboration necessary to enable a language 'to be learnt as a subject and [to become] the medium in which all modern knowledge can be taught at an advanced level'. However, Scott and Tiun (2007) admit that this view is by no means universally accepted by all the people in Taiwan and, as Chen (2005) reports, this difference in point-of-view accounts for the marginalizing attitude that some LLE teachers hold toward the teaching of local languages.

Internationalization-driven Language Planning

Policy change: From English for the elite to English for all people

While the indigenization of Taiwan in the process of multilingualism and multiculturalism was raging, the parallel process of internationalization or globalization was rapidly developing. This process basically advocates that every citizen in Taiwan should acquire enough English proficiency to become a qualified citizen in the coming together of the global village. The advocates of English also claim that learning English at an earlier age constitutes an effective means of promoting English proficiency nation-wide. This English language movement was initiated partly under peer pressure from such neighbouring Asian countries as Japan and South Korea (Chou, 2005) and by politicians, and later it was supported by scholars, parents of students, school administrators and ESL practitioners.

Actually, as early as 1990s, people's awareness of the importance of English was aroused by the government's efforts to promote Taiwan to become an Asian-Pacific business centre. This awareness was constantly reinforced throughout the 1990s by the government's efforts to promote English teaching. By the turn of the century, in the minds of most government officials and the general public, there was a virtual consensus that the first step in internationalizing Taiwan was to increase its citizens' English proficiency. Anyone who lacks English proficiency is subject to criticism for lacking a proper sense of internationalization. A case in point is the incumbent president Chen Shui-bian, who was criticized for his inability to take an international perspective because he was not proficient in English (*Liberty Times*, 1998, June 12: 11). This strong association of English proficiency with the internationalization of Taiwan was evidently the primary cause for the reformulation of the English-in-education policy in 2001, allowing the teaching of English in elementary schools nation-wide, although many city and county governments gave permission to teach English in elementary schools as early as 1993, about the same time that local language education was launched, as previously noted.

Thus, English language, which has long been a subject in the high school curriculum, was, in 2001, moved to the fifth grade of the elementary school curriculum. The MOE, in announcing its decision, gave the following reasons:

(1) to develop in students an international perspective;
(2) to maximize students' critical period of language acquisition in language learning;
(3) to optimize the timing of the implementation of the new nine-year integrated curriculum; and
(4) to follow the trends of the new era and to fulfil parents' expectations (MOE, 1998a, cited from Lin, 2006: 816–817).

It is interesting to note in this connection that 'parents' expectation' has to be included in the fourth point. It is included, perhaps, as a sign to indicate how democratic Taiwan is and to announce to the people that their expectations are an important factor in education policy decisions. But parental expectations in Taiwan's context might be regarded as a double-edged blade that cuts both ways. The expectations might have the effect of expediting the process of policy making, but it might also have the effect of putting too much pressure on the government and thus making the government act too rashly. I tend to agree with a number of scholars (Chou, 2005; Crombie, 2006; Lin, 2006) who argued that the latter case was exactly what happened in Taiwan. Two years after the previous policy change, the English-in-education policy changed again, due in large part to continuing pressure from parents, by moving the onset of instruction to the third grade. While it is debatable whether the third grade is the optimal time for the introduction of the English instruction into Taiwan's elementary curriculum, it is certainly a case of bad planning to change the policy after only two years of implementation, a point that we will pick up in our discussion of implementation, which follows.

Implementation of the English-in-education (EE) policy

Like our previous discussion of the LLE implementation, the following discussion of EE policy implementation includes the following subtopics adapted from Kaplan and Baldauf (2003): target population, syllabus, teacher supply, facilities and resources, and evaluation. The same framework as we used in our previous discussion of LLE implementation has been chosen deliberately to facilitate comparison between the two.

Unlike the LLE policy in which every student in the target population may choose any one of the three local languages to meet the requirement, in the new EE policy all the students are required to receive English education.

As we mentioned previously, as of Fall 2005, students from the third grade on were to receive at least one class period of English education per week. This decision by the MOE, like many previous ones, was intended to serve only as a minimum standard. Such being the case, many local governments introduced English at even lower grade levels. For example, Taipei city, Taichung county and Hsinchu county decided to introduce English to students in the first grade and to continue instruction throughout the elementary school years. In addition, many local governments (for instance Taipei city and Tainan city) allot two class periods instead of one to English instruction. To make the matter even more complicated, a number of counties/cities (e.g. Taoyuan county, Taichung city and Taichung county) allot one or two periods per week, allowing each school to make its own decision. As can be expected, these different implementation plans resulted in great discrepancies among different areas of the country, which has caused quite a number of problems in supervising the quality of teachers, teaching materials and syllabus. It has also widened the gap between the urban sector and the rural sector in the quality of English learning and teaching.

In sharp contrast to the 'old' EE curriculum standard, with its focus on the development of reading and writing for academic, professional and technological purposes, the new EE curriculum standard aims to develop English oral proficiency along with literacy, for international communication. To facilitate this change of focus new teaching methods were introduced. The most significant changes in teaching methodology, according to Yeh and Shih (2000) are:

(1)   the adoption of a communicative language teaching approach to English teaching and the use of phonics rather than phonetic symbols to teach pronunciation in the elementary school curriculum;
(2)   the attempt to use English as the medium of instruction in English classes in order to increase input and English proficiency.

Both of these approaches diverge from the structure-based approaches that dominated English teaching over the past fifty years.

Also unlike the old EE policy, where only one set of standardized textbooks was provided, the new policy opened up the textbook market, allowing publishers and language institutions to develop textbooks on condition that they are reviewed and screened by the National Institute of Compilation and Translation. The new policy thus enables English teachers to choose from a selection of approved textbooks on the basis of the need and proficiency level of the students and their personal preference. This sounds ideal in theory but in actual practice, since the teachers are untrained in the selection of textbooks, and often there is a certain amount of profit involved, the decision is often made collectively, either at the county/city level or at school level. English teachers have yet another problem to face. They are constantly under parental pressure to select something more advanced in content for their students, since their parents all have high expectations for their children, and they do not want their children to learn what they think is too rudimentary for them. In short, it seems clear from the description of the textbook situation, in both EE policy and LLE policy, that government, parents, and publishers all show a far more enthusiastic attitude toward the teaching of EE than towards the teaching of local languages.

Similar to the situation of LLE, at the inception of the implementation of EE policy, a severe shortage of qualified English teachers was anticipated so that, to meet the urgent demand, the government took several actions:

(1)   in 1999, a proficiency test was administered which 45,000 people took and 3,500 (7%) passed;
(2)   among those who passed the test, 1,900 successfully went through a two-year training course (Scott & Chen, 2004).

The training programs stand in sharp contrast to those for LLE teachers held at about the same time in which trainees took 15 required courses and eight elective courses, each lasting from 3–8 hours. Because of this marked difference between the two training programs, the government was criticized for practicing 'covert discrimination' (Scott & Tiun, 2007).

To return to the topic of EE policy implementation, of 1,900 who completed the training program only a small portion actually took full-time teaching positions at an elementary school. This is so because the training programs were far too long, and those who could pass the test and complete the training courses could easily find a job elsewhere. Thus, the situation appeared to be rather like that found in the case of LLE; i.e. there were three types of teachers with the majority belonging to the second or the third categories:

(1) well-qualified, full-time English teachers holding elementary school English teaching certificates;
(2) substitute or part-time teachers who may be proficient in English to a certain degree but do not have an official elementary school teacher certificate;
(3) regular homeroom teachers who did not receive special training in English teaching but were assigned, for some reason, to teach these courses.

The central government, well aware of the shortage of teachers, has taken the following measures to increase the pool of qualified teachers:

(1) to allow normal colleges to set up new English teaching programs;
(2) to step up efforts to recruit teachers certified under the 1999 MOE training scheme;
(3) to encourage colleges to offer different types of summer English teaching programs to train more qualified English teachers;
(4) to allow some colleges to offer post-graduate English teaching programs in which students with a Bachelor Degree can take classes for one year and spend the second year in teaching practicum;
(5) to import foreign English teachers from English-speaking countries on a national level;
(6) to recruit certified teachers who have sufficient English proficiency (i.e. at least 213 points on the computer-based TOEFL) or the third level of Taiwan's General English Proficiency Test (GEPT) (*Taipei Times*, July 7, 2004: 3); and
(7) to provide funds for in-service training in English teaching to certified elementary school teachers who may lack English proficiency or English teaching training.

Among these, the recruiting of native English teachers has spawned the most controversies and has produced some far-reaching repercussions. This provision has aroused serious criticism for the following reasons:

(1) it would deprive local English teachers of employment opportunities;
(2) it would result in students' to experience confusion of cultural identity;
(3) it is argued that being native English speakers does not guarantee the teaching ability of foreign teachers;
(4) in some cases at least, foreign English teachers might burden local teachers

with extra administrative work and teaching load, due to their lack of communicative ability in Mandarin and sometimes due to their attitude of superiority over local cultures (*United Daily News*, Jan. 19, 2003).

So far it has produced some repercussions in at least two areas:

(1)	the employment regulations by which foreigners were not allowed to teach in and below secondary schools were revised; and
(2)	it is believed the sustained efforts to bring in large numbers of native English speakers may contribute to the development of the international atmosphere needed for the spread of English.

Another matter related to but not restricted to English teachers in elementary schools is the government's attempt to raise the level of English teachers' English proficiency to a satisfactory level by 2008. Those who are teaching English in any educational level are expected to pass the GEPT (General English Proficiency Test) at the intermediate-high level.[2] This was written into the Challenge of the 2008 Education White Book by the MOE in 2004 (Chen, 2005: 21). This is seen as yet another effort to promote English teaching in conjunction with the new EE policy.

In sharp contrast to the situation of local language teaching where only limited facilities are available for teaching, a wide variety of facilities and resources are available for the teaching of English. In addition to five or six sets of textbooks approved by the MOE for each elementary grade, there is a wide variety of supplementary material easily accessible to the teachers. Besides, there are teaching tools – e.g. electronic equipment, audio- or multi-media language laboratories, and even spacious classroom specially designed for the performance of language tasks and interaction activities in English (Chen, 2005). This example provides yet another indication that the government and school administrators have put a great deal of effort into the teaching of English.

The EE policy suggests that both formative and summative measures of learner achievement should be used. According to Yeh (2000), formative measurement focuses on the use of portfolios and summative measurement aims to evaluate students' oral as well as written ability in English. Many teachers have made attempts to apply both methods, but they have found formative evaluation very time-consuming and difficult to apply to large numbers of students. To make the matter worse, many parents who are asked to help out with their children's evaluation have turned in a large quantity of portfolios in order to achieve a higher grade for their own children.

In addition to teachers' evaluation, quite a few city / county governments (e.g. Taipei city, Taipei county, Chiayi county) have made a practice of administering city-wide or county-wide written tests in their region in order to gauge the level of achievement of their students; in other words, local governments and administrators are very interested in finding out how well their schools and teachers have been doing in their implementation of the EE policy.

In the previous discussion, we have made several comparisons with respect to various facets of implementation between EE policy and LLE policy. We can summarize our comparisons in Table 1 adapted from Chen (2005). It is clear from the comparisons that the government, the community, school administrators and teachers have all exhibited a strong bias in favour of the EE policy.

Table 1 Comparison between LLE and EE policies and implementation

		LLE		EE	
		Policy	Implementation	Policy	Implementation
Target population		Students are required to learn one from among three languages	Most students are offered Southern Min classes	All students are required to learn English	Same as policy
Syllabus	Years	1st–6th grades	Not strictly implemented	3rd–6th grades	1st–6th grades
	Hours	1 hour per week	0–2 hours	1–2 hours per week	1–2 hours
	Contents	Related to ethnic groups	Left to individual schools and teachers	Related to inter- & intra- cultural communication	Same as policy
	Methods	Not specified	Same as policy	Communicative approach	Same as policy
Teacher qualification		Qualified	Few qualified and others from different backgrounds	Qualified	Qualified or College graduated with an English major
Resources	Language policy legislation	Written in the curriculum	Meet or fall short of the minimum requirements	Written in the curriculum	Meet or exceed the minimum requirements
	Textbooks	Textbooks sponsored by MOE or local government	Very little or no selection	Commercial textbooks that are authorized by MOE	A wide selection facilitated by each board of education
	Facilities	Not specified	Limited	Not specified	A wide variety
Assessment		Not specified	Either included as part of Mandarin class or as an independent class	Regulated (Formative and summative assessment)	Same as policy, and additional proficiency tests

Other related issues

In the preceding two sections, the target population of English education that used to be restricted to the elite for its instrumental functions of having access to the world of science, professionalism and technology has been officially extended to all people for the purpose of becoming world citizens capable of international communication. Consequently, the new EE policy requires students to take one to two periods of English instruction from the third grade on. In addition to the reasons previously given, there is one that is often left implicit in the official account of the policy change and that is Taiwan urgently needs to make itself internationally visible for its ambiguous national status, but most people, seeing neither a China-centered state nor a Taiwan independent state as viable, tend to focus their attention on the economic opportunity offered by English. Therefore, they have an extraordinarily high expectation for their children's English ability. This easily translates itself as parental pressure, which had the regrettable effect of causing the government to act too rashly, as pointed out earlier.

A second issue that has frequently been brought up in the discussion is the simultaneous implementation of LLE policy and EE policy (Chen, 2004; Lin, 2006; Crombie, 2006; Scott & Tiun, 2007). It is quite common for advocates of indigenization to set up policies in which language education serves as a vehicle to promote the vitality of indigenous languages (see May, 1996) similar to what has happened in Taiwan. It is also very common for countries to promote internationalization by requiring their citizens to take English instruction in their early schooling years, as has occurred in Israel (Spolsky & Shohamy, 1997, 1999). It is, however, rare for a country in the contemporary world to call for both internationalization and indigenization at the same time and to implement both types of language policy simultaneously. The reasons are not hard to discover. A country may, at the same time, strive for internalization and indigenization, but the government would normally hesitate to carry out the policies simultaneously, knowing full well that these two types of policy will vie for the limited resources that the country has, and in the end it is very likely that the EE policy will win out, leaving the other policy under-funded and under-staffed. This undesirable situation, unfortunately, is developing in Taiwan, and I can only hope that the indigenous Taiwanese people may manage to persist over the difficult period.

Third, more should be said about the status of Mandarin Chinese in Taiwan. It is true, as previously pointed out, that the successful promotion and propagation of Mandarin in Taiwan was achieved through high-handed hegemonic enforcement, and the KMT regime should be condemned for that, but the fact remains that it has become a language spoken by a large number of young people as their native language in Taiwan, and it serves as a lingua franca for interethnic communication. Outside the country, it is also a useful lingua franca in Greater China (Li, 2006)[3], and with increasing trade dependence throughout Greater China, it has gained in importance as a language of business; unless some other languages can take its place, pragmatism would dictate that it be retained as a default national language. This is exactly the position taken by the government despite the contention of radicals who view it as 'Beijing dialect' and hence unfit for official status in Taiwan (Chen, P., 2001; Cheng, 1993).

Finally, while the present writer has been working on this update, a new issue has emerged. Previously, the MOE has set up committees engaged in a moderate revision of the curriculum standards for the various subjects in the Nine-year (G1 to G9) Integrated Curriculum. There are altogether 18 subjects, and five of them belong to the 'language study area': Mandarin, Southern Min, Hakka, the Aboriginal Austronesian Languages, and English. Since, as reported earlier, the term *Guoyu* (national language), referring specifically to the study of Mandarin in the old curriculum standards, will have to be changed since the term is now defined plurally. In the revision, the suggested term is *Huayu* (Chinese language). Likewise, the term *guozi* (national characters) will be changed to *Hanzi* (Han characters). Other terms involving the character *guo* (national) such as *guohua* (national painting), *guoyue* (national music), *guoju* (national opera) are likely to be changed to *shui mou hua* (water-ink-painting), *chuantong yinyue* (traditional music) and *jingju* (Peking opera) respectively. But the change of these terms and many others are only suggestions for future textbooks writers and will not take effect until 2010 or 2011 when the new curriculum standards go into effect. (*China Times*, Feb. 14, 2008, p. A2)

Summary and Conclusion

This discussion began with the turn of the 21st century, and continued to explore the new policies in association with the two tremendous driving forces: indigenization and internationalization. These policies were analyzed by taking into account Taiwan's social and political history, current discussion about identity, language rights, distribution of resources and representation, economic development and concern about Taiwan's status in the international community. Special attention was given to the interplay of the two driving forces: indigenization and internationalization. The discussion also focused on the implementation of these policies, pointing out their strong points and defects along the way.

In conclusion, it is important to call particular attention to two points that were only made implicitly in the previous discussion:

(1) Taiwan's unique situation illustrates how the complex relationship between language, ethnicity, national identity, economic competitiveness and global participation interact to shape the language policies and their implementation;

(2) Taiwan has made a great step forward over the past in the sense that present tolerance rights are practised under which the usage of any Sinitic language and any variety of the Austronesian languages have been saved from discrimination, and yet this is only the first step; we should not stop here. We should continue to work toward the institutionalization of multilingualism and multiculturalism, so that Taiwan will eventually become a truly multilingual and multicultural society

Notes

1. This legal problem does not affect the broader interrelation of the term *guoyu* (nation language) in the title because the Chinese noun in this case is not marked for number.
2. The level is believed to be equivalent to 213 points in the new-style TOEFL.
3. Greater China, as defined by Li (2006), comprises four more or less distinct polities: China, Taiwan, Hong Kong, and Macao.

References

Chen, Ping (1999) *Modern Chinese: History and Sociolinguistics*. Cambridge: Cambridge University Press.

Chen, Ping (2001) Policy on the selection and implementation of a standard language as a source of conflict in Taiwan. In N. Gottlieb and P. Chen (eds) *Language Planning and Language Policy. East Asian Perspectives* (pp. 95–110). Richmond: Curzon Press.

Chen, Su-chiao (2004) Linguistic vitality in Taiwan: A sociolinguistic study. A NSC Study Report.

Chen, Su-chiao (2005) Indigenization and internationalization: New language-in-education planning in Taiwan. In *The Proceedings of 2005 Conference on Taiwan Culture: Linguistics, Literature, Culture and Education* (pp. 1–30). Taipei: Crane Publishing Co.

Cheng, Robert L. (1993) Hu tsa te tsu-ti yu chi-hui tu tai-yu hsieh Tai-yu (Let our children have opportunities to read and write Tai-yu). *Tai-wan wen-i (Taiwan Literature)* 136, 173–80.

China Times (2008) *China Times*, Feb. 4.

Chiung, Wi-vun Taiffalo (2001) Language attitudes towards written Taiwanese. *Journal of Multilingual and Multicultural Development* 22 (2), 502–521.

Chou, Chung-tien (2005) ELT in East Asia: Lessons to be learned from our neighbors. In *Proceedings of the 5th Annual Wenshan International Conference.* Taipei: Department of English, National Chengchi University.

Corcuff, S. (2002) The symbolic dimension of democratization and the transition of national identity under Lee Teng-hui. In S. Corcuff (ed.) *Memories of the Future* (pp. 73–102). New York: M. E. Sharpe.

Crombie, W. (2006) Taiwan and New Zealand: Some critical issues in languages policy and planning. In *the Proceedings of 23rd International Conference on English Teaching and Learning in the Republic of China – Changes, Chances, and Challenges in English Teaching & Learning* (pp. 1–11). Kaoshiung, Taiwan: Kaun Tang International Publications.

Gazette of the Legislative Yuan (1993).

Gazette of Ministry of Education (1997).

Hornberger, N. (1990) Bilingual education and English-only: A language planning framework. *The Annals of the American Academy of Political and Social Science* 508, 12–26.

Hornberger, N. (1994) Literacy and language planning. *Language and Education: International Journal* 8, 75–86.

Hsiau, A-chiu (1997) Language ideology in Taiwan: The KMT's language policy, the Tai-yu language movement, and ethnic polities. *Journal of Multilingual and Multicultural Development* 18 (4), 302–315.

Huang, Shuanfan. (1995) *Yuyan, Shehui yu Zuqun Yishi [Language, Society and Ethnicity]* (2nd edn). Taipei: Wenhe Chubanshe.

Kaplan, R. B. and Baldauf, R.B., Jr. (1997) *Language Planning: From Practice to Theory.* Clevedon: Multilingual Matters.

Kaplan, R. B. and Baldauf, R.B., Jr. (2003) *Language and Language-in-Education Planning in the Pacific Basin.* Boston: Kluwer Academic.

Li, D. C. S. (2006) Chinese as a lingua franca in greater China. *Annual Review of Applied Linguistics* 26, 149–176.

Liberty Times (1998) *Liberty Times*, June 12.

Lin, Han-Yi. (2006) The implications of extending English education in Elementary Schools in Taiwan. In *the Proceedings of 23rd International Conference on English Teaching and Learning in the Republic of China – Changes, Chances, and Challenges in English Teaching & Learning* (pp. 814–824). Kaoshiung, Taiwan: Kaun Tang International Publications.

May, S. 1996. Indigenous language rights and education. In J. Lynch *et al.* (eds) *Education and Development: Tradition and Innovation,* 1 (pp.149–71). London: Cassell.

MOE (Ministry of Education, 教育部). (1998) *The Assessment Report of Implementing Elementary English Education. (國小實施英語教學評估報告)* Retrieved August 6, 2001 from the World Wide Web at: *http://www.edu.tw/minister/copool/pres362.htm.*

Scott, M. and Pi-fen Liu Chen (2004) English in elementary schools in Taiwan. In P. Lee and H. Azman (eds) *Global English and Primary Schools: Challenges for Elementary Education* (pp. 51–71). Melbourne: CAE Press.

Scott, M. and Tiun, Hak-khiam. (2007) Mandarin-only to Mandarin-plus: Taiwan. *Language Policy* 6 (1), 53–72.

Spolsky, B. and Shohamy, E. (1997) Planning foreign-language education: An Israeli perspective. In T. Bongaerts and K. de Bot (eds) *Perspectives on Foreign-Language Policy* (pp. 99–111). Amsterdam: John Benjamins.

Spolsky, B. and Shohamy, E. (1999) *The Languages of Israel.* Clevedon: Multilingual Matters.

Taipei Times (2002) *Taipei Times*, August 14.

Taipei Times (2004) *Taipei Times*, July 7.

Tse, John Kwock-ping (2000) Language and a rising new identity in Taiwan. *International Journal of the Sociology of Language* 43, 151–164.

United Daily News. (聯合報) (19 Jan. 2003) Foreign English teachers, walking CD players? (外籍英語教師，會走的錄放音機), p.6.

Yeh, Hsi-nan, Chan, Hui-chen, and Cheng, Yuh-show (2004) Language use in Taiwan: Language proficiency and domain analysis. *Journal of Taiwan Normal University Humanities & Social Science* 49 (1), 79–107.

Yeh, H.N. and Shih, Y.H. (2000) A new era for foreign language education in Taiwan: English teaching in the elementary schools. Paper presented at the Conference of ELT Curriculum for the Young Learners in East Asia 2000. Taipei, Taiwan.

Yeh, R.S. (2000) Duo yuan hua ping liang [Multiple assessment]. In *Guo min zhong xiao xue ying yu jiao xue huo dong she ji ping liang zhi yin* [The Nine-Year Integrated Curricula: Guidance of Design of Teaching and Assessment Activities] (pp.41–73). Taipei: The Ministry of Education.

The Authors

Sonia Eagle, now retired, was a professor in the English Department at Kanda University of International Studies (*Kanda Gaigo Daigaku*), Japan, where, for twelve years, she has taught anthropology and sociolinguistics. Born in Canada, and now residing in Port Moody, BC, she completed her education at the University of Illinois, Purdue University, Indiana University and the University of Southern California. She holds a doctorate in anthropology from Purdue University and studied Applied Linguistics at the University of Southern California. She has conducted anthropological fieldwork on the Salasaca of Ecuador, the Passamaquoddy of Maine and the Basque of southern California. She spent ten months in Nepal collecting data on language planning and multilingualism. She has published a number of articles on language and culture and one textbook/reader.

Nanette Gottlieb is ARC Professorial Fellow in the Japan Program, School of Languages and Comparative Cultural Studies at the University of Queensland in Brisbane, Australia. She has published widely on the sociology of language in Japan, most recently *Language and Society in Japan* (Cambridge University Press, 2005) and *Linguistic Stereotyping and Minority Groups in Japan* (Routledge, 2006). Her current research project is 'Immigration, Technology and Citizenship: Key Challenges for Language Policy in a Changing Japan'.

Feng-fu Tsao is Professor of Linguistics at the Graduate Institute of Linguistics and in the Department of Foreign Languages, National Tsing Hua University, Hsinchu, Taiwan. He was Dean of the College of Humanities and Social Sciences from August 1999 to July 2002. As of August 2005 he has been appointed Distinguished Professor of Linguistics. Since obtaining his PhD degree in Linguistics from the University of Southern California in 1977, he has been devoted to teaching and research in the area of grammar, sociolinguistics and applied linguistics at various universities in Taiwan, Hong Kong and the United States and has published widely both at home and abroad. His publications include seven books and some ninety articles.

Zhao Shouhui (PhD, University of Sydney) is Research Fellow at the Centre for Research in Pedagogy and Practice (CRPP), NIE at Nanyang Technological University, Singapore. A professional language teacher by training, Zhao has been teaching and researching in Chinese applied linguistics for the past 19 years at seven universities in five countries beginning in 1988, when he completed his MA in Chinese Applied Linguistics at Renmin University of China (Beijing). Zhao is a member of All-China Society of Teaching Chinese as a Foreign Language and the Singapore Association of Applied Linguistics. He has published in the areas of linguistics and education. Zhao is the primary co-author of three dual-authored Chinese language textbooks and the co-compiler of two dictionaries. He has also contributed a number of ephemeral pieces (e.g. prose, short stories, film reviews, etc.) to a range of literary publications, websites and broadcasts.